THE RECKLESS DECADE

H. W. Brands

◆

THE RECKLESS DECADE
America in the 1890s

The University of Chicago Press
Chicago and London

The University of Chicago Press, Chicago 60637
The University of Chicago Press, Ltd., London
Copyright © 1995 by H. W. Brands

All rights reserved. Originally published 1995
University of Chicago Press edition 2002
Printed in the United States of America
17 16 15 14 13 12 11 10   5 6 7 8 9
ISBN-13: 978-0-226-07116-9
ISBN-10: 0-226-07116-2

Library of Congress Cataloging-in-Publication Data

Brands, H. W.
    The reckless decade : America in the 1890s / H. W. Brands.
        p. cm.
    Originally published: New York : St. Martin's Press, 1995.
    Includes bibliographical references (p.   ) and index.
    ISBN 0-226-07116-2 (pbk. : alk. paper)
        1. United States—History—1865–1898.   2. Spanish-
    American War, 1898.   3. Eighteen nineties.   I. Title.
    E661 .B795   2002
    973.8—dc21
                                        2001057009

CONTENTS

◆

NOTE TO THE PAPERBACK EDITION

This book was written during the 1990s, a century-ending decade that exhibited certain parallels with the 1890s, the decade the book is about. Although I tried to avoid excessive present-mindedness in the writing, the parallels naturally informed aspects of the book's approach to its subject matter.

The 1990s are now history, and the perspective of readers encountering the book in the first decade of the twenty-first century will inevitably be different from that of the book's original readers. Yet I have resisted the temptation to rewrite the book, and perhaps thereby make myself appear wiser than I am. Two considerations motivate this decision. First, the book is about the 1890s, not the 1990s, and if several additional years' hindsight affords a better view of the 1890s, that view is not so much better that a rewrite would necessarily improve the book. Second, to the degree the book manifests the perspective of the 1990s, readers might be interested to see how that perspective now appears dated (or doesn't).

In one regard, though, this paperback edition *is* different from the hardcover. The realities of economics have prevented the inclusion of the original illustrations. The fight against rising costs continues; a new decade hasn't changed that.

PROLOGUE

◆

COMING OF AGE, OR COMING APART?

There is something about the end of a century that sets people to thinking about their collective prospects and ultimate destiny. The current final decade of the twentieth century (and of the second millennium, which exacerbates the tendency) hadn't even begun before America's airwaves, newspaper columns, and bookstores were filled with a debate over whether the United States was commencing a post–Cold War renaissance as the planet's sole superpower and the linchpin of a new world order, or entering an era of decline, finally overtaken by the economic competitors that had been nipping at America's heels for most of the 1970s and 1980s. American triumphalists stressed the demise of the Soviet Union as freeing America from the worries and constraints that had dominated American life for two generations, and contended that while Japan and Germany might give the United States a good run for its economy, neither came close to matching America's combination of military, political, and economic resources. American declinists countered with all manner of bleak statistics regarding federal finances, trade balances, patent applications, household savings, educational test scores, and out-of-wedlock births. The triumphalists looked hopefully ahead, seeing a future bright with the potential for fulfilling Americans' dreams for their country and the world; the declinists argued that America's best days were past and that Americans would have to get used to being citizens of just another world power.

This fin-de-siècle soul searching had happened before. During the 1890s, Americans agonized over what the twentieth century about to begin held for their country. To many of them, America's finest hours were behind it. The continent was filling up and the vast open spaces that had characterized

American life were quickly disappearing. The symbolism of the vanishing frontier was even more traumatic than the reality. A "frontier" interpretation of American history, pioneered and popularized by Frederick Jackson Turner, attained the status of revealed truth during the 1890s. According to this view, American democracy, self-reliance, and prosperity—in short, the distinctive traits that made Americans what they were—depended on the ready availability of free land. With the disappearance of this free land, an epoch of American history was ending. Whether what would follow would match what had come before was very doubtful; at the least it would be decidedly different.

During both century-ending decades, the vertiginous sense of standing at the brink of a new era was most pronounced in America's cities. The future seemed closer, and often more ominous, in such places as Los Angeles in the 1990s and Chicago in the 1890s. America's cities straddled the cutting edge of America's nineteenth-century industrial revolution, as of its twentieth-century post–industrial revolution, and the poor people of America's cities in both ages had the wounds to prove it. Cities attracted the powerful and proficient, but also the powerless and deficient. Their abundant opportunities fed the dreams of those who dwelt on the right side of the law, but also the greed of those who cruised on the wrong. The cities drew their denizens from all races, regions, and cultures; yet the very diversity that was one of the glories of Houston in the 1990s and New York in the 1890s was also the dynamite that threatened to blow each city apart. To much of the rest of the country, the cities were foreign ground, home to a class of humanity that seemed alien and unassimilable.

In each decade, the cities were the product of forces that were reshaping the American and world economies. At the top of the economic food chain of the 1890s were the captains of industry and finance, men such as John D. Rockefeller, Andrew Carnegie, and J. P. Morgan, who created vast empires of wealth and who by virtue of their wealth wielded enormous influence over the lives of millions of Americans. At the bottom were those who labored for dimes a day, when they labored at all. During much of the 1890s they didn't, for the nation's worst depression to date seared the slums and working-class neighborhoods, casting millions into despair. The top of the pyramid during the 1990s was somewhat less sharp than a century earlier—largely as a result of lessons learned then—but the base of the pyramid was as broad as ever. If life at the bottom was now slightly less tenuous than a century earlier—again due to lessons learned during that earlier period and after—it was almost equally devoid of hope.

And the whole pyramid often appeared as precarious as before. The industrializing of America in the 1890s was accomplished by the consolidation of industrial power in the hands of the titans; it was accompanied by violent protest on the part of those who found themselves at the mercy of the new conquistadors. While the deindustrializing of America during the 1990s saw nothing so violent as the Homestead strike of 1892 or the Pullman strike of 1894, its myriad mergers, acquisitions, downsizings, outsourcings, and offshorings created anxieties that, if anything, were more pervasive than those facing Americans a century earlier. Nor, in either period, were ordinary workers the only ones to feel the economy tremble; coupon-clippers were shaken too. Repeatedly during the 1890s the dollar was savaged by overseas speculators; on one occasion, the pressure on the greenback forced the Treasury Department to turn to J. P. Morgan and a coalition of big American and British bankers for relief. During the 1990s, relief was more likely to be spelled in Japanese characters, as the dollar swooned against the yen and other currencies. But America's exposure to the whims of financial fortune recalled the conditions of a century before.

In each decade, the stomach-churning changes, economic and otherwise, evoked a variety of attempts at accommodation, amelioration, and denial. When industrialization and immigration made the cities of the 1890s ungovernable by received rules and practices, urban bosses like Richard Croker rewrote the rulebook. Despised by the more respectable classes, Croker and his colleagues in cities across the country made it their business to help others equally despised—and, in the time-honored American manner, to help themselves in the process. Yet if Croker was a hero to his New York constituents in the 1890s, he was hardly more so than Marion Barry was to the Washington voters of the 1990s who recalled him from prison to the mayorship of the nation's capital. A vote for Barry was a protest vote, but it was also a vote for pride by those who often had little else to be proud of.

Fear and resentment pervaded the politics of both decades. Each time, the sense of sliding over a cliff into an alien future prompted unprecedented efforts at heel-digging, and it produced a conspicuously conspiratorial brand of political rhetoric. In the 1990s, the mantra was traditional values, and the enemy a ubiquitous, iniquitous liberalism that was soft on crime, high on taxes, profligate on public spending, hostile to American institutions, and scornful of the real people. The nest of the liberals was the nation's capital; the home of virtue was the heartland, defined as anything beyond the Beltway and outside the inner cities. In the 1890s, the mantra was also traditional values, which in this case meant the way of life of American farmers, those sons and daughters of the soil who had nurtured the nation from its youth and who still represented its last best hope for the future. The enemy was the money power, centered in the cities of the East and sapping the strength of the South and West. In each decade, the distrust and hostility on the part of the aggrieved gave rise to a populist reaction: in the 1990s, a populism of Rush Limbaugh, Pat Robertson, and the Republican right; in the 1890s, a populism of Mary Lease, Tom Watson, and the Populist left.

The dirty secret of each brand of populism was race. In the 1890s, the nation addressed the unfinished business of Reconstruction by mandating the separation of blacks from whites; the 1896 Plessy case stamped the Supreme Court's seal of approval on the Jim Crow system. In the 1990s, the business of Reconstruction was still unfinished, and a major part of what remained was undoing the damage wrought by the work of the 1890s. The question of separate treatment for blacks (and other minorities) still vexed the country, although this time the issue was whether government ought to weigh in on the side of African-Americans rather than weigh down upon them. And in the 1990s, as in the 1890s, racial matters rent the black community. Some embraced affirmative action as a needed corrective to the Plessy legacy; others denounced it as paternalistic and stigmatizing. This division echoed the 1890s split between Booker T. Washington and W. E. B. Du Bois. Washington, a man of the people if ever one existed, was willing to tolerate short-term social and political inequality in order to play a longer game of economic betterment and self-reliance. Du Bois, an unabashed elitist, insisted that rights surrendered without a struggle would never be recaptured; besides, the birthright of political and moral equality that came with the Declaration of Independence couldn't be sold for a mess of material pottage.

Although domestic concerns dominated the politics of each decade, neither could escape involvement in the affairs of the larger world. The collapse of the Soviet Union in the early 1990s rendered irrelevant a half century of received wisdom regarding America's international role, and the new world disorder that followed required a redefinition of American national interests. Could America be safe in a world of Saddam Husseins? Could America's sense of morality and self-respect survive acquiescence in Serbian "ethnic cleansing"? On the other hand, would foreign intervention become a snare and a distraction from problems at home? Analogous questions exercised Americans during the 1890s. American expansionists contended that the United States had an obligation to share the blessings of liberty with other nations and peoples, to shine the light of democracy where the darkness of despotism reigned. Skeptics claimed that American energies would be better employed employing the out-of-work and housing the homeless at home. When a brutal colonial war in Cuba ravaged that island, Americans agonized for more than two years before deciding that decency and national interest required intervention. As wars almost always do, the Spanish-American War brought surprises, including possession of an American overseas empire. It also set the United States on the path to a globalism that would be the predominant feature of international life during the twentieth century; whether to try to sustain this globalism would lie at the heart of the 1990s debate over appropriate American attitudes and policies after the Cold War.

During each decade, the attitudes adopted toward America's role in the world reflected the deeper feelings regarding America's future. Optimists of the 1890s, like optimists of the 1990s, believed that the nation's best days were ahead, and that the United States had much to offer the world, including moral and political leadership. Pessimists of both periods doubted that America had much to offer itself, let alone anyone else. America may once have been great, but greatness was passing to other countries and peoples. Each time, each side had plenty of evidence to support its asser-

tions. Pessimists cited changing economic conditions that put the livelihoods of many millions at risk, divisions of class and race that made a
mockery of the American promise of equality and fair play, politics that
rewarded shortsightedness and cynicism, and international circumstances
that tempted America to save other people while ignoring its own. Optimists countered by interpreting economic change as a leading indicator of
economic health; by admitting that while racial and class differences remained, they paled next to what had gone before; by accepting, even ap-
plauding, raucous politics as a natural feature of democracy; and by
embracing the opportunity to provide American leadership to a world
sorely in need of guidance.

For Americans living in the 1990s, the events of the 1890s would be
worth exploring even if they imparted no insight into the present. Life on
the edge frequently evokes the best and worst in people and societies. It
did so during the 1890s, when the United States produced more than its
normal quota of demagogues and dedicated reformers, scoundrels and par-
agons of goodwill, when the American people lived up to their better selves
and down to their worse. What follows is the story of an extraordinary
time, and one that requires no extrinsic justification.

Yet the story of the 1890s also possesses significance beyond its inherent
color and drama. How America survived the last decade of the nineteenth
century—how it pursued its hopes, occasionally confronted and frequently
fled its fears, wrestled its angels and demons—reveals much about the
American people. What it reveals can be of use to a later generation of
those people, situated similarly on the cusp between an old century and a
new one.

Chapter 1

THE LOST FRONTIER

I

Fred Sutton had watched the earlier rushes into Oklahoma; he had seen friends no smarter, tougher, or more deserving than himself grab homesteads; and when word came that the government in Washington was going to open up the Cherokee Strip to settlement, he determined that this time he'd get a piece of the action. Folks with families and a hankering to grow crops and raise livestock usually went for the quarter-section farms—there would be forty thousand this time around—but Sutton fixed his sights on a town lot. He might start a store or build a boardinghouse; maybe he'd just sell it to someone who would. The previous rushes had shown that towns were where the big money was to be made. Oklahoma City hadn't been anything at all before April 22, 1889; overnight it became the crossroads of the territory. Lots there had changed hands several times, and those folks who had got in at the start were now sitting pretty.

Sutton studied maps of the Strip, plotting his strategy. He considered journeying to Kansas and entering from the north, but decided he'd have better luck coming in from the south. He'd been through part of the Strip, despite the fact that neither the Cherokees who had owned the land until recently nor the Texas cattlemen who had leased it were especially pleased at having visitors. Visitors invariably became "boomers," agitators for opening up Indian lands to white settlement; and between the boomers and the do-gooders who wanted to make Indians like white people, with farms of their own and churches and schools and stores and graveyards and all the rest, and who would accomplish their goal by forcing the Indians to give up their "surplus" land, Congress couldn't resist opening up more territory. Politicians had always been good at giving away what belonged to other people, and they probably always would be. The Cherokees, the shrewdest of the tribes in the Indian Territory, maybe the shrewdest of all the tribes in America, had fought off the boomers and the reformers for years, but finally the boomers and reformers had won. Not completely, though: while the Cherokees had given up 6 million acres, they had received $8.5 million in return. The land was worth more than that—after September 16, 1893, it would be worth a lot more—but $8.5 million was nothing to sneeze at. Most other tribes that had dealt with the government would have been happy to come away with that kind of cash.

Fred Sutton selected Wharton, a junction about a dozen miles from the southern boundary of the Strip, as his destination. Right now Wharton hardly bore noticing, but once the hundred thousand or so people who looked likely to make the run planted their markers and filed their claims and started getting hungry and thirsty and bored, Wharton would be as lively as any town in the territory. An enterprising young man should have no trouble making money there.

In July 1893, during the heat of the Oklahoma summer, Sutton traveled to Oklahoma City. Just looking around the city set his palms to itching: Who was to say Wharton wouldn't be the next Oklahoma City? The bustle simply reconfirmed Sutton's desire to be the first person to get to Wharton and the person to get the choicest lot there.

The initial step in his plan was to buy a good horse. For twenty-five dollars he found a snow white mustang, a wild animal that had never felt saddle or bridle. Sutton spent several days breaking the horse and getting it used to him. Then he began riding it, short distances at first, gradually increasing in length. By August, the two were making regular.training runs across the plains outside Oklahoma City. At one stretch they covered eighteen miles a day for two weeks.

Confident that he and his mount were in condition for the race, Sutton proceeded to register for the event. The first opening in 1889, as well as smaller openings in 1891 and 1892, had been attended by widespread cheating. "Sooners" had slipped across the line ahead of the official opening and snatched the prime locations. The cheating caused considerable violence and no end of bad feeling. Since then the federal authorities had adopted a tougher set of regulations designed to prevent jumping the gun. In the days before the opening of the Cherokee Strip, prospective settlers had to register at land offices established on the border of the Strip. When they subsequently filed their claims for land, the claims would be checked against the initial registration forms. Though this wouldn't eliminate soonering entirely, it would curtail the practice, since as the opening got closer the boundary grew thicker with soldiers and harder to cross surreptitiously.

Sutton arrived at the land office in Orlando, the town closest to Wharton, only to find a very long line of landseekers. It stretched for over a mile, snaking around the town, and was moving very slowly, what with the marginal literacy of many of the registrants. For a moment Sutton reconsidered his plan, but only for a moment. He took his place in line, and for two blazing days and two windy nights he inched his way forward. By the second night he was parched, starved, and exhausted. According to his later, doubtless exaggerated recollection, the only thing that saved him from death right there in line was the fortuitous arrival of a friend with a sandwich and a bottle of beer. Revived, he stuck out the last few score yards to the desk of the land officer and got his certificate of registration.

At this point there was nothing Sutton wanted more than a square meal, a bath, and a good night's sleep. He got none of them. The impending bonanza of land had swollen the population of Orlando from a couple hundred to thirty thousand. Meals were almost impossible to come by; when available, they fetched astronomical prices. Even drinking water was in desperately short supply, and what could be found often went first to the horses and other animals that were going to make the race. Water for bathing was out of the question. As for a place to sleep, only the most extravagant could afford the few hotel rooms in Orlando. Even if Sutton had had the money—and if he had, he wouldn't have been going to all this trouble to win a small plot of land—he couldn't leave his horse unattended. He'd been smart to buy his pony two months ahead of time; as race day approached, any steed that looked as though it might make a dozen miles drew covetous and often larcenous gazes. Sutton decided he needed to guard his pony in order to keep thieves at a distance.

Sutton hoped that at least on the morning of the appointed day he might manage to scrounge up a meal. But thirty thousand other people had the same idea at the same time, and he reconciled himself to making the run on an empty stomach.

He then turned to the problem of finding a good spot to begin the race. Hours before the noon start, thousands of people jostled for position on the boundary, stretching out for miles on either side of the town. Men, and boys who thought they could pass for men, stood beside horses that pawed the ground and snorted and shied at all the excitement. Men and women sat uneasily in wagons hitched to mules or oxen, getting out every few minutes to check harnesses or lubricate wheels for the tenth time. Cows unaccustomed to hauling carts tried to flick flies from their backs, only to have their tails catch in the traces. Those souls who needed the land most made ready to walk or run across the line.

At quarter to twelve, Sutton pushed his way to the front. He squeezed just to the right of a large, formidable character, obviously a veteran of innumerable frontier scrapes. This desperado had a wooden leg and a visage of the kind that caused children to cry, women to tremble, and men to cross the street. He stood in his stirrups on an Indian paint pony that appeared too small to carry him; he brandished a black-barreled Colt 45; he swore at the top of his lungs for the sheer pleasure of terrifying any fainthearts in the throng. Sutton wasn't a faintheart, but neither did he get any closer than he had to—which, by the crushing nature of the situation, was pretty close.

On the other side of Sutton was an unlikely-looking rusher, a young woman of perhaps eighteen years, dressed in black tights and skullcap. The girl's mount matched her apparel: a coal black Kentucky thoroughbred trained for speed and snorting to get started. Sutton was intrigued by her appearance, as well as by the fact that someone of her sex, years, and attire should be making the race. Hoping to impress her, he said he was going to Wharton and surely would be the first person there. She laughed and said she was going the same direction; she patted her horse on the neck and said she'd show him the way.

At a few minutes before noon, voices began to fall silent and riders and drivers tried to calm their beasts as every ear ached to hear the starter's shot. "Steady now!" shouted the army captain in charge of the Orlando line. All held their breath. At the stroke of twelve, his raised pistol roared and set the flood in motion.

Sutton spurred his mustang for all it was worth, pointing the horse for a wagon road that led across the plain toward Wharton. The wild man on his left had the same idea; so did the girl on his right. The three reached the road at the same time, with the man and his paint claiming one smooth wheeltrack, the girl and her thoroughbred the other wheeltrack, and Sutton and his snow white pony—no longer snow white amid the dust of fifty thousand hooves, wheels, and feet—caught in between. As one or another of the three momentarily pulled ahead, that person's horse claimed the best route, but the others refused to fall back and whipped their mounts to overtake the leader.

The three stuck close together for several miles. Sutton was as determined as ever to make Wharton first, but the one-legged man looked as if he'd kill rather than be bested. As his horse tired, the man took to beating the exhausted animal about the neck and shoulders with the barrel of his Colt. The poor beast couldn't help slowing down; the man pistol-whipped it the more. As Sutton passed the desperado, the paint stumbled and threw its rider headlong. Sutton looked back only long enough to see the one-legged man disappear under the trample of horses and riders that were following too rapidly and single-mindedly to halt.

The black thoroughbred and the black-dressed girl hung on longer, but eventually they too started to fall back. She, having seen the horrible end to which the one-legged man had come, resorted to no such frenzied and fatal efforts to drive her horse on.

The weeks Sutton had spent running his mustang across the prairie now came to his aid, and the pair gradually distanced themselves from the pack. The pounding hoofbeats and the furious exhortations and curses of the riders faded into the background. Success—Wharton—loomed, almost within reach.

Then, mounting a rise, Sutton saw a low cloud in the distance. His first thought was that it must be dust, but he couldn't figure out what might be raising it. He was sure none of the other racers were ahead of him. As he drew closer, he realized it was smoke. In the dead of night, just hours before the land rush was to begin, some sooners had bribed their way past the soldiers guarding the boundary line. With morning they had torched the prairie to slow down those who would come behind them. After a long, dry summer the blue-joint grass—taller than a man in places—quickly became a wall of flames.

The fire terrified Sutton's pony, which balked and tried to turn away. But Sutton spurred and whipped the horse toward a break in the flames, and the pair plunged through. Fortunately, the area of the grass still actively burning wasn't many yards deep, and though the flames blistered Sutton's face and burned all his hair off and singed the pony badly, they were past the inferno in a few seconds. Glad to be alive, they kept racing toward Wharton.

The fire reminded Sutton of his and the horse's need for water. About a mile beyond the scorched earth, they came upon a lone man—perhaps one of the arsonists, perhaps not. Sutton didn't raise the issue, since on the back of his wagon the man had a barrel of water. At that moment water was more important than the fire—which anyway was now working in Sutton's favor against those behind him. Sutton approached the man, intending to ask for a drink of water. The man pulled a gun. "This is my land," he said, "and the sooner you are off it the longer you will live." Sutton assured the man he had no designs on his claim; he was headed for Wharton. He only wanted some water. The man thought the matter over for a few moments while Sutton nervously looked back up the road to see if his competitors had made it past the fire. Finally the man agreed to sell some water for a dollar a pint. At that price Sutton decided to go thirsty himself but bought two pints for his horse. He wetted his bandanna and swabbed down the face and nose of the mustang. Lacking a container, he soaked the material and placed it in the horse's mouth, letting the animal suck what moisture it could out of the bandanna. Then Sutton remounted and, still under the gun of the mistrustful man, resumed his race.

All went well until horse and rider were within rifle shot of their destination. They had left the road and were dashing across the open plains through tall grass when the ground suddenly fell away beneath the horse's feet. The rare but torrential rains that fall in that part of the country had carved a sheer-sided ravine, perhaps twenty feet deep and somewhat wider. It was too late to stop or turn around; Sutton had no choice but to try to leap his horse across. He dropped the reins to give the animal its head and held on for dear life to the saddle horn. The pony gamely sprang for the far side, but after twelve miles of hard riding its haunches just didn't have the strength to propel horse and rider across. Its front legs landed on the other side, but its hind legs fell short, and it pitched backward into the ravine. While the horse was going down, Sutton kicked his feet free from the stirrups and scrambled off. Although Sutton escaped the fall unhurt, the horse broke something. Its hind legs were paralyzed, and it couldn't get to its feet.

For a moment Sutton was unable to decide whether to stay with the horse or finish the race afoot. Loyalty to the animal that had carried him this far held him to the spot; land hunger pulled him forward. The latter won out, and after convincing himself there was nothing he could do for the horse (which in fact died the next day), he ran on.

As he had intended, he was the first—of the honest rushers anyway—to reach Wharton. He planted his flag on a choice site and hurried to find a government official to file his claim.

During the next six hours, Sutton watched Wharton grow from nearly nothing to a town (albeit a tent town) of ten thousand. The Territory of Oklahoma, which had been created out of the Indian Territory in 1889, added seven new counties that afternoon. They were temporarily designated Counties K, L, M, N, O, P, and Q (previous letters having already been assigned). In the process, 6 million acres of land passed from the public domain to private hands. In later years the federal government would be stingier with its property, and privatizing public assets would require more time and paperwork. But in the 1890s, public ownership of land was generally thought to be a temporary aberration, and the quicker the land passed to private individuals the better.

On the afternoon of September 16, 1893, Wharton, Oklahoma Territory, was a frantic place and an expensive one. An entrepreneur named R. W. Black and his assistant Mr. Williams sold "Pale Malt Tonic" at a dollar a bottle, with ice optional at ten cents a pound. H. C. Finley opened a restaurant that served a cup of coffee and a stale sandwich for a dollar and a half. A watermelon dealer, taking advantage of the hot weather and lack of potable water, sold a carload of melons at a dollar each. Saloons and dancehalls started up in midafternoon; by sundown their roulette wheels, poker tables, and escort services were doing business at the same pace the land office had been doing all afternoon.

Squabbles over land claims led to fights; the fights frequently involved the firearms that nearly everyone had brought along. To prevent matters from getting out of hand, the local authorities had sent a message to nearby Guthrie—itself a result of the 1889 rush—asking for Bill Tilghman, a law enforcement officer who had won a reputation as a no-nonsense law-and-order man during the earlier rushes. Tilghman immediately produced a calming effect on Wharton; as Sutton described the situation later, the marshal's "pleasant smile and cheery voice, to say nothing of his brace of silver-mounted 45s and a sawed-off Winchester, soon restored the confidence of the better element."

Some members of the worse element required a little more time to catch on. One roughneck known as Crescent Sam, on account of the flaming semicircular scar on his left temple, ran into Tilghman on the main street of Wharton. "Hello, Crescent," Tilghman said. "When did you leave the Horseshoe outfit, and when are you going back?" Sam replied with a snarl, "I left this morning and will go back when I feel like it, and not before." Tilghman gently suggested that the prudent thing would be for Sam to remove himself from Wharton by sundown. Sam retorted that he intended to stick around awhile and would certainly be in town that night. Tilghman responded matter-of-factly, "If you are I shall have to kill you."

Tilghman went about his business for the rest of the day. An hour after sunset, as he approached the rowdiest of Wharton's tent saloons, he spied Crescent Sam under one of the coal-oil lamps that already lit the major thoroughfares. At first Sam didn't see Tilghman; he was too busy declaiming that he was a wolf and this was his night to howl. He defied anyone to send him home. To punctuate his remarks, he fired several shots in the general direction of the moon.

As he turned to swagger down the street, still blaspheming boisterously, he saw Tilghman. Sam instantly fell quiet. For a moment he and Tilghman stood silent in the yellow glow of the lamp, sizing each other up. Slowly Sam's left hand reached for his holster; Tilghman's eyes tracked Sam's slightest shiver. Just as he was about to draw his left gun, Sam suddenly fired the pistol in his right hand, which had seemed to be out of bullets.

Two shots cracked out, so close together as to sound almost one. Neither man moved for a long second. Then Sam slumped to the dusty street. Tilghman lifted his own left arm to examine a neat hole in his coat and shirt just below the armpit. He blew the smoke and powder blacking from his gun barrel and calmly reloaded. Then he walked over to where Sam lay dead, muttered "Poor devil," and dragged the body off the street into the saloon from which Sam had emerged. He laid the corpse along one tent-wall of the saloon, carefully crossing the arms over the chest. The gamblers briefly looked up from their cards and dice, but when they saw there was nothing to get excited about they went back to their game. Sam lay in state for two nights and a day before the smell started bothering the patrons. The management then arranged to have the body removed.

Fred Sutton had watched the shootout from the side of the street. He strolled about the town for a bit longer before returning to his claim. He raised a small pup tent he had brought for the purpose and as a pillow arranged the saddle he had retrieved from his unfortunate horse. Within seconds he drifted off to sleep.

Some time later—he couldn't tell just how much later—he awoke to a gunshot fired from close range. The bullet tore through the canvas wall of his tent, zinged past his ear, ricocheted off the saddle horn, and exited through the roof. After lying still for a minute to see if anyone was going to shoot back, Sutton got up. He reached for a match; in doing so he stumbled over a prostrate young man, evidently breathing his last. Sutton decided the dying man was beyond assistance, and besides he wasn't sure where to turn for help. So he lay back down and soon fell asleep again. This time nothing disturbed his well-earned slumber.

In the morning he looked the deceased over more closely. He was a handsome fellow, dressed all in black: black silk shirt and tie, black cotton jeans, and an expensive pair of tooled leather boots. Perhaps Sutton mused that he would have made a fitting match for the girl on the thoroughbred. The dead man carried no identification, and if someone in town knew who he was, no one was talking. The young man was buried a short while later, an early occupant of the newly established potter's field.

Fred Sutton proceeded to make good on his claim—a wise move, since the opening of the Cherokee Strip was the final major rush into Oklahoma, as well as the biggest. The 1889 rush had provided homesteads to some fifteen thousand families, carved out of roughly 3 million acres. A much smaller opening in 1891 had been followed in 1892 by the allotment of

3.5 million acres. In the rush to the Cherokee Strip, approximately forty thousand families divided up 6 million acres, not counting those people like Sutton who claimed town lots. An opening of Kickapoo Indian lands in 1895 was again a small one. It was also the last of the one-day wonders: a subsequent land opening in 1901 was conducted in accordance with a lottery scheme. Applicants for land filled out tickets with their names, sealed them in envelopes, and had them placed in large revolving drums. On opening day the land commissioner and his assistants spun the drums and pulled out names. The winners were allowed to file claims according to the order in which their names were drawn. In 1906, the remaining "surplus" Indian lands were made available for general settlement. This time the government decided to maximize revenues: lots were auctioned to the highest bidders. The next year Oklahoma entered the Union as the forty-sixth state.

II

After all the land-rushing, the Indians of Oklahoma were left with only a rump of the original Indian Territory. Dispossessing the natives of what would become the United States had been a protracted process, stretching back to the first English arrivals in Virginia and Massachusetts in the early seventeenth century. The penultimate phase had begun in the late 1860s when the Union Pacific Railroad had crossed the Great Plains, splitting the buffalo herd of the plains into two parts. A few years later leather workers in the East discovered an economical way to tan buffalo hides; during the next decade, professional buffalo killers slaughtered the huge stupid beasts at the rate of millions per year. By 1883, a scientific expedition could discover only two hundred buffalo in the entire plains region. The extermination of the buffalo left the Indians of the plains bereft of their major source of food, shelter, and clothing. For some time the American government had been trying to talk the Indians onto reservations; in many instances, military coercion accompanied the talk. The extermination of the buffalo delivered the coup de grâce to the Indians' hope of surviving outside the reservations. A few hard-core reservation rejectionists retreated north to Canada; the rest gave up and moved onto the reservations.

But though the reservations allowed the Indians far less land than they had been accustomed to inhabit, to many whites the reservations seemed larger than necessary. Even before all the Indians had resigned themselves to life on the reservations, whites began chipping away at the reservations' boundaries. In 1877, for example, the Sioux had been forced to give up the Black Hills of Dakota—demonstrating, if such demonstration were necessary, that while the Indians might have won the Battle of the Little Big Horn against George Custer and his men, the whites would win the war.

The most direct assault on the reservations came in 1887, with the passage of the Dawes Act. The Dawes Act authorized the president to order the surveying of the Indian reservations; after the surveys were completed the reservations would be divided among tribe members, with each head of a family receiving 160 acres, each single adult and each orphan child 80 acres, and each other child 40 acres. Where the land was fit only for grazing, the acreage allotments would be doubled. Title wouldn't be transferred to individuals at once, lest unscrupulous land sharks swindle the new owners out of their property; the federal government would hold the title in trust for twenty-five years. In the event that some Indians resisted the allotment of tribal lands, the government was empowered to assign land to those who refused to select land for themselves. Indians would become citizens of the United States, subject to federal laws and the laws of the states or territories in which they resided. In effect, the tribes would no longer legally exist.

Support for the Dawes Act came from two sources. One wished the Indians well; the other didn't. The well-wishers believed that individual ownership of land would be in the best interests of the Indians, in that individual ownership would facilitate the assimilation of the Indians into the larger American society. So long as tribal lands were held in common, there was no incentive for individual Indians to improve their lands: the lazy and shiftless would freeload on the backs of the hardworking and thrifty. By the grant of individual titles, Indians would acquire this incentive.

The second group that supported the Dawes Act, the group that didn't wish the Indians well, simply wanted to seize more of their land. The Dawes Act accomplished this quite neatly. Basic arithmetic showed that 160 acres times the number of Indian families, plus 80 acres times the number of single adults and orphans, plus 40 times the number of other children, totaled far less land than the reservations comprised. What was left over would be made available to whites.

At first the Dawes Act didn't apply to the so-called Five Civilized Tribes: the Cherokee, Choctaw, Chickasaw, Creek, and Seminole. But a variety of legal devices gradually eroded this exemption. In the case of the Cherokee Strip—from which the Cherokees derived a tidy income in the form of leasing fees from Texas cattle ranchers—President Harrison in 1890 declared the leases illegal and ordered all cattle removed. This ruling drastically lowered the value of the Strip to the Cherokees, which was the whole idea, and it caused the Cherokees to cut the deal with the government that gave Fred Sutton his opportunity.

During the next few years the assault on the status—and lands—of the Five Tribes continued. Eventually the assailants persuaded Congress to add the Five Tribes to the Dawes list of those whose lands might be subdivided even against their will. In 1898, Congress delivered the final blow to tribal autonomy: it did away with tribal courts in Oklahoma. By this action all inhabitants of Oklahoma became subject to the same territorial laws. The consequence was to emasculate the tribal governments, since without legal enforcement powers those governments meant little. Acceding to force majeure, the governments of the Five Tribes decided to liquidate operations, which they did just before Oklahoma became a state.

In the same year—1890—that President Harrison revoked the Cherokee leases, the Sioux chief Sitting Bull received a visitor on the Standing Rock reservation in South Dakota. Kicking Bear, a Sioux from the Cheyenne River reservation, brought strange and wonderful news from the far Southwest. Kicking Bear said a voice had commanded him to find the spirits of dead Indians who were waiting to return to earth; with his brother-in-law Short Bull and several other Sioux, he had traveled by train westward until the steel rails stopped. There the search party had been greeted by two Indians who welcomed them as brothers, though the searchers had never laid eyes on the two before. These Indians spoke of a messiah, a man named Wovoka who foretold a return of the past days of peace and plenty. To see him, they must continue to the west. They traveled for four days on foot until they came to a camp of Paiutes near Pyramid Lake in Nevada. The Paiutes said they must travel still farther, to Walker Lake where the Messiah would speak to them.

When Kicking Bear and his fellow pilgrims arrived at Walker Lake, they discovered hundreds of other Indians from dozens of tribes, all eager to hear what the Messiah had to tell them. On the third day the Messiah appeared. He was the same Messiah the white missionaries called the Christ, but instead of having a white skin, this man was an Indian. He said he had been sent by God once before, many years ago. The white people had misused him, beating and wounding him, and he had gone back to heaven. Now he had returned as an Indian to try once again to teach the people how to live, and to restore the earth to the way it had been before the white men had taken all the Indians' land.

He said that when the grass next grew in the spring a wave of new soil would cover the earth, burying the white men. From the new soil would sprout new grass, tall and lush; fresh creeks and rivers would flow among new groves of trees. The buffalo would return, and life would be as before.

Lest they too be buried by the wave of soil, the Indians must learn a new dance. Those who practiced this Ghost Dance would be lifted up to the sky when the earth-wave came. The wave would pass beneath their feet, and after it did they would descend softly to the ground, where they would walk among the returned spirits of their ancestors.

Wovoka then demonstrated his dance. He danced for hours, late into the night. Kicking Bear and the others joined him, and all danced again on subsequent nights.

When they had learned the dance well enough to teach it to their own kinsmen, Kicking Bear and his friends were instructed to leave Walker Lake. They went back to the railroad and returned to their homes. Kicking Bear spread the knowledge of the Ghost Dance among his people on the Cheyenne River; Short Bull and the others taught the dance to the Sioux elsewhere in Dakota Territory.

Sitting Bull listened intently to Kicking Bear's story. The Sioux chief had heard of this dance that was gaining converts on nearly all the reservations. He wasn't sure he believed that the ghosts of dead Indians would return to life, and he had serious doubts that a wave of earth would sweep the white men under. But his people, discouraged at their plight on the reservations and desperate for an escape, if only spiritual, wanted to dance, and he wouldn't tell them not to. Besides, it would be prudent to be ready in case the Messiah's message did turn out to be true.

All the same, Sitting Bull worried that the Ghost Dance would cause trouble with the white soldiers. The whites didn't like anything that seemed subversive, and now that the Sioux were on reservations the whites had them at their mercy.

Kicking Bear and Short Bull said there was nothing to fear: the dancers wore special "ghost shirts" that were impervious to the white soldiers' bullets.

This worried Sitting Bull even more, and it continued to worry him after Kicking Bear and Short Bull left. He knew enough about the whites to realize that Sioux warriors dancing what the whites would interpret as a war dance and convinced they couldn't be killed would seem very threatening. In the past, the whites had responded to Indian threats by attacking. There was no reason to think they wouldn't do so now.

Events soon confirmed Sitting Bull's worries. As the cult of the Ghost Dance spread across the Great Plains, word came from Washington to suppress it. At best the cult would encourage the Indians to resist the ways of white civilization; at worst it would incite them to rebellion.

Suppressing the Ghost Dance without triggering violence would have required a steady head and an ability to inspire confidence among distrustful Indians—talents in short supply among the white officials who dealt with Indians. The agent in charge of the Pine Ridge reservation, several days' ride south of Standing Rock, was particularly deficient. Daniel Royer was a doctor and failed politician who owed his job as Indian agent to his friendship with South Dakota Senator Richard Pettigrew. For years Indian agencies had been easy pickings for small-time grafters; Royer was in the tradition. He knew next to nothing about Indians and scarcely more about human relations in general.

The Sioux at Pine Ridge recognized the kind of person they were dealing with; they dubbed Royer "Young-Man-Afraid-of-Indians." As the Ghost Dance took hold on the reservation, Royer blustered for the dancers to stop. They refused. Their refusal convinced Royer they were bent on insurrection; his failure to follow up on his threats of punishment convinced the Indians they could do more or less as they chose.

The situation grew increasingly tense through the autumn of 1890. The Ghost Dancers abandoned other activities in order to dance day and night. Helped along by hunger and exhaustion, they danced themselves into a state of self-hypnosis. They collapsed and hallucinated; when they revived they related visions of the Messiah, of heaven, of the new white-free world to come. The dancing attracted other Sioux to Pine Ridge, some of them dancers, some simply onlookers. The growing numbers frightened Royer the more, and he frantically called for troops to prevent an uprising.

Royer's superiors understood that he was the kind to cry wolf when no wolf was nearby, and they let him cry for a few weeks without responding. But toward the end of November, he seemed more alarmed than usual. "Indians are dancing in the snow and are wild and crazy," he cabled Washington. "We need protection and we need it now."

Protection arrived in late November in the form of U.S. Army troops. The soldiers' arrival increased the tension, as some experienced Indian-watchers had predicted it would. One former Indian agent, asked how he would handle the Ghost Dancers, remarked, "I should let the dance continue. The coming of the troops has frightened the Indians. If the Seventh-Day Adventists prepare their ascension robes for the second coming of the Savior, the United States Army is not put in motion to prevent them. Why should not the Indians have the same privilege? If the troops remain, trouble is sure to come."

But this was a minority viewpoint. The troops stayed—and trouble came. With the appearance of the troops, the leaders of the Ghost Dancers, including Kicking Bear and Short Bull, removed themselves and their followers to a remote corner of the Pine Ridge reservation, to a mesa called the Stronghold. There they continued to dance and prepared to defend themselves and their religious beliefs against the white intruders. Three thousand strong, they seemed—to nervous whites in the area, anyway—to pose a serious threat to white control of western South Dakota.

The army commander for the district, General Nelson Miles, summoned reinforcements, until he had five thousand troops on hand. Miles wasn't eager to storm the Stronghold; initially he sought to negotiate the Ghost Dancers down from the mesa.

But an event beyond his control irreparably undermined his credibility with the Sioux. During the first part of December, James McLaughlin, the Indian agent at Standing Rock, received reports that Sitting Bull was preparing to leave his home there and join the Ghost Dancers at the Stronghold. Though no longer the terror of the plains he once had been, the revered leader was still a potent symbol of Sioux resistance, and the thought of his linking up with the Ghost Dancers sent shudders through whites all across the northern plains.

McLaughlin decided to preempt any move by Sitting Bull: he ordered the chief arrested. He dispatched a contingent of Indian police—Indians hired to enforce white laws and regulations against their fellow Indians—to arrest Sitting Bull at his cabin. The police surprised Sitting Bull before dawn on December 15, but they in turn were surprised by a larger group of Sitting Bull's supporters. Wild shooting erupted in the dark December morning; before the shooting ended, a dozen dead bodies lay sprawled on the frozen ground, among them Sitting Bull's.

The assassination of Sitting Bull—for so his death appeared to most of the Sioux—snapped relations between the whites and the Sioux. Even relatively friendly Sioux took to the hills, apparently in preparation for battle. The army worried especially about the chief Big Foot, who was known to have embraced the Ghost Dance. When word arrived at General Miles's headquarters that Big Foot and his followers had left the Cheyenne River and were headed toward Pine Ridge, the general assumed they were aiming to join Kicking Bear and Short Bull at the Stronghold. This assumption was probably wrong: Big Foot, a relative pacifist among his people and one who currently was suffering from pneumonia, more likely was trying to avoid a fight than to pick one. But Miles wasn't taking any chances, and he sent cavalry units to scour the countryside and intercept the chief and his band.

Miles's soldiers caught up with Big Foot on the banks of Wounded Knee Creek. To prevent his getting away, the soldiers, under the command of Colonel James Forsyth, surrounded Big Foot's camp. They mounted four small Hotchkiss cannons on a rise above the camp just to make sure— although, with over two hundred women and children in his entourage, Big Foot couldn't move very fast.

On the morning of December 29, Forsyth attempted to disarm Big Foot and his warriors. The Indians realized they were outnumbered and out-gunned, and most appeared ready to hand over their weapons. But a medicine man began to dance the Ghost Dance, and he urged his fellows to fight. He reiterated the promise that their ghost shirts would protect them from the soldiers' bullets. This made the soldiers more nervous than ever. One attempted to seize the rifle of a deaf man who wasn't quite sure what was happening; the rifle fired.

As soon as it did, guns on both sides began blasting away. Indians and soldiers, standing just yards from each other, went down in clumps. Troopers in the rear opened up on the camp, raking the tents with their rifles and the Hotchkiss cannons. The soldiers' fire continued long beyond the end of return fire from the Indians; most of the last victims were obvious noncombatants. When the firing finally ceased, one hundred and fifty Indians, including many women and children, were dead, and scores more were wounded. The soldiers lost twenty-five killed and thirty-nine wounded, several to bullets from their own comrades.

The battle—or massacre—at Wounded Knee at once utterly alienated nearly all the Sioux and demoralized most of them. Cooperation with the whites was hopeless, but so was the Ghost Dance. The "ghost shirts" hadn't saved anyone at Wounded Knee; all they did was produce more ghosts.

General Miles capitalized on the demoralization, as well as on dissension among the Sioux leadership. He surrounded the camps of the Ghost Dancers and forced their surrender. The last ones gave up on January 15, 1891.

III

The battle-massacre at Wounded Knee was the last significant armed confrontation between Indians and U.S. troops. As such it signaled the passing of the Indian frontier on the northern plains, just as the land rushes into Oklahoma denoted the passing of the frontier in the south. In each case, the frontier's passing was a matter of both geography and psychology. Geographically speaking, Oklahoma and Dakota filled with settlers, erasing the distinction between settled and unsettled territory. Psychologically, the area that once had been wild was now tamed. The psychological element was fully as important as the geographical, for the frontier had always been a state of mind as much as a state of anything else. The frontier was that region where the unknown and unpredictable began. Advancing the frontier—winning the West—meant increasing the area of the predictable and diminishing the area of the unpredictable. Some people lamented this change; more didn't.

Among those who did was Frederick Jackson Turner. In July 1893, at the time Fred Sutton was breaking his mustang for the race into the Cherokee Strip, Turner read a paper to a Chicago gathering of his colleagues in the historical profession. That July wasn't quite as hot in Chicago as in Oklahoma, but it was more humid. The city sweltered through the summer doldrums; and only occasionally did a breeze off Lake Michigan lift the heat. Not many of those breezes found their way into the halls where the historians were meeting—and neither, for that matter, had many of the country's most prominent historians. Although Henry Cabot Lodge, Edward Eggleston, Hermann von Holst, and Albion Small were all specifically asked to come to the conference, each decided he had better things to do. The few well-knowns who did show up—Edward Everett Hale, Frederic Bancroft—were drawn more by the Columbian Exposition down the street than by the historians' conference, which in fact had been convened to lend an air of intellectual respectability to the world's fair.

The schedule of papers for Wednesday, July 12, included some yawners. One professor spoke on "English Popular Uprisings in the Middle Ages," another on "The Social Compact and Mr. Jefferson's Adoption of It," a third on "Early Lead Mining in Illinois and Wisconsin." By the time Fred Turner got up to read his paper on "The Significance of the Frontier in American History," those who hadn't fled the hall for the more lively happenings at the fair needed something to snap them out of their somnolence.

Turner didn't provide it. Such at least was the judgment of those in attendance. One listener recalled that the predominant mood was bored indifference; no one bothered after Turner finished to challenge the speaker or even ask questions. Only one of the Chicago newspapers noticed Turner's talk, giving it a perfunctory paragraph in the goings-on-about-town section. A magazine account of the conference had good things to say about the lecture on lead mining but overlooked Turner entirely.

Turner in 1893 was an easy man to overlook. Of medium height and pleasing but unremarkable appearance, he was thirty-two in the year of the Columbian Exposition. He had been born and raised in Portage, Wisconsin, a hamlet within gunshot of the upper Midwest's frontier. His relatives were frontier folk; he later remembered, "My people on both sides moved at least every generation and built new communities." Turner added, "My father was named Andrew Jackson Turner at his birth in 1832 by my Democratic grandfather, and I still rise and go to bed to the striking of the old clock that was brought into the house the day he was born, at the edge of the Adirondack forest." Turner recalled his early years fondly as he grew older. He recounted Indian-guided canoe trips down the Wisconsin River through "virgin forests of balsam firs"; he recollected "seeing deer in the river—antlered beauties who watched us come down with curious eyes and then broke for the tall timber; hearing the squaws in their village on the high bank talk their low treble to the bass of our Indian polesman; feeling that I belonged to it all."

Frontier life was not uniformly idyllic, though it never lacked color or excitement. "I have seen a lynched man," Turner said, "hanging from a tree when I came home from school in Portage, have played around Fort Winnebago at its outskirts, have seen the red-shirted Irish raftsmen 'take' the town when they tied up and came ashore, have plodded up the 'pinery' road that ran past our house to the pine woods of Northern Wisconsin, have seen Indians come in on their ponies to buy paint and ornaments and sell their furs, have stumbled on their camp on the Baraboo, where dried pumpkins were hung up, and cooking muskrats were in the kettle, and an Indian family were bathing in the river."

Portage still had less than five thousand inhabitants when Turner left for the University of Wisconsin in 1878. The school at Madison had little reputation, deservedly, although a few compelling teachers graced its faculty. The one who most influenced Turner was W. F. Allen, a Harvard graduate who had subsequently studied in Germany. Allen taught in the history department, which was small enough that he had to cover several fields, lecturing on ancient and medieval history in addition to American. Turner greatly admired Allen, and from Allen acquired an appreciation for large themes in history. Allen also inspired in Turner a determination to discover how diverse aspects of history fit together.

For a time after graduation, Turner considered a career in journalism, his father's field. But the undeadlined world of academia was more to his taste, and he returned to Madison for a master's degree. He taught history at his alma mater until the university's new and ambitious president decided to make Turner a part of his faculty-upgrading program. He essentially kicked Turner out, telling him he might return with Ph.D. in hand.

Several Wisconsin acquaintances of Turner had gone to Johns Hopkins University in Baltimore, and Turner followed their lead. Hopkins was then the most prominent graduate school in America, having staffed itself with a cohort of European-trained (usually German-trained) scholars. Herbert Baxter Adams lorded over the history department, stamping his students with his distinctive but not then unusual approach to the study of history. Adams's approach reflected both his own European educational background and the contemporary widespread enchantment with the scientific method, especially those aspects associated with the evolutionary theories of Charles Darwin. Adams held that American social practices and institutions—American democracy, for instance—had evolved out of practices and institutions that had previously arisen in Europe. "The science of Biology no longer favors the theory of spontaneous generation," Adams wrote a few years before Turner arrived at Hopkins. "Wherever organic life occurs, there must have been some seed for that life. History should not be content with describing effects when it can explain causes. It is just as improbable that free local institutions should spring up without a germ along American shores as that English wheat should have grown here without planting. Town institutions were propagated in New England by old English and Germanic ideas brought over by Pilgrims and Puritans."

What Adams asserted was incontrovertible: nothing in history springs from nothing. The controversy started when historians attempted to assign weights to the various precursors and determinants of social institutions. Adams and other "germ" theorists gave greatest weight to the ideas Europeans brought over from the Old World and much less to the conditions in the New World that modified those ideas in American practice. Trained in Europe by European teachers, Adams and the germists stressed continuity with European roots in the development of American democracy.

Turner wasn't persuaded, and he would say so before long. He earned his doctorate in 1890, by which time he was back teaching at Wisconsin. Classroom duties occupied most of his waking hours during the next few years; of those he stole from the classroom he devoted a major portion to fishing on Wisconsin's innumerable lakes and streams. His fishing expeditions afforded him plenty of opportunity to think but not much to write—which may partly have explained his lifelong affinity for angling: Turner constantly sought excuses to avoid putting pen to paper. During the early 1890s he published little, and what he did publish didn't appear in journals that attracted much attention. His most substantial piece of work was his dissertation, a study of trading posts in Wisconsin. Turner's teaching earned him a modest reputation on campus in Madison, but students weren't exactly thronging his classroom.

So it wasn't surprising that when Turner announced a new approach to the interpretation of American history in his 1893 Chicago paper, the importance of what he had to say took a while to sink in. Turner had noted the opening of Oklahoma and the suppression of the Ghost Dancers, and he reflected on what the passing of the frontier portended for American civilization. He adopted as his point of departure a statement contained in the 1890 federal census report: "Up to and including 1890 the country had a frontier of settlement, but at present the unsettled area has been so broken into by isolated bodies of settlement that there can hardly be said to be a frontier line."

Turner contended that the existence until the very recent past of this frontier of settlement had largely determined the course of American history and the development of American institutions. "The existence of an area of free land," he asserted, "its continuous recession, and the advance of American settlement westward explain American development." The frontier, which he defined as "the meeting point between savagery and civilization," was the region of "most rapid and effective Americanization." On the frontier, immigrants and the descendants of immigrants were refashioned into a new people, no longer English or German or Irish or Swedish but American. The characteristic traits of Americans—individualism and self-reliance, practicality, impatience with forms and traditions, energy, inventiveness, egalitarianism, confidence that the future would be better than the present—were the direct result of the frontier experience. On the frontier, people made their mark based on their own abilities, not on the status of their parents. The frontier offered opportunity to all comers; in America, no one had to accept permanent disadvantages.

The frontier had been the fountainhead of American democracy, Turner declared. With each stage in the march of settlement westward, Americans had been required to reinvent government, and this continual reinvention precluded the congealing of a political system in which power begot privilege and privilege monopolized power. "The peculiarity of American institutions is the fact that they have been compelled to adapt themselves to the changes of an expanding people, to the changes involved in crossing a continent, in winning a wilderness, and in developing at each area of this progress, out of the primitive economic and political conditions of the frontier, the complexity of city life." Where land was abundant and cheap, no one needed to kowtow to landlords or employers. Economic independence begot political independence; democracy was the child of the frontier, the natural consequence of free land.

The frontier had offered an escape valve for the excess energies Americans developed. "What the Mediterranean Sea was to the Greeks, breaking the bond of custom, offering new experiences, calling out new institutions and activities—that, and more, the ever retreating frontier has been to the United States." Excess energy in Europe gave rise to wars and other forms of social turmoil; in America it was vented productively in settling the frontier.

Turner saw the decade of the 1890s as a watershed in American history. The vast expanse of free land that had made America what it was had disappeared. No more would the frontier guarantee that America would be different from Europe. The escape valve had been screwed shut. The frontier was gone, and with its passing ended the first phase of American history.

Turner's message wasn't original, though his packaging of it was. As

Theodore Roosevelt remarked upon reading a printed copy of the lecture, Turner put "into shape a good deal of thought that has been floating around rather loosely." The floating thought included the ideas of both Americans and Europeans. Émile Boutmy, a French writer whose treatise *Studies in Constitutional Law* appeared in English translation in 1891, held that a strong central authority was needed to maintain order in the crowded countries of Europe, but that in the wide open spaces of America, political institutions could develop along more independent and democratic lines. Another French writer, André Churillon, argued in the *Review of Reviews* in 1892 that the equality of opportunity afforded by the abundance of land on the frontier enforced a social equality unknown in Europe. From social equality sprang political equality, whose principal manifestation was democracy. The English journalist and political economist Walter Bagehot had contended in *Physics and Politics* that the constant struggle against nature was what gave American politics and American society their distinctiveness. Bagehot explained that the "eager restlessness" and the "high-strung nervous organization" foreigners commonly remarked in Americans were precisely those attributes best suited to taming the wilderness and pushing the frontier westward. Turner didn't read Italian but had friends who did; those friends brought to his attention a recent volume by Achille Loria, a political economist whose *Analisa della Proprietà Capitalista* described a causal connection between decreasing availability of land and the rise of freedom-stifling aristocracy. Until recently the United States had been spared what Europe had suffered for centuries; with free land running out, America wouldn't be spared much longer.

Some of Turner's countrymen likewise contributed to the molding of his frontier thesis. Reformer Henry George's 1879 *Progress and Poverty* offered a scheme for replacing the diverse taxes on which the different layers of government in the United States depended with a single tax on the appreciation in land values consequent to settlement and development. George's reformism appealed to Turner, a fellow progressive at heart; but more important for Turner as a theorist of history and politics was George's emphasis on the existence of "unfenced land" in the shaping of the American character. Free land, George said, was what gave Americans the independence of mind, the resourcefulness and the optimism that typified their world view. Turner agreed. Brown University professor Francis Walker, in an 1889 essay entitled "The Growth of the Nation," outlined the evolution of the American character; the westward movement, he said, accounted for the most important aspects of that evolution, especially the emergence of the practical intelligence and public-mindedness that set Americans apart from other people. Walker subsequently read the same census report that caught Turner's attention, and he forecast a dismal future for America now that the frontier had vanished. In 1892 he warned, "No longer can a continent of free virgin lands avert us from the social struggle which the Old World has known so long and so painfully."

Perhaps partly because of the fundamental familiarity of the frontier thesis, Turner's interpretation didn't immediately make much noise. Another part of the delay resulted from the circumstance that most of the mandarins of the American historical profession—men like Herbert Baxter Adams—were still devoted to the germ approach to American democracy (also labeled the Teutonic School, after the supposed Teutonic origins of American democracy). Related to the germ theory was the conception of New England as the seat of American development. The New England town meeting was thought to be a variant on the tribal councils of the Black Forest; American legislatures were the descendants of the German *moot*.

Turner's frontier thesis challenged both the germ theory and the primacy of New England. Turner contended that the critical element in the emergence of American democracy was not some idea transplanted from the Old World to the New but the frontier soil in which the idea took root. Turner never denied that American institutions had European antecedents, yet he held that the antecedents mattered far less in the development of the institutions than the conditions in America in which they developed. And he declared that the most important of those conditions were found not in New England, except for a very brief time, but on the frontier, which for the majority of American history had meant the West. Proponents of the New England school had long held that the real America lay within a hundred miles or so of Boston; Turner argued just the opposite. The real America, he said, existed beyond the first range of mountains, in the river valleys and on the prairies and plains of the West.

Though the mandarins, many of them New Englanders, opposed Turner's ideas, other Americans found the frontier thesis compelling. Americans have usually thought they were exceptional; if they had wanted to be like the Europeans, they would have stayed in Europe. Turner told them they *were* exceptional and that their exceptions were their own doing rather than the remnant of some Teutonic tribal custom. Additionally, Turner's theory had the attractive feature of being adaptable to a variety of political agendas. American expansionists could argue that the United States needed to push its frontier overseas—into Asia, for example—in order to preserve the American way of life. Anti-expansionists could counter by reminding that the important feature of the frontier was vacant land; the countries of Asia were far from vacant, with China being the most crowded place on earth. Social Darwinists could cite the evolution of American institutions on the frontier as evidence in support of their belief that human societies, much like biological species, adapted according to the laws of natural selection. Social scientists could credit Turner with devising a theory that provided the logical apparatus of cause, effect, and connecting mechanism they held dear and that substantiated their contention that human behavior could be explained as scientifically as the motion of the planets.

Few fresh paradigms of social or scientific thought take hold by convincing confirmed skeptics. What usually happens is that new practitioners in a field adopt the novel approach while the unreconstructed old fogies die off or retire. Such was the fate of Turner's frontier theory, which became conventional wisdom only after the Herbert Baxter Adamses of the historical profession passed from the scene.

Meanwhile the young Turks embraced it enthusiastically. Among those most taken by Turner's ideas was Woodrow Wilson, who had been a visiting instructor at Johns Hopkins when Turner was there and who now contributed frequently to popular journals (with half an eye toward an eventual political career). Wilson employed Turner's approach in an assault on traditionalism in American history. Reviewing a conventional history of the United States, Wilson upbraided the author for adopting an outdated New Englandist perspective. It was not in New England, Wilson contended, but in the Middle Colonies and, by the nineteenth century, the trans-Appalachian West that American history had been made; in the crucible of the frontier experience had the American character been fashioned. Writing elsewhere, Wilson expanded on the frontier thesis. He compiled a "Calendar of Great Americans" that neglected seaboard giants Alexander Hamilton, John Adams, and John Calhoun in favor of sundry smaller figures who had been touched by the "true American spirit" that came from personal experience of the frontier. He wrote in *Forum* magazine that expansion was "the central and determining fact in our national history," which instilled in Americans "a new temper, a new spirit of adventure, a new impatience of restraint, a new license of life."

No one, however, did more to spread Turner's message than Turner himself. Shortly after his 1893 address, Turner received an invitation to contribute to *Johnson's Universal Encyclopedia* from a consultant to the project who also happened to be the president of the University of Wisconsin—the man who had prodded Turner to get his doctorate. Turner provided an essay on "The Frontier," laying out for the general readership of the encyclopedia the fundamentals of his theory. In the meantime he sent a copy of his 1893 address to Walter Hines Page, the editor of *Atlantic Monthly*. Page was favorably impressed and subsequently commissioned Turner to write an article on how and why the politics of the West was different from the politics of the East. The question was particularly pertinent in light of the rise of the Populist Party and the looming electoral showdown between William Jennings Bryan and William McKinley. Turner predictably traced the difference to the frontier. Page liked the article and asked Turner to write a series of similar pieces for the magazine. Turner accepted the offer.

One of these pieces appeared in the April 1897 issue of *Atlantic*. But then Page discovered what a succession of editors and publishers would learn about Turner: that like many of the frontier migrants he wrote about (although he didn't dwell on this regional deficiency), he lacked the patience to stick to a task that required a long-term commitment of energy. For a person who became one of the most influential of all American historians, Turner published very little—just two books, exclusive of his collections of essays. Turner couldn't stay with large projects: he continually allowed himself to be distracted by extraneous matters, and he succumbed to the historian's occupational hazard of wanting to fill the very last notecard before beginning to write. Turner promised much to various publishers and signed one contract after another, but the books kept retreating into the future.

As an excuse not to write, yet also as a way to spread the frontier message—and to earn lecture fees—Turner accepted numerous requests to speak before audiences of all kinds. Commencement and Phi Beta Kappa addresses filled his appointment book; he talked to veterans' groups, high school teachers' meetings, alumni conferences, geographical societies. Canny, and not one to burden himself with overwork, he recycled lectures shamelessly. A favorite was "Pioneer Ideals and the State University," which was heard by audiences at the Universities of Kansas, Michigan, Wisconsin, Indiana, and doubtless elsewhere.

Always Turner made the same point: The frontier had been the source of that which was distinctively American, the wellspring and proving ground of American social and political institutions. The frontier was the source of American greatness. If not for the frontier, Americans wouldn't be Americans.

IV

Turner lamented the passing of the frontier, but his lament lacked the depth of that of some other Americans. For Henry and Brooks Adams, the passing of the frontier seemed simply to reinforce a national decline that had been under way for decades. The Adams family had figured centrally in American political affairs since before the Revolutionary War. John Adams had helped Thomas Jefferson write the Declaration of Independence, had represented the new government of the United States in the capitals of Britain and France, and had served as vice president and president. John's son John Quincy Adams had been an American ambassador abroad, congressman and senator, secretary of state, and president. John Quincy's son Charles Francis Adams had been minister to Britain during the Civil War; in that post he had helped persuade London to stay out of the war and let the North strangle the South unmolested.

Charles Francis Adams had three sons who made names for themselves. Charles Francis, Jr., went into railroads—first as an analyst and historian of their development, second as a government regulator, third as chairman and then president of Union Pacific. He had the honor of being crowbarred out of the last position in 1890 by railroad-wrecker Jay Gould. Henry Adams, the second son, became a historian and a man of letters. He was one of the first intellectuals to attempt residence in Washington; the experiment was a qualified success. Brooks Adams, the third son, dabbled in law for a few years before joining Henry in the study of history. Like all the other Adamses, Brooks traveled throughout Europe; unlike them, he added to his itinerary extensive journeys through more exotic regions such as the Middle East and India. While Henry wrote chiefly about American and occasionally European matters, Brooks ranged widely across the spectrum of global history and covered the chronological ground from the earliest civilizations to the present.

Henry and Brooks—and to a lesser extent Charles Jr.—bemoaned a decline in family fortunes. None of them came close to achieving the public distinction of their great-grandfather, grandfather, or even father. Henry, in particular, being the most introspective of all the Adamses, pondered how much of the decline owed to the lack of gifts of his generation of the family and how much to the times in which he and his brothers lived. He inclined toward both explanations. Like his brothers, Henry had grown up in the shadow of his illustrious forebears; to a greater degree than they he never learned to feel he could step outside that shadow. He tried teaching at Harvard for a time. Finding the lecture system there uncongenial and unproductive, he abandoned lectures for seminars and succeeded in cultivating a group of students willing to devote days and weeks to the individual pursuit of knowledge. Many of the students were bound for law school, so Adams chose the history of law as the general frame of reference. "The boys worked like rabbits," he remarked afterward, "and dug holes all over the field of archaic society; no difficulty stopped them; unknown languages yielded before their attack, and customary law became familiar as the police court; undoubtedly they learned, after a fashion, to chase an idea, like a hare, through as dense a thicket of obscure facts as they were likely to meet at the bar." Yet Henry couldn't escape the feeling that he was doing his charges a disservice by encouraging in them an independence of mind they would never be able to use. "Their teacher knew from his own experience that his wonderful method led nowhere, and they would have to exert themselves to get rid of it in the Law School even more than they exerted themselves to acquire it in the college."

Henry considered other reforms of the educational system. Believing wisdom, or at least knowledge, to be the byproduct of the competition of ideas, he proposed an adversarial approach to pedagogy. In the classroom, opposite his own desk, he would seat a rival professor whose sole business would be to challenge his views. This motion died quickly for want of a second. "Of all university freaks, no irregularity shocked the intellectual atmosphere so much as contradiction or competition between teachers," Adams explained. He left teaching after seven unrewarding years; the chapter of his autobiography describing the period carried the simple title "Failure."

Henry went on to become editor of *North American Review*. The magazine was respected but dull. Adams found editing as unrewarding as teaching, since the chief function of an editor seemed to be selling advertising space. "Ten pages of advertising made an editor a success; five marked him as a failure." At times he wished he were back at Cambridge. "A professor had at least the pleasure of associating with his students; an editor lived the life of an owl."

Owlishness was in Henry Adams's blood, a condition he recognized and one that made him cherish his few friends. John Hay, the former personal secretary of Abraham Lincoln, was one of Adams's two closest intimates. Clarence King, the geologist and surveyor of the West, was the other.

For Adams, King became a symbol of the times. Adams met King in 1871, following an invitation from a scientist acquaintance to join him and a field party of the government's Fortieth Parallel Survey in its work. Adams took a train west to Laramie where he missed his acquaintance but hooked up with another group headed south into Colorado. Although he knew nothing about geology or minerology or botany or zoology or any other discipline of use to the surveyors, the government was footing the bill for the expedition, and the professionals allowed him to tag along.

Mounted soldiers accompanied the Fortieth Parallel Survey, yet the geologists and topographers spent little time worrying about hostile Indians over the next ridge; they concentrated rather on the minerals and potential railroad grades that lay beneath their feet and before their eyes. They took for granted that the West would be won; their job was to assess the spoils of victory.

Adams spent most of his time hunting and fishing. He preferred the latter. Though he didn't mind killing deer and elk and bear, he shrank from skinning and butchering the beasts, and no one volunteered to do the unpleasantness for him. Fish, on the other hand, he could eviscerate with only mild compunctions, and so he searched the canyons and valleys of Colorado's Front Range for the perfect trout stream and the denizens thereof.

One morning when the survey party was working the flank of Long's Peak, high above Estes Park, he pointed his mule down into that gladed valley. The day was sunny and warm, the sky mostly clear, with a hint of smoke from some forest fire many miles away. Adams had the valley to himself, and for a moment imagined he had somehow found his way into a huge, carefully tended English garden. The sun traced its arc westward while he tried one fishing hole after another. Before he realized the time, the sun had disappeared over the Continental Divide. The rapidly lengthening shadows of the peaks plunged the park into darkness.

Adams knew more or less where he was but not how to get back whence he had come, and certainly not in the dark. The next morning he would have no difficulty retracing his steps; the hours until then, however, promised to be cold and hungry. He had been told of a cabin at the entrance to Estes Park, used by travelers in just such predicaments as his. Though he had no confidence in his own ability to locate the cabin, he trusted his mule, and he gave the animal its head. Mule and rider ambled slowly down the valley floor, stars brilliant overhead and mountain ridges jaggedly black against the barely less black sky. After a couple of hours, Adams spied a light in the distance. The mule brought the light closer, until it took shape as the door of the cabin. Adams, by now fatigued, ravenous, and saddlesore, almost fell off the mule, into the arms of Clarence King.

It was love, or admiration certainly, at first sight. "King had everything to interest and delight Adams," Adams wrote thirty-five years later, in the clinical third person. King seemed utterly experienced and wise. "He knew more than Adams did of art and poetry; he knew America, especially west of the hundredth meridian, better than anyone; he knew the professor by heart, and he knew the Congressman better than he did the professor. He knew even women, even the American woman, even the New York woman, which is saying much." Adams continued, "His wit and humor; his bubbling energy which swept everyone into the current of his interest; his personal charm of youth and manners; his faculty of giving and taking, profusely, lavishly, whether in thought or in money as though he were Nature herself, marked him almost alone among Americans. He had in him something of the Greek—a touch of Alcibiades or Alexander. One Clarence King only existed in the world."

To Adams, King represented both science and the West. King had organized the Fortieth Parallel Survey and persuaded the federal government to fund it. The survey would provide the most detailed compendium of scientific information in history about the heart of the North American continent, and would set a standard against which future surveys would be measured. And when the survey was finished, King would be better placed than anyone else to take advantage of the knowledge it provided. The West was full of riches: King would know where they lay hidden.

Or so things had seemed in 1871 when, as Adams said, "the West was still fresh and the Union Pacific was young." Twenty years later the Union Pacific was showing its age, creaking under the strain of Jay Gould, who had just ousted brother Charles from the front office; and the West had filled in with a rapidity unimaginable two decades before, dispossessed of its riches as fast as greedy men could grab them.

Surprisingly—to Adams anyway—Clarence King was not among those benefiting from the opening of the West. Since the 1870s, nearly all evidence of ethics in American public affairs had vanished. Men less capable than King but more ruthless in their pursuit of wealth had pushed him aside. Though King had, as Adams anticipated, resigned from the government to enter private business, success commensurate with his capacities eluded him. He lost the assurance Adams had found so impressive in 1871; while there might still be but one Clarence King in the world, he wasn't what he had been.

Fate hadn't been much kinder to John Hay, Adams's other close friend. Hay had done duty in the State Department during the administration of Rutherford Hayes, yet had failed to move up the diplomatic bureaucracy and had left little mark. His biography of Lincoln took a decade to write (even with the help of co-author John Nicolay), and while it had won critical respect, to many it seemed a relatively thin harvest for the effort Hay had plowed into it.

As for Henry Adams, the twenty years ending in the early 1890s had not been unproductive, but he himself put scant store in what he accomplished. He published biographies of Albert Gallatin and John Randolph, as well as two novels. His largest project had been a multi-volume *History of the*

United States from 1801 to 1817, which many considered (and some still do) a landmark in American historiography. Yet the death by suicide of his wife in 1885, when he was right in the middle of writing the book, cast a pall over what otherwise should have seemed a noteworthy achievement. And in any event Adams regularly undervalued his literary endeavors—not least since he held a low opinion of himself, tending to believe that whatever he could accomplish couldn't be worth much.

From this combination of causes, the early 1890s found Adams—and Hay and King, at least in Adams's perception—in a chronic condition of ennui. He felt the problem to be collective and national as well as personal. "In 1892, neither Hay, King, nor Adams knew whether they had attained success, or how to estimate it, or what to call it; and the American people seemed to have no clearer idea than they. Indeed, the American people had no idea at all; they were wandering in a wilderness much more sandy than the Hebrews had ever trodden about Sinai; they had neither serpents nor golden calves to worship." Americans didn't even worship money, Adams remarked. "Worship of money was an old-world trait: a healthy appetite akin to worship of the Gods, or to worship of power in any concrete shape." That Americans didn't worship money was evidenced by the manner in which they squandered it. "The American wasted money more recklessly than anyone ever did before; he spent more to less purpose than any extravagant court aristocracy; he had no sense of relative values, and knew not what to do with his money when he got it, except use it to make more, or throw it away."

Adams found particularly distressing the waste of the riches of the West. "Except for the railway system, the enormous wealth taken out of the ground since 1840 had disappeared." San Francisco was a monument to what Americans had thrown away. The gold and silver mines of the Sierra Nevada should have made that port city the envy of North America; instead, the Californians had created an embarrassment of mindless ostentation. "Probably, since human society began, it had seen no such curious spectacle as the houses of the San Francisco millionaires on Nob Hill." San Francisco was the worst indictment of the banality of the West but not the only one. "West of the Alleghenies, the whole country might have been swept clean, and could have been replaced in better form within one or two years."

Adams sought refuge from the banality by setting off for Europe. Leaving in the early summer of 1893, he traveled in the company of Senator James Cameron and the senator's attractive and intriguing wife. The party toured England, then crossed over to the Continent. Adams, who constantly measured himself against others and sought large meanings in the measurement, reflected that between Cameron and himself existed the difference between the Pennsylvanian and the New Englander. The latter quibbled about procedures and methods and fine points of ethics; the former got things done and didn't worry much how. The Pennsylvanian epitomized the energy of America, whether in terms of political logrolling or of the manufacture of steel. "When one summed up the results of Pennsylvanian influence, one inclined to think that Pennsylvania set up the Government in 1789; saved it in 1861; created the American system; developed its iron and coal power; and invented its great railways."

The Camerons and Adams discussed the pressing issues of the day as they journeyed across France to Switzerland. No issue pressed more insistently than the currency question. Adams discovered that though the interests of his class and family favored gold, his temperament and intellectual inclinations spoke for silver. Writing of himself, Adams explained, "He thought it probably his last chance of standing up for his eighteenth-century principles: strict construction, limited powers, George Washington, John Adams, and the rest. He had, in a half-hearted way, struggled all his life against State Street, banks, capitalism altogether, as he knew it in old England or new England, and he was fated to make his last resistance behind the silver standard."

The Panic of 1893 transplanted Adams's abstract theorizing about money to the realm of the crushingly concrete. On arrival at Lucerne, he received a packet of letters from home: Charles and Brooks insisted that he return to Boston at once. The dive had devastated the family, and he was probably a beggar.

Adams found the situation incomprehensible. Just months before, he had paid off every debt he knew himself to owe. How then could the financial panic have ruined him? Answering the question formed an important part of his continuing education. "As a starting point for a new education at fifty-five years old, the shock of finding oneself suspended for several months over the edge of bankruptcy, without knowing how one got there or how to get away, is to be strongly recommended."

In Boston, Adams discovered debts of which he had been unaware, contracted indirectly in the course of other financial transactions. These debts were being called in—frantically—by the banks to which they were owed, the banks themselves being in an even more precarious state than Adams.

Adams judged the whole predicament proof that things had gotten seriously out of control. "The more he saw of it, the less he understood it. He was quite sure that nobody understood it much better. Blindly, some very powerful energy was at work, doing something that nobody wanted done." Adams went to his bank to withdraw one hundred dollars he had deposited there; the bank told him he could have only fifty. He didn't complain, reasoning that since he couldn't pay his debts there was no reason for the bank to pay what it owed. "Each wanted to help the other, yet both refused to pay their debts, and he could find no answer to the question which was responsible for getting the other into the situation." Everyone seemed as perplexed as he. "No one knew what it meant, and most people dismissed it as an emotion—a panic—that meant nothing." But dismissing the situation as an emotion didn't diminish the effects of the collapse. "Men died like flies under the strain, and Boston grew suddenly old, haggard, and thin."

Adams philosophized—or later said he did, speaking from the safe distance of a decade after the fact—that the crisis afforded an edifying case study in the revolution that was sweeping over American life. "Great changes had taken place since 1870 in the forces at work; the old machine ran far behind its duty; somewhere—somehow—it was bound to break down, and if it happened to break precisely over one's head, it gave the better chance for study."

After doing all he could in Boston, Adams headed west. His object was to visit Chicago's Columbian Exposition, which to his mind captured the essence of the America that was rapidly coming into being. Adams (who arrived too late to hear Frederick Jackson Turner's paper) found the fair astonishing in both its reality and its symbolism. The exhibit by the Cunard Company showed what steamships currently were and what they presently would be; working generators afforded a glimpse of a brilliant, electrically lit future; a score of other exhibits demonstrated mechanical and chemical principles that were making obsolete much of what Americans of Adams's generation had taken for granted. "Here was a breach of continuity, a rupture in the historical sequence," he wrote. "Men who knew nothing whatever—who had never run a steam-engine, the simplest of forces, who had never put their hands on a lever, had never touched an electric battery, never talked through a telephone, and had not the shadow of a notion what amount of force was meant by a watt or an ampere or an erg or any other term of measurement introduced within a hundred years—had no choice but to sit down on the steps and brood as they had never brooded on the benches of Harvard College, either as student or professor, aghast at what they had said and done in all these years, and still more ashamed of the childlike ignorance and babbling futility of the society that had let them say and do it."

The exposition challenged Adams—and, Adams presumed, the American people—as nothing before had. "Chicago asked in 1893 for the first time the question whether the American people knew where they were driving." Adams certainly didn't know, and he decided that the American people knew no more than he.

V

Adams determined to try to enlighten himself, to complete his education. In the endeavor he consulted brother Brooks, who had spent the previous decade brooding on this general topic. Where many Americans of his generation, including Henry, tended to think that their country was going to hell in a handbasket, Brooks Adams expanded the container to include all of Western civilization. Brooks's writings reflected the major intellectual trends of his day, especially the economic determinism of the Marxian socialists, the natural selectionism of the Social Darwinists, and the logical reductionism of the physical scientists. His first book, the 1887

Emancipation of Massachusetts, hinted at what was to come. Frederick Jackson Turner would have approved of Brooks's attack on the ancestor worship that commonly passed for history in New England—although it is by no means certain Turner read the book, since almost no one did. Yet more important than Adams's assault on the smugness of the New England aristocracy was his attempt to formulate the laws he believed dictated the course of human history. Biologists and medical scientists had achieved signal success describing the principles that governed the workings of the human body; Adams was convinced that the actions of the human mind were governed similarly. He went so far as to say, of body and mind: "I believe they are one and subject to the same laws."

Brooks Adams devoted the next several years, indeed much of the rest of his life, to teasing out these laws. His efforts carried him far afield—intellectually and physically—from Massachusetts and New England. But notwithstanding his desire to discover timeless and universal laws of human conduct, he also wanted to have an impact on the contemporary world. In a period when the gold versus silver debate was rending American political parties and spawning new alignments, Adams heard echoes of an earlier era. "I can see myself now," he wrote later, "as I stood one day amid the ruins of Baalbek, and I can feel the shock of surprise I then felt, when the conviction dawned upon me, which I have since heard denounced as a monstrous free-silver invention, that the fall of Rome came about by a competition between slave and free labor and an inferiority in Roman industry."

It was at this moment, Adams asserted, that he hit upon the idea underlying *The Law of Civilization and Decay*. This second book, published in 1895, was an ambitious effort to explain the rise and fall of empires, particularly what the author saw as the rise of Asia and the East and the fall of Europe and the West, including the United States. Brooks's ambition at times outstripped his exposition, and it wasn't always easy to figure out exactly what he was saying. Brother Henry did as well summarizing the message as anyone. After reading a draft, Henry wrote Brooks:

> On your wording of your Law, it seemed to me to come out, in its first equation thus, in the fewest possible words:
>
> All Civilisation is Centralisation.
> All Centralisation is Economy.
> Therefore all Civilisation is the survival of the most economical (cheapest).

> Darwin called it fittest, and in one sense fittest is the fittest word. Unfortunately it is always relative, and therefore liable to misunderstanding.

Your other formula is more difficult.

> Under economical centralisation, Asia is cheaper than Europe.
> The world tends to economical centralisation.
> Therefore Asia tends to survive, and Europe to perish.

This was a fair approximation of what Brooks was up to, but it didn't do justice to the wide-ranging variety of examples and evidence he adduced to sustain his thesis. On a tour that took the reader from republican Rome to imperial China and back to industrial Europe, Adams relentlessly hammered home the point that human beings behave according to strict, ineluctable laws. Sometimes the tour took strange twists; the author meandered for pages and pages through a single decade, then vaulted across centuries in a sentence. He offered few roadsigns to indicate where he was going, and he rarely stopped to recapitulate where he had been.

To make his argument easier to understand, Brooks issued a second edition just months after the appearance of the first, and included an interpretive preface. On the first page of the 1896 edition Adams stated his understanding of the task of the historian, which he deemed much the same as that of the natural scientist. "The value of history," he wrote, "lies not in the multitude of facts collected but in their relation to each other, and in this respect an author can have no larger responsibility than any other scientific observer." Adams declared that his impartial observation of the facts of history had forced him to the conclusion that the conscious thoughts of people have very little to do with the way they act. "At the moment of action," he asserted, "the human being almost invariably obeys an instinct, like an animal; only after action has ceased does he reflect. These controlling instincts are involuntary, and divide men into species distinct enough to cause opposite effects under identical conditions. For instance, impelled by fear, one type will rush upon an enemy, and another will run away; while the love of women or of money has stamped certain races as sharply as ferocity or cunning has stamped the lion or the fox."

Instincts were strongly hereditary. As a result, individuals' fates were largely determined by how closely the biological and psychological heritage they acquired from their ancestors fitted the world of their day. "It is plain that as the external world changes, those who receive this heritage must rise or fall in the social scale according as their nervous system is well or ill adapted to the conditions to which they are born." Getting personal, Adams continued, "Nothing is commoner, for example, than to find families who have been famous in one century sinking into obscurity in the next, not because the children have degenerated"—perish the thought—"but because a certain field of activity which afforded the ancestor full scope has been closed against his offspring."

Adams then outlined the grand theme of his project. "I want to offer an hypothesis by which to classify a few of the more interesting intellectual phases through which human society must, apparently, pass, in its oscillations between barbarism and civilization, or, what amounts to the same thing, in its movement from a condition of physical dispersion to one of concentration." This notion of dispersion and concentration provided the link Adams sought between the Newtonian physical world and the realm of human history. "The theory proposed is based upon the accepted scientific principle that the law of force and energy is of universal application in nature, and that animal life is one of the outlets through which solar energy is dissipated." Human thought and feelings, being aspects of animal life, were outlets for solar energy; on their path to dissipation they took two forms, fear and greed. Fear, which stimulated the imagination, gave birth to superstition and belief in the invisible and ultimately produced a priesthood. Greed fostered aggression, which found release first in war but eventually in trade.

Though Adams dressed up his argument in elaborate and obscure theoretical language ("The velocity of the social movement of any community is proportionate to its energy and mass, and its centralization is proportionate to its velocity"), the thrust of his message was that human societies moved along a path leading from fear to greed as the compelling intellectual and psychological force. In societies that were just emerging from barbarism, the ruling classes identified with the priesthood, the group that exploited humanity's instinctive fear of the unknown and uncontrollable. Over time, as the portion of reality that was known and controllable grew larger, fear diminished and the hold of the priests on the popular imagination decreased. Greed took over as the primary motivating force, and a new ruling class of warriors and merchants, expert in the exploitation and satisfaction of greed, came to power.

Adams didn't lament the passing of the priests: their superstitions prevented people from seeing the world as it really was. But he objected to the subsequent transition during the age of greed from the warriors to the merchants. During this period of human evolution the honest martial virtues of the barracks gave way to the decadent cleverness of the counting-house. Adams was fascinated by what he considered the greater virility of warriors compared to clerks. The decline in virility was obvious—to Adams anyway—by the time of the later Roman Empire. Of the Romans of that era, Adams declared, "They lacked the martial and amatory instincts. As a general rule, one salient characteristic of the later reigns was a sexual lassitude yielding only to the most potent stimulants." Men who loved money couldn't love women. "Women seem never to have more than moderately appealed to the senses of the economic man. The monied magnate seldom ruins himself for love, and chivalry would have been as foreign to a Roman senator under Diocletian as it would be now to a Lombard Street banker."

Indifference bred—so to speak—infertility, and greed-directed societies lost their ability to reproduce. As a result, they guaranteed their own decline. Nature sifted among the economic personalities, "culling a favored aristocracy of the craftiest and subtlest types, choosing, for example, the

Armenian in Byzantium, the Marwari in India, and the Jew in London." The process pushed relentlessly on. "As the costly nervous system of the soldier becomes an encumbrance, organisms which can exist on less successively supplant each other, until the limit of endurance is reached. Thus the Slavs exterminated the Greeks in Thrace and Macedonia, the Mahrattas and the Moslems dwindle before the low caste tribes of India, and the instinct of self-preservation has taught white races to resist an influx of Chinese." The outcome of the twin processes of selection—in favor of the effete and cunning, against the virile and brave—was inescapable. "When nature has finished this double task, civilization has reached its zenith. Humanity can ascend no higher." It could only descend.

If the future looked bleak on this global scale, it looked hardly better with regard to an issue that was narrower but still of surpassing importance for Americans. With the ascendance of the commercial classes, control over matters of currency fell into the hands of creditors. These creditors saw to it that governments enacted policies guaranteed to support and indeed enhance the value of their credits. The commonest such policies were designed to restrict the amount of money in circulation, thereby increasing the value of the money in circulation—and, of necessity, driving down commodity prices. The commonest method of restricting the money supply was to enforce a gold standard.

Brooks Adams traced at length the conflict between creditors and debtors—or, as it commonly appeared, between producers and bankers. He distilled to essentials the struggle over money, whether the struggle took place in the Old World or the New. "To the producer, the commodity was the measure of value; to the banker, coin. The producer sought a currency which should retain a certain ratio to all commodities, of which gold was but one. The banker insisted on making a fixed weight of the metal he controlled the standard from which there was no appeal."

As Adams told the tale, the contest was nasty and mean. He showed how bankers deliberately manipulated the value of currency so that debtors were forced into bankruptcy, their property then passing to the bankers. He demonstrated how farmers were driven to the brink of subsistence in good times, to early graves in bad times. He related how prosperity for the masses accompanied accidental—from the standpoint of the bankers—increases in the money supply, such as that following the California gold strike of 1848, and how the bankers subsequently worked feverishly—and successfully—to rein in the currency once more. He described the initial victories of the bankers at midcentury in Britain and their final triumph in America in the 1870s. Summarizing, he wrote: "These bankers conceived a policy unrivalled in brilliancy, which made them masters of all commerce, industry, and trade. They engrossed the gold of the world, and then, by legislation, made it the sole measure of values. What Samuel Loyd"—an English champion of the gold standard—"and his followers did to England in 1847 became possible for his successors to do to all the gold standard nations after 1873"—the year the U.S. Treasury stopped minting silver.

"When the mints had been closed to silver, the currency being inelastic, the value of money could be manipulated like that of any article limited in quantity, and thus the human race became the subjects of the new aristocracy."

Brooks Adams intended to provoke with his *Law of Civilization and Decay*, and he succeeded. "Few more melancholy books have been written," Theodore Roosevelt asserted in a long and detailed review. Roosevelt praised the scope of Adams's work, calling it "a marvel of compressed statement," in which the author displayed adeptness at "presenting the vital features of a subject with a few master-strokes." Roosevelt was not usually one to equivocate; regarding people, ideas, and causes, he liked to be entirely in favor or unalterably opposed. Yet he couldn't help feeling ambivalent about Adams's message. "This is not a pleasant theory," Roosevelt said. "It is in many respects an entirely false theory; but nevertheless there is in it a very ugly element of truth."

Roosevelt, a gold man, thought Adams overstated the importance of the currency question in history. An advocate of a strong military establishment, he thought Adams exaggerated the demise of the soldier in modern life. A believer in the capacity of individuals and nations to fashion their own fates, he rejected Adams's biological and sociological determinism. On the other hand, Roosevelt thought Adams entirely right regarding the failed fecundity of civilized societies. No quality in a race, Roosevelt wrote, atoned for an inability to produce abundant and sturdy children. "The problem upon which Mr. Adams here touches is the most serious of all problems, for it lies at the root of, and indeed itself is, national life."

Roosevelt similarly concurred with Adams's gloomy description of the debilitating effects of modern commercial activities on the collective psyche. "There is no use blinding ourselves to certain of the tendencies and results of our high-pressure civilization. Some very ominous facts have become more and more apparent during the present century, in which the social movement of the white race has gone on with such unexampled and ever-accelerating rapidity." Chief among these ominous facts were "a certain softness of fibre" and a loss of "flexibility" that together foreshadowed defeat in "those contests through which alone any great race can ultimately march to victory."

On the whole, Roosevelt accepted Adams's diagnosis but not his prescription. Though Adams might be right about the crumbling of previous civilizations, America needn't follow the pattern. Roosevelt was an ardent American exceptionalist, and he thought Rome, Byzantium, India, and China had little to teach this "great modern state where the bulk of the population are wage-earners, who themselves decide their own destinies; a state which is able in time of need to put into the field armies composed exclusively of its own citizens, more numerous than any which the world has ever before seen, and with a record of fighting in the immediate past with which there is nothing in the annals of antiquity to compare."

Criticism didn't much bother Adams. It deflected him as little from the path of his theory hunting as, in his opinion, the wishes of individuals deflected a civilization from the course of its emergence and decline. He continued to monitor world events, especially the enervating economic depression of the 1890s, with an eye toward discovering more about the laws that governed human existence. His observations gave rise to a pair of books—*America's Economic Supremacy* and *The New Empire*—in which he elaborated on the theme of his earlier work. Despite the upbeat tone of the titles, gloom remained the prevailing mood.

Adams cited figures showing the historic ascent of the United States to world economic preeminence. During the mid-eighteenth century, he reported, Britain, France, and Germany had been roughly equal in industrial production. By the early part of the nineteenth century, however, the wheel of industrial supremacy had turned westward and Britain was outproducing its two Continental rivals combined. But Britain's predominance was temporary; the wheel continued to turn. During the second half of the nineteenth century the United States surpassed all three countries, and in 1898 American plants produced nearly 10 million tons of pig iron, compared with 9 million for Britain, 7 million for Germany, and less than 3 million for France.

Adams buttressed these statistics with many more, all of which demonstrated the American economic supremacy of his title; yet where most Americans found encouragement in this trend, Adams perceived cause for worry. In the first place, economic supremacy carried a high price tag. As much as American factories produced, American salesmen had to dispose of. The American market was saturated—a fact painfully demonstrated in the decade's depression. Disposing of American goods therefore necessitated acquiring and defending foreign markets. This wasn't a matter of choice but of grim necessity: the United States "must protect the outlets of her trade or run the risk of suffocation." Already the struggle for markets had begun; the Spanish-American War of 1898 was nothing less. Anti-imperialists might argue for a policy of avoiding foreign entanglements, but their arguments were fatuous. "It is in vain that men talk of keeping free of entanglements. Nature is omnipotent, and nations must float with the tide. Whither the exchanges flow, they must follow, and they will follow as long as their vitality endures." Human intervention couldn't prevent the disasters the contest over markets inevitably entailed. "These great catastrophes escape human control."

Adams perceived another cause for worry beyond the foreign entanglements America's economic power dictated. The wheel of economic supremacy had turned in a direction that currently favored Americans, but there was absolutely no reason to think it would cease turning. The experience of centuries demonstrated that nothing could stop it. The depression of the 1890s, rather than the war with Spain or any other apparent American success, was the seminal event of the decade. Adams saw the depression, which was a global as well as American phenomenon, as evidence of the continued westering of the center of economic power. The depression had jolted the British, whose trembling in turn had shaken a large part of the rest of the planet. "Few unprejudiced observers have ever doubted that much of the financial stringency which prostrated Argentina, Australia, and America between 1890 and 1897 originated in the withdrawal of English capital." Britain never quite recovered from the depression; America, after being knocked momentarily backward, emerged as the world's economic leader.

But even as the depression eroded Britain's strength, its effects on the Atlantic's western side demonstrated that the United States' economic might rested on a flimsier foundation than most Americans realized; in addition it suggested that the moment of America's preeminence would be briefer than those of its predecessors at the top of the economic heap. Already Japan was arising as the dominant power in the Far East; there, Adams asserted, lay the future. Japan's condition was analogous to Britain's a century before, namely that of a crowded island country containing much human energy but few natural resources. Yet Japan enjoyed the advantage of being able to learn from the example of the West. Modernizing in the age of steam and electricity, Japan was accomplishing in a generation what had required centuries in Europe and almost as long in America. The center of commerce and civilization had migrated from the European continent across the Atlantic to the United States; just so would it continue west across the Pacific. "Each man can ponder the history of the last fifty years," Adams wrote, "and judge for himself whether the facts show that Great Britain apparently lies in the wake, and Japan in the path, of the advancing cyclone."

For the moment, America stood at the center of economic activity. "The vortex of the cyclone is near New York. No such activity prevails elsewhere; nowhere are undertakings so gigantic, nowhere is administration so perfect; nowhere are such masses of capital centralized in single hands." Nonetheless, the cyclone maintained its westward course, gaining speed as it went. "Society is moving with intense velocity, and masses are gathering bulk with proportionate rapidity." The present configuration of forces was unstable. Noting that changes in price levels had allowed America to eclipse Europe economically, Adams warned: "If so apparently slight a cause as a fall in prices for a decade has sufficed to propel the seat of empire across the Atlantic, an equally slight derangement of the administrative functions of the United States might force it to cross the Pacific."

Adams detected various causes that would derange America. "Under any circumstances, an organism so gigantic as the American Union must generate friction." Under the circumstances of the 1890s, friction—between farm and city, between labor and capital, between borrower and lender—was undeniable. This friction was the likely doom of America's economic hegemony. "America holds its tenure of prosperity only on condition that she can undersell her rivals, and she cannot do so if her administrative machinery generates friction unduly."

Regardless of the unfavorable odds, the United States had no choice but to wage the contest for economic supremacy. "Americans in former generations led a simple agricultural life. Possibly such a life was happier than ours. Very probably keen competition is not a blessing." But the old life had vanished, never to return. "We cannot alter our environment. Nature has cast the United States into the vortex of the fiercest struggle which the world has ever known. She has become the heart of the economic system of the age, and she must maintain her supremacy by wit and by force, or share the fate of the discarded." The weight of world history was against Americans in this struggle, and Adams held out little hope for his country.

VI

Brooks and Henry Adams were more pessimistic than most of their compatriots, but many shared their dismal view of the future. Not everyone accepted Frederick Jackson Turner's frontier thesis in detail, but nearly all agreed that the passing of the frontier and the filling in of the formerly wide open spaces of the West portended a serious change in the American way of life. A great many expected the change to be for the worse. There would be no more Oklahomas for scores of thousands to populate in a day; future Fred Suttons would have to devise different schemes for getting ahead. Even the final suppression of Indian resistance, while applauded by a majority of Americans, left others somewhat wistful for the days when the West was wild.

In a certain objective sense, the fears that accompanied the passing of the frontier were overblown. By no means had America run out of available land: history would show that more homesteaders took up claims *after* the 1890 census declared the frontier nonexistent than before. And a century later visitors from Europe and Asia flying across the western half of the United States would be struck by how empty it seemed.

But the passing of the frontier in the 1890s was no less significant for being principally symbolic. As a people, Americans had long cherished the idea that off in the West existed an unclaimed area where people might go if things got really tough in the East. Plenty of people *did* go west and make new lives for themselves; to those who didn't, the mere thought that they might was reassuring. As long as the frontier existed, so did an escape hatch from the pressures and burdens of everyday life. The frontier was what had made America different from other countries, and in the national mythology nothing was more important than the conviction of American uniqueness. Laws of history, of the rise and fall of empires, applied to other countries; American history was a law unto itself. It *had* been, at any rate. Whether it would continue to be so, with the frontier now gone, was another question—and a very disturbing one.

Chapter 2

IN MORGAN WE TRUST

I

It was entirely fitting that Frederick Jackson Turner delivered his account of the significance of the vanishing frontier in Chicago at the 1893 Columbian Exposition. No city in the country captured so well the two visions of America—the one looking forward and the other back—and no single event summarized so succinctly the swiftness with which the future was overtaking the past and present. Within the living memory of people not yet middle-aged, Chicago had been as raw and rough as any frontier town, and even now there remained some pretty wild territory not a day's travel from the city's heart. As for the Columbian Exposition, while commemorating the four centuries since the arrival of Columbus in the New World, it celebrated the latest triumphs of America's corporate technology and forecast many more. Of the two faces of this Janus, the one looking ahead was far more arresting than the one looking back.

When Turner arrived in Chicago in July 1893, the exposition was in its third month and had three more to go. The fair had been considerably longer in the planning. In 1890, the U.S. Congress had considered how to celebrate the upcoming fourth centenary of the discovery of the New World; Chicago's boosters, anxious to erase the memory of the Haymarket riot of 1886, which had linked the city in the public mind to anarchism and violence, lobbied aggressively to receive the honor. No other city pressed its claim so vigorously, and Congress said yes to the pushy men from the shores of Lake Michigan.

Chicago's city fathers gave charge of the planning to the architectural firm of Burnham & Root, the most prominent in the area. John Wellborn Root had won a reputation for originality in designing office buildings, including the Monadnock Building, a graceful seventeen-story tower that belied the heaviness usually associated with masonry construction. Daniel Burnham was the go-getter of the partnership. Burnham had built up the firm following the 1871 fire that had gutted the center of Chicago; with dozens of major buildings to be raised, Burnham had convinced much of Chicago's business community that he and Root were the team to raise them. Now he had helped convince Congress that Chicago was the place to hold America's world's fair.

Burnham and Root expected to profit from the fair; so did many others in Chicago. The city government of Chicago, like the governments of most large American cities in the 1890s, had a marked tendency toward crooked dealing, and nowhere was the tendency more marked than in public works. Building contracts were floated to friends of aldermen, and kickbacks floated the other way. The elaborate physical structures of the exposition, to be erected at Jackson Park on the lakeshore five miles south of the Chicago business district, would cost tens of millions of dollars and would afford innumerable opportunities for graft. There were fortunes to be made, and those on the inside of the city government were in the best position to make them.

With the aldermen aboard, Burnham also brought in some of America's most noted architects. Frederick Law Olmsted, the guiding spirit behind the development of New York's Central Park and recently the designer of the campus of Stanford University, received a commission to oversee the landscaping. Louis Sullivan, Boston-born, Paris-trained, and now Chicago-based, and fresh from the triumphal completion of his Chicago Auditorium, would design the main transportation building. Frank Lloyd Wright, a junior member of Sullivan's firm but already showing remarkable promise, would assist Sullivan.

Burnham envisioned for the fair a "White City" built along classical lines. Pillars, arches, and porticoes would predominate, and the entire grounds and all the buildings would be united in a harmonious whole—a "city beautiful" that would serve as a model for urban planning around the world. Not everyone agreed with Burnham's vision. Louis Sullivan thought the emphasis on classical Greece and Rome a bunch of hokum. A new nation such as America mustn't be chained to the dead past, Sullivan said, nor to forms that once served a purpose but now were merely decorative. Sullivan, the chief exponent of the "Chicago School" of architecture, which stressed that form should follow function, refused to adhere to Burnham's scheme. As things turned out, his modernistic transportation building was the hit of the show.

In bidding for the contract on the exposition, Burnham had pointed to his record of getting projects completed on time. He succeeded again with this one, although his success did not come easily. When work commenced at the end of 1890, the site consisted of dunes and bogs. Burnham took up residence there and gathered an army of seven thousand workers, whom he drove relentlessly through some of the worst weather the Midwest could muster. When snow covered the ground, Burnham's men shoveled it aside; when the ground froze, they switched shovels for pickaxes. The work was dangerous: seventeen men died before the job was finished.

The last months prior to opening saw the pace of construction increase from fast to frenzied. Groundsmen slopped through mud, imploring grass to grow before the soil was warm enough to sustain it; masons slapped stucco on walls too cold to let the coating set properly. Stucco was, in any event, a poor choice of material for Chicago's continental climate, but the exposition was intended to make an immediate impact on visitors, not last for decades.

When the fair opened on May 1, 1893, it definitely made an impact. Five hundred thousand people jammed the grounds the first day to gaze at and listen to President Grover Cleveland, Illinois Governor John Peter Altgeld, the Infanta Eulalia of Spain, two direct descendants of Columbus, and sundry other dignitaries; but mostly they wanted to experience what seemed a marvel of the ages. "Sell the cook stove if necessary and come," young Hamlin Garland wrote his parents. "You *must* see this fair." One elderly visitor was heard to remark to his wife, "Well, Susan, it paid, even if it did take all the burial money." The curious converged on Chicago by the millions, selling cookstoves, raiding funeral funds, and otherwise depleting rainy-day reserves for railway tickets to Chicago and the price of admission.

The human spectacle by itself was worth the expense. The crush of the crowds jeopardized life and limb, prompting fathers to lift their babies above their heads and out of danger. Pursesnatchers and pickpockets battened on the crush; Jane Addams, who took a day off from Hull House, almost lost her handbag to a young thug. Fortunately for her, an alert officer of the fair's honor guard confronted the thief, drawing his sword and threatening dire harm unless the scoundrel returned the lady's purse.

Visitors ogled the most modern inventions—as well as some exhibits that qualified for distinction only by their novelty, such as a detailed map of the United States composed entirely of pickles. On display were an enormous telescope donated by traction magnate Charles Yerkes to the University of Chicago, a monster cannon forged by the Krupp works of Germany, and two of Thomas Edison's latest: an improved phonograph and a prototype motion picture machine called the Kinetoscope. Fairgoers with friends in New York could talk to them over the American Bell Telephone's new long-distance line—and be glad that the patent on the Bell telephone expired while the fair was on, opening the door to lower rates and wider service offered by Bell's competitors. The clocks of the fairgrounds were connected by electrical wire to the Naval Observatory in Washington: each day precisely at noon (Eastern time; eleven o'clock in Chicago) the observatory sent a signal the thousand miles to Chicago and set bells and alarms ringing and buzzing. Sleek, shiny cattle and breathtakingly huge hogs reminded visitors of the livestock industry that formed a mainstay of the local economy. Grapefruit brought in from Florida on some of the first mechanically refrigerated railcars promised a transformation of the American diet.

Reformers took advantage of the crowds to proselytize for their causes. Prohibitionists fought a vain battle against alcohol: Chicago nearly washed away on an ocean of booze during the fair. Feminists agitated for greater rights for women, especially including the vote. Children's advocates urged the passage of child-labor laws. Consumer watchdogs railed against conditions in the Chicago stockyards and packinghouses. Bicyclists—a group whose numbers were exploding following the recent introduction of the safety bicycle—campaigned for better roads. Labor spokespersons demanded measures to relieve unemployment. Free-silverites preached the merits of an enlarged money supply. Gold-bugs extolled the honesty of the yellow metal.

Off the grounds, gamblers and prostitutes did unprecedented business catering to all the guests. Chicago's police let the games and frolics proceed more or less uninhibited; the officers didn't wish to dampen the festival spirit, and in any event they were often paid to look the other way. The purveyors of pleasure had plenty of palm-greasing money: one outfit headed by Tom O'Brien, the self-styled "King of the Bunko Men," cleared half a million dollars. The madams did even better. Vina Fields, proprietress of the largest house in the city, doubled her work force to handle the influx of out-of-towners. Carrie Watson paraded sixty girls about the verandas and balconies of her capacious brownstone; a trained parrot called out, "Carrie Watson! Come in, gentlemen!" They did, hundreds every night.

By the time the fair closed in the autumn of 1893, 27 million visitors—a total equivalent to one out of every four Americans—had passed through the turnstiles. The bill for the exposition topped $30 million, which was considerably more than the gate receipts returned. Yet the overrun produced relatively few complaints. Most of those involved with the fair were willing to accept it as the price of progress, as the cost of displaying, in the words of one visitor, "all the contrivances of civilization, ancient and modern, that helped to elevate and ennoble man, refine his tastes, enlarge his ideas, and further his deliverance from the despotism of nature."

II

The big story of the fair, as any visitor who arrived after dark immediately saw, was electricity. What the visitors could not see, even by the light of the tens of thousands of incandescent and arc lamps that kept the Midway Plaisance brilliant until the wee hours, was the bitter contest that marked the development of the American electrical industry during the early 1890s.

One of the contestants was the former boy wonder of American invention, Thomas Edison, now in his fifties and an established figure of American business. Edison had come to the electrical industry via the telegraph. Almost totally lacking in formal education—he attended school for three months in Port Huron, Michigan, then dropped out to get on with life—Edison taught himself the Morse code and became a telegraph operator at the age of fifteen. The job offered young Edison both an entree into the world of electrical technology and a ticket to see the country. From earliest childhood Edison had been a tinkerer, and he immediately began reflecting on how he might improve the telegraphic equipment he was working with. The stream of messages he had to attend to slowed drastically at night, providing plenty of time for reflection—but not enough for Edison. Company rules required night operators to check in with a regional dispatcher every hour: they sent the simple message "6" to assure the dispatcher they were awake and alert. Edison found this repetitive task a nuisance and a distraction from his thinking, and he devised a machine that automatically sent the required signal on each hour. Edison's supervisor eventually found out what was going on. This wasn't Edison's first offense against conventional practice, nor was it his last, and before long he got his walking papers.

He wandered across the continent from job to job. Everywhere he went—from Michigan to Ontario to Indiana to Ohio to Tennessee to Louisiana to Kentucky to Massachusetts—he tinkered, fiddling with the equipment to make it more powerful or easier to use. Sometimes his fiddling produced a valuable working device, such as the Morse repeater he put together in Indianapolis; sometimes it simply led him deeper into the field of electricity, where his future increasingly appeared to lie.

In 1869, Edison went into fiddling full time. In that year he received his first patent (of more than a thousand in his career), for an electrical vote recorder. Subsequently he improved the stock-ticker, rendering it more readable for nervous investors, and developed systems that allowed telegraph lines to carry several messages simultaneously.

Edison believed that creativity, or at least innovativeness, could be marshaled and thrown against technological problems just as soldiers were thrown against the wall of a besieged fortress. He gathered the best troops he could find and installed them in a research laboratory at Menlo Park, New Jersey. The first important achievement of the Menlo Park lab was the phonograph; the second was the incandescent light bulb. The phenomenon of electrical incandescence had been common knowledge for decades, but no one before Edison had managed to find a filament that would generate lots of light without incinerating itself in a short while. Edison's researchers painstakingly tried one material after another, then one mixture of materials after another, then one combination of materials and surroundings after another, until they hit upon the idea of placing a carbonized thread in a vacuum tube.

Edison was no ivory tower scientist devoted to knowledge for its own sake. He expected to make money with his inventions. To advertise his most recent breakthrough, he threw a grand New Year's Eve party for visitors to Menlo Park from across the Hudson. Special trains from New York brought the revelers to watch Edison flip a switch and turn on a bank of forty of his new bulbs. Edison briefed fascinated reporters on how he had sent agents all around the globe looking for the perfect filament—to the rain forests of Brazil, the jungles of Sumatra, the bamboo thickets of Japan. The search continued; no invention couldn't be improved. But in the meantime the public could enjoy the blessings of safe, inexpensive artificial light produced by a filament whose precise composition he preferred not to divulge while patents pended.

The public could enjoy said blessings, however, only after the requisite system of electrical generators and transmission lines was completed. Edison commenced construction of such a system, utilizing direct current, the simplest and most straightforward variety of electrical current. But direct current has some significant drawbacks, the worst being the difficulty with which direct current voltages are raised and lowered. Intractable laws of physics dictate that low-voltage currents lose unacceptable amounts of power when sent long distances; beyond a few miles the losses are economically prohibitive. High-voltage currents conserve power much more effectively. The trouble is that high voltages are dangerous. With alternating current, as opposed to direct current, the trouble is minimized through the use of transformers, which efficiently raise and lower voltages. In an alternating current system, electricity is transmitted from the generating plant to substations over high-voltage lines that are safely separated from people (although not always from birds and other unwary fauna). At the substations the voltage is stepped down, and it is stepped down again closer to the consumer until the current that people might accidentally encounter is comparatively harmless. The consequence of all this is that in alternating current systems, generating plants can be located farther from end users, and thus the alternating current systems can be bigger than direct current systems.

Edison envisioned electrical grids serving cities primarily. A large city might have several direct current generating facilities; from these facilities, lines would spread out to factories, offices, shops, and homes. Because of the dense populations in cities, enough customers could be found within a few-mile radius of each generating plant to make the direct current system pay.

But Edison's vision wasn't the only one available. George Westinghouse had a different dream. Just four months older than Edison, Westinghouse was the other great American inventor of the late nineteenth century (winning more than four hundred patents in his lifetime). Where Edison came to electricity via the telegraph, Westinghouse arrived by train. Westinghouse's single most important achievement was the railway air brake, unveiled in the same year Edison opened his research laboratory. Ante-Westinghouse, stopping a train had been a tricky and slow business; brakemen had to go from car to car, setting each car's brakes individually. Quick stops were impossible; derailments were a regular feature of railroad life. (Before he came up with the air brake, Westinghouse invented a machine for re-railing derailed cars.) With the Westinghouse brake, the train's operator could brake all the cars at once. The new device not only improved safety; it also allowed trains to run at much higher speeds, thereby substantially enhancing the efficiency of the nation's railroads.

Westinghouse made a great deal of money off his brake, which was swiftly adopted throughout the industry. Most of the money he reinvested in the company he named after himself. For several years the company concentrated on other improvements in railroading, especially automatic signal systems. The signals were electrically operated and required the transmission of current over long distances; this led Westinghouse to investigate the possibilities and limitations of long-distance electrical transmission. It also led him into competition with Edison.

The struggle between Edison and Westinghouse—headline writers billed it as the "battle of the currents"—developed slowly. In 1880, Westinghouse visited Edison at Menlo Park. Then in their early thirties, both men were celebrities in their respective (and still largely separate) fields. The meeting was friendly enough. But the friendliness soon evaporated. "Tell Westinghouse to stick to air brakes," Edison muttered to a mutual acquaintance, when he discovered that Westinghouse wasn't.

Westinghouse took a page from Edison's notebook in lining up a group of bright young researchers. The brightest of these was Nikola Tesla, an immigrant from Croatia who initially had come to America to work for Edison. An Edison lieutenant had encountered Tesla in France and recommended him highly. "I know two great men," Edison's scout wrote to the boss. "You are one of them. The other is this young man." Edison didn't like being compared to an unknown apprentice, and Tesla turned out not to like working for Edison. A rupture occurred following a financial misunderstanding between employer and employee. While thinking about possible improvements in electrical generation, Tesla hit upon some ideas he believed would boost efficiency significantly. He described these ideas to Edison, who remarked, "There's fifty thousand dollars in it for you if you can do it." Tesla did, then returned to Edison for his bonus. Edison refused to pay, insisting he had been joking. Tesla didn't appreciate Edison's sense of humor and stormed out of the laboratory. He soon found his way to George Westinghouse, who immediately recognized his good fortune.

Tesla helped Westinghouse solve various technical problems regarding alternating current. By the late 1880s most of the bugs had been exterminated, and Westinghouse was ready to pursue the construction of alternating current networks. In contrast to Edison's idea of many self-contained direct current systems, Westinghouse saw regional grids in which monster generating stations fed alternating current over hundreds of miles of wire to millions of people. Of the two visions, Westinghouse's more closely reflected the consolidating corporate tendencies of the 1890s; it would exploit economies of scale and appeal to the kinds of investors who were underwriting the great trusts that were coming to dominate the American economy.

Edison wasn't a person to yield ground gracefully. At any given time he was engaged in scores of lawsuits defending his patents against persons and firms he felt were cutting into his profits; to guard his turf against Westinghouse, he launched a scorched-earth (or perhaps scorched-flesh) campaign of negative public relations. Edison and his lawyers and public relations people did their best to frighten potential customers about the dangers inherent in the high voltages Westinghouse's scheme employed. To demonstrate the lethal power of such high voltages, Edison's technicians wired stray dogs and cats to generators and switched on the current. As the unfortunate animals fried, Edison's publicists described the "experiments" in lurid pamphlets that extrapolated the results to human beings.

One unintended side effect of these grisly activities was to persuade the New York state legislature to adopt electrocution as a form of capital punishment. In the course of the Edison-Westinghouse fight, penal officials came to wonder just how large a blow electricity could produce. Killing dogs and cats was one thing; could it dispatch a full-grown man? Edison's experts contended that they could kill an elephant with enough voltage. Experiments were arranged in which a calf was sizzled, then a horse. The legislature was convinced, saving the elephants of the world from being sacrificed to electrical and penal science. Westinghouse duly won the contract to furnish the (alternating current) generators that powered the state's new "electric chairs." A convicted murderer named William Kemmler earned the dubious distinction of being the first person intentionally put to death by electrocution.

The salesman in Edison begrudged Westinghouse this minor victory, but at the same time he took comfort from the fact that the electrocution provided prima facie evidence that alternating current was as dangerous as he had always contended. Making the best of the situation, Edison remarked that murderers now faced being hanged or being "Westinghoused."

Yet despite Edison's efforts at negative advertising, people registered little concern about the hazards associated with alternating current. Perhaps they didn't really understand the issue, since it was rather technical; perhaps they were simply growing inured to the dangers of life in an industrial age, as a result of the existing high rate of accidents in factories, mines, and the like.

In any event, when Westinghouse bid aggressively for contracts—as he usually did—and offered prices lower than Edison's, he generally won out. The year 1893 witnessed two signal Westinghouse victories. The first involved the Columbian Exposition: Westinghouse beat Edison in a head-to-head fight for the right to power the world's fair. It was a brilliant victory for alternating current—even though much of the brilliance came from incandescent bulbs of Edison's design.

The second victory won Westinghouse the contract to build electrical generating facilities at Niagara Falls. Although lighting the Columbian Exposition brought Westinghouse greater immediate prestige and visibility, harnessing Niagara provided the better measure of the manner in which Westinghouse and alternating current were leaving Edison and direct current behind. As recently as the 1880s, the Niagara project would have been impossible: alternating current technology was too undeveloped to handle the massive amounts of power the greatest waterfall in North America produced (estimated at 50 million horsepower), and the location was too far from heavily populated areas for direct current to be feasible. But by the mid-1890s, alternating current had come of age. Two years after Westinghouse won the Niagara contract—partly due to the endorsement of the eminent British physicist Lord Kelvin—the first of three 5,000-horsepower generators went into operation. The other two followed before long. Transmission lines carried 11,000-volt alternating current across the countryside of upstate New York to Buffalo and points beyond.

In the heat of the battle of the currents, Edison and the direct currentists had championed their version of electricity as the more democratic form. Users wouldn't depend on huge electrical grids, which inevitably would be controlled by impersonal and unaccountable giant corporations; instead, they would rely only on smaller distribution companies more susceptible to local control. There was much to this argument, and in later years many consumers of electricity would balk at the extent of their dependence on the powerful electric utilities.

Yet Westinghouse and the alternators had a counterargument that was also persuasive. While Edison's scheme might grant cities electrical autonomy, it would leave small towns and farms in the kerosene age. Rural communities couldn't use enough electricity to pay for their own generating facilities; under Westinghouse's plan, they wouldn't have to. They could simply hook into the big electrical grids, paying only the cost of stringing the wires to their doorsteps. For the most isolated villages and farms, the stringing cost might still be excessive, but for the millions not quite at the end of beyond, the Westinghouse arrangement placed them on an equal footing with city dwellers. Since time immemorial, country life had been more primitive than city life; with the coming of alternating current, the country took a big step toward catching up with the city.

Ironically, just at the time Westinghouse was gaining the edge on Edison, further technological developments made direct current more practical than before. During the mid-1880s an Englishman named Charles Parsons invented a steam turbine that efficiently converted thermal power—provided by coal, oil, or occasionally wood—to electrical power. Since coal or oil could be hauled to any location, this invention allowed generating facilities to be located almost anywhere—in particular, close to consumers, as direct current generators had to be.

But Westinghouse beat Edison to acquiring the American rights to Parsons's invention; in 1896, Westinghouse won a North American monopoly and shut Edison out. Soon Westinghouse adapted the steam turbine to use with alternating current, and by decade's end 100,000-horsepower jumbos were producing alternating current in recently unimaginable quantities.

The widespread electrification that accompanied the wiring of America to Westinghouse's alternating current marked the second stage of the American industrial revolution. Steam had powered the first stage, allowing machines to accomplish what human muscles had accomplished for millennia, and to accomplish much more as well. But steam engines had to be big to be efficient, and many industrial processes are small. In a steam-powered plant, belts and pulleys and drive shafts connected the various tools to the central steam engine, severely constraining the placement of the tools and the pace at which they functioned. Electric motors, by contrast, could be small and still be efficient; electrification allowed each tool operator to possess his own engine and therefore be the master of his own tool. In addition, steam-powered factories gulped massive amounts of water and consequently had to be located near lakes or streams. Electrically powered plants operated dry; they could be placed more conveniently for suppliers and markets.

Electrification reshaped American life in other ways besides making industry more flexible and efficient. Modern urban activities would have been impossible without electricity. Lamps burning oil, kerosene, or gas had lifted some of the shadows from after-hours city life, but not until the advent of electrical lighting did cities really remain alive past dark. Where previously lamps had to be lit one by one, now whole neighborhoods switched on at a single throw. Indoor illumination became much safer with the snuffing of millions of flames; the new incandescent bulbs were nearly fail-safe, since they burned out instantly once their vacuum seal was broken. Fire, the scourge of cities for centuries, was brought largely under control. (Exceptions like the San Francisco fire of 1906, which raged wildly for days after the terrible earthquake of that year broke the water mains and thereby prevented the fire department from doing its job, proved the rule.)

Electricity powered the elevators that carried occupants and visitors to the tops of the new skyscrapers; no one would have wanted a top-floor office if it meant climbing twenty flights of stairs. Elevators had been in use since the 1850s, when Elisha Otis demonstrated the safety of his model by riding one of his cars to the top of its shaft, then cutting the cable with his own hand; Otis's automatic brake saved him from a sudden end and made his name synonymous with building hoists. But the early steam-powered elevators moved slowly, not more than 50 feet (or about four floors) per minute. Only with the fitting of electric motors to the elevators did they become much faster than taking the stairs. By the 1890s, elevators were flying up their shafts at more than 600 feet per minute.

While moving people up the new skyscrapers, electricity also moved air and water through the buildings. Electricity spun the fans that provided ventilation, making central heating (and later cooling) possible. Electricity powered the pumps that pushed water clear to the penthouses, making high-rise apartment life attractive to the middle and upper classes. (The poor in the tenements had learned to get along without indoor plumbing.)

Electricity powered the streetcars that delivered workers to offices and factories. The coming of electricity spared the horses and mules that previously had drawn the streetcars and usually had died after a few years on the job. One electric-streetcar promoter named Sprague advertised his product with handbills declaring, "Lincoln set the slaves free; Sprague set the mule free." Electricity also spared the city dwellers who had had to fight off the flies, smell, and disease that arose from what the horses and mules left behind. Steam-powered cable cars had been tried in some cities, drawing their motive force from a cable driven by a single central engine. But these were always awkward, often unnerving to ride, and generally suffered the usual weakness of centralized systems: a malfunction in any part could bring the entire system clanking to a halt. Although cable cars survived in San Francisco and a few other places where steep hills frustrated electric motors, nearly everywhere else the electric streetcars caught on quickly. By the end of the 1890s, more than twenty thousand miles of streetcar lines were in operation.

If electricity allowed Americans to get to work more quickly and to work more efficiently once they got there, it also opened new avenues of frivolity. The Kinetoscope that Edison displayed at the Columbian Exposition was an early version of a technology that would transform the way tens of millions of Americans spent their Saturday afternoons. As early as the 1830s, the Englishman William Horner had demonstrated that the eye could be fooled into perceiving motion by a swift succession of slightly varying still pictures. Adaptations of Horner's idea became parlor toys during the subsequent decades. The development of photographic techniques allowed would-be moviemakers to consider capturing motion on film. A prime, albeit unwitting, contributor to the technology was Leland Stanford, the railroad tycoon and part-time horse breeder, who bet a friend that the four feet of a galloping horse are off the ground simultaneously at some point during the course of each stride. Stanford wagered $25,000, then proceeded to spend $100,000 winning the bet. The proof of Stanford's contention came in a series of photographs shot by Eadweard Muybridge showing one of Stanford's racehorses in motion. Muybridge rigged a row of cameras at the side of a track; to each camera he connected a light tripwire. As the horse galloped by, it tripped the wire and caused its picture to be taken. When the resulting photographs were viewed in swift succession, the horse appeared to gallop before the viewer—and sure enough, all four feet left the ground in midstride.

Muybridge was on the right track, but as long as he had to use dozens of cameras to produce his separate frames, there were severe restrictions on the kinds of motion he could reproduce. Not until the 1880s did a Frenchman, Étienne-Jules Marey, devise a method for taking a rapid series of photos with a single camera.

Edison entered the motion picture field through the back door of phonography. Having learned to capture a succession of sounds and play them back, Edison thought he ought to be able to do the same thing with a succession of sights. Initially he intended to use motion pictures to make his phonographs more attractive and therefore more profitable. During the late 1880s and early 1890s, Edison and his researchers tested various methods of exposing film to motion and of playing back the exposures. By 1891 he was ready to file for patents, one for the "Kinetograph" (the special camera that made the exposures) and another for the "Kinetoscope" (the device that played them back).

As was his custom, Edison paid close attention to how he could squeeze the most money out of his invention. One of his researchers had been investigating the possibility of projecting the motion pictures onto a screen for viewing by a large audience. Edison rejected this line of research in favor of the development of his Kinetoscope, a peephole-in-a-box arrangement that required users to watch the film one at a time. Edison reasoned that he could sell more Kinetoscopes than devices that played to hundreds at a sitting.

This proved to be a bad choice, like Edison's preference for direct current. Though the Kinetoscope drew big crowds at the Columbian Exposition, competitors quickly crowded the market with projection systems. Edison's own chief researcher into projection left to join a rival firm. Ultimately Edison himself had to come up with a projector; in the meantime he sued everyone he could think of for patent infringement.

By the end of the 1890s motion picture technology had reached the stage where it no longer could thrive simply on its newness. Viewers increasingly demanded longer films with more-involved plots. Moviemakers complied, producing such features as Edwin Porter's *Great Train Robbery*, which packed vaudeville halls across America—leaving Edison's one-at-a-time Kinetoscopes to fill attics and barns and other final resting places for bypassed technology.

IV

The bruising contest between Edison and Westinghouse for control of the direction of the second stage of the American industrial revolution was merely one of several similar battles during the 1890s. It was far from the largest, for while Edison and Westinghouse were fighting for markets that counted annual sales in the hundreds of thousands of dollars, other industrial barons were dueling for markets that totaled in the hundreds of millions.

No baron was more powerful than John D. Rockefeller, and none guarded his fiefdom so jealously. A native New Yorker, Rockefeller had early moved with his parents to Cleveland; he completed high school before entering the business world as an office boy to a retail trading company there. He quickly demonstrated his capacity for commerce, including an uncanny way with figures and a passion for mastering details. At the ripe age of twenty, Rockefeller left his employer to form a start-up with a friend. His timing couldn't have been better, for hardly had the commodity brokerage of Clark & Rockefeller opened its doors than the Civil War erupted. The war sent demand for commodities of all kinds soaring, almost guaranteeing the success of the venture.

One of the commodities in greatest demand during the war was lubricating oil, which kept the trains the Union rode to victory running. The

1859 discovery of oil in western Pennsylvania had touched off a boom in the hinterland behind Cleveland, and Rockefeller determined to cash in on the boom. More quickly than others, Rockefeller perceived the tremendous future for petroleum products; accordingly, in 1863 he organized a company devoted to refining and marketing oil and its derivatives. The war gave Rockefeller's new firm a running start; the running start gave Rockefeller the funds and financial standing to buy out three of his partners.

The economic boom continued, in the North and West at any rate, from the surrender at Appomattox to the Panic of 1873. During that period Rockefeller climbed to the pinnacle of the petroleum industry—at the same time that the industry was growing at a fantastic rate. No sector of the American economy during the nineteenth century underwent a more spectacular transformation than oil. In 1855, petroleum had been a curiosity sold in patent medicine bottles; it was often thought a nuisance for fouling springs and infiltrating water wells. Within a decade it had become a necessity: an industrial lubricant, solvent, and fuel, and a household illuminator. Commercial production hadn't existed before 1859; during the next decade it approached 10 million barrels per year. Petroleum technology evolved at a breathtaking pace. New drilling methods eased the search for oil; pipeline networks collected the crude into large storage tanks; ever bigger and more efficient refineries processed it; elaborate distribution systems delivered the refined products by pipeline, barge, tanker, and railcar.

The burgeoning oil industry suited Rockefeller's gifts perfectly. Rockefeller was neither inventor nor, strictly speaking, innovator. But he was an organizer, and at this frenetic time in the development of the oil industry, organization was what was called for. The earliest days of oil had been dominated by the hard-driving, hard-living types that characterized most mineral booms; the oil towns of western Pennsylvania during the 1860s looked very much like the gold camps of California during the 1850s, only grimier. Few early oilers kept close track of expenses; few could tell what their output was during any given week or month. Rockefeller could. His passion for careful accounting amounted at times to an obsession. On one occasion, when the Standard Oil Company was raking in revenues by the millions, he dropped in on an obscure junior accountant. "Permit me," he said, then proceeded to review the young man's ledger books. "Very well kept—very, indeed," he congratulated the nervous fellow. He flipped a few more pages, until his eye caught something. "A little error here. Will you correct it?" he said. The accountant who later told the story stated that he had then gone back over the whole ledger book. "And I will take my oath that it was the only error in the book," he insisted.

In a business in which the common unit of volume was the gusher, Rockefeller lay awake nights figuring out how to wring an extra drop out of each step of the production and refining process. He ordered his engineers to capture and save byproducts other refiners threw away—such as gasoline, which didn't yet have much of a market and which was commonly dumped into the Cuyahoga River, often to be torched by bored tugboat men who shoveled hot coals onto the gasoline to watch it blaze. As Rockefeller's engineers found uses for his byproducts, they became products in their own right, adding to the steady swelling of his profits.

No detail was too small to warrant Rockefeller's attention. The story of how he reduced from forty to thirty-nine the number of beads of solder used to seal his five-gallon kerosene cans became a legend in the industry. As another cost-cutting measure, he decreed that the overlap in the iron hoops binding each of his wooden barrels be reduced from five inches to two. He had tested the new design and found that it didn't reduce the strength of the barrels; the iron saved would net the company thousands of dollars per year.

Rockefeller drove hard bargains. He demanded and received special treatment from the railroads that hauled his petroleum products. These secret rate reductions, or rebates, later became highly contentious, ultimately provoking Congress to outlaw them. To Rockefeller, they were simply a sound business practice. "Each shipper made the best bargain that he could," Rockefeller remarked afterward, pointing out that a large shipper such as Standard Oil deserved lower rates than small shippers because it provided so much more business to the railroads.

Rockefeller drove even harder bargains with his competitors. He believed most competition to be wasteful, a needless duplication of effort. He had no compunctions about forcing competitors to the wall: they were less efficient than he and therefore deserved to be devoured or dismantled. As Standard Oil's share of the market for refined petroleum products grew, its costs continued to fall. No one could stand up to Standard in a price war. Those who surrendered without a fight often were glad they did, for when they took their payment in Standard stock, Rockefeller subsequently made them wealthy. Those who chose to fight usually wished they hadn't.

Tom Scott and Joseph Potts fell into the latter category. Scott was the president of the Pennsylvania Railroad, at that time the largest hauler of freight in the world and the most powerful corporation in the United States. In 1875, the Pennsylvania's net earnings came to $25 million. Potts was the head of the Empire Transportation Company, a conglomerate linked to the Pennsylvania and having interests in rail, steamships, and pipelines. Scott and Potts had watched with growing alarm as Rockefeller nearly perfected Standard Oil's monopoly of petroleum refining; they feared that the Standard octopus would soon stretch an arm into the oil transportation business as well. "We reached the conclusion," Potts said afterward, "that there were three great divisions in the petroleum business—the production, the carriage of it, and the preparation of it for the market. If any one party controlled absolutely any one of these divisions, they practically would have a very fair show of controlling the others."

Potts and Scott judged that to protect their oil carriage business, they must break Rockefeller's stranglehold on preparing petroleum for market— that is, refining. Early in 1877 they agreed to a scheme whereby the Empire would acquire oil refineries with the help of the Pennsylvania and would ship the output of such refineries exclusively over its own lines and those of the Pennsylvania; the Pennsylvania would transport the Empire's oil at preferential rates.

Rockefeller soon learned of the Pennsylvania-Empire pact. He warned the principals to cease and desist. "The Pennsylvania and its subsidiary the Empire are carriers," he told Scott. "The Empire has no business whatever in the field of refining." Rockefeller requested that the Empire withdraw from the deal. He didn't exactly threaten; he didn't have to. Scott was fully aware that Standard accounted for most of the oil traffic on the Pennsylvania. Rockefeller had only to hint that should the Pennsylvania-Empire combination persist in its encroachment into refining, the Pennsylvania might have to look for other customers to fill a big gap in its shipping revenues.

Scott could have retorted that Standard, a refiner, had no business being in transportation but nonetheless owned and operated pipelines. Rockefeller doubtless would have responded that pipelines weren't railroads. Standard had never directly assaulted the Pennsylvania by acquiring railroads, but now the Pennsylvania was directly assaulting Standard by acquiring, through the Empire, refineries.

Scott hoped Rockefeller was bluffing. After all, large though Standard was, it was still smaller than the Pennsylvania. Standard needed the Pennsylvania more than the Pennsylvania needed Standard, or so Scott thought.

Yet Rockefeller, ever a man for details, had laid his battle plans carefully. He had enlisted the support of two of the Pennsylvania's most bitter railroad rivals, the New York Central and the Erie. In addition, Rockefeller had been building up Standard's financial reserves ever since its incorporation in 1870. During twenty years in business Rockefeller had watched scores of ventures fail for want of cash to carry them through the slumps that regularly afflicted the American economy. There was money to be made in hard times, but making money required having money. Rockefeller determined always to have money. When Scott and Potts threw down the gage, Rockefeller's war chest was full.

Rockefeller's first move was to cancel his shipping contract with the Pennsylvania; next he slashed the price of kerosene in all the markets where Standard was competing with the Empire. He ordered the rush construction of six hundred new tank cars, which he persuaded the New York Central and the Erie to haul on their tracks. He directed Standard's purchasing agents to bid fiercely for crude oil wherever the Empire's agents were also bidding; he would starve the Empire of supplies. Likewise he instructed Standard's sales agents to lowball the Empire in both domestic and foreign markets. He persuaded the New York Central and the Erie to cut their freight rates; when the Pennsylvania matched the cuts, Rockefeller's two allies cut again. He closed down his Pittsburgh refineries in order not to have to ship a single gallon of Standard's oil over the Pennsylvania lines.

Rockefeller's barrage staggered the Pennsylvania-Empire coalition. The rate cutting and the loss of Standard's traffic sapped the Pennsylvania's financial foundation, which, like most American railroads' during the last quarter of the nineteenth century, wasn't very solid to begin with. Through the spring and early summer of 1877, Scott watched the Pennsylvania's slim reserves vanish, and he tried frantically to reassure the railroad's creditors. The Pennsylvania was forced to trim dividends even below what it had paid during recent recession years; on Wall Street the Pennsylvania's stock slid sharply, further limiting the line's ability to borrow.

Rockefeller's offensive forced the Pennsylvania to reduce wages, which sparked a walkout by the railroad's employees. The Pennsylvania's workers had hated Scott for years; of all of the despised class of railroad managers, he was the most despised. He ran the road like a plantation, where a worker's place was to do as he was told, accept what wages he was offered, and be happy to have a job. Scott didn't help his image among the working class of the state of Pennsylvania by flaunting his influence in the state's political process. The wage cuts forced by Rockefeller's attack were the last in a long series of provocations. When the Pennsylvania's workers walked out, employees of other lines followed suit, and the years of bad blood soon gave rise to violence. Mobs roamed Pittsburgh, burning railcars, smashing windows, looting shops, and stoning militiamen. The militiamen fired at the crowds, killing dozens of people. Beyond the human tragedy, the financial losses mounted to the tens of millions of dollars. Damage to the Pennsylvania's rolling stock and fixed plant came to more than $4 million.

Scott had no choice but to run up the white flag. When Rockefeller offered to buy out the Empire's refineries and recommended that the Pennsylvania take over the Empire's rail facilities, Scott agreed. Joseph Potts objected loudly, not wishing to see his company cut right out from under him. But by the terms of his alliance with Scott, he had little alternative. For whatever consolation it afforded, the buyout made Potts a very wealthy man and eventually quieted his complaints.

The crushing of the Pennsylvania-Empire combination left Rockefeller and Standard with nearly complete control of American oil refining; yet even this wasn't enough for Rockefeller. In creating his leviathan, Rockefeller had been forced to resort to a variety of ad hoc measures, with the result that the Standard Oil combination exhibited a certain legal untidiness. Most persons would hardly have noticed: Rockefeller possessed the power, including more than 90 percent of American refining capacity; what did he care for the forms? But Rockefeller couldn't stand untidiness, since untidiness entailed waste. To eradicate waste was his life's mission.

As a remedy for the untidiness, Rockefeller turned to something new in American economic history: the trust. By this device, control of the various corporate entities that constituted the Standard combination passed to a single board of trustees. Traditionally, the word "trust," as used in a legal sense, had connoted a trusteeship: the holding and administering of property on behalf of another. In its new guise the term retained this meaning but added the idea of a concrete business structure, a kind of super-corporation.

Trusts were highly controversial, since the transparent purpose of trusts was to curtail competition and thereby boost prices and profits. Rockefeller knew that the Standard trust would cause a stir; for several years after its 1882 establishment he and the other Standard trustees kept the precise nature of their compact a secret. But by the beginning of the 1890s the secret had spilled, and Rockefeller's example became the model for consolidation in other industries.

Nor was the trust the last word in consolidation. The predictable public outcry against trusts triggered legislative action to curb the monopolists. In 1890 Congress passed the Sherman Antitrust Act, which empowered the federal government to prevent the establishment and operation of manufacturing combinations that restrained trade. Although for more than a decade the Sherman Act was largely unenforced—and unenforceable, on account of Supreme Court rulings that sharply distinguished between trade, which the Constitution allowed the federal government to regulate, and manufacturing, which it didn't—the wave of protests against trusts prompted Rockefeller and the Standard directors to consider new devices to guarantee coordination among the constituent parts of their empire. In 1892, under pressure from the state of Ohio, which had antitrust laws of its own, the Standard board decided to dissolve the trust. After further study of alternatives, Rockefeller's lawyers recommended the creation of a holding company.

Holding companies—corporations that owned the stock of other corporations—had typically been illegal or at least quite exceptional before the late 1880s. In 1888, however, the state of New Jersey passed a law allowing corporations to own other corporations; the law was broadened in 1889, 1893, and 1896. Without the use of a holding company, a firm that wished to take over ten $10 million corporations had to find $100 million to purchase their assets. The use of a holding company, by contrast, allowed the purchase of the stock of the target companies rather than their assets. By acquiring 51 percent of each company, for a total of $51 million, (give or take something for the difference between asset values and stock prices), the holding company gained control of the same assets as before but at little more than half the expense. In addition, buying stock was straightforward and convenient and didn't require the approval of the management of the targeted companies, while buying assets was complicated and difficult and did require management approval.

Rockefeller perceived the advantages of the holding company approach, and to that end the Standard Oil Company of New Jersey was chartered in June 1899. This new holding company controlled twenty constituent companies that formerly had been part of the Standard Oil Trust; the new company was capitalized at $110 million. One of the largest and most powerful industrial combinations in the world at its moment of birth, it immediately began gobbling up other companies. Its net profits in 1900 totaled more than $55 million, and it grew stronger daily.

V

Yet enormous as Standard Oil of New Jersey was, it wasn't the biggest corporation in America. That honor went to United States Steel, which was the godchild of the only two men in America who rivaled Rockefeller for industrial and financial primacy.

The first of the godfathers was Andrew Carnegie. When the drafters of the American dream created their rags-to-riches legend, Carnegie was the man they had in mind. Carnegie had emigrated from Scotland to America at the age of twelve with scarcely a penny in his pocket but with ambition, intelligence, and grit enough for a dozen people. Like Edison, Carnegie got his start in the telegraph business; he was one of the first persons to master the art of reading Morse code by ear. His skill impressed one of the telegraph company's customers, the Pennsylvania Railroad, sufficiently that the Pennsylvania offered him a job. Carnegie took the job and stayed with the railroad for a dozen years, moving up the ranks to superintendent of the Pittsburgh division. Among the innovations he promoted was the Pullman sleeping car, which soon became the standard of luxury in American rail travel.

During the railroad building boom of the 1850s and 1860s, Carnegie noted how much money the roads were paying for iron and steel, and he decided to chart his course in the direction of those metals. In 1865, he formed the Keystone Bridge Company, which specialized in iron bridges. For the next few years he dabbled in other business ventures, but by the early 1870s he was ready to devote himself to a ferrous future. In 1872 he created a company to manufacture steel according to the state-of-the-art Bessemer process.

Carnegie brought to the steel business an acute mind (like Rockefeller's), a charismatic personality (totally unlike Rockefeller's), and an absolute mania for organization and efficiency (Rockefeller in spades). This last quality gave Carnegie a critical advantage over his competitors in steel (just as it had Rockefeller in oil). Describing his introduction to steel manufacturing, Carnegie later remarked: "I was greatly surprised to find that the cost of each of the various processes was unknown. Inquiries made of the leading manufacturers of Pittsburgh proved this. It was a lump business, and until stock was taken and the books balanced at the end of the year, the manufacturers were in total ignorance of the results. I heard of men who thought their business at the end of the year would show a loss and had found a profit, and vice versa."

Carnegie was certain he could do better, and he spent the next quarter century proving it. He tightened up the bookkeeping in order to identify where improvements needed to be made. "One of the chief sources of success in manufacturing is the introduction and strict maintenance of a perfect system of accounting, so that responsibility for money or materials can be brought home to every man," he wrote. "Owners who, in the office, would not trust a clerk with five dollars without having a check upon him, were supplying tons of material daily to men in the mills without exacting an account of their stewardship by weighing what each returned in finished form."

Carnegie devised a system for keeping close track of every stage of the manufacturing process; he utilized his system in an unceasing effort to cut costs. Carnegie didn't worry about profits, concentrating instead on cutting costs. The profits, he believed, would take care of themselves. As he exhorted the managers of his steelworks: "Show me your cost sheets. It is more interesting to know how well and how cheaply you have done this thing than how much money you have made, because the one is a temporary result, due possibly to special conditions of trade, but the other means a permanency that will go on with the works as long as they last."

In his quest for lower costs, Carnegie invested incessantly in the latest technology. He built Bessemer converters when they were the finest in the business; when the open-hearth furnace appeared, he junked his Bessemers for open-hearths. He believed that every month his company stuck with outdated equipment was a month forever lost to inefficiency. Once, talking shop with a British steelman, Carnegie listened to an explanation of how British companies liked to wring the last ton of steel out of old equipment before retiring it. "We have equipment we have been using for twenty years, and it is still serviceable," the Englishman declared with evident satisfaction. To which Carnegie retorted, "That is what is the matter with the British steel trade. Most British equipment is in use twenty years after it should have been scrapped. It is because you keep this used-up machinery that the United States is making you a back number."

Carnegie at times carried his quest for the latest technology to extremes. On one occasion he ordered Charles Schwab, his chief lieutenant, to tear out a rolling mill that had been installed only three months before, when Schwab said he had found a more efficient design.

Carnegie's obsession paid off. During the 1880s, his costs fell from $40 a ton to $30 to below $20. Meanwhile output climbed from less than 10,000 tons per month to 15,000 and on past 20,000. Profits, as Carnegie had predicted, took care of themselves, rising to more than $1 million annually.

This didn't put Carnegie quite in the category of Rockefeller, not yet anyway; but it did attract Rockefeller's attention. Though Rockefeller had objected, to the point of industrial warfare, when the Pennsylvania and the Empire had invaded Standard Oil's petroleum turf, he exhibited no compunctions about poaching on Carnegie's steel territory. In fairness to Rockefeller, by the 1890s the oil king had a problem, albeit one few of his contemporaries could appreciate, let alone sympathize with. Rockefeller's stake in Standard Oil was netting him between $10 million and $15 million per year. Already he was plowing millions back into the company; it couldn't usefully absorb any more. His personal wants were satisfied. He was giving away millions to assorted benefactions, including the college he had recently endowed, the University of Chicago. What else could he do with his money? Where could he invest it?

Being a natural-resources man, Rockefeller naturally looked to other resources besides oil. Starting in the mid-1880s, he had made minor (for him; major for anyone else) investments in iron properties. To this time, apparently, he had entertained no grand designs on the iron and steel industry as a whole; he had plenty of work left to do in oil. He was simply looking for some place to invest some money.

The properties Rockefeller purchased were scattered about the Western Hemisphere. One of the largest was in Cuba near Santiago. Developing this property absorbed a fair amount of Rockefeller's spare cash: the mine itself had to be surveyed and shafts sunk; a railroad connecting the ore body to the sea had to be built; dock facilities for loading the ore onto ships had to be constructed. The preparations proceeded during the early 1890s; the mine was ready to begin production when the Panic of 1893 hit. Like so much else at that time, Rockefeller's Cuban mine went into suspended animation.

Closer to home, Rockefeller purchased rights to iron in Wisconsin, in the Gogebic Range; the two most promising tracts included the Aurora and Tilden mines. Additional properties were located in Michigan and Minnesota; these represented something of a flier, since no one knew just what they contained. For twenty years reports had drifted down from the cold north woods above Lake Superior about dirt that rusted and mountains that deranged compass needles. But whether the reports reflected solid truth, delusions of prospectors too long in the forest, or propaganda of unscrupulous promoters remained to be seen.

The most enthusiastic of the reports came from a family of brothers, the Merritts, formerly of upstate New York and now resident in the vicinity of Duluth. Leonidas Merrit—commonly called Lon—and his five brothers had begun their explorations of the Lake Superior region cruising pine timber. While tramping about the hills and lakes, they had encountered iron-veined rocks scattered across the hillsides and valleys. The greatest concentration centered on the Mesabi Range, which, they became convinced, held iron in quantities never before seen in North America.

Despite their conviction, Lon and his brothers failed to secure the kind of proof necessary to convince outside investors. The problem wasn't that the iron wasn't there; it was. But the ore was a different sort than was common in other iron areas. Elsewhere iron prospectors had found iron-bearing strata in cliffs and outcroppings above the surface; in the Mesabi, the ore lay in flat beds below the ground.

Despite their failure to find funding, Lon and his brothers persisted. They had never really expected to get rich, and like so many other persons who left the civilized parts of the country for the frontier—upper Minnesota was still plenty wild in the early 1890s—they were happy enough to spend extended periods on their own beyond the edge of settlement. Their timbering kept them in boots, blankets, and grub, and allowed the occasional blowout in town. They would discover unmistakable proof of the Mesabi iron, they believed, if not sooner then later; in the meantime they filed claims against the day when their persistence would pay off. In 1890, Lon alone took out more than one hundred leases; the brothers and even some nephews filed additional claims. At the same time they organized the Bi-wabik Mountain Iron Company to exploit such strikes as they might make. Though land- (or lease-) rich, the company almost entirely lacked capital.

In 1891, the Merritts found the proof they had been seeking. Thirty miles into the woods north of Superior's shore, in a basin that soon would gain fame as the Mountain Iron Mine, they prepared to sink a shaft to test the formations below the ground. The German driller they had brought along refused to drill in the center of the basin, insisting that ore could be found only under mountain slopes. Lon Merritt and the others compromised with the German, agreeing to drill halfway up a nearby slope. They later regretted the compromise. "If we had gotten mad and kicked the ground right where we stood," Lon said, "we would have thrown out 64 percent ore—if we had kicked it hard enough to kick off the pine needles." As matters turned out, they struck paydirt at fourteen feet. They took a quantity of the ore into Duluth to be assayed and discovered that this indeed was the bonanza they had been looking for.

Or rather it *would* be the bonanza they had been looking for if they could raise the money to get the ore out of the ground, out of the woods, and off to the steelmakers who could do something useful with it. They tried to talk a couple of the railroads already in the area into extending spurs to their claims, but neither one had the cash to risk the venture.

The boys weren't about to lose the prize they had pursued so doggedly for so long merely because of the shortsightedness of some railroad managers. They decided to build the railway themselves. They created their own company for the purpose, scrounged a little cash, and commenced construction. By the time the snows of autumn stopped the building during the last months of 1892, they had completed forty-five miles of line. The following spring they started shipping ore out of the woods and down to a terminal on Lake Superior.

Their prospects were sufficiently promising that a Pittsburgh investor, Henry Oliver, offered them a tempting price for a piece of the action. Oliver said he'd pay a $75,000 cash bonus on signing and royalties of 65 cents for each ton hauled out. He guaranteed to take at least 400,000 tons per year.

The Merritts, never having seen this kind of money before, eagerly signed. They drank down a sizable portion of the $75,000 bonus celebrating, and when they sobered up they began figuring out how to spend the rest.

But becoming millionaires wasn't quite so easy. In order to build their railroad and acquire additional property, the Merritts had hocked themselves deeply. At the end of 1892 they owed more than $2 million; during the first months of 1893 they ran further into the red.

To ease their cash flow problems, they sought additional outside invest-ment. Most helpful in their search was Charles Wetmore, a New York financier with connections to the Rockefeller group. Lon and a couple of brothers traveled to New York and joined Wetmore for lunch at Delmon-ico's; they convinced him of the worthiness of their enterprise, and he agreed to sell $1.6 million worth of bonds to support it.

Wetmore then went to Rockefeller, who immediately purchased $400,000 of the bonds. The other $1.2 million sold more slowly, but Wet-more wasn't worried. With each passing month, ore from the Mesabi would be moving from mine to mill; as the world became aware of the value of the rim of iron around Lake Superior, Mesabi bonds would sell easily.

Then the Panic of 1893 hit. Consumers stopped purchasing, retailers canceled orders, factories shut down, workers drew pink slips, and com-modity prices plunged. The iron and steel business was flattened overnight. Big, well-financed corporations retrenched and lived off reserves; smaller firms dissolved. Credit contracted with a suffocating sound. The best bonds went begging; unproven ventures like the Merritts' drew derisive laughs from investors fortunate enough to be still liquid.

In a twinkling, the Merritts watched their net worth vanish. Their cred-itors closed in, demanding payment and threatening to seize assets if they didn't get their money. Unless Lon and the boys could arrange new fi-nancing, they would lose everything they had spent more than a decade discovering and building.

During the summer of 1893, the Merritts' predicament grew ever more desperate. Their debts were increasing by $10,000 per day; they couldn't pay interest on the bonds they had issued; creditors were bringing lawsuits; their workers were muttering about a strike. Fistfights and even knife fights broke out when the workers' pay envelopes came up short; one group of irate laborers entered company offices in Duluth and demanded their wages at gunpoint.

Pushed to the brink, the Merritts looked to the one person they knew of who might rescue them. Lon and the brothers reckoned that Rockefeller stood to lose his $400,000 if the situation didn't turn around; they reck-oned further that he might be willing to bail them out in order to save his investment.

The Merritts and Wetmore pitched this proposal to Rockefeller in July. The oil baron appreciated the logic of their argument; he also recognized that here was an opportunity to grab some valuable property at a fire-sale price. For several days Rockefeller's high-powered lawyers talked to the Merritts' overmanned and rather overawed attorneys; on July 12, the two sides struck a bargain. By the terms of the deal, Rockefeller consented to cover the Merritts' debts; he advanced them $500,000 to meet immediate obligations; subsequently he added another $1.5 million. In exchange they transferred their mines and railroads and associated properties to a newly chartered holding company, the Lake Superior Consolidated Iron Mines

Company, into which would also be folded Rockefeller's other iron interests in North America and the Caribbean. The Merritts got most of the stock in the new company; Rockefeller took $4.3 million in first-mortgage bonds.

To close the deal, Lon Merritt visited Rockefeller in New York. The weatherbeaten prospector and the industrial magnate were a study in contrasts, but they chatted affably for some time about the rigors of the Minnesota climate and the bright future of the Mesabi. Eventually Rockefeller indicated that he had another appointment, and he bade Merritt good day. The two never met again.

Lon and the boys exulted in their narrow escape. Only weeks before, they had been staring bankruptcy in the face. Now they were millionaires, at least on paper. Characteristically for the times, they inflated their paper value by watering the stock of the new company—which was one reason why Rockefeller took his cut of the deal in bonds rather than stock. As a matter of fact, however, the Mesabi mines proved to be so immensely valuable that Rockefeller could have taken even watered stock instead of bonds and come out ahead.

The creation of Lake Superior Consolidated made Rockefeller one of America's principal players in iron and steel. In the near wake of the 1893 Panic this wasn't an obvious boon. Prices of iron products had fallen off a cliff: from a high of more than $24 per ton in 1889, Bessemer pig iron had plummeted to $11 by the autumn of 1893. Prices of iron ore had slumped commensurately. Compounding Rockefeller's problem was the fact that the Mesabi ores, though vast, were of a loose, granular consistency unlike that which the major steel mills were accustomed to processing. The first attempts to make metal out of them were disappointing, sometimes spectacularly so. The ore tended to pack down in the furnaces, often congealing in dense clumps, occasionally ripping the furnaces to shreds in tremendous explosions. The force of the blasts would shower the countryside for miles around with a fine coating of hot dust. The steel mills' neighbors had gotten used to a lot in the name of progress and jobs, but this was too much for many of them, and they brought suit for damages. Eventually the steel companies learned to cope with the Mesabi ore, but for several years it created chronic troubles, and the troubles depressed its price.

Between the woeful state of the iron and steel industry generally and the refractoriness of the Mesabi ore, Rockefeller's investment looked to be a money loser for some time to come. He continued to have to pour money into the venture to keep it from sinking under the weight of its debts. Yet he stuck with it and indeed lengthened his position by purchasing the properties of other companies—firms pushed to the brink by the same forces that were squeezing the Consolidated. As Rockefeller recalled afterward, "Everybody seemed to want to sell. The stock was offered to us in alarming quantities." Rockefeller paid cash and snatched up some enticing bargains.

Rockefeller's entry into iron and steel couldn't help causing concern to those already in the business, especially those, like Andrew Carnegie, who had the most at stake. By the mid-1890s, Carnegie was far and away the leading figure in American steel; his mills produced the metal by the millions of tons at the lowest costs in the world. Against anyone besides Rockefeller, Carnegie might have felt impregnable. But no one in America could match the resources Rockefeller commanded, and no business leader had shown the combination of shrewdness and ruthlessness Rockefeller had displayed time and again in building the Standard Oil monopoly. Carnegie couldn't help wondering what Rockefeller intended. Would he try to capture the market in iron ore the way he had captured the oil market? Would he expand into steel production?

The looming confrontation between Carnegie and Rockefeller electrified the country. The penny papers spilled barrels of ink covering the combat between the colossi of steel and oil. At one end of the lists was the charismatic Scotsman, whose sparkling eyes and snowy beard make him look like Santa Claus, and who in fact preached that great wealth brought great responsibilities, including the responsibility to distribute that wealth to the less fortunate. "The man who dies rich, dies disgraced," Carnegie said. Carnegie was giving away money at a rapid rate, endowing libraries, schools, hospitals, and the like; yet still his wealth accumulated. And though he increasingly looked to the hereafter, he hadn't lost the ambition and competitive instinct that had carried him to the apex of the steel industry.

At the other end was the dour, driven Rockefeller. Rockefeller's grim joylessness couldn't have contrasted more with Carnegie's congeniality; in this contest it was clear who was the villain. Rockefeller made enemies unnecessarily; he had a knack for bungling public relations. While he usually paid fair prices for companies he took over, he had nonetheless gained a reputation for ruining those he bested and for driving widows and orphans to the poorhouse. Rockefeller provided an easy target, for he believed a dignified silence to be the appropriate response to the charges leveled against him. To many, his silence often seemed an admission of guilt.

The fight between Carnegie and Rockefeller threatened to shake the American economy to its foundations. Each man controlled an industrial empire more powerful than most countries; each held the fate of armies of workers, contractors, customers, and creditors in his hands. An all-out struggle between Carnegie and Rockefeller might lay several states to waste. The rail strike of 1877 that had accompanied Rockefeller's battle with the Pennsylvania Railroad, or the more recent but likewise bloody Homestead strike at Carnegie's flagship steelworks, might well pale by comparison with the wreckage of a war between the emperor of oil and the strongman of steel.

As the contestants squared off, rumors abounded regarding their strategies. Rockefeller's agents were reported skulking about the Great Lakes, looking for locations to build huge, ultramodern steel mills. Carnegie fueled speculation of a similar sort by declaring that Pittsburgh was no longer so well suited to the manufacture of steel as it once had been, and hinting that the Carnegie company was considering establishing steelmaking operations in the Upper Midwest and Great Lakes region.

Rockefeller kept his own counsel regarding his intentions. Privately he thought it surprising that Carnegie and his associates hadn't perceived their weakness before. "I was astonished," Rockefeller declared afterward, "that the steelmakers had not seen the necessity of controlling their ore supply." He added, "The lands which contained a good many of our best ore mines could have been purchased very cheaply before we became interested." But they hadn't been, and Rockefeller found his opening.

Rockefeller upped the ante by establishing a line of ore boats on the Great Lakes to deliver to market the ore the Consolidated's railroads were bringing out of the woods. He appeared to be repeating the pattern that had won him success in the petroleum business. There he had first acquired control of his sources of supply, then had mastered the means by which his supplies were transported. Now he was doing the same with iron ore.

Carnegie grew worried as Rockefeller expanded his rail and shipping network. Using one of his sarcastic sobriquets for Rockefeller, the steel king wrote: "Remember that Reckafellows will own the R.R. and that's like owning the pipelines. Producers will not have much of a show."

Carnegie was determined to have a show. He opted for an oblique defense, preferring not to take on Rockefeller directly. Though Carnegie believed he might win an all-out battle, the cost would be high. Nothing would be more wasteful than a ruinous fight with Rockefeller, and Carnegie abhorred waste. Besides, Carnegie had suffered a severe public relations setback in the violence that surrounded the Homestead strike, and he didn't desire to do anything that would further tarnish his carefully burnished image.

Rockefeller wasn't so worried about popular perceptions of himself, but he detested waste as much as Carnegie did. This common detestation was a major reason the two giants decided at the last minute to avoid a declaration of war. Through an intermediary, Carnegie proposed a preemptive truce. He offered to lease Rockefeller's iron mines for fifty years; the Carnegie group would underwrite the development and operation of the mines and pay Rockefeller 25 cents per ton on annual production of at least 600,000 tons. In addition, Carnegie agreed to ship this ore and at least 600,000 tons annually from other mines over Rockefeller's rail and ore-boat network. Rockefeller accepted the offer.

The agreement suited both sides well. Without putting any money down, Carnegie acquired an assured supply of inexpensive ore (the going rate recently had been 50 to 65 cents per ton and most likely would be at least that again as soon as the current depression lifted). Rockefeller relieved himself of the cares of entering a new field of production which he never had been really enthusiastic about—iron didn't get in his blood the way oil had. At the same time, the deal guaranteed that his freshly purchased rail lines and lake steamers wouldn't want for traffic.

The Rockefeller-Carnegie compact hit the American business world like a mortar shell. The prospect of a war between the two titans had driven prices of almost everything related to iron and steel upward, albeit from a depressed level. The compact immediately exploded this speculative bubble. Companies that had survived the shakeout thus far found themselves in deeper trouble than ever, their shares trading at a steep discount. Carnegie and his confederates snapped up several of the troubled firms, adding further to their strong position in Great Lakes ore.

Iron Age, the principal journal of the iron and steel industry, described the Rockefeller deal as Carnegie's most brilliant coup. "It gives the Carnegie Company a position unequalled by any steel producer in the world," the trade paper asserted. Carnegie himself particularly liked the way he had blunted Rockefeller's foray into iron and steel. "It does my heart good to think I got ahead of John D. Rockefeller on a bargain," he said.

VI

Rockefeller didn't agree that Carnegie had got ahead of him; the oil magnate was happy with the way the Mesabi business turned out. Carnegie himself had to admit that he didn't always come out ahead in tough transactions. In the biggest deal of the decade, the steel leader conceded that he was bested by the third member of America's economic triumvirate, J. P. Morgan.

John Pierpont Morgan was just as smart as Carnegie and Rockefeller; to his native intelligence he added a ferocious personality. When photographer Edward Steichen arranged to take a picture of Morgan, he found his subject truly frightening. Steichen had shot portrait photos of other formidable and powerful personages, but Morgan made them all seem like pretenders. Morgan arrived for the sitting and curtly informed Steichen that he could have two minutes to do his business, no more. Steichen motioned Morgan to a chair; the great financier sat bolt upright, gripping the armrests as though he might rip them off and glaring at the camera. And at the cameraman: Steichen recalled afterward that looking into Morgan's blazing hazel eyes made him think of standing on a railroad track at night in the glaring headlight of an express train hurtling straight toward him.

It required eyes like Morgan's to draw a viewer's attention away from the other outstanding feature of his face. Morgan's nose—"huge, more or less deformed, sick, bulbous," in Steichen's words—was legendary by the 1890s. Cartoonists and caricaturists drew the nose, and instantly their audiences recognized the man they intended. It had always been large, but as Morgan grew older it developed the blotched, inflamed aspect characteristic of the *acne rosacea* that ran in the family. Children stared and sometimes cried upon seeing it. Men doing business with Morgan tried not to let their gaze dwell on the nose, instead focusing on his eyes—and got run over by the express train.

Steichen was photographing Morgan because the banker lacked the patience to sit for a painted portrait. Morgan had commissioned Fedor Encke to paint him, and Encke had made a start, but Morgan lost interest and refused to hold still long enough for Encke to finish. Encke thereupon asked Steichen to photograph Morgan; he would work from the photo. Steichen agreed. He met Morgan and Encke and quickly took the photo Encke needed. While he had Morgan there, he took another for his own use. Steichen suggested a particular pose. Morgan tried it, then said in an irritated tone that it was uncomfortable. Steichen told him to find a position he found comfortable. Morgan shuffled and shrugged a bit before returning to the position Steichen had suggested. By this point Morgan was nearly out of patience and Steichen was nearly out of his allotted time. The photographer quickly made his exposure and thanked Morgan for his cooperation. Morgan left the room, pleased at Steichen's efficiency if not at the general idea of the sitting. In the hall outside the studio he pulled his money clip from his pocket and peeled off five hundred-dollar bills—about half a year's wages for a skilled worker. He handed the money to Encke with instructions to give it to Steichen.

Morgan wasn't so happy when Steichen returned with the prints. Steichen had done only minor retouching of the Morgan nose, judging the banker to be the kind who wanted himself to be seen with warts and all. Whether Morgan had been expecting a more thorough cleanup or just didn't like this particular picture, he expressed disgust at the print Steichen showed him. "Terrible!" he snorted, and he tore the photo to pieces.

Steichen had been hoping for a more favorable response, perhaps accompanied by another generous payment. But undismayed, he went back to his darkroom and made more prints, one of which he gave to his friend and fellow photographer Alfred Stieglitz.

The photo remained with Stieglitz for many years. After several of those years, Morgan's librarian saw the Steichen photograph. The passage of time hadn't been kind to Morgan's appearance, a fact that a succession of photographers and painters hadn't been fully able to hide. The librarian thought the photo captured the real Morgan and asked Stieglitz if she might show it to him. Stieglitz consented.

Morgan apparently had forgotten his initial reaction; he too now liked the photo. He said he wanted it for his own collection and would pay $5,000 for it. At that price he expected to get it—such an amount was then unheard of for a photograph. But Stieglitz also liked the photo; he refused to sell. Morgan eventually settled for copies, which Steichen took his time delivering.

Morgan didn't appreciate not getting his way, since for most of his life he had usually gotten it. He was born into wealth in Hartford, Connecticut, in 1837, a year of financial panic. The Morgan family survived the panic and came out stronger than ever, as Morgans generally did. The Morgan money had originated in sharp real estate investments and in steamship and railroad lines. Morgan's grandfather employed some of this money to make

Hartford a center of the insurance industry; he helped found the Aetna Insurance Company.

Morgan's father, J. S. Morgan, branched out into the dry-goods business, moving to Boston when operations outgrew Hartford. Cotton formed a staple of the business, and the elder Morgan and his partners soon fattened on the trans-Atlantic cotton trade. Credit was required to keep cotton afloat on the high seas, and in order to ensure that his credit lines stayed open, Morgan linked up with the London banking house of George Peabody. The deal made much money for both men, and when Peabody retired in the early 1860s, J. S. Morgan assumed control.

This was the business Pierpont Morgan grew up in. He loved it from the time he was a child. Other boys played at soldiering or exploring the wilderness; Morgan played at accounting. All his life he prided himself on his ability to scan a ledger sheet and instantly spot errors.

Had Morgan been healthier as a child he might have undertaken more vigorous pursuits. But a series of childhood maladies, the most serious being a case of inflammatory rheumatism that prompted his parents to send him to the Azores to recuperate, removed what little inclination he had to join the rough and tumble of his peers. It was about the time he contracted rheumatism that he also developed the initial signs of the *acne rosacea* that had been in the family for generations and eventually gave his nose its distinctive appearance.

Morgan received the kind of international education American business executives would learn to appreciate only several generations later. He attended the English High School in Boston until his father moved the family to London, at which point Pierpont went to Switzerland to continue his studies. Afterward he traveled north to Germany, where he enrolled in the University of Göttingen. He showed himself to be an exceedingly apt pupil; his mathematics professor tried to talk him into staying on as his assistant. Morgan thanked the professor for the thought but said he had business to attend to.

Shortly before the Civil War, Morgan accepted an offer of employment from the Wall Street firm of Duncan, Sherman & Company. He began as a junior accountant, but his insight into markets and finances showed from the start and he quickly moved up. On a visit to New Orleans on matters relating to the cotton trade, he came across a cargo of coffee that had lost its buyer. Though he had no authority to do so, he purchased the coffee for Duncan, Sherman at a sharply discounted price. Before his reprimand arrived from the front office in New York, Morgan found a new buyer at a much higher price, turning a neat profit for his company and turning aside the chastening.

The Civil War disrupted some established patterns of trade, especially those involving cotton, but it created new ones as well. Morgan took advantage of the opportunities the war provided; in 1862, he founded the firm of J. Pierpont Morgan & Company and began trading on his own account. He was an immediate success. The war afforded ample scope for

Morgan's combination of audacity and prudence, and it rewarded the successful with profits far beyond those available during the dull days of peace. In 1864, Morgan, then twenty-seven years old, earned more than $50,000—roughly what a skilled worker made in a lifetime.

The opportunities for profit taking diminished after the war, but not Morgan's success. In 1871 he formed a partnership with the Drexel firm of Philadelphia, creating the financial house Drexel, Morgan & Company, headquartered at the corner of Wall and Broad Streets in New York. The merger enhanced Morgan's power, making him one of the country's most influential financiers, at the same time that it made him one of America's wealthiest individuals. During the 1870s he regularly earned half a million dollars annually—while a depression was causing incomes across the continent to slump sharply.

Morgan declined to enter the conspicuous-spending competition indulged in by other American millionaires; his style of living, though comfortable to the point of luxury, was frugal next to that of such Manhattan neighbors as Cornelius Vanderbilt. Morgan concentrated instead on business. In 1879, he helped William Vanderbilt sell $18 million worth of stock in the New York Central Railroad. Morgan's fees earned him another mound of money; more important, the transaction landed him on the board of directors of the railroad. This was typical of Morgan's method, and it demonstrated the growing power of financial capital in the management of the American economy.

The railroad industry during the 1870s and 1880s was the Wild West of American business, with outlaws (takeover artists like Jay Gould) preying on peace-loving townsfolk (small shareholders). Morgan arrived on the scene like a marshal wise enough in the ways of the outlaws to beat them to the draw. As did Rockefeller and Carnegie, Morgan detested wastefulness; he especially resented the graft and corruption that had gone into building the railroads and still characterized their operation. Many parts of the American rail system were overbuilt, with more lines competing for business than the traffic could sustain. Directors commonly ran roads for their own benefit and that of their friends; the interests of stockholders took a distant third place. Watered stock was endemic; another typical scam had the directors of a railroad award construction contracts at grossly inflated prices to a separate business they controlled. The frequent result was that directors and their cronies made killings while stockholders were left holding the empty shells of worthless roads.

Cutthroat competition exacerbated the railroads' troubles. Managers used all sorts of tactics in their struggle for market share, from secret rebates—of the kind Rockefeller exploited so thoroughly—to, occasionally, dynamite. Some fortunately situated shippers benefited from the rate wars; others were hurt as the railroads tried to make up for below-cost pricing on trunk lines by raising rates elsewhere. The country as a whole suffered from the chaos that reigned in this critical sector of the economy.

Morgan determined to straighten things out. Believing that reasonable men like himself could come to reasonable agreements regarding the proper approach to running the railroads, he invited the heads of his own New York Central and the competing Pennsylvania to join him aboard his yacht *Corsair* on the Hudson River. The New York Central was close behind the Pennsylvania in the race for railroad supremacy in the United States, and the two companies were locked in a strangling struggle. The Central had invaded the Pennsylvania's territory by starting construction of a line from Pittsburgh to Philadelphia. The invasion had the full support of Andrew Carnegie and other steelmen who until now had been paying monopoly prices to the Pennsylvania. The Central's William Vanderbilt had asked Carnegie what he thought of the scheme; Carnegie replied, "I think so well of it that I and my friends will raise five million dollars as our subscription."

The Pennsylvania could hardly complain, since it was trying to steal traffic from one of the Central's main routes. Several years before, Jay Gould had launched a plan to lay track parallel to the Central's lucrative line from New York City to Buffalo. The venture was typical of its era: Gould and the others didn't really want to complete the new line; rather, they wanted the Central to pay them *not* to complete it. But Vanderbilt and the Central called Gould's bluff and refused to come up with his blackmail money. The scheme collapsed, as Vanderbilt had anticipated it would. The collapse pleased Vanderbilt—but only until he learned that a group of speculators associated with the Pennsylvania was buying up Gould's devalued assets.

The prospect now loomed of an all-out war between the two rail giants. The prospect appalled Morgan. In the first place, it offended his taste for efficiency. The Central and the Pennsylvania were duplicating each other's efforts; the waste was already great and would grow. Second, Morgan as a director of the New York Central didn't want to see the company engage in such profit-draining behavior. Avoidable competition was bad business. Finally, construction of Gould's New York–Buffalo line had necessitated major blasting along the Hudson River just below Morgan's summer home. The racket was deafening. In the interests of his own peace and quiet, Morgan wanted the construction halted for good. Besides, the construction crews were an unsavory lot, a bad influence on his children and their friends if not a downright danger to the neighborhood. Already Morgan had had to curtail the kids' vacation rambles, and he didn't like it a bit.

So Morgan, as would become his custom, brought together the principals to the contest. The group—George Roberts and Frank Thomson of the Pennsylvania, Chauncey Depew and Morgan himself of the New York Central—settled into chairs on the afterdeck of the *Corsair* for a cruise up the Hudson. Roberts and Depew did most of the talking, with Morgan interjecting an occasional comment. Both sides agreed that the competition they were engaged in was counterproductive. Depew was ready to call off the contest, but Roberts didn't relish giving the appearance of succumbing to the will of Morgan. The Pennsylvania president refused to budge as the *Corsair* steamed upriver as far as West Point; he held out while the cruiser returned downstream past New York harbor and out to Sandy Hook. He was still resisting when the yacht approached its berth at Jersey City. Only at the last moment, following some final arguments by Depew and Morgan, did Roberts consent to a truce. "I will agree to your plan and do my part," he told Morgan and Depew as he left the banker's boat.

The plan was simple in conception, though a bit more complicated in practice. Essentially the Pennsylvania abandoned all designs on the alternate route to Buffalo; the Central canceled its work on the Pittsburgh-Philadelphia line.

Not everyone appreciated the outcome of the deal cut on the *Corsair*. Carnegie and the Pittsburgh steelers were exceedingly annoyed, as were others who liked the idea of competition in rail services. But the powers-that-were in American railroading and finance applauded Morgan for a solution that promised to restore sanity and profitability to the railroad industry and enhance the stability of the American industrial system over-all.

The New York Central–Pennsylvania deal tremendously enhanced Morgan's reputation; his enhanced reputation brought him even more business than before. And the increase in business gave him greater ability to negotiate other such deals. Through the late 1880s, Morgan became the nation's foremost industrial peacemaker and railroad reorganizer. He arranged plans for restructuring several of the country's biggest railroads, including the Chesapeake & Ohio, the Baltimore & Ohio, and the Reading.

In December 1888, Morgan hosted a summit meeting of American railway presidents. The previous year Congress had approved the Interstate Commerce Act, which forbade some of the more egregious forms of inequity in rail service and rate setting. Though the new law lacked sufficient sanctions and enforcement provisions to measurably modify the railroads' behavior, the presidents desired to nip any reformist tendencies in the bud. Morgan invited them to his Madison Avenue brownstone for a series of strategy sessions.

The sessions were less than peaceful and less than a complete success. Nearly all the nation's major roads were represented, and they had been battling each other too long to drop their differences in just a few days. Some of the railroaders took the opportunity to lob a few rocks in the direction of their rivals; others castigated Morgan for providing the financing that allowed destructive competition in road building and operation to continue. Morgan offered to desist from such financing and get his fellow bankers to do likewise if the railroaders could agree among themselves to halt their beggar-thy-neighbor policies.

The Madison Avenue meetings produced a pledge on the part of the presidents to abide by the strictures of the Interstate Commerce Act, to avoid rate wars, and to submit disputes to arbitration. But the accord contained no measures to compel compliance, and how long it would hold up was an open question.

Not long, as events proved. In fact, before the year was out Morgan felt forced to call another meeting of the railroad chieftains. This second summit accomplished no more than the first. If anything, the highly visible gathering of the rulers of the nation's railway system spurred reformers to work for stronger antitrust measures. It also focused public attention on Morgan, who more and more appeared the arbiter of American finance and industry.

This appearance, though perhaps exaggerated in the popular mind, wasn't all that far from reality. Grover Cleveland, at any rate, knew where to turn when events subsequent to the Panic of 1893 threatened the stability and indeed very existence of the American financial system. In the 1890s, as Brooks Adams and other prophets of doom complained, the U.S. government stuck to the gold standard. For years advocates of easier money had tried to pry Washington loose from the yellow stuff, but to date the greenbackers and silverites had been unsuccessful. By adhering to the gold standard, the American government pledged to redeem American paper currency for gold upon the demand of currency holders. Most currency holders didn't usually want gold, which is unwieldy and wears holes in pockets, but in times of economic distress people fled paper for gold, which has the distinct merit of being rare and beyond the power of governments to reproduce.

The period following the Panic of 1893 was definitely one of economic distress, and people by the hordes fled paper for gold. The U.S. Treasury kept a large supply of gold on hand for just such emergencies. At first the Treasury's supplies sufficed to meet the demands of worried paper-holders. But the depression deepened and continued longer than anyone expected. Persons who in the normal course of events would have gotten over their jitters and reexchanged their gold for paper held onto the gold and in many cases demanded more. Exacerbating the Treasury's troubles was the fact that the depression sent the federal budget sharply into deficit. In order to cover the gap between revenues and outlays, the Treasury dipped into the gold reserve. Moreover, the depth and length of the depression frightened European investors. During the 1890s, the United States as a nation remained a heavy debtor and consequently subject to the whims of foreign confidence or lack thereof. The depression undermined European confidence in American prospects, causing the Europeans to unload their American securities and exchange their American paper for gold.

The negative influences fed on themselves. The more people demanded gold, the less confidence they had in the government's ability to redeem their paper with gold. The less confidence people had in the government, the less they tended to have in the economy in general. The less confidence they had in the economy, the less willing they were to spend the money required to pull the economy out of the depression. The longer the depression lasted, the greater was the drain on the Treasury. The greater the drain on the Treasury, the more people demanded gold.

By January 1895, the situation had grown critical. Conventional wisdom on Wall Street and elsewhere in American financial circles held that the

Treasury needed to keep $100 million in gold on hand. If the Treasury's reserve should fall below the $100 million mark, people would begin to panic—again—and the entire American financial structure would be in jeopardy. The Treasury's reserve had flirted with the $100 million floor in the past but had always bounced back up. Now, though, it hit the floor so hard it plunged right through, and it kept plunging. By the morning of January 28, the Treasury's stockpile had fallen to $58 million. During the course of that Monday's business almost $4 million more disappeared. On Tuesday, $3 million vanished. Wednesday witnessed the loss of nearly another $4 million.

President Cleveland and Treasury Secretary John Carlisle frantically weighed various methods to stanch the bleeding. The most obvious was to ask Congress for emergency help in the form of a public bond issue. There were drawbacks to this course, though. Cleveland, a conservative Democrat, was already in trouble with the populist—and largely silverite—Western and Southern wings of his party. The president would get himself deeper in trouble defending the gold standard, which the West and South saw as serving the interests of the Eastern financial establishment. Besides, announcing a public bond issue would aggravate the very condition it was supposed to ease. The announcement would be interpreted by American and European investors as a distress signal, an indication that the government was on the edge of insolvency. Finally, floating a public bond issue would take too long. By the time the Treasury arranged the details and conducted the auction, the government's credit might already have vaporized.

Cleveland and Carlisle decided to act at once. In 1895 there was but a single person to turn to in such a situation, a sole individual who commanded both the financial resources and the confidence of the American and international business communities to save the United States government from bankruptcy.

On Thursday, January 31, Cleveland contacted Pierpont Morgan. The assistant secretary of the treasury, William Curtis, met with Morgan and August Belmont, a financier with close connections to the European house of Rothschild. Curtis asked for Morgan's views regarding appropriate and necessary measures for dealing with the current emergency.

Morgan suggested that the Cleveland administration make a private contract with a syndicate of investors he would organize for the immediate sale of $50 million in government bonds; the syndicate should receive an option on another $50 million. The contract would be confidential, not to be divulged until the sale was completed.

Morgan thought such a measure necessary to stem the run on the Treasury, a result essential to the economic health of America—not to mention to the house of Morgan. In a message wired to his branch office in London just after his meeting with Curtis, Morgan explained: "We all have large interests dependent upon maintenance of the sound currency of the United States." While preventing the corruption of the currency was vital, it would also prove profitable. "We think that if this negotiation can be made, it will be most creditable to all parties and pay a good profit."

Curtis gave no immediate answer to Morgan's proposal. Instead he returned to Washington to speak to the president and the treasury secretary. But Wall Street was (and is) a small village, and news of Curtis's meeting with Morgan quickly spread. The news and the rumors it generated had an instant effect on the bond and stock markets. Pierpont Morgan was coming to the rescue of the government. The rumors possessed sufficient plausibility to slow the pace of gold withdrawals and reassure the stock market, which closed the day on an upbeat after weeks of gloom.

But the optimism was premature. Cleveland wasn't quite ready to accept Morgan's terms, which entailed the political risk of seeming to sell out the government to Morgan and the big bankers. For several days Cleveland and his close advisers fretted and paced their offices. Was the danger of default so great as to warrant the hazards of hopping into bed with Morgan? Ironically—or so it appeared to Morgan—the very confidence the financial community derived from the thought that Morgan would save the day tended to convince Cleveland he didn't need Morgan's help after all. The gold supply stabilized momentarily, thereby removing some of the pressure on the president.

Morgan understood the source of the improvement, but he feared that Cleveland didn't. He believed that if the government refused a deal at this point, after hopes had been raised, the consequences would be more dire than if no bargain had been bruited. "The effect of abandonment upon all interests would now be worse than if never begun," he said.

Cleveland was whipsawed by economic necessity and political expedience. Prominent Democrats were lambasting him for even contemplating a deal with Morgan. If the government needed a loan, the critics declared, it ought to turn to the people rather than to the money trust. If there was profit to be made defending the faith and credit of the government—and there must be, since otherwise Morgan wouldn't be involved—that profit ought to accrue to the people.

Morgan had always distrusted politicians, and he distrusted the politician in Grover Cleveland. On Monday morning, February 4, Morgan remarked to his agents in England, regarding the situation in Washington: "We are completely at a loss to understand it." He described conditions as "critical," adding with dismay, "The politicians seem to have absolute control."

Time was running out. The breathing spell couldn't last; with each day that brought no news of a loan, optimism faded and more investors demanded gold. Without prompt and vigorous action, the government would soon run out of gold. The failure of the government to honor its most basic financial pledge would shatter the confidence of the entire country and much of the world. The Panic of 1893 would be nothing next to the panic that would follow a government default. Such a default must be averted at all costs. Morgan saw only one way to avert it—to travel to Washington and confront the president directly.

Morgan took a train to the capital, arriving in the early evening of February 4. The seriousness of the situation was symbolized by the fact that Morgan was greeted not by the secretary of the treasury or one of his assistants but by the secretary of war. Daniel Lamont thanked Morgan for coming; then he said President Cleveland could not meet with him. Lamont didn't have to explain that Cleveland's political enemies would like nothing better than to spot Morgan pulling up to the White House with the evident purpose of acting as receiver for the federal government. Morgan replied simply that he had come to Washington to see the president. "I am going to stay here until I see him."

While awaiting the summons from the White House, Morgan visited an old friend of the family who lived just several blocks from the executive mansion. Morgan and Mrs. J. Kearney Warren exchanged pleasantries; he puffed his cigar and baked out the winter chill in front of her fireplace. After an hour, the telephone rang. On the other end was a Morgan assistant, who explained that Richard Olney, the attorney general, wanted to speak with him.

Morgan wished good night to Mrs. Warren and took a cab to Olney's residence. Olney hoped to draw Morgan out and save the president the embarrassment of a face-to-face meeting. Morgan refused to be drawn, insisting that an agreement as delicate and crucial as the current emergency required could be arranged only in a personal conference between the responsible parties. When the president was prepared to meet with him, he said, he would discuss the matter further. Until then he had nothing to say.

Morgan went from Olney's house to the Arlington Hotel, his regular address in Washington. As he approached the desk in the hotel lobby, an alert reporter from the *New York Times* spotted him. The reporter asked the banker if he had come to Washington to negotiate a deal with the Cleveland administration. Morgan refused to comment.

In his usual suite, Morgan settled down to wait for the invitation he was confident would come. Morgan habitually played solitaire before going to bed: the game demanded just enough attention to soothe the mind but not so much as to tax it. Now he pulled out a deck of cards and dealt a game. He played once, then again, then again. An hour passed, and another. No message came.

Finally, long after nearly all of Washington had retired for the night, the summons arrived from 1600 Pennsylvania Avenue. The president would see Mr. Morgan at his convenience after breakfast.

Though that Tuesday morning was cold by the standards of Washington Februarys, Morgan chose to walk the short distance to the president's house. August Belmont accompanied him, as did one of Morgan's junior assistants and his chief lawyer—who just happened to have been a law partner of President Cleveland before Cleveland entered politics.

On arrival at the president's house, Morgan and the others were shown upstairs to the living quarters. The atmosphere was harried, befitting the occasion. Aides rushed in and out with the latest news from New York regarding gold withdrawals. Telephone calls pulled the president away from Morgan; various minor crises needed tending to.

Cleveland told Morgan he had resolved upon a public borrowing. Without specifying his reasoning, Cleveland made clear he found the political expense of a private loan forbidding. A public issue was much to be preferred. Treasury Secretary Carlisle seconded the president. Cleveland asked Morgan for his opinion on the matter.

Morgan must have wondered what Cleveland's game was, since if the president had really resolved on a public issue he didn't need to talk to him. The banker responded directly that a public loan would never do. The run on the government's gold had started again—Morgan's sources were better than Cleveland's—and would continue until investors saw irrefutable evidence that the president was acting with enough boldness to right the situation. A public issue of bonds would be too slow; the Treasury would be empty before the government got the funds it needed.

More important, a public issue wouldn't send the signal the president needed to send; it would simply be an S.O.S. the moment before the ship slipped beneath the waves. Europe had no confidence in public issues, and the Europeans were the ones who mattered at this crucial juncture. On the other hand, the Europeans had confidence in the house of Morgan and the other houses Morgan could line up behind a private bond issue. Morgan reminded Cleveland of the positive effect the mere mention of a Morgan-backed loan had produced the previous week; if the president needed evidence of the ability of a Morgan syndicate to turn the tide, there it was.

At this point in the conversation Morgan mentioned a device that would enable Cleveland to deflect likely charges of political shenanigans in arranging a private deal. Morgan had traded bonds and gold during the Civil War, and he recalled a law passed then and still on the books that authorized the president to buy coin money and pay for it with bonds. Morgan suggested that the Treasury purchase gold coin from his syndicate and pay for it with newly issued bonds.

Cleveland was intrigued. He called for the statute books to consult the article Morgan referred to. There in section 3700 of the Revised Statutes was the provision, just as Morgan had described it.

Cleveland was still skeptical. "I had a feeling, not of suspicion, but of watchfulness," the president recalled afterward. He queried Morgan, "What guarantee have we that if we adopt this plan, gold will not continue to be shipped abroad; and while we are getting it in, it will go out so that we will not reach our goal? Will you guarantee that this will not happen?"

Cleveland was asking quite a lot. Essentially he wanted Morgan to pledge to stop the drain on the Treasury. This meant overriding the actions and fears of investors around the world by whatever means were required. The U.S. government had been unable to stop the drain; now the government was turning to Morgan.

The banker didn't blink. "Yes, sir," he declared. "I will guarantee it during the life of the syndicate, and that means until the contract has been concluded and the goal has been reached."

Morgan's decisiveness and general air of certainty worked a change in Cleveland's skeptical attitude. "My doubts disappeared," the president remembered. "I found I was in negotiation with a man of large business comprehension and of remarkable knowledge and prescience." Cleveland added that he was most favorably impressed by Morgan's "clear-sighted, far-seeing patriotism."

The two men—the elected leader of the United States and the unelected but hardly less powerful head of the country's most powerful financial empire—parted with a handshake. They didn't discuss the details of the agreement Morgan had suggested; this they left to their subordinates. Until the details were agreed upon, of course, there remained a possibility the deal would fall through. An eighth of a percent might still foil the plan.

But this wasn't likely to happen, and it didn't. Too much was at stake—for Cleveland and the Democrats, for Morgan and the financial community, for the United States as a nation—for either party to block the bargain on account of a detail. Morgan certainly didn't expect any insuperable difficulties to arise. "We have carried our point and are more than satisfied," he cabled his London office the afternoon of his meeting with Cleveland.

Beyond working out the financial terms of the accord, Cleveland had some political ends to tie up. The administration had proposed a measure for dealing with the financial crisis to the House of Representatives, and the legislators had greeted the bill with a conspicuous lack of enthusiasm—which suited the administration well enough, since the purpose of the bill was merely to show that the administration was exhausting all other means before turning to Morgan. On Thursday, February 7, the bill was voted down as expected. Morgan immediately returned to Washington where he met briefly with Cleveland again. On Friday, Morgan visited the Treasury for the necessary exchange of signatures.

When news of the bargain broke, the pressure on the government's gold instantly eased. It was one thing for the Cleveland administration to place the full faith and credit of the U.S. government behind the country's currency; under present circumstances this was a dubious guarantee. It was another thing to pledge the full faith and credit of the house of Morgan. Investors had much more confidence in Morgan than in Cleveland and the government.

And just as the pressure on gold had fed upon itself when on the rise, so the easing of pressure encouraged further easing. The auction price of government bonds quickly rose, indicating investor trust that Washington would be able to repay what it was borrowing. By the middle of February the crisis was clearly over. Gold began flowing back into the Treasury, slowly at first, then more rapidly as the weeks passed without a relapse. By June, the government's reserves had again topped $100 million.

Yet though the economic crisis ended within days of the Cleveland-

Morgan agreement, the political storm had only begun. The return once more of confidence persuaded many of the president's foes that the situation had never been so desperate as Cleveland had judged. It certainly hadn't been so desperate, on this view, as to justify selling out to the Morgan syndicate. William Jennings Bryan, the young Democratic congressman from Nebraska, denounced the deal as evidence that the American government was being administered on behalf of big money rather than of the people. The *New York World* castigated the agreement as "an excellent arrangement for the bankers." The *World* continued, "For the nation it means a scandalous surrender of credit and a shameful waste of substance."

The scandal and apparent waste grew larger when Morgan and his associates began selling the bonds they had just purchased from the government. The government had transferred the bonds to Morgan's group at an interest rate that corresponded to a price of 104.5; within days the price shot up to 120. Morgan and his syndicate pocketed the difference—to the apoplectic outrage of William Jennings Bryan and his fellow populists.

So bitter were the attacks that the Senate convened an investigation of the matter. Morgan received a call to testify, and again he journeyed to Washington. The Republicans on the investigating committee treated the banker with respect and even gratitude, but some of the Democrats grilled him as though he were the defendant in a grand larceny trial. The prosecutors wanted particularly to know how rich Morgan had grown on the deal. "What profit did your house make upon this transaction?" demanded Senator George Vest of Missouri.

"I decline to answer," Morgan replied. He offered to reveal "every detail of the negotiation up to the time that the bonds became my property and were paid for"—which wasn't promising much, since the negotiation was now a matter of public record—but beyond that was his business alone. "What I did with my own property subsequent to that purchase I decline to state, except this, that no member of the government in any department was interested directly or indirectly in connection therewith." Morgan's last remark was intended for persons who were charging Cleveland with having made a fast buck off the bond sale.

Despite continued badgering by Vest and others, Morgan resolutely refused to reveal how much money he had made. He took the secret to his grave. Estimates of his profit varied wildly, from $250,000 to $16 million. The truth probably lay toward the lower end of the range of speculation. However large his cut might have been, Morgan doubtless deemed it no more than a fair recompense for having rescued the government of the United States from potential default. He believed that no one else could have accomplished the feat, and he was probably right.

VII

There was a curious sidebar to the story of Morgan's bailout of Cleveland and the American government. Shortly after the onset of the Panic of 1893, as confidence in the American economy and the American government began its precipitous decline, Grover Cleveland visited his doctor with a request to have a sore spot on the roof of his mouth examined. Cleveland had long indulged a fondness for cigars, and although he was used to a certain irritation of the mouth, this time the tenderness wouldn't go away. For several weeks during the spring of 1893 it bothered him, but the crashing stock market and the failure of hundreds of banks kept him too busy to tend to it. Finally, though, it hurt so much he couldn't ignore it any longer.

Dr. Robert O'Reilly, the White House physician, sat Cleveland down and had him lean far backward. O'Reilly shone a light into the president's mouth and discovered a raw, inflamed area about an inch in diameter on the left side of the roof of the mouth. He scraped the area—to Cleveland's intense pain—in order to get samples of tissue. He then sent a sample to Dr. William Welch of the Johns Hopkins medical faculty. Welch was one of America's foremost pathologists. O'Reilly sent a second sample to the staff of the Army Medical Museum. He informed neither Welch nor the museum staff of the identity of the patient.

A couple of days later O'Reilly received the two reports. They both declared that the tissue was malignant. O'Reilly wasn't especially surprised, since cancer of the mouth and throat was common among heavy cigar smokers. Just a few years earlier former president Ulysses Grant had died of throat cancer, evidently the consequence of too many cigars over too many years. Cleveland wasn't Grant in most respects, but O'Reilly feared that, sharing a liking for cigars, they might also share a mortal malady.

When Cleveland heard the diagnosis, he insisted on the utmost secrecy regarding the entire affair. The country already was experiencing a crisis of confidence. Should reports surface that the president was suffering from a potentially fatal condition, public confidence in the administration's ability to lead the nation out of the current difficulties would slip still further. Vice President Adlai Stevenson, a man of silverish tendencies, had been added to the Democratic ticket in 1892 to steal some of the silverites' thunder; no one in the Democratic leadership, least of all Cleveland, had ever intended that Stevenson should become president.

As to how Cleveland should deal with the malignancy, there seemed no choice but to operate. The president called in his old friend and family doctor, Joseph Bryant of New York. Bryant examined the biopsy reports and looked at the president's mouth, then concurred with the diagnosis. When Cleveland asked what he ought to do, Bryant replied, "Were it in my mouth, I would have it removed at once." Cleveland accepted Bryant's advice and directed that preparations begin immediately.

Keeping secrets in the 1890s was easier than it would be a century later, but Cleveland didn't want to take any chances. He summoned Dan Lamont, who before being appointed secretary of war had been the president's press secretary; the two devised an elaborate scheme to keep knowledge of the surgery from the press and the American people.

On the afternoon of June 30, Cleveland left the executive mansion in the company of Lamont and Dr. Bryant. The three caught a northbound train out of Washington and headed for New York. Although the departure wasn't announced, Cleveland's spokesman was prepared to say that the president was leaving town for a few days to join his pregnant wife at their summer home on Buzzards Bay, Massachusetts. Both Lamont and Bryant were known to be longtime associates of the president; their accompanying him would raise no eyebrows.

The train arrived in New York as night was falling. Cleveland quietly slipped off the train and with Lamont and Bryant caught a cab for the Hudson River. If the driver noticed who his riders were, the generous tip he received encouraged his silence. (In those days before television and ubiquitous news photos, he probably didn't recognize them.) At the waterfront Cleveland and his two companions rendezvoused with a boat from the yacht *Oneida*, anchored in the river. The yacht's owner, Elias Benedict, was a friend of Lamont and had patriotically agreed to let the vessel be used for the secret mission.

Cleveland, Lamont, and Bryant were the last arrivals on the yacht that evening; earlier in the day the ship's boat had inconspicuously picked up Dr. O'Reilly and three other distinguished physicians: oral surgeon William Keen of Philadelphia, noted physiologist Edward Janeway, and New York surgeon John Erdmann, who was Bryant's partner. Ferdinand Hasbrouck, a New York dentist and an expert in the use of anesthetic nitrous oxide, rounded out the surgical team.

That night and the next day the *Oneida* plied the waters around Manhattan and Long Island. The summer heat had settled upon the city, and many of those who could afford to had likewise taken to the water. While the members of the secret surgical squad and the object of their attentions remained below deck and out of sight, Lamont and Benedict made themselves obvious above. To all appearances the yacht's owner and the secretary of war were simply starting their Independence Day break a little early.

The main saloon of the ship had been transformed into a fully equipped surgical theater. Dr. Hasbrouck's nitrous oxide tank was backed up by a supply of ether. Dr. Janeway had brought instruments to monitor the president's pulse, blood pressure, and respiration. A magneto-cauterizing machine was available to control bleeding. Drs. Bryant and Keen had laid out their scalpels, scrapers, and other instruments. To accommodate the patient, a chair had been tied to the main mast.

At noon on July 1, Cleveland was brought in. His mouth had been washed out and disinfected several times during the morning; now he was strapped to the chair with his head tilted back at an uncomfortable angle. The discomfort didn't last long. Hasbrouck began administering the nitrous oxide—preferred over the ether, which would put the patient under so deeply that in the event of complications he couldn't be easily aroused—and Cleveland soon drifted off. Hasbrouck proceeded to extract two of the president's teeth, which would get in the way of the surgeons' instruments and fingers. Hasbrouck packed the resulting gaps with cotton to stem the bleeding.

Dr. Bryant then started cutting away at the tumorous area. The actual cutting wasn't especially difficult, and was made easier by a device recently brought from Paris by Dr. Keen: a cheek retractor that pulled Cleveland's jowls out of the way of Bryant's scalpel. Bryant's one big worry was that he might accidentally slice too deeply, into Cleveland's eye socket.

Bryant cut carefully for the better part of an hour. Hasbrouck hadn't counted on the operation lasting this long, and at quarter past one he reported signs that the nitrous oxide was wearing off. Despite the greater risks the surgical team decided to give Cleveland a shot of ether, which sent him into a fully unconscious state.

Bryant continued cutting, excising the tumor and everything around it that looked suspicious. He finished just after two o'clock, then tidied up by tying off one large blood vessel and cauterizing several smaller ones. He plugged the golf-ball-sized hole that now existed inside the president's head with gauze and ordered the patient taken to his stateroom. Around three o'clock, Cleveland began to waken. Bryant gave him a shot of morphine. The chief surgeon then administered himself a shot of alcohol and prescribed the same for the other members of the surgical team. They joined him in a toast to a successful operation.

Medically speaking, the hard part was over. Cleveland, despite habitual heavy eating and nearly no exercise, was in generally hearty health, and a swift recovery could be anticipated. On the afternoon of the day after the operation, he felt strong enough to get up and try out his legs. He walked about his stateroom, but remained beneath deck and away from any prying eyes.

Dan Lamont, in charge of security surrounding the surgery, had ample reason to fear prying eyes. The original plan had been for all to stay aboard for a few days, partly to keep watch on the president's recovery and partly to keep the members of the surgical team away from the press. Dr. Hasbrouck, however, had scheduled another operation and demanded to be put ashore. Lamont and the others resisted his entreaties for twenty-four hours, but when no complications developed in the president's condition they relented. Lamont, the former press man, realized that forfeiting Hasbrouck's goodwill would be tantamount to blowing the cover off the whole affair.

With Hasbrouck's departure from the ship, Lamont knew it would be only a matter of time before reporters came poking around. Already the press was wondering where the president was, since he hadn't shown up at Buzzards Bay. People were starting to worry—which was just what Cleveland and Lamont were trying to prevent.

By July 5, the patient was strong enough to be put ashore, at Buzzards Bay. Lamont attempted to field the inevitable questions and allay suspicions at an impromptu press conference in the barn on Cleveland's estate. He declared that the president had suddenly developed a pair of ulcerated teeth, which had had to be removed. Beyond this his recurrent rheumatism had been flaring up.

The reporters were plainly distrustful. There had been stories of a malignancy, they said. Was there anything to them?

Preposterous, Lamont replied. The president had merely had some teeth pulled. What would the rumormongers think of next? Lamont's ridicule succeeded in quieting the questions for the moment, if not in convincing the reporters who asked them.

Cleveland spent the next four weeks at Buzzards Bay. During the first two of these he rested and occasionally went fishing in a rowboat. An orthodontist, Dr. Kasson Gibson, came up from New York to fit the president with a rubber plug for the hole in the roof of his mouth. The plug served the dual purpose of preventing food particles from collecting in the hole and restoring the customary fullness to Cleveland's face.

In the middle of July, Cleveland started work on a message he was slated to deliver to Congress on August 7. The president had called a special session of the legislature to convene that day; his purpose was to effect repeal of the 1890 Sherman Silver Purchase Act. The silver law had required the Treasury to buy virtually the entire output of America's silver mines and to issue, against the silver, notes redeemable in either silver or gold. Since the Panic of 1893 almost all the note-holders had been demanding gold. Together with the other pressures on the government's gold reserve, the Sherman Act was seriously jeopardizing the nation's economic health. Cleveland demanded that it be repealed. On August 7 he would make his case to Congress, and he was determined to make his case effectively.

Unfortunately for the president's plans, he suffered a mild setback in late July, necessitating that Dr. Bryant do a little more cutting and scraping. The extra operation took its toll. When Richard Olney arrived to help the president draft his message, the attorney general expressed shock at Cleveland's haggard and worn appearance. "My God, Olney," the president replied, "they nearly killed me!"

Cleveland wrote most of his message at Buzzards Bay, but returned to Washington on August 5 to apply the finishing touches, as well as to twist a few reluctant silverite arms. Two days later, he exhorted the legislators in the special session to reject "financial experiments opposed to the policy and practice of other civilized states" and to return America to "a sound and stable currency." Then, having given the cause his best effort, he retired again to Buzzards Bay to await the outcome of the congressional debate and deliberation.

While the repeal question hung in the balance, the story of the president's surgery and deception began to leak a little more. The source of the new leak was Dr. Hasbrouck, who had explained his tardiness in the operation he had left the *Oneida* for by dropping the president's name to his co-surgeon. This physician in turn had notified a newsman friend, E. J. Edwards of the *Philadelphia Press*, who pursued the lead. Edwards first visited Hasbrouck. The correspondent intimated that he knew the whole story but just wanted to verify some details. Hasbrouck fell for the ruse and told all, including even the names of the rest of the surgical team.

Edwards and the *Press* might have published the story at this point; in doing so they would have revealed both Cleveland's perilous physical condition and the duplicity the president was employing to keep his condition secret from Congress and the American people. Needless to say, such a revelation would have damaged Cleveland politically and might have ruined his chances for repealing the Sherman Act. The silverites constantly charged the gold forces with conspiracy; here was proof the charges were true.

But Edwards first wanted to check what Hasbrouck told him with the other men involved. Fortunately for the Cleveland administration and the gold standard, the others stuck to the cover story. The president had had some dental work done and nothing more, they asserted. Hasbrouck was telling bald-faced lies. Coordinating their stonewalling, they claimed that Hasbrouck had fouled up on his part of the teeth-pulling and had been fired; evidently his scandal-spreading was his way of venting his anger.

So vehement and convincing was the multiple denial that the Philadelphia paper sat on the story. Through August, Congress debated repeal. The silverites, led by William Jennings Bryan, thundered against repeal, calling it a crime against the common people. But the administration's allies on Capitol Hill came through; on August 28 the House of Representatives, the crucial chamber on this issue since it was the one more influenced by populist and silver sentiments, voted in Cleveland's favor for repeal.

The very next day the *Press* finally summoned the nerve to print its story—too late to influence the crucial House vote. By this time Cleveland had completely recovered and was making regular public appearances. The continued denials by the conspirators and the president's evident robustness enabled the administration to shrug off the truth as merely more of the scurrilousness the silverites customarily substituted for reason and sense. It didn't hurt Cleveland's case that on September 9 his wife bore him a robust baby girl. How could a man so obviously vigorous and virile have been at death's door?

Silver senators delayed the passage of the administration's repeal measure in the upper chamber for a few weeks, but in October their filibuster failed. The special session having achieved his purpose, Cleveland signed the repeal bill and sent the legislators home. He breathed a double sigh of relief: for his health and for the gold standard.

VIII

Cleveland remained healthy through the end of his term; the gold standard likewise survived although with some further close calls. Prosperity returned to America beginning in 1897, aided by large new discoveries of gold in South Africa and the Yukon. The new discoveries increased the world's gold supply and thereby accomplished some of the same inflationary results the silverites had desired. More-efficient means of separating gold from gold ore also increased the amount of the yellow metal available for financial purposes.

The return of good economic times helped trigger another wave of corporate consolidation. The biggest firms in all sorts of industries—leather, lead, copper, agricultural equipment, machine tools, life insurance, steel pipe, and a dozen others—combined forces to allocate markets and elevate profits. One merger, however, dwarfed the rest. A fitting coda to the decade of consolidation, it linked the forces of the three giants of the American economy: Morgan, Carnegie, and Rockefeller.

In the late summer of 1897, Morgan received a visit from Elbert Gary, a Chicago corporate lawyer. Gary was representing John Gates, a wire manufacturer who had devised a scheme to gather together several of his competitors into a single company that would control the market for their products. Morgan knew of the scheme and had reservations about it, principally relating to Gates. Morgan once declared that the most important consideration in any business dealing was character. "A man I do not trust could not get money from me on all the bonds in Christendom," he said. Morgan didn't trust Gates, a speculating type with a reputation for corner-cutting and gambling with other people's funds. Morgan declined to back the project Gary described.

Yet though he didn't like Gates, Morgan developed a high opinion of Gary, and he subsequently underwrote other mergers Gary orchestrated. One of these led in 1898 to the creation of the Federal Steel Company, which became the second largest steel firm in America.

Federal Steel immediately proved profitable; its success prompted Morgan and Gary to contemplate forming an even greater combination. Only one steel company was bigger than Federal. If that company and Federal and a few smaller firms merged, the resulting supercorporation would have a hammerlock on steel production throughout the United States.

The sole hitch in this scheme was that that other company belonged to Andrew Carnegie, and Carnegie didn't want to merge. On the contrary, as plans for the big merger surfaced, Carnegie indicated that he would fight it. Gary and the leaders of the some of the smaller companies, including the wire combine Gary had put together with John Gates, tried to pressure Carnegie into going along. Gates's wire company canceled contracts with Carnegie for raw steel and announced that henceforth it would manufacture its own.

Carnegie had been pondering retirement, but this new challenge revived his competitive instinct. Hitherto Carnegie Steel had concentrated on manufacturing raw steel; it had left to others the finishing of that steel into products like wire, pipe, tubes, and nails. Now that the finishers were going into manufacturing, however, Carnegie decided to go into finishing. From his vacation home in Scotland, Carnegie cabled a declaration of war. "Prompt action essential," he wrote. "Crisis has arrived. Only one policy open: start at once hoop, rod, wire, nail mills." Carnegie ordered further measures, then closed with a rousing admonition: "Have no fear as to the result; victory certain."

Carnegie's counterattack threatened to savage the entire American steel industry. As long as steel manufacturers and steel finishers had kept out of each other's way, the industry had been relatively stable. In particular, Carnegie had refrained from swallowing up the smaller companies. But with the boundary between manufacturing and finishing being erased, the smaller fish looked to be in grave danger from the monster of the industry. Carnegie Steel had the lowest costs and the deepest pockets of any steel firm; no other company could withstand its concerted assault.

Nor did Carnegie appear to be content with devastating steel. Upon the outbreak of this steel war, Carnegie resurrected his earlier plan for building a railroad from Pittsburgh to the Atlantic seaboard; his idea was to protect his lines of transport. The incipient steel war seemed about to trigger a new railroad war.

This last prospect especially alarmed Morgan, the great railroad peacemaker and reorganizer. Morgan predicted to a friend: "Carnegie is going to demoralize railroads just as he has demoralized steel." He would, at any rate, unless something were done to stop him.

In an effort to do just that, Morgan met with Carnegie's right-hand man Charles Schwab. Curiously for someone whose company had just embarked on what looked like a major offensive against the rest of the steel industry, Schwab expatiated on the blessings of cooperation. If the steel companies could learn to cooperate, Schwab said, to the point of combining their talents and resources into a single centrally directed unit, they could lower costs so far that profits would soar even as prices to consumers fell. All would benefit.

Morgan listened with interest. Was this a proposal for a cease-fire? Was it an offer to join the steel combination? Morgan pumped Schwab for details, and though nothing concrete came of their discussions on this particular night, Morgan left the meeting believing Carnegie might come to terms.

Several days later, Morgan again met with Schwab. They spoke more specifically about the prospects of cooperation among the big steel companies. Just as the meeting was ending, Morgan asked Schwab to find out whether Carnegie would be willing to consider selling out to the new combination. If so, what would be his price?

Schwab was reluctant to raise the matter with Carnegie, fearing his boss's reaction. Some days Carnegie seemed to want to get out of business and into full-time philanthropy; other days he was as zestful for industrial combat as ever. But Schwab decided to take a chance. On the advice of Carnegie's wife—who was eager to see her husband retire—he invited Carnegie to a round of golf; afterward he broached Morgan's offer.

Perhaps Carnegie had threatened the steel war simply to drive up the price Morgan might pay; perhaps he was just in a retiring mood the afternoon Schwab relayed Morgan's offer. Whichever, Carnegie didn't take long to respond. He grabbed a slip of paper, scribbled a few figures on it in pencil, and told Schwab to give it to Morgan.

By this informal document Carnegie agreed to sell Carnegie Steel for approximately $400 million. His own personal share would come to a little more than $225 million.

Schwab quickly carried the paper back to Morgan. The banker was by this time one of the world's best-known art collectors. He was also famous for never haggling over price. He simply noted what the dealer was asking, and if it seemed fair he paid it. If it didn't, he walked away. Morgan adopted the same decisive approach in business negotiations. In the Carnegie case he took one look at the terms Carnegie proposed and told Schwab, "I accept."

Drawing up the contracts effecting the merger required a few weeks. When the papers were in order, Morgan paid a visit to Carnegie at the latter's New York residence. The financier and the steel manufacturer spoke affably for a quarter of an hour, at the end of which Morgan extended his hand. "Mr. Carnegie," Morgan said, "I want to congratulate you on being the richest man in the world." Carnegie accepted the congratulations.

Morgan walked away well pleased, for even at the unprecedented price he was paying Carnegie he thought he had made a good bargain. Carnegie presently thought so too. A couple of years later, Carnegie and Morgan encountered each other on board an ocean liner. Carnegie mentioned the merger and commented, "I made one mistake, Pierpont, when I sold out to you."

"What was that?" queried Morgan.

"I should have asked you a hundred million more than I did."

"You would have got it if you had."

Carnegie's agreement to sell removed the biggest obstacle to Morgan's design of creating a single steel corporation that would dominate the market and eliminate duplication and competition in the most basic of American industries. Yet other obstacles remained. Among these the most worrisome involved John D. Rockefeller.

Although Carnegie had turned aside Rockefeller's foray into iron and steel in the mid-1890s, Morgan now feared that all the activity in the industry might encourage Rockefeller to try again. It was becoming apparent that the Mesabi was the richest source of iron ore on earth, and notwithstanding his lease agreement with Carnegie, Rockefeller had other properties in the area he could develop. Rockefeller's fleet of ore boats—built up partly as a consequence of his deal with Carnegie—was the most efficient on the Great Lakes. Controlling his own ore and transportation, all Rockefeller had to do was put up steel works somewhere on the lakes and he would be able to give any steel company in America, present or projected, a harrowing run for its money. Morgan judged that in order to avert such a contest, he must buy Rockefeller out, as he had bought Carnegie out.

Elbert Gary agreed. But getting Rockefeller to go along might be difficult, Gary warned. There was only one way to handle the purchase. Morgan must talk to Rockefeller personally.

Morgan was taken aback. "I would not think of it," he replied.

"Why?" asked Gary.

"I don't like him," Morgan said.

This time it was Gary who was surprised. He thought Morgan was being silly, and he frankly told him so. "Mr. Morgan," Gary said, "when a business proposition of so great importance to the steel corporation is involved, would you let a personal prejudice interfere with its success?"

Morgan thought the issue over. "I don't know," he muttered.

Eventually Gary's reasoning got the better of Morgan's dislike of Rockefeller, and Morgan consented to talk to the oil chief. The visit wouldn't be easy, since Rockefeller disliked Morgan as much as Morgan disliked him. "Very haughty, very much inclined to look down on other men" was how Rockefeller characterized Morgan. "I have never been able to see why any man should have such a high and mighty feeling about himself." Yet Rockefeller similarly concluded that in a matter of such significance and involving such immense amounts of money, personal taste had to be subordinated to business.

The meeting between Morgan and Rockefeller was brief and to the point. "We had a few pleasant words," Rockefeller recalled; but only a few. The meeting didn't have to be long to serve Morgan's purpose.

"I have done it," Morgan announced, when Gary entered his office the next morning.

"Done what?"

"I have seen Rockefeller."

"How did he treat you?"

"All right."

"Did you get the ore lands?"

"No," Morgan admitted. But he said he thought he would be getting them shortly. "I just told him we ought to have them and asked him if he would not make a proposition."

As it turned out, Rockefeller chose not to make a proposition, preferring that Morgan be the one to state a price. Morgan declined in turn. For a moment the bargaining stuck, but before long the two sides agreed to let Henry Frick, a veteran iron man each trusted, determine a price. Frick set $80 million as fair.

Elbert Gary deemed this figure too high, since it was $5 million above the $75 million he and Morgan had earlier defined as their absolute upper limit. "That is a prohibitive sum," Gary told Morgan.

Morgan wasn't about to quibble. "Judge Gary," he said, "in a business transaction as great as this, would you let a matter of $5 million stand in the way of success?"

Gary reminded Morgan that the $75 million figure was supposed to be a ceiling, not a starting point for negotiations.

Morgan rejoined, "Well, put it this way: Would you let those properties go?"

"No," Gary conceded.

"Write out an acceptance," Morgan ordered. And the deal was done.

The successful conclusion of the negotiations with Rockefeller basically completed the creation of the United States Steel Corporation, which announced its existence to the world at the beginning of 1901. At birth U.S. Steel was the largest corporation on earth, capitalized at $1.4 billion. Its creation made Carnegie and Rockefeller considerably richer than they already were, and each took the occasion to retire from the active conduct of business affairs.

The creation of U.S. Steel and the retirement of Carnegie and Rockefeller also indicated how the direction of American industry was passing from the industrialists themselves to the financiers—to the people like Morgan who commanded the financial resources that commanded all else. Carnegie and Rockefeller stepped off the stage; Morgan moved squarely to the center, more powerful than ever.

Chapter 3

HOW THE OTHER HALF LIVED

I

"Down below Chatham Square," journalist Jacob Riis wrote in 1890, "in the old Fourth Ward, where the cradle of the tenement stood, we shall find New York's Other Half at home, receiving such as care to call and are not afraid. Not all of it, to be sure, there is not room for that; but a fairly representative gathering, representative of its earliest and worst traditions." Riis continues: "Leaving the Elevated Railroad where it dives under the Brooklyn Bridge at Franklin Square, scarce a dozen steps will take us where we wish to go. With its rush and roar echoing yet in our ears, we have turned the corner from prosperity to poverty. We stand upon the domain of the tenement."

Riis invites his readers to follow him into a dark alley, shut in by high brick walls and wholly cheerless. "The wolf knocks loudly at the gate in the troubled dreams that come to this alley, echoes of the day's cares. A horde of dirty children play about the dripping hydrant, the only thing in the alley that thinks enough of its chance to make the most of it: it is the best it can do. These are the children of the tenements, the growing generation of the slums; this is their home."

Riis spots a dog scavenging for food. "Vain hope, truly! Nothing more appetizing than a bare-legged ragamuffin appears. Meat bones, not long since picked clean, are as scarce in Blind Man's Alley as elbow room in any Fourth Ward back-yard. The shouts of the children come hushed over the housetops, as if apologizing for the intrusion. Few glad noises make this old alley ring. Morning and evening it echoes with the gentle, groping tap of the blind man's staff as he feels his way to the street. Blind Man's Alley bears its name for a reason. Until little more than a year ago its burrows harbored a colony of blind beggars, tenants of a blind landlord, old Daniel Murphy, whom every child in the ward knows, if he never heard of the President of the United States." Dan Murphy had made his fortune— $400,000, he told Riis—off his blind tenants in years past, only to grow blind himself in old age.

Riis has been to Blind Man's Alley before. While trying to take a picture inside one of the buildings, he accidentally allowed the flash powder to set fire to a pile of paper and rubbish against a wall. There were six people in the attic room at the time of the accident: Riis and five blind men and women. Only Riis knew at once of the danger to them and the other dozen or so households in the building. He thought first of racing down the rickety stairs and calling for help, but decided that the fire would probably be beyond control before help arrived. Instead, he tried to put out the fire himself. After several frantic moments beating the flames he succeeded in extinguishing them. Yet he feared that invisible smoldering embers might reignite the fire, and now that the immediate danger was past he hurried to inform the authorities of the need for additional action. He ran into a policeman on the street and explained the situation. The policeman burst out laughing. Riis was shocked. Only after the officer caught his breath did he tell Riis the cause of his mirth. "Don't you know?" he said. "That house is the Dirty Spoon. It caught fire six times last winter, but it wouldn't burn. The dirt was so thick on the walls, it smothered the fire!"

On his guided tour of tenement life, Riis takes his readers farther into the slums, to Gotham Court, a double row of five-story tenements built back to back under a single roof and stretching from the street more than two hundred feet deep. He explains that the project is notorious as one of the unhealthiest in the city. During a recent outbreak of cholera, the mortality rate approached 200 per 1,000 inhabitants. As a result the city government has mandated improvements in sanitation, including grates placed over the sewers that connect the court to the city's main sewers. Beyond sanitation, a reason for the grates is to prevent the "Swamp Angels," a gang of thieves that hides out in the larger sewer tunnels, from easily entering and leaving their lair.

Past Gotham Court, Riis comes to the head of an alley where there was a tragic fire a few years before. The fire had started in a tenement one morning after most of the men had gone to work, leaving their wives and children—those wives and children who didn't themselves work—at home. Although the building possessed fire escapes, they were so narrow and obstructed that many of the women and children had been unable to flee and had been burned alive.

Riis proceeds to a street called Penitentiary Row, after an old prison. He explains the changing demographics and economics of the neighborhood. "Within recent days it has become peopled wholly with Hebrews, the overflow from Jewtown adjoining, pedlars and tailors, all of them. It is odd to read this legend from other days over the door: 'No pedlars allowed in this house.' These thrifty people are not only crowding into the tenements of this once exclusive district—they are buying them. The Jew runs to real estate as soon as he can save up enough for a deposit to clinch the bargain. As fast as the old houses are torn down, towering structures go up in their place, and Hebrews are found to be the builders. Here is a whole alley named after the intruder, Jews' Alley. But abuse and ridicule are not weapons to fight the Israelite with. He pockets them quietly with the rent and bides his time. He knows from experience that all things come to those who wait, including the houses and lands of their persecutors."

Riis's tour continues. He points out a man giving his son a ride on an ashcart; the young boy, though grimy and ragged, appears as happy as could be. Riis and his readers come to a tenement called "the Ship." Some local historians explain that the building got its name in an era when the river was closer than at present and boats moored nearby. Others contend that the name refers to the interior of the building, which with its ladders, instead of stairs, and maze of passages reminds one of the inside of a ship.

Riis guides his readers into one of the tenements. "Be a little careful," he warns. "The hall is dark and you might stumble over the children pitching pennies back there. Not that it would hurt them; kicks and cuffs are their daily diet. They have little else. Here where the hall turns and dives into utter darkness is a step, and another, another. A flight of stairs. You can feel your way, if you cannot see it. Close? Yes! What would you have? All the fresh air that ever enters these stairs comes from the hall-door that is forever slamming, and from the windows of dark bedrooms that in turn receive from the stairs their sole supply of elements God meant to be free but man deals out with such a niggardly hand.

"That was a woman filling her pail by the hydrant you just bumped against. The sinks are in the hallway, that all the tenants may have access— and all be poisoned alike by their summer stenches. Hear the pump squeak! It is the lullaby of the tenement-house babes. In summer, when a thousand thirsty throats pant for a cooling drink in this block, it is worked in vain. But the saloon, whose open door you passed in the hall, is always there; the smell of it has followed you up.

"Here is a door. Listen! That short hacking cough, that tiny, helpless wail—what do they mean? They mean that the soiled bow of white you saw on the door downstairs will have another story to tell—Oh! a sadly familiar story—before the day is at an end. The child is dying with measles. With half a chance it might have lived; but it had none. That dark bedroom killed it.

" 'It was took all of a suddint,' says the mother, smoothing the throbbing little body with trembling hands. There is no unkindness in the rough voice of the man in the jumper, who sits by the window grimly smoking a clay pipe, with the little life ebbing out in his sight, bitter as his words sound: 'Hush, Mary! If we cannot keep the baby, need we complain—such as we?'

"Such as we! The words ring in your ears as we grope our way up the stairs and down from floor to floor, listening to the sounds behind the closed doors—some of quarreling, some of coarse songs, more of profanity. They are true. When the summer heats come with their suffering, they have meaning more terrible than words can tell. Come over here. Step carefully over this baby—it is a baby, spite of its rags and dirt—under these iron bridges called fire-escapes, but loaded down, despite the incessant watchfulness of the firemen, with broken household goods, with wash-tubs and barrels, over which no man could climb from a fire.

"This gap between dingy brick walls is the yard. That strip of smoke-colored sky up there is the heaven of these people. Do you wonder that the name does not attract them to the churches? That baby's parents live in the rear tenement here. She is at least as clean as the steps we are now climbing. There are plenty of houses with half a hundred such in. The tenement is much like the one in front we just left, only fouler, closer, darker—we will not say more cheerless. The word is a mockery. A hundred thousand people lived in rear tenements in New York last year.

"Here is a room neater than the rest. The woman, a stout matron with hard lines of care in her face, is at the wash-tub. 'I try to keep the childer clean,' she says, apologetically, but with a hopeless glance around. The spice of hot soapsuds is added to the air already tainted with the smell of boiling cabbage, of rags and uncleanliness all about. It makes an over-powering compound.

"It is Thursday, but patched linen is hung upon the pulley-line from the window. There is no Monday cleaning in the tenements. It is wash-day all the week round, for a change of clothing is scarce among the poor. They are poverty's honest badge, these perennial lines of rags hung out to dry, those that are not the washerwoman's professional shingle. The true line to be drawn between pauperism and honest poverty is the clothes-line. With it begins the effort to be clean that is the first and best evidence of a desire to be honest."

But honest poverty, Riis says, is still poverty and all too often hopeless poverty. He relates the story of a German family of nine—husband, wife, grandmother, and six children—that lived in two rooms, the larger measuring ten feet by ten feet. The rent for the two rooms was $7.50 per month, which stretched the family budget to the breaking point. The wife struggled for years to help make a decent home and life for them all, but finally the strain got too great. She threw herself from a window of the tenement to her death on the street below. The striking thing about the event was not the suicide itself but the fact that it passed nearly unremarked among the neighbors. They sympathized with the dead woman; more than a few had been tempted to the same fate. But they couldn't spend much time mourning her, for their lives allowed no such luxury.

Riis's tour of New York includes several other stops. He takes his readers to "Chinatown," to "Jewtown," to the Italian section, and to various other districts. He lingers longer than usual in the black neighborhood, for it occupies a special place in the urban mosaic. "The color line must be drawn through the tenements to give the picture its proper shading," he says. "The landlord does the drawing, does it with an absence of pretense, a frankness of despotism, that is nothing if not brutal. The Czar of all the Russias is not more absolute upon his own soil than the New York landlord in his dealing with colored tenants. Where he permits them to live, they go; where he shuts the door, stay out. By his grace they exist at all in certain localities; his ukase banishes them from others. He accepts the responsibility, when laid at his door, with unruffled complacency. It is business, he will tell you.

And it is. He makes the prejudice in which he traffics pay him well, and that, as he thinks it quite superfluous to tell you, is what he is there for."

The discrimination against blacks persists in spite of their efforts to better their condition. Riis reports that blacks are "immensely the superior" of many of the whites with respect to cleanliness and maintaining the premises. All the same, landlords charge blacks higher rents than whites. Riis reproduces the testimony of a representative of one of the largest real estate firms in New York: "We would rather have negro tenants in our poorest class of tenements than the lower grades of foreign white people. We find the former cleaner than the latter, and they do not destroy the property so much. We also get higher prices. We have a tenement on Nineteenth Street, where we get $10 for two rooms which we could not get more than $7.50 for from white tenants previously." The reason for the landlords' ability to get higher rents from black families is simple enough: the blacks are restricted to certain neighborhoods, thereby curtailing the supply of housing available to them.

The denizens of the tenements don't make common cause against their common oppressors; far from it. The area where the different groups rub against each other brings out the evil in each, Riis says. "The border-land where the white and black races meet in common debauch, the aptly-named black-and-tan saloon, has never been debatable ground from a moral standpoint. It has always been the worst of the desperately bad." Fights constantly break out, and when they do, blood soon flows. "As the Chinaman hides his knife in his sleeve and the Italian his stiletto in the bosom, so the negro goes to the ball with a razor in his boot-leg." The blade-wielders know their work, and they know how to create work for others. "There is always a job for the surgeon and the ambulance."

If life is difficult for adults, it is harder still for children, especially orphans and others thrown out on their own. "The Street Arab," Riis explains, using the term for these wild, wily youths, "is as much of an institution in New York as Newspaper Row, to which he gravitates naturally, following his Bohemian instinct." Circumstance distinctively shapes character. "The Street Arab has all the faults and all the virtues of the lawless life he leads. Vagabond that he is, acknowledging no authority and owing no allegiance to anybody or anything, with his grimy fist raised against society whenever it tries to coerce him, he is as bright and sharp as the weasel, which, among all the predatory beasts, he most resembles."

The street arabs' life in the newspaper neighborhood is rough but independent. In winter, they huddle for warmth about the grated ventholes that let warm air and steam out of the underground pressrooms; in summer, they play craps and seven-eleven on the curb. Of persons who make a profession of trying to do them good, as well as of others less charitably inclined, they are ever wary. "Here the agent of the Society for the Prevention of Cruelty to Children finds those he thinks too young for 'business,' but does not always capture them. Like rabbits in their burrows, the little ragamuffins sleep with at least one eye open, and every sense alert to the approach of danger: of their enemy, the policeman, whose chief business in life is to move them on, and of the agent bent on robbing them of their cherished freedom. At the first warning shout they scatter and are off. To pursue them would be like chasing the fleet-footed mountain goat in his rocky fastnesses. There is not an open door, a hidden turn or runway which they do not know, with lots of secret passages and short cuts no one else ever found.

"To steal a march on them is the only way. There is a coal chute from the sidewalk to the boiler-room in the subcellar of the Post Office which the Society's officer found the boys had made into a sort of toboggan slide to a snug berth in wintry weather. They used to slyly raise the cover in the street, slide down in single file, and snuggle up to the warm boiler out of harm's way, as they thought. It proved a trap, however. The agent slid down himself one cold night—there was no other way of getting there—and, landing right in the midst of the sleeping colony, had it at his mercy."

The boys tried to maintain their headquarters, but after repeated raids they had to abandon it. They moved to the waterfront, where they fitted up a clubhouse under one of the East River banana docks. The clubhouse served as home for thirty or forty boys "and about a million rats." There the street arabs found safety—such as it was—from the long arm of the law and the Society. And from there, like the tens of thousands of others who inhabited the realm of the tenement, they continued the struggle that constituted their daily existence.

II

Riis's tour of the slums of New York, published as *How the Other Half Lives*, shocked many of its middle-class readers even as it enlightened them; in doing both it set the tone for the most influential journalism of the 1890s and early twentieth century. The leading journal of the muckrakers—to use Theodore Roosevelt's subsequent label—was *McClure's* magazine, founded in 1893. Publisher S. S. McClure targeted a readership beyond that of the staid big four of the time: *Harper's, Scribner's, Century,* and *Atlantic Monthly.* Where those journals focused on literature and the arts, with James Russell Lowell's *Atlantic* occasionally venturing into nature and travel subjects, *McClure's* dealt with topics of interest to a wider variety of readers, particularly politics. Nor did McClure hesitate to take sides, in contrast to the genteel standoffishness of the publishers of the established magazines.

As important as McClure's editorial policy was his marketing strategy. McClure set his price at fifteen cents, well below the twenty-five and thirty-five cents charged by the upscale periodicals. Within a short time, competition from other magazines edited and marketed similarly—especially *Munsey's* and *Cosmopolitan*—caused McClure to lower his price to a dime. The low price, in turn matched by *Munsey's* and *Cosmopolitan*, made

McClure's and the other two available to a much larger segment of the American population than had formerly read monthly journals. As the older magazines struggled to retain their readers, and as more new publications opened, the magazine business became one of the liveliest in the country. By the estimate of Frank Munsey, whose guess was probably as good as anyone's, the magazine-purchasing public in America more than tripled by the end of the 1890s, to some 750,000.

The new magazines—and the older magazines under the pressure from the new—dealt with diverse contentious topics. The condition of the urban poor, so well documented by Jacob Riis, was one such topic; the tariff was another. In 1890, Congress passed the McKinley tariff, the first blatantly protectionist tariff (with duties designed to keep foreign goods out rather than generate revenues) in decades. The McKinley tariff touched off a political storm that lasted to the end of the century and beyond, polarizing the country by occupation and region, as the agrarian West and South lined up against the tariff and the industrial Northeast lobbied in favor. Writers in several magazines argued the merits of protection versus free trade. A majority of journals took a side and stuck with it; others ran articles on both sides of the issue. In the latter category, the *North American Review*, for example, opened its pages not only to Republican stalwart James G. Blaine, an apostle of protection, but also to former British prime minister William Gladstone, one of the foremost fighters for free trade.

Related to the issue of the tariff was the consolidation of economic power in America. The rise of the likes of Rockefeller, Carnegie, and Morgan alarmed many magazine readers, as alert editors noticed. In 1891, *Forum* published an article entitled "The Coming Billionaire," which pointed out that at a time when four fifths of the nation's families earned less than $500 annually, more than one hundred Americans had incomes of over $1 million. William Dean Howells asked in the *North American Review* in 1894, "Are we a plutocracy?" and concluded that we were. *The Nation* deplored the fact that the Rockefellers, Carnegies, and Morgans had become for American youth what Roland had been to youngsters of the Middle Ages: the primary model of achievement and object of emulation.

The most powerful blast against the consolidation of economic power burst from the pen of Henry Demarest Lloyd. The son of a Dutch Reformed minister, Lloyd gained a national following on the strength of an 1881 article, "The Story of a Great Monopoly," published in *Atlantic Monthly*. Lloyd's article traced the growth of Rockefeller's Standard Oil Company, and did so damningly. The continuing growth of Rockefeller's oil trust during the 1880s incensed Lloyd all the more, prompting him to expand his indictment into a book published in 1894 as *Wealth Against Commonwealth*.

Lloyd charged Rockefeller with subverting the American republic by the unfair business practices his enormous economic power made possible. "Liberty produces wealth, and wealth destroys liberty," Lloyd wrote. America's cities, America's factories, and America's private fortunes were "the obesities of an age gluttonous beyond its powers of digestion." Democracy had failed to stem the onslaught of industrialization. "The locomotive has more man-power than all the ballot-boxes, and mill-wheels wear out the hearts of workers unable to keep up beating to their whirl." Nor had America seen the worst. Anticipating the shift in power from the Rockefellers and Carnegies to the Morgans, Lloyd warned: "Beyond the deep is another deep. This era is but a passing phase in the evolution of industrial Caesars, and these Caesars will be of a new type—corporate Caesars." That dire day wasn't far off. "The corn of the coming harvest is growing so fast that, like the farmer standing at night in his fields, we can hear it snap and crackle." Those who opposed the trend of events often misunderstood the nature of the contest. "We have been fighting fire on the well-worn lines of old-fashioned politics and political economy, regulating corporations, and leaving competition to regulate itself. But the flames of a new economic evolution run around us, and we turn to find that competition has killed competition, that corporations are grown greater than the State and have bred individuals greater than themselves, and that the naked issue of our time is with property becoming master instead of servant, property in many necessaries of life becoming monopoly of the necessaries of life."

Lloyd, whose dismay at the excesses of capitalism drove him first to the Populist Party and then to the Socialists, carried his critique of current trends in the American political economy farther than most muckrakers. Partly because they wrote for magazines that were profit-making ventures (or aspired to be), most investigative journalists during the 1890s remained well within the general philosophical framework of capitalism. Indeed, some remained so well within the capitalist framework as to applaud the activities of the great industrial and financial empire builders. Upon the announcement of the formation of United States Steel, Ray Stannard Baker registered admiration in *McClure's* for what the titans of capitalism had accomplished in creating the great steel trust. *Cosmopolitan* author John Brisben Walker was even more enthusiastic, calling the alliance of Carnegie, Rockefeller, and Morgan "the beginning of the most wonderful revolution in the world's history."

Yet indignation, sometimes to the point of outrage, was the dominant mood of the muckrakers. In the cover editorial to an issue of *McClure's* containing articles by his three musketeers of muckraking—Baker, Lincoln Steffens, and Ida Tarbell—S. S. McClure described the trio of articles as "three arraignments of American character such as should make every one of us stop and think." The authors depicted "capitalists, workingmen, politicians, citizens—all breaking the law or letting it be broken." McClure asked, "Who is there left to uphold the law?" He answered, "There is no one left—none but all of us."

The muckrakers formed the advance guard of the Progressive movement, that groundswell for reform that swept across America starting in the 1890s and extending until World War I. The Progressives had a wide and varied agenda, including political reforms such as the initiative and referendum, social reforms such as child labor laws and prohibition, economic reforms such as utility regulation and trust busting, and consumer protection reforms such as pure food and drug laws. But what most of the items on the Progressive agenda embodied in common was a desire to remedy the ills consequent to the industrialization and urbanization that transformed American life during the last half of the nineteenth century.

The America that fought the Civil War was still largely a rural, agricultural society; by the 1890s it was well on the road to becoming a predominantly urban, industrial society. In 1850, scarcely 15 percent of the American population lived in cities or towns of more than 2,500 inhabitants; by 1900, the proportion was nearly 40 percent. The gain in absolute numbers was even more dramatic: in 1850, the population of American cities and towns totaled 3.5 million; by 1900, it had reached over 30 million.

All these newcomers needed places to live. Some fared better than others, some worse—as Jacob Riis graphically described. In the 1890s, approximately three out of every four American city dwellers lived in rental housing; for the working class, the rate was far higher. While the middle and upper classes moved to the suburbs where homes were newer and better maintained, working-class families, most of whom couldn't afford suburban homes or often even the carfare to get from the suburbs to their jobs, remained in the inner city. The pressure of increasing populations translated into increasing demand for housing and drove up real estate prices. In turn rents went up, forcing many families to take in lodgers.

To meet the rising demand, property owners multiplied the housing units on their lots. Single-family houses were divided into two or more units; warehouses were converted into apartments. In some cities, row houses were the predominant form of urban housing: Philadelphia and Baltimore saw the construction of thousands of two-story row houses that each accommodated four to six families. Three-deckers—long, narrow buildings with three floors and a loft—were the norm in Boston and other New England cities. In New York, tenement buildings of five and six stories were specially designed to fit the 25-by-100-foot lots into which most of Manhattan had been subdivided in the early nineteenth century. With four apartments per floor and many apartments housing more than one family, a single building might contain thirty or more families—on a lot originally intended to shelter one family. New York's large city blocks—200 feet by 1,000 feet—were often home to 2,500 families or more. The population density of the neighborhoods of these blocks—where Riis's Other Half lived—was as great as that of any city in the Western world.

The luckier residents of these neighborhoods lived in tenements of recent design, known as "dumbbells" for their characteristic narrow-in-the-middle, wider-at-the-ends shape. In 1879, regulations had been passed requiring that every room in new tenements have a window. (Older buildings escaped the regulations.) The dumbbell shape allowed lot owners to build right up to their lot lines and meet the requirement. Unfortunately, although the air shaft that resulted when two dumbbells were built next to each other, as they usually were, allowed a certain amount of light and air to penetrate the apartments, it also provided a tempting dumping ground for the garbage of the apartments' inhabitants. Flies, roaches, and rats fed on the refuse that piled up at the bottom of the shaft, becoming a nuisance and a danger to public health. Mortality statistics testified to the danger: on average, dwellers of the tenement districts died at a rate two to three times that of other urban neighborhoods.

Yet life in the dumbbells was an improvement over what had gone before. In many of the older buildings, indoor plumbing was a pipe dream. Privies and faucets were located in nearby alleys or in cellars—which helped explain why the upper floors commanded lower rents than the ground and second floors. In most older buildings there was nothing that resembled a kitchen, and residents were lucky to have a woodstove for heat.

In 1867, the New York Board of Health passed a set of regulations establishing minimum standards for new housing. The standards included fire escapes (which often became blocked, as Riis saw) and indoor plumbing: one toilet per twenty residents and one water faucet per building. The standards were subsequently tightened so that the dumbbell tenements built during the 1880s and 1890s typically had two toilets and one faucet on each floor.

The new buildings, though grossly overcrowded, were an improvement over the old in another way as well. Fire was the bane of the eighteenth- and nineteenth-century American city. The 1871 Chicago fire ravaged 1,700 acres and consumed $200 million in property. In 1872, a huge blaze roared through Boston, wreaking similar destruction. Part of the problem was that cities were built mostly of wood, which made them great piles of kindling. Part of the problem was that fire codes were often either nonexistent or unenforced. Part of the problem was that municipal fire departments were often as confused and haphazard as the fire codes; equipment was insufficient and firefighting techniques outdated.

But during the last two decades of the nineteenth century the situation improved. New steel-frame buildings resisted burning; new fire codes (instituted at the insistence of the big insurance companies) specified the inclusion of fire-walls and other barriers to combustion. The adoption of electrical lighting decreased the risk from kerosene lamps and candles. Fire departments became professionalized, purchasing more-powerful pumps and better support machinery.

The professionalization of fire departments benefited entire cities, although, as one might have guessed, the firefighters paid closest attention to the neighborhoods of the wealthy and powerful. Yet many of the other improvements meant little to the millions of residents of buildings constructed prior to the establishment of the new codes. Predictably, those residents were overwhelmingly the poor, the people who had the fewest options regarding where to live.

Those options were circumscribed by more than poverty. As Jacob Riis reported—and as any city dweller with open eyes and ears quickly learned—different neighborhoods reflected different ethnic and racial backgrounds. Italian immigrants clustered in Little Italy; Poles congregated in Polishtown; Russian Jews inhabited Jewtown; Asian immigrants settled in Chinatown; African-Americans from the South took up residence in the colored district. To a certain extent the groupings were voluntary: a recent arrival from Greece or Bohemia often found life more congenial among fellow Greeks or Bohemians than among people who neither knew the language nor appreciated the customs of the fatherland. To a certain extent the groupings were forced: to move outside the neighborhood considered acceptable for one's group, especially if one was black, was typically either imprudent or impossible. As immigrants became acculturated to American ways, leaving the ethnic neighborhood grew easier; and many immigrants and especially their children eventually did leave. For African-Americans the problem was more persistent: while the sons and daughters of immigrants from Poland or Russia might be indistinguishable from the children of most native-born Americans, the sons and daughters of black immigrants from the South were still obviously black.

IV

For many city residents during the 1890s, the journey to their urban home had started somewhere far away. The largest number hailed from Europe. Earlier immigrants from across the Atlantic had come mostly from the countries of Western and Northern Europe: from the British Isles (then including Ireland), Germany (or rather the many small states that would become Germany), and Scandinavia. But during the last couple of decades of the nineteenth century, a growing portion of the immigrants arrived from Eastern and Southern Europe, as leaving those regions for America became politically and economically less difficult than before.

For the average immigrant, probably a young man, probably unattached but possibly with a family, deciding to start the journey to America wasn't exactly easy. The village where he was born and raised comprised most of what he knew. He might have traveled a few miles to market or to the wedding of a cousin or even to a nearby town on a lark. But his life revolved around the village, and leaving the village took courage. It usually also took a big push: a series of bad harvests, the cumulative burden of debts and taxes and falling prices (these last partly the result of American competition), general economic depression, or a renewed outbreak of anti-Semitism if he happened to be a Jew.

Many of those who left the villages of Europe emigrated merely to the cities of Europe. Urbanization was a global phenomenon, and the same attractive forces that were drawing people from American farms to American cities were drawing people from European farms to European cities. But European cities were growing less rapidly than American cities and producing fewer jobs. And for those many migrants whose families had been farmers for countless generations, the prospect of cheap land in America was often irresistible. Europe had nothing comparable to offer.

Though most European peasants knew relatively little about the outside world, nearly everyone knew something about America. Perhaps a brother had traveled to America and sent letters home; maybe the nephew of a friend had done so. This kind of communication was the most credible available, although the news the letters contained—about the low price of land, about the high wages—often sounded quite *in*credible. Somewhat less believable but also influential was the publicity put out by many of the states of the American Midwest and West. These states possessed land they wanted to sell, and in order to do so they established offices in European countries to drum up business. American railroad companies, which likewise had land to dispose of, did the same. Steamship lines, having found the emigrant traffic a lucrative source of income, hired agents in several European countries.

The United States didn't have a monopoly on immigration from Europe, of course. Canada, Mexico, and Central and South America claimed large numbers of the dissatisfied Europeans. Yet partly because of the advertising efforts of the states and the corporations and partly because the United States was the biggest, richest, most dynamic, and most democratic country of the Western Hemisphere, it drew the largest portion of the emigrant stream.

Crossing the Atlantic during the 1890s was much easier than it had been a generation earlier. The inception of regular steamship service made the journey far faster, safer, and more predictable. It also made the journey less of an irrevocable decision. With Europe only ten days away from the port cities of America's East Coast, a person could sample life in the United States and give it up if it proved unrewarding. Even if the relocation worked out, the emigrant could hope to return to the ancestral village on a reasonably regular basis. Most people in fact didn't get back as often as they thought they would—if they got back at all—but the mere possibility made it easier for them to undertake the journey in the first place.

While crossing the ocean was less trying than it had been, entering the United States wasn't. Immigrants still had to pass muster with the immigration officials at the ports of entry. The greatest number of immigrants entered at New York through the clamorous halls of Ellis Island. New arrivals had to demonstrate that they wouldn't become a burden on the public, which usually meant that they had to have some money in hand

and had to show that they were physically fit to work. But carrying money could be dangerous on shipboard, not to mention during the earlier part of the journey between the home village and Hamburg or Genoa or Liverpool or wherever the point of embarkation had been. A person didn't want to be known for carrying lots of cash. As for work, a person had to show that he *could* work but not that he already had a job lined up: trade unions in America had succeeded in getting Congress to ban contract labor. Nor could the immigrants exhibit signs of infectious disease. The insane and the mentally retarded were likewise barred.

Once the new arrivals surmounted the tests of the immigration officials, there remained the problems of adjusting to life in America. Most of those who came from farm villages aimed to resume farming. Perhaps they would work as tenants or laborers for a time, but eventually they would acquire land of their own. For some, this scenario actually played out. The ones who had the best chance of seeing it do so were those who had fled their old homes for reasons other than economic necessity. Religious and political refugees were more likely to leave with a fair amount of money than were economic refugees, and money made many things possible. With money, a peasant family could buy land. With money, a man who had been a merchant could purchase some inventory and open a shop. But the majority left their homes for economic reasons, scraping together barely enough cash to get them across the ocean and into the United States. Almost on arrival they had to figure out how to make more money: to buy food, to rent a place to live, to purchase clothes for the children.

Fortunately, there were people willing to help the immigrants find jobs and accomplish the adjustment to their new lives. Compatriots from the homeland lent a hand; this was what made the Little Italys and the Polish-towns so attractive. In the ethnic neighborhoods the newcomers could find plenty of folks who spoke the language of their fathers and mothers, plenty who had survived the shock of arrival, plenty who had found jobs and new homes and who could show the new arrivals how to do likewise.

V

Fewer in number but more visible to the American public at large were individuals who made it their vocation to assist immigrants and other city dwellers adjust to life in industrial America. Jane Addams established the model for American social workers with her work at Hull House in Chicago. Addams had been born in Cedarville, Illinois, in 1860. Her father was a prosperous Quaker who instilled in all of his eight children a sense of responsibility toward the society they lived in. He encouraged Jane, obviously the brightest of the lot, to educate herself in preparation for a career of service. She attended college in Rockford, then moved to Philadelphia for medical school. But poor health—a chronic problem—forced her to withdraw from medical school and left her at loose ends as to what to do with her future.

For a few years she drifted, living the life of cultured ease that her father's material success made possible. She traveled to Europe a number of times and took in the attractions popular with visiting Americans, as well as some sights not on the typical grand tour. In London she was appalled and at the same time fascinated by the poverty evident in the city she had only read about in Dickens. She described her reaction in her memoirs, written decades later. It was on a Saturday night, she explained, when she received an "ineradicable impression" of the wretchedness of the East End. She and a few others had been taken by a city missionary to witness the sale of decaying vegetables and fruit, which, owing to Sunday laws, couldn't legally be sold again until Monday. "On Mile End Road, from the top of an omnibus which paused at the end of a dingy street lighted only by occasional flares of gas, we saw two huge masses of ill-clad people clamoring around two hucksters' carts. They were bidding their farthings and ha'pennies for a vegetable held up by the auctioneer, which he at last scornfully flung, with a gibe for its cheapness, to the successful bidder. In the momentary pause only one man detached himself from the groups. He had bidden in a cabbage, and when it struck his hand, he instantly sat down on the curb, tore it with his teeth, and hastily devoured it, unwashed and uncooked as it was." Addams examined others in the crowd that night; the predominant memory she carried away was of "that most unlovely of human expressions, the cunning and shrewdness of the bargain-hunter who starves if he cannot make a successful trade."

Addams remained in London for some time afterward. She went about the city "almost furtively," she said, "afraid to look down narrow streets and alleys lest they disclose again this hideous human need and suffering." Even when sightseeing in the affluent parts of the city, she couldn't erase from her mind the images of the poor neighborhoods. After a while she could think of nothing else. "All huge London came to seem unreal save the poverty in its East End."

Addams gradually grew convinced she must do something about this awful state of affairs, but she couldn't figure out just what. She continued to travel about Europe, hoping to find some answers. She observed work being done among the poor in England and elsewhere by college-educated reformers, people of talents and temperament much like herself, and she formed a vague plan to purchase or rent a house in Chicago where she and other young women might balance their formal classroom education with practical experience among the poor. But this scheme remained nebulous and indefinite until a visit to Spain.

"We had been to see a bull fight," she wrote, "rendered in the most magnificent Spanish style, where greatly to my surprise and horror, I found that I had seen, with comparative indifference, five bulls and many more horses killed. The sense that this was the last survival of all the glories of the amphitheater, the illusion that the riders on the caparisoned horses might have been knights of a tournament, or the matador a slightly armed gladiator facing his martyrdom, and all the rest of the obscure yet vivid associations of a historic survival, had carried me beyond the endurance of any of the rest of the party. I finally met them in the foyer, stern and pale with disapproval of my brutal endurance, and but partially recovered from the faintness and disgust which the spectacle itself had produced upon them. I had no defense to offer to their reproaches save that I had not thought much about the bloodshed; but in the evening the natural and inevitable reaction came, and in deep chagrin I felt myself tried and condemned, not only by this disgusting experience but by the entire moral situation which it revealed. It was suddenly made quite clear to me that I was lulling my conscience by a dreamer's scheme, that a mere paper reform had become a defense for continued idleness, and that I was making it a *raison d'être* for going on indefinitely with study and travel. It is easy to become the dupe of a deferred purpose, of the promise the future can never keep, and I had fallen into the meanest type of self-deception in making myself believe that all this was in preparation for great things to come. Nothing less than the moral reaction following the experience at a bull-fight had been able to reveal to me that so far from following in the wake of a chariot of philanthropic fire, I had been tied to the tail of the veriest ox-cart of self-seeking."

Addams made up her mind that she would put her plan into action at the earliest possible moment. She returned to America, and with a close friend, Ellen Starr, moved into a boardinghouse in Chicago. Addams and Starr searched the neighborhoods of the city until they found what they were looking for on the West Side: a rundown mansion formerly owned by real estate developer Charles Hull, which somehow had managed to survive the great fire of 1871. They arranged to rent most of the house and took possession in the autumn of 1889.

They had no fixed agenda, but aimed to base their work loosely on the model of Toynbee Hall, the famous social mission in London. By early 1890, they commenced an educational program that eventually included classes in English and other subjects relating to successful adaptation to life in America, "reading parties" featuring important works of American and English literature, lectures on art and music and associated uplifting topics, youth activities designed to channel adolescent energies in useful directions, job training for the unskilled, and counseling of all kinds for those who thought they could benefit from it.

The educational influences of Hull House worked in both directions. Jane Addams discovered in herself capacities she hadn't realized were there. She overcame an aversion to the crowding, filth, and poverty that marked slum life, and she ventured boldly into parts of the city where she never would have set foot before. Her compassion acquired a pragmatic and nonjudgmental bent. One night a burglar broke into Hull House. Addams caught him in the act, but rather than summon the police she told the man to come back at nine the next morning. When, perhaps to her surprise, he did, she found him a job earning an honest living. She learned much she had never known about children, including how to deliver a baby, a feat she accomplished on more than one occasion.

Partly from its novelty and partly from Addams's energy in publicizing its work—the better to raise money to expand that work—Hull House soon gained a national and then an international reputation. Fellow reformers as well as the merely curious flocked to the house on Halsted Street. They came from all across America and around the world. Henry Demarest Lloyd, an Addams friend and supporter, called Hull House "the best club in Chicago." Sidney and Beatrice Webb, the British socialists, arrived for a look, as did Keir Hardie, the leader of the British Labour Party, and Aylmer Maude, Tolstoy's translator.

Before she fully realized what she had started, Addams found herself at the head of a movement. By the end of 1891, there were at least half a dozen settlement houses comparable to Hull House in cities across the country; by mid-decade, perhaps two score; by the turn of the century, over one hundred. Requests for advice and invitations to speak and write poured into Addams's office. Though she couldn't accept all the invitations, she did accept many. Soon she was one of the best known and most admired women in the United States. A Philadelphia editor expressed the view of millions in America and other countries when he wrote, "The name of this woman stands as the synonym of the best type of womanhood." More than a few referred to her as "Saint Jane"; one man was so taken by her spirit of solidarity with the poor that he wrote to say he wanted simply to touch the hem of her skirt in order to absorb a little of that spirit.

VI

Jane Addams liked working with immigrants better than with their American-born children or grandchildren. "It is much easier to deal with the first generation of crowded city life than with the second and third," she said. The first generation was "more natural and cast in a simpler mould" and retained some of the attractive traditional ways. "Italian and Bohemian peasants who live in Chicago still put on their bright holiday clothes on a Sunday and go to visit their cousins. They tramp along with at least a suggestion of having once walked over plowed fields and breathed country air. The second generation of city poor have no holiday clothes and consider their relations a 'bad lot.' "

Certain other people who worked in the cities likewise appreciated those just off the boat. In every large American city during the 1890s there existed a class of professional greeters, people who made it their business to ease the immigrants' transition to American life. These people helped immigrants secure jobs, sometimes in the private sector but often on the public payroll; they explained how the American legal system functioned, especially stressing which laws were rigorously enforced and which allowed a certain flexibility; they interceded with local authorities when the immigrants overstepped the line between the acceptable and the forbidden, posting bail for rambunctious teenage sons who got into fights and speaking to judges on behalf of those who found the American courts intimidating and incomprehensible. If a fire destroyed the meager possessions of a family, these helpers arrived with a bundle of clothing and a few pairs of boots. If the family's principal breadwinner got laid off before the holidays, they left a basket of groceries and a box of coal on the doorstep. They attended weddings and wakes, toasting the bride and groom, eulogizing the deceased, and helping cover the expenses.

All they asked in return was loyalty, particularly on election day. The immigrants formed the basic constituency of many of the big-city political machines of the late nineteenth and early twentieth centuries. Few of the immigrants came from countries where anyone had ever asked them to participate in the political process; democracy was as new to them as English. Fewer still arrived with any well-developed sense of an abstract "public interest" toward which political leaders ought to bend their efforts. For the immigrants—as for most voters in most democracies at most times—the political issues that really mattered were the bread-and-butter questions of how to get from one day to the next. During the 1890s, there existed almost nothing in the way of a government-guaranteed safety net to catch people slipping off the social and economic ladder. The philosophy of government had not kept up with the reality of urban industrial life. Unemployment was an invention of the industrial age; in the days when the great majority of people lived on farms, economic slumps didn't throw millions out of work. Prices might fall and families might have to stretch their resources farther than usual, but there was always work to do and almost always food to eat, if only the vegetables from the garden and the milk from the cow. Generally there was a roof over the family's head. If things stayed really bad for several years, a family might lose the farm, but that was unusual in the days when land was cheap and mortgages small.

As people moved to the cities, society lost this shock-absorbing capacity. A man who worked in a factory and got a pink slip was deprived of his sole means of support. He had no money to buy groceries, so his children faced hunger. He couldn't pay the rent, so his family was threatened with eviction. If anyone in the family became sick, he couldn't afford a doctor. He was at the mercy of economic cycles and market forces he hardly understood; his fate could be determined by a rate war on the railroads or a change in tastes for shoes.

For the immigrants, the difficulty was doubled by the loss of the family and community ties that held village life together in the old country. In the old country, when times got hard there were always relatives nearby to help out. In the old country, a tenant family might have worked the land of the same landlord family for five or ten generations; such longevity of service bred a sense of obligation in landlords that helped ease the strain of trying times.

But the journey across the ocean sundered the ties that held the peasant's world together. In the new country, there were no such longstanding connections; that was what made it new. The factory owner had nothing to do with the thousands of souls who operated his machines, beyond paying them wages in exchange for services rendered. Everything was reduced to a cash transaction. When the cash ran short, obligations ceased. Workers drew their last pay envelope and that was that.

The political machines cushioned the shift from the Old World and the old way of doing things to the New. In an otherwise indifferent political economy, they held out a helping hand. They were called "machines," but that was merely a label borrowed from the lexicon of industrialization. If anything they were the opposite of machines, for they provided a human touch in an age marked by the inhumanity of real machines. Their agents knew the families in their neighborhoods by name; they knew when babies were born, when youths married, when grandparents died. They knew, and they cared, after their own fashion. Eventually governments would assume many of the responsibilities they fulfilled, but for the time being they furnished the compassionate element without which life in the cities would have been unbearable for millions of people.

Compassion came with strings, however. The political bosses, the men who ran the city machines, expected to do well for themselves in doing good for their constituents. A reporter once asked Richard Croker—"King Richard" of New York's Tammany Hall—if he was working for his own interests. "All the time," Croker replied. "The same as you."

Croker typified the bosses of the 1890s. He had left Ireland with his parents at the age of three when the potato crop failed during the 1840s. The family landed in New York's Lower East Side, where he joined the Fourth Avenue Tunnel Gang as a teenager. By force of personality and a wicked right jab, he rose to preeminence in the gang and was recruited into the Tammany machine of William "Boss" Tweed during the 1860s. Croker worked loyally for the machine, gradually climbing the pyramid to the top, which he reached by the late 1880s.

Like many political bosses, Croker could be disarmingly forthright, even with those who wished him ill. Lincoln Steffens, the foremost muckraker of urban political corruption, wrote: "Richard Croker never said anything to me that was not true, unless it was a statement for publication." Croker's friends, who included tens of thousands of New York's poor, treated him as a hero. When he attended the opera, the orchestra played "Hail to the Chief"; when he left the city for his annual vacation in Europe, throngs of well-wishers crowded the pier to wish him bon voyage.

On one of Croker's trips to Europe, in 1897, he granted an interview to William Stead, a noted English journalist and reformer. Reporting the encounter, Stead described the demeanor of the boss, then at the height of his power: "Mr. Croker is not a silk-stocking dude, but he is a gentleman in his bearing and in his conversation." Many of Stead's readers, if not Stead himself, found this surprising, since they were accustomed to thinking of the bosses as a grasping, grubby lot. "To all outward appearance," Stead continued, "there was no one on board ship who was less exposed to the accusation of vulgarity, forwardness, bad manners, or bad language. He behaved himself as seemly as anyone could desire. He vaunted not himself, he talked quietly and intelligently to those to whom he was introduced, and so far as in him lay, he contributed as much as anyone on board, and more than most, to the amenity of the voyage." Stead hazarded the guess that most of those on board the ship who knew Croker by reputation had formerly felt they would need "a very long spoon" to sup with the New York boss. "But none of those who had the good fortune to meet with him in his endless constitutional up and down deck but liked him as a companion and parted with him with regret."

Croker's shipmates might have liked him less had they heard what he told Stead about the operations of Tammany Hall. At the least some would have thought him a hypocrite. Yet Stead, after lengthy conversations, came to believe in Croker's sincerity, even while differing on matters of interpretation. Croker explained that Tammany Hall had been much maligned in the press. The very fact that it had thrived for so many years demonstrated that it was accomplishing worthwhile results. "Although wrongdoing may endure for a season," Croker asserted, "right must in the long run come to the top. Human nature is not built so that roguery can last."

Stead reminded Croker that the Tammany slate had been turned out of office in the last election. Didn't this suggest that there might be something amiss in Croker's reasoning—or that his own argument could be used against him?

"No, sir," Croker said. "In a moment of restlessness, the people put in what they called a Reform Administration, but after three years' experience they have had enough of it, and Tammany is coming out on top once more. It's bound to, for Tammany is honest and Tammany is true. And you have only to go on being honest and true to come out on top—not every time, for we have our reverses; but on the whole, Tammany has come out on top most of the time."

Stead inquired about the spoils system. How did Croker square the practice of giving offices to friends with the principle of being good and true?

"Politics are impossible without the spoils," Croker answered. "It is all very well to argue that it ought not to be so. But we have to deal with men as they are and with things as they are. Consider the problem which every democratic system has to solve. Government, we say, of the people, by the people, and for the people. The aim is to interest as many of the citizens as possible in the work—which is not an easy work, and has many difficulties and disappointments—of governing the state or the city. Of course, in an ideal world every citizen would be so dominated by patriotic or civic motives that from sheer unselfish love of his fellow men he would spend nights and days in laboring for their good. If you lived in such a world inhabited by such men, I admit there could be no question but that we could and would dispense with the spoils system. But where is that world to be found? Certainly not in the United States, and most certainly not in New York."

The so-called reformers—"mugwumps," in the bosses' term—couldn't sustain the effort required to do the work of governing, Croker said. They talked a good game, but when it came to the messy, sweaty business of actually administering the city, they faltered. Why? Because they disdained to rub shoulders with the people who made up the bulk of the city's population.

"Think what New York is, and what the people of New York are," Croker said. "One half, more than one half, are of foreign birth. We have thousands upon thousands of men who are alien born, who have no ties connecting them with the city or the state. They do not speak our language, they do not know our laws, they are the raw material with which we have to build up the state." People abused Tammany Hall for currying the favor of the immigrants. Croker accepted the charge but not the implication. "There is no denying the service which Tammany has rendered to the Republic. There is no such organization for taking hold of the untrained friendless man and converting him into a citizen. Who else would do it if we did not? Think of the hundreds of thousands of foreigners dumped into our city. They are too old to go to school. There is not a mugwump in the city who would shake hands with them. They are alone, ignorant strangers, a prey to all manner of anarchical and wild notions. Except to their employer, they have no value to anyone until they get a vote."

Stead asked, smiling, "And then they are of value to Tammany?"

"Yes, and then they are of value to Tammany," Croker answered. "Tammany looks after them for the sake of their vote, grafts them upon the Republic—makes citizens of them, in short. And although you may not like our motives or our methods, what other agency is there by which so long a row could have been hoed so quickly or so well? If we go down into the gutter, it is because there are men in the gutter, and you have got to go down where they are if you are to have anything to do with them."

Croker declared that much of the criticism of Tammany reflected an animus against the foreign-born. "Tammany is everywhere spoken against because it is said to be a foreign organization," Croker said. This criticism was both mistaken and misguided. "Tammany, on the contrary, is a distinctively American organization founded on much more thoroughgoing American principles than those which find favor with the framers of the Charter of Greater New York [a reform group], for instance. It makes me tired to hear their talk about foreigners. Where would America be today without foreigners?"

Stead responded that it would still be in the hands of the Indians.

Croker nodded and went on. "This discrimination against citizens because of their place of birth seems to me un-American and unjust. Do not these men pay taxes, found homes, build up states, and do a great deal more in the government than our assailants? They may have been born under another flag. But they forswear their own nationality; they swear allegiance to our flag; they filled the ranks of our armies in the great war [the Civil War]; everywhere they fulfill the duties and accept all the burdens of the citizen. And yet we are told they are foreigners."

Croker's voice took on a tone of special earnestness. "Sir, in Tammany Hall there is no discrimination against citizens on account of race or religion. We meet on the common ground of one common citizenship. We know no difference of Catholic or Protestant, of Irishman, German or American. Everyone is welcome amongst us who is true to the city and true to the party." Tammany was an example to the nation. "It is of the people, created for the people, controlled by the people—the purest and strongest outcome of the working of democratic government under modern conditions."

Stead remarked that a fellow passenger, a Republican, had asserted that the Democratic Tammany machine was far from democratic, that it was under the absolute despotism of the men in office. Where many other political organizations had difficulty enforcing discipline, Tammany ruled with an iron hand.

"How can that be?" objected Croker. "You talk of Tammany and those who are in office as if they had an authority whatever beyond the popular vote freely expressed. What is Tammany? I am the boss, they say. But I hold no office. If I am boss, it is simply because what I may say or think goes with the Executive Committee. You or any man might be a boss tomorrow if you could convince those who hear you that you are a sensible man who has a sincere regard for the party and the city. They cry Tammany Hall! Tammany Hall! But what is Tammany Hall? It is simply an executive committee of the Democratic party of New York, elected annually at primaries or open public meetings held subject to the law, which makes strict provisions against any fraud or wrongdoing. New York is divided into thirty-four assembly districts. Each of these districts holds a public meeting, which every member of the party resident in that district is free to attend. At these primaries, representatives are selected by the free vote of the citizens present. These representatives elect one of their number in whom they have confidence as their leader. This leader becomes their representative on the Executive Committee of Tammany Hall. He may be reelected year after year. But he can be superseded in twelve months if he cannot retain the confidence of the people in his own district."

Stead asked if members of the Executive Committee ever got turned out.

"Certainly," Croker answered. "They are always changing. Their only authority depends on their personal influence. You hear a great deal about my being the boss, as if I were lord and master of Tammany Hall. I hold no office. I have no power, not an atom, except what I can exercise because of the confidence which the people have in me. They know that I am honest, that I am true, that I care for the party and the city; and that is all there is to it. Boss Tweed no doubt was a bad boss. But we met him in the primaries, and we turned him down, and put Honest John Kelly in his stead. When Kelly died, there was some discussion as to his successor. I said, let us appoint no successor, or rather let us all be his successors.

Instead of one boss, let us all thirty-four be bosses. And it was agreed. But somehow when people found that what I said went, they got into the habit of saying I was boss. But I could not help that."

Stead inquired wherein Croker perceived his strength to lie. Croker responded that it lay in trust. He had always trusted the people, and the people had always trusted him. He had never been crooked, and he had never tolerated crooked people under him. As soon as anyone was found to be corrupt, he was out of a job. The people recognized this intolerance of corruption, and they rewarded him with their trust.

Stead asked Croker if there were any more specific secrets of his success. Croker pondered the question awhile, then answered that there were two. The first was his decision to divest himself of direct responsibility for doling out patronage. Previous bosses had kept job appointments to themselves; as the patronage list lengthened, they were left with no time for anything else. Croker said he had delegated the responsibility to the thirty-four district leaders. They made the appointments in their districts, freeing him to deal with larger matters.

The second secret, also an innovation, was his decision to encourage the appointment of younger men to office. He himself had got ahead when young, and he had always appreciated the opportunity. Other bright young men valued similar opportunities. "If you get a reputation for picking out young fellows and giving them a show six or ten years sooner than anybody else, all the smartest lads will crowd around you, and naturally. You are giving them the chance they want today, while the other fellows only promise it next week."

There was an additional reason for pushing young men to the front. "I favored young men on principle on a calculation which worked right every time. If you get the young men, you get their fathers and their elder relations. That is invariable. It is quite otherwise with the old. If you get the father, you probably won't get the son, whereas if you get the son you always get the father." This was merely a matter of human nature, at least as manifested in America. "There is no motive which operates more constantly in American life than the desire of every father to secure for his children a better education than he has had himself. That motive, far more than any greed for the dollar, takes most men into politics. They want to see their boys better educated." (In his report of the conversation, Stead interjected here that Croker evidently meant education in the broad sense of training for life rather than mere academic learning.) "And when they see their boy taken hold of and put into place early, they are true to the party that pushes their boy."

In this exchange and several others on their Atlantic crossing, Croker didn't quite convince Stead that the New York machine was a philanthropic organization, but the boss did convince the journalist that he envisioned it as one. "Thus, by slow degrees, and during the course of many conversations," Stead wrote, "I gradually began to perceive, as it were, some glorified image of Tammany Hall and its Boss as he evidently loved to dwell upon them in his dreams, and it was not far from the Kingdom of Heaven. For it was based upon the great principle of human brotherhood; it has as its foundation the doctrine that in Tammany there is neither Jew nor Gentile, Barbarian or Scythian, bond or free; and it has as its habitual rule of life the serving of the Brethren. Instead of being an excrescence upon the State, it was the great digestive apparatus of the Republic, upon whose rude strength and capacity for assimilation depended the health of the Commonwealth. And today, while Citizens' Unions and Charter Committees, and all the great and learned and influential of the city are going astray from the true Democratic faith, and seeking to cast out municipal evils by having resort to elective Caesarism, Tammany stands forth fearless and undismayed, the very Abdiel, faithful among the faithless found, in its unswerving allegiance to the pure original principles of free popular elective self-government."

VII

Richard Croker wasn't the only Tammany leader willing to elaborate on the principles of democracy. George Washington Plunkitt was one of Croker's lieutenants, the ward boss of the Fifteenth Assembly District. Plunkitt was a year older than Croker and a native of Manhattan. Like Croker he had worked his way up the Tammany organization, and although he didn't quite reach the top, he did well enough. By the 1890s, his income allowed him to live in fine style.

Plunkitt always insisted that what affluence he achieved came honestly. Some people might have considered it hair-splitting, but Plunkitt detected an important difference between what he called "honest graft" and "dishonest graft." "Everybody is talking these days about Tammany men growing rich on graft," Plunkitt told William Riordon, a reporter for the *New York Evening Post*. "But nobody thinks of drawing the distinction between honest graft and dishonest graft. There's all the difference in the world between the two. Yes, many of our men have grown rich in politics. I have myself. I've made a big fortune out of the game, and I'm getting richer every day. But I've not gone in for dishonest graft—blackmailing gamblers, saloonkeepers, disorderly people, etc.—and neither has any of the men who have made big fortunes in politics.

"There's honest graft, and I'm an example of how it works. I might sum up the whole thing by saying: 'I seen my opportunities and I took 'em.' Just let me explain by examples. My party's in power in the city, and it's going to undertake a lot of public improvements. Well, I'm tipped off, say, that they're going to lay out a new park at a certain place. I see my opportunity and I take it. I go to that place and I buy up all the land I can in the neighborhood. Then the board of this or that makes its plan public, and there is a rush to get my land, which nobody particularly cared for before. Ain't it perfectly honest to charge a good price and make a profit on my investment and foresight? Of course it is. Well, that's honest graft.

"Or supposing it's a new bridge they're going to build. I get tipped off and I buy as much property as I can that has to be taken for approaches. I sell at my own price later on and drop some more money in the bank. Wouldn't you? It's just like looking ahead in Wall Street or in the coffee or cotton market. It's honest graft, and I'm looking for it every day of the year. I will tell you frankly that I've got a good lot of it, too.

"I'll tell you of one case. They were going to fix up a big park—no matter where. I got on to it, and went looking about for land in that neighborhood. I could get nothing at a bargain but a big piece of swamp, but I took it fast enough and held on to it. What turned out was just what I counted on. They couldn't make the park complete without Plunkitt's swamp, and they had to pay a good price for it. Anything dishonest in that?

"Up in the watershed I made some money, too. I bought up several bits of land there some years ago and made a pretty good guess that they would be bought up for water purposes later by the city. Somehow I always guessed about right, and shouldn't I enjoy the profit of my foresight? It was rather amusing when the condemnation commissioners came along and found piece after piece of the land in the name of George Plunkitt of the Fifteenth Assembly District, New York City. They wondered how I knew just what to buy. The answer is—I seen my opportunity and I took it."

Plunkitt cited yet another example. The City of New York was repaving a street and had several hundred thousand old granite blocks to sell. Plunkitt decided to make a bid for them. But on auction day he discovered that some of Tammany's enemies had conspired to "do"—that is, undo—him. They had leaked news of what was supposed to be a quiet deal, and rival bidders had come to the auction. Plunkitt explained how he foiled the attempt to foil him: "I went to each of these men and said, 'How many of these 250,000 stones do you want?' One said 20,000 and another wanted 15,000, and another wanted 10,000. I said, 'All right, let me bid for the lot, and I'll give each of you all you want for nothing.' They agreed, of course. Then the auctioneer yelled, 'How much am I bid for these 250,000 fine paving stones?' 'Two dollars and fifty cents,' says I. 'Two dollars and fifty cents!' screamed the auctioneer. 'Oh, that's a joke. Give me a real bid.' He found the bid was real enough. My rivals stood silent. I got the lot for $2.50 and gave them their share. That's how the attempt to do Plunkitt ended, and that's how all such attempts end."

Plunkitt asserted that most politicians accused of feeding at the public trough made their money the same way he did. "They didn't steal a dollar from the city treasury. They just seen their opportunities and took 'em. That's why, when a reform administration comes in and spends half a million dollars trying to find the public robberies they talked about in the campaign, they don't find them. The books are all right. The money in the city treasury is all right. Everything is all right. All they can show is that the Tammany heads of departments looked after their friends, within the law, and gave them what opportunities they could to make honest graft."

Plunkitt contended that such activities would never hurt Tammany with the voters. "Every good man looks after his friends, and any man who doesn't isn't likely to be popular. If I have a good thing to hand out in private life, I give it to a friend. Why shouldn't I do the same in public life?"

Plunkitt cited another variant of "honest" graft: increasing the salaries of civil servants. He granted that reformers caused a ruckus when public salaries went up, but he said Tammany could take the heat. "Don't you know that Tammany gains ten votes for every one it lost by salary-raising? The Wall Street banker thinks it shameful to raise a department clerk's salary from $1500 to $1800 a year, but every man who draws a salary himself says, 'That's all right. I wish it was me.' And he feels very much like voting the Tammany ticket on election day, just out of sympathy."

Of course Tammany had other ways of cultivating the sympathy of voters. Plunkitt had made a science of winning popular favor. "You must study human nature and act accordin'," he told Riordon. He added, "You can't study human nature in books. Books is a hindrance more than anything else. If you have been to college, so much the worse for you. You'll have to unlearn all that you learned, before you can get right down to human nature. And unlearnin' takes a lot of time. Some men can never forget what they learned at college. Such men may get to be district leaders by a fluke, but they never last."

To learn human nature required constant application. "You have to go among the people, see them and be seen. I know every man, woman and child in the Fifteenth District, except them that's been born this summer— and I know some of them too. I know what they like and what they don't like, what they are strong at and what they are weak in, and I reach them by approachin' at the right side."

Plunkitt illustrated by explaining how he gathered in the young men. "I hear of a young feller that's proud of his voice, thinks that he can sing fine. I ask him to come around to Washington Hall and join our glee club. He comes and sings, and he's a follower of Plunkitt for life. Another young feller gains a reputation as a baseball player in a vacant lot. I bring him into our baseball club. That fixes him. You'll find him workin' for my ticket at the polls next election day. Then there's the feller that likes rowin' on the river, the young feller that makes a name as a waltzer on his block, the young feller that's handy with his dukes—I rope them all in by givin' them opportunities to show themselves off. I don't trouble them with political arguments. I just study human nature and act accordin'."

Plunkitt acknowledged that this approach didn't cover all cases. He said that "high-toned fellers," the college and Citizens' Union types, resisted this technique. He had other methods for such persons. "I ain't like the patent-medicine man that gives the same medicine for all diseases. The Citizens' Union kind of young man! I love him! He's the daintiest morsel of the lot, and he don't often escape me."

Plunkitt prefaced his explanation of how he swallowed these morsels with some general comments on the Citizens' Union. Before a recent election, he said, the reform group had listed four or five hundred voters from the Fifteenth District on its roster. The organization had a handsome head-quarters office, with rugs, rolltop desks, and all the rest. "If I was accused of havin' contributed to fix up the nest for them," Plunkitt remarked, with a wink, "I wouldn't deny it under oath. What do I mean by that? Never mind. You can guess from the sequel, if you're sharp."

Election day arrived, and the Citizens' Union candidate polled five votes in the entire district, against more than 14,000 votes for Plunkitt. "What became of the 400 or 500 Citizens' Union enrolled voters in my district?" asked Plunkitt mischievously. "Some people guessed that many of them were good Plunkitt men all along and worked with the Cits just to bring them into the Plunkitt camp by election day. You can guess that way too, if you want to. I never contradict stories about me, especially in hot weather. I just call your attention to the fact that on last election day 395 Citizens' Union enrolled voters in my district were missin' and unaccounted for."

Returning to the question of how to capture young men of reformist tendencies, Plunkitt boasted, "I have a plan that never fails. I watch the City Record to see when there's civil service examinations for good things. Then I take my young Cit in hand, tell him all about the good things and get him worked up till he goes and takes an examination. I don't bother about him any more. It's a cinch that he comes back to me in a few days and asks to join Tammany Hall. Come over to Washington Hall some night and I'll show you a list of names on our rolls marked 'C.S.,' which means 'bucked up against civil service.' "

Plunkitt had strategies for pulling in older people as well. In response to a query from Riordon whether he used campaign handbills or other printed material, Plunkitt said he didn't. "You ain't goin' to gain any votes by stuffin' the letter-boxes with campaign documents," he sniffed. "Like as not, you'll lose votes, for there's nothin' a man hates more than to hear the letter-carrier ring his bell and go to the letter-box expectin' to find a letter he was lookin' for, and find only a lot of printed politics. I met a man this very mornin' who told me he voted the Democratic state ticket last year just because the Republicans kept crammin' his letter-box with campaign documents."

What captured the loyalty of ordinary people wasn't political philosophy but practical consideration. "What tells in holdin' your grip on your district is to go right down among the poor families and help them in the different ways they need help. I've got a regular system for this. If there's a fire in Ninth, Tenth, or Eleventh Avenue, for example, at any hour of the day or night, I'm usually there with some of my election district captains as soon as the fire-engines. If a family is burned out, I don't ask whether they are Republicans or Democrats, and I don't refer them to the Charity Organi-zation Society, which would investigate their case in a month or two and decide they were worthy of help about the time they are dead from star-vation. I just get quarters for them, buy clothes for them if their clothes were burned up, and fix them up till they get things runnin' again. It's philanthropy, but it's politics too—mighty good politics. Who can tell how many votes one of these fires brings me? The poor are the most grateful people in the world, and, let me tell you, they have more friends in their neighborhoods than the rich have in theirs."

Plunkitt explained that he dispensed jobs to deserving people along with the emergency relief. "I make it a point to keep on the track of jobs, and it seldom happens that I don't have a few up my sleeve ready for use. I know every big employer in the district, and in the whole city, for that matter, and they ain't in the habit of sayin' no to me when I ask them for a job."

Neither did Plunkitt overlook the children—"the little roses of the district." "They know me, every one of them, and they know that a sight of Uncle George and candy means the same thing." Children were the best kind of vote-getters. "I'll tell you a case. Last year a little Eleventh Avenue rosebud, whose father is a Republican, caught hold of his whiskers on election day and said she wouldn't let go till he'd promise to vote for me. And she didn't."

The common people wanted to look up to their leaders for certain things, Plunkitt said, but not too far up and not for everything. "Puttin' on style don't pay in politics. The people won't stand for it. If you've got an achin' for style, sit down on it till you have made your pile and landed a Supreme Court Justiceship with a fourteen-year term at $17,500 a year, or some job of that kind. Then you've got about all you can get out of politics, and you can afford to wear a dress-suit all day and sleep in it all night if you have a mind to. But before you have caught onto your life meal-ticket, be simple. Live like your neighbors even if you have the means to live better."

Plunkitt warned particularly about the perils of the dress suit. "You have no idea of the harm that dress-suits have done in politics. They are not so fatal to young politicians as civil service reform and drink, but they have scores of victims." Plunkitt mentioned one especially sad case. "After the big Tammany victory in 1897 [in which Croker's prediction to Stead of a Tammany triumph came true], Richard Croker went down to Lakewood to make up the slate of offices for Mayor Van Wyck to distribute. All the district leaders and many more Tammany men went down there too, to pick up anything good that was goin'. There was nothin' but dress-suits at dinner at Lakewood, and Croker wouldn't let any Tammany men go to dinner without them. Well, a bright young West Side politician, who held a three-thousand dollar job in one of the departments, went to Lakewood to ask Croker for something better. He wore a dress-suit for the first time in his life. It was his undoin'. He got stuck on himself. He thought he looked too beautiful for anything, and when he came home he was a changed man. As soon as he got to his house every evenin' he put on that dress-suit and set around in it until bedtime. That didn't satisfy him long. He wanted others to see how beautiful he was in a dress-suit, so he joined dancin' clubs and began goin' to all the balls that was given in town. Soon he began to neglect his family. Then he took to drinkin', and didn't pay any attention to his political work in the district. The end came in less than a year. He was dismissed from the department and went to the dogs. The other day I met him rigged out almost like a hobo, but he still had a dress-suit vest on. When I asked him what he was doin', he said. 'Nothin' at present, but I got a promise of a job enrollin' voters at Citizens' Union headquarters.' Yes, a dress-suit had brought him that low!"

Plunkitt told Riordon he steered well away from any such vices. "No-body ever saw me puttin' on any style. I'm the same Plunkitt I was when I entered politics forty years ago. That is why the people of the district have confidence in me. If I went into the stylish business, even I, Plunkitt, might be thrown down in the district. That was shown pretty clearly in the senatorial fight last year. A day before the election, my enemies circulated a report that I had ordered a $10,000 automobile and a $125 dollar dress-suit. I sent out contradictions as fast as I could, but I wasn't able to stamp out the infamous slander before the votin' was over, and I suffered some at the polls. The people wouldn't have minded much if I had been accused of robbin' the city treasury, for they're used to slanders of that kind in campaigns, but the automobile and the dress-suit were too much for them."

As in attire, so in speech. "If you're makin' speeches in a campaign, talk the language the people talk. Don't try to show how the situation is by quotin' Shakespeare. Shakespeare was all right in his way, but he didn't know anything about Fifteenth District politics. If you know Greek and Latin and have a hankerin' to work them off on somebody, hire a stranger to come to your house and listen to you for a couple of hours; then go out and talk the language of the Fifteenth to the people. I know it's an awful temptation, the hankerin' to show off your learnin'. I've felt it myself, but I always resist it. I know the awful consequences."

VIII

Not surprisingly, critics of Croker, Plunkitt, and the rest of the bosses took a less flattering view of the activities of the machines. Even William Stead, who found Croker so personally charming, attacked the machines quite vigorously. Stead visited Chicago for the Columbian Exposition and extended his stay to investigate the politics of the city. What he discovered deeply dismayed him; his dismay took form in a scathing exposé entitled *If Christ Came to Chicago.* The upshot of the book was that Christ wouldn't be pleased. Stead objected as much to the immorality that flourished in Chicago, especially during the summer of the exposition, as he did to the political corruption. He compiled and included in his book a black list of owners and operators of "property used for immoral purposes," and drew a map of the reddest of the red-light districts, with the brothels, saloons, and other low dives plainly marked. He decried the exploitation of unfortunate women by the madams. Of Carrie Watson, he wrote, "She has made a fortune of her trade in the bodies of her poorer sisters." He described the lot of the homeless and destitute, who survived on the charity of the churches, the saloonkeepers, and anyone else who would help out.

But it was political corruption that allowed the immorality to flourish. Stead depicted how elected officials, judges, and police conspired with the panderers, turning a blind eye and an open palm to those who catered to human weakness. Stead revealed widespread manipulation of tax assessments, so that though Chicago had grown enormously since 1873, its assessed valuation was currently less than it had been at that time. The city council he characterized as utterly corrupt. "The boodling aldermen," he said, were "the swine of our civilization."

Although Stead's book attracted great attention throughout most of America and in England as well, Chicagoans took it in stride. Some denounced it as sensationalistic—"a guide book to the brothels and other places of evil resort in Chicago," according to one sardonic reviewer. Some accused Stead of sanctimony. Some simply objected to the bad publicity at a time when Chicago was trying to win the respect of the rest of the country. But almost no one disputed the essential veracity of his charges, since nearly everyone who paid attention to such matters recognized that Stead could have told much more.

He might, for example, have disclosed the activities of "Bathhouse John" Coughlin and "Hinky Dink" Kenna. John Coughlin and Michael Kenna were the lords of "the Levee," Chicago's First Ward. Beginning in the early 1890s, "the Bath" and "Hinky Dink" established a political fiefdom that survived until well into the twentieth century. They made an odd couple, the Laurel and Hardy of American machine politics. No one ever accused Bathhouse John of being brilliant, but he had the street savvy other bosses like Plunkitt respected. When people asked him how he had decided to enter politics, he used to cite the Chicago fire, which burned down his father's grocery store, as the instrument of his salvation. "I'm glad that fire came along and burned the store," he said. "If not for that bonfire, I might have been a rich man's son and gone to Yale—and never amounted to nothing." (Yale presumably was equally relieved.) The Bath loved what life had to offer in the way of sensory gratification; he especially valued expensive and ostentatious clothing (being an exception that perhaps proved Plunkitt's rule). One memorable occasion, a fund-raising ball (with the local charity of Coughlin & Kenna the prime beneficiary), saw Coughlin decked out in a tailcoat of billiard-cloth green, a mauve vest, lavender pants and cravat, pink gloves, yellow shoes, and a top hat of shiny black silk.

Though intellectual inspiration occasionally visited the Bath (so named for his start as a rubber in a Chicago bathhouse), especially when the topic was boodling, Hinky Dink Kenna was the brains of the First Ward. Small (whence the nickname), Hinky Dink barely came up to Bathhouse John's boutonnière; where the Bath pumped hands and slapped backs with a hail-fellow-well-met air, Hinky Dink stood to the side with a skeptical eye and a dry wit. Paul Douglas, later United States senator from Illinois, once said half seriously that Hinky Dink had the makings of a great idiomatic Latin scholar; Douglas cited as evidence the legend above the bar in Hinky Dink's saloon—"In Vino Veritas"—and the proprietor's succinct translation—"When a man's drunk, he gives his right name." (Among Hinky Dink's colleagues were some who could appreciate such learning. In 1895, "One-Eyed" Jimmy Connelly visited the Silver Dollar, a newly converted saloon run by Bathhouse John, himself newly converted to the cause of free silver. In keeping with the name, the walls and ceiling of the saloon had been painted to show piles of silver dollars. The coins depicted showed no dates; instead they bore inscriptions such as "Silver Money," "Easy Money," "Workingman's Money," and "Matrimony." Each dollar did display the familiar "E pluribus unum," which One-Eyed Connelly translated phonetically as "He brews us new rum.")

It said much about the Bath and Hinky Dink that they gained reputations for boodling in a city notorious for municipal corruption. The racket that produced the most money for elected officials and unofficial hangers-on was the sale of concessions to operate streetcars, railroads, and other public utilities to private corporations. In a rapidly growing city like Chicago, which in addition was rebuilding after the 1871 fire, construction projects were the meat-and-potatoes of the local economy. Chicago aldermen battened on "honest" graft, but they supplemented their incomes with bribes for approving ordinances such as those allowing a gas company to lay pipes in one neighborhood, a traction company to build a trolley line in another, a factory to extend its warehouse into the alley behind.

As in Plunkitt's New York, the Chicago boodlers had perfected schemes to keep the city's books balanced. Typically an ordinance requested by a particular corporation would be referred to a committee. The sponsoring corporation would send a representative to meet with a committeeman thought to be persuadable and offer to hire legal counsel to give expert advice regarding the ordinance. Perhaps a particular member of the committeeman's law firm would be acceptable? Quite acceptable, the committeeman would say. The counsel would be hired at an exorbitant fee and would split the fee with the cooperating committeeman. The latter would find the arguments for the ordinance persuasive, and—perhaps after similar treatment of other committee members—the committee would approve the ordinance. Occasionally such arrangements would come to light, but because the form of the transaction was legal and correct—the committee had simply sought counsel in order to protect the public interest, and anyway economic development was good for the community—whatever storm developed usually blew over without incident.

All manner of firms had got into the boodling business. Eight streetcar and elevated-train lines operated by the rules the boodlers laid down; three gas and electric companies required rights to burrow under the avenues; in the First Ward alone, sixty enterprises, running everything from foundries to laundries to taverns to shops, had obtained variances to grant them portions of the city's thoroughfares; assorted railroad companies had taken over a quarter of the ward's streets. Payments varied from as little as $100 per favorable vote on an ordinance to $25,000, the amount a railroad paid in 1890 to each of four aldermen. Most of the time the payments were for positive actions: putting new ordinances on the books; less frequently the payments served to prevent blackmail measures from being enacted. So pervasive was the boodling that even the comparatively honest members of the city council felt obliged to turn blind eyes to the grafting. The boodlers had elevated logrolling to an art: if the honest members wanted any cooperation on issues close to their own hearts—or districts—they had to cooperate with the boodlers. "Either you go along with us," warned John Powers ("Johnny de Pow," sometimes called the "Prince of Boodlers"), speaking to a newcomer to the council, "or you won't get a can of garbage moved out of your ward till hell freezes over."

Although the boodlers held the sizable advantage of controlling access to publicly owned property, their clients—the purchasers of their favors—weren't without leverage. The most formidable client was Charles Yerkes. A Philadelphia native and the son of a bank president, Yerkes had followed his father's footsteps into finance during the 1860s. He bought and sold municipal bonds at a time when cities were growing swiftly; in doing so he made a great deal of money and gained a reputation as a high flier. But he flew a little too high, for when the Chicago fire of 1871 precipitated a panic in the municipal bond market, he was caught short. Criminally short: charged with and convicted of embezzlement, he was sentenced to two years and nine months in prison. He served seven months and then was pardoned.

The prison stretch having damaged his credibility in relatively staid Philadelphia, Yerkes decided to move west. He picked Chicago as providing ample opportunities for an ambitious sort like himself. Yerkes was a prickly fellow, and he hadn't been in Chicago long before he got on the wrong side of Joseph Dunlap, the publisher of the *Chicago Dispatch*. In the Chicago press wars the *Dispatch* had won a well-deserved reputation for scandalmongering; Dunlap assigned a reporter to dig into Yerkes's background to find some dirt. The reporter quickly unearthed the fact of Yerkes's prison record and wrote a story revealing it. Dunlap sent the reporter to Yerkes to verify the story and give him a chance to tell his side of the tale. "You're damn right it's true," Yerkes replied, anger giving his voice a threatening edge. "And you tell that God-damned Dunlap that if he ever publishes a line or tells a soul I'll kill him the first time I see him." Dunlap evidently took Yerkes seriously: he decided to kill the story rather than risk Yerkes's killing him.

Yerkes went into the transportation business. He borrowed funds from some of his Philadelphia friends and purchased a controlling stake in several traction lines serving Chicago. The centerpiece of what soon became a small empire was the North Chicago Street Railway, which linked up with subsidiary lines to give Yerkes the lion's share of the Chicago transportation market. By fair means (replacing horse power with cables and electricity) and foul (watering stock and bribing aldermen), Yerkes earned a fortune and made himself one of the most powerful men in Chicago.

Power bred arrogance. Besides threatening newspaper publishers, Yerkes showed open contempt for his customers. When the unruly behavior of some riders upset him, he closed down the line concerned, forcing everyone in the neighborhood to walk until they learned their lesson not to cross Charles Yerkes. When an associate, noticing overcrowding on his lines, suggested that he add more seats on his lines, Yerkes responded, "Why should I? It's the strap-hangers who pay the dividends."

Like most entrepreneurs doing business in Chicago, Yerkes required the assistance of the city council. He had the money to secure the assistance, and he got it, usually working through Johnny Powers of the Nineteenth Ward. A sketch in the *Chicago Times-Herald* described Powers and the way he operated: "Powers has piloted, either openly or covertly, nearly every boodle ordinance in the city council since the embodiment of the pernicious influence that has dictated municipal legislation for many years. In the Nineteenth, Mr. Powers is not called the Prince of Boodlers. He's called the Chief Mourner. The shadow of sympathetic gloom is always about him. He never jokes; he has forgotten how to smile. He never fails to visit the bedside of the dead, nor to distribute Christmas turkeys to the poor. Those who know Powers best will tell you that no meaner miser ever rivalled Shylock. The only way he can get votes is by hypocritical posing as a benefactor filling the role of friend in need when death comes. He has bowed with aldermanic grief at thousands of biers. He is bloodless, personally unattractive. His demeanor is one of timid alertness and anxiety to please, but he is actually autocratic, arrogant, and insolent."

Powers made the ideal match for Yerkes. The alderman was especially useful in keeping down the assessments on Yerkes's property. Yerkes lived in a mansion that boasted a Japanese Room, an Empire Room, a Yellow Room, a palm garden (in Chicago, no less), a private museum containing an art collection that later sold for three quarters of a million dollars, a library, and stables that housed several proven thoroughbreds; with Powers's assistance the property was assessed at $1,337.

Effective though the Yerkes-Powers alliance was, it left something to be desired. The Chicago boodlers had honed their skills to the point where getting anything through the council was maddeningly slow and exorbitantly expensive. Extending a streetcar line required buying council approval on a block-by-block basis. Eventually Yerkes grew frustrated with this retail grafting and decided to go wholesale. He sent his agents to Springfield to deal with the Illinois state legislature. Yerkes's men persuaded a friendly state senator to introduce a measure effectively taking control of matters touching Yerkes's vital interests out of the hands of the Chicago city council and bestowing it on the state legislature.

This end run united both the reform-minded in Chicago, led at this time by Mayor Carter Harrison, Jr., and the boodlers. The reformers recognized Yerkes's maneuver as an attempt to get gold-plated franchise rights, guaranteed far into the future, for a song. (State legislators were known to be willing to sell their votes more cheaply than Chicago aldermen—doubtless from lack of experience.) The reformers argued that the people would be the losers. The boodlers, including Bathhouse John and Hinky Dink, realized that if Yerkes succeeded in cutting them out of the boodling process, others would follow his lead and a major source of their income would dry up.

The combined forces of indignant reform and frightened boodle succeeded in blocking passage of the Yerkes bill. The traction king settled for a diluted version that left control of Chicago's streets in the hands of the city council but streamlined, at least potentially, the process of transferring control to private interests. In effect, the battle between Yerkes and the Coughlin–Kenna–Harrison coalition moved back to Chicago.

Yerkes strengthened his side in the contest by purchasing a Republican newspaper, the *Inter-Ocean*, and luring the sharp-penned George Hinman away from the *New York Sun* to assassinate his opponents in its editorial columns. Hinman immediately began earning his salary. He screamed that the journals of the "Trust Press" were opposing Yerkes because he had refused to pay them their required bribes of $50,000 to remain silent. He lambasted one opposing publisher as a "sanctimonious churchgoer" who nonetheless profited from his stake in two horse tracks. A pair of opposition papers were alleged to be controlled by gambling rings; a rival publisher was said to have sold out to the big banking interests in Chicago; another publisher, who in fact had excoriated Governor Altgeld for pardoning the surviving Haymarket rioters, was characterized as an "anarchist."

Meanwhile Yerkes tempted the members of the city council with offers more lucrative than anything they had ever seen. To those with an interest in mining, he promised contracts to supply coal to his powerhouses; to aldermen connected to the garment trade, he dangled the chance to furnish uniforms to his motormen and conductors; to those with broker friends, he said he'd throw his insurance and real estate business their way. The aldermen—including Bathhouse John and Hinky Dink—listened carefully. Some signed on, others—including Coughlin and Kenna—held out, perhaps to say no, perhaps just angling for a higher payoff.

The contest came to a head when a Yerkes alderman laid a proposal before the city council, granting a fifty-year extension of Yerkes's franchise at steeply reduced rates. Yerkes mobilized all his forces to support the proposal. He had sympathetic aldermen steer the proposed ordinance into committees chosen for their willingness to be bought. He had his allies on the council blow smoke in the faces of opponents by offering complicated amendments that ostensibly raised the rates to be paid by Yerkes to the city but which in fact did almost nothing of the sort. He increased his offer to Bathhouse John and Hinky Dink; reliable reports pegged the offer at $150,000 cash split between the two, generous financial backing at election time, and first option on various lucrative contracts awarded by his company. As additional encouragement to accept the offer, Yerkes's paper, the *Inter-Ocean*, promised a scorched-earth campaign against the Bath and Hinky Dink if they refused. On several pages in each issue, the paper emblazoned a bold-faced warning: "The alderman who votes against a fair ordinance for the street car companies in order to help the Trust Newspapers extort money from the traction companies thereby becomes accessory to blackmail and extortion. His name will be placed in the pillory among those who prostitute their convictions to the interests of blackmailers and corruptionists. The brand of dishonesty and cowardice will be upon him for life!" By way of indicating more precisely what was in store for those who opposed Yerkes, the *Inter-Ocean* ran a story charging Coughlin and Kenna with operating an illegal numbers racket and lording over "a vast illicit empire of 400 opium resorts, 100 gambling dens, 7,000 saloons and other haunts of sin, and over a population which is 18 percent criminal."

All Chicago watched to see whether Bathhouse John and Hinky Dink would succumb to Yerkes's combination of bribes and brickbats. Chicago papers daily carried the story of the fight as front-page material; one paper ran a regular feature: "Bulletins of Franchise War News!" On rumors that Coughlin and Kenna were leaning this way or that, the value of Yerkes's streetcar stocks rose or fell, sometimes by millions of dollars in a day. When the stocks rose, wavering aldermen increased the price they demanded for a favorable vote on the Yerkes ordinance; when the stocks fell, Yerkes and his friends faced the loss of large amounts of money. Neither occurrence placed Yerkes in a very good mood, and both aggravated his belligerency.

As the climactic test of strength approached, Mayor Harrison invited Coughlin and Kenna to his office. "Boys," he said, "now is the time to finish Yerkes. I'm depending on you to help."

The two aldermen kept still, waiting to hear more.

"John, Mike," Harrison went on, "I hope you're going to be loyal to me. I need your help. Your name will be remembered forever if you fight with me."

After a pause, Bathhouse John addressed the mayor. "Mr. Mayor," he said slowly. "I was talkin' a while back with Senator Billy Mason, and he told me, 'Keep clear of the big stuff, John. It's dangerous. You and Mike stick to the small stuff; there's little risk and in the long run it pays a damn sight more.' Mr. Mayor, we're with you. An' we'll do what we can to swing some of the other boys over."

Bedlam descended on City Hall as the council took up the proposed traction ordinance. The gallery was packed, with people sitting two to a seat and standing in the aisles. From the First Ward, Bathhouse John and Hinky Dink had collected some of the toughest characters they could find; their job was to intimidate aldermen wavering in Yerkes's direction. The goons began by shouting abuse at those not clearly on the side of their patrons. In the front row of the gallery, silent but determined, sat an additional dozen unsavory types, each dangling a hangman's noose over the rail.

In the corridor outside the council chambers, a brass band from a German neighborhood blared "The Battle Hymn of the Republic." A news photographer took a picture, the flash of his powder prompted council member "Hot Stove" Jimmy Quinn to joke, "The Dutchies up north just shot an alderman who won't vote on the mayor's side." A Yerkes alderman close by, not sure Quinn was kidding, turned pale and made himself as small a target as possible. One council member declared that Yerkes wasn't paying enough for the privilege of using the public's rights-of-way. "We need all we can get from the traction companies," he declared. Taunters replied from the gallery: "How much are you getting?" When another speaker, Mike McInerney, blasted the anti-Yerkes papers and was met with hisses from the balcony, he shouted back, "I come from a country where only snakes hiss."

Amid further heckling and threatening, the issue reached a vote. By some parliamentary maneuvering, the ground of battle had been shifted to a procedural matter, a motion to suspend the rules and delay consideration of the Yerkes ordinance pending action by the state legislature. If two thirds of the council backed the motion, Yerkes was finished then and there. Various members cast their yeas and nays, with neither side gaining a decisive edge until Bathhouse John's turn came. The Bath rose slowly, gazed this way and that, savored the drama of the moment, waited for silence, drew out the silence, then finally boomed out, "I vote yea!" Hinky Dink immediately jumped up, out of turn, and likewise said, "Yea!"

The gallery exploded. Backers of both sides screamed and stomped their feet: one group in pleasure, the other in rage. Threats continued to rain down; blows were exchanged. Eventually the sergeant-at-arms managed to restore a semblance of order, and the voting proceeded.

The votes of Bathhouse John and Hinky Dink broke the back of Yerkes's support. By the time the last votes were tallied, the procedural motion had fallen short of the two thirds necessary for passage, but it had garnered comfortably more than a majority. This latter fact was crucial, for if this majority could hold together on the substantive vote, Yerkes was beaten.

The majority did hold together. Despite furious eleventh-hour lobbying and some devilishly involved parliamentary intrigue, the Coughlin–Kenna–Harrison coalition carried the day.

The Yerkes fight made Bathhouse John and Hinky Dink more famous— or notorious—than ever among Chicagoans. The backers of the two predicted a brilliant future for their heroes; the Bath was widely spoken of as a candidate for the next mayor of Chicago. On the other hand, the opponents of the two—and even a few of their recent allies—forecast trouble. The *Tribune* guessed that Johnny Powers would exact vengeance. Describing orders Coughlin had customarily introduced to the council granting favors to friends, the *Tribune* asserted, "The word has gone out that every order of this kind he introduces shall be sent to committee, there to be buried."

The Bath and Hinky Dink professed not be worried, and in fact nothing fatal came of Powers's ire. The increased reputation of the two also brought them greater attention from reformers. The Municipal Voters' League had a memory that stretched back beyond the fight against Yerkes, and when Kenna came up for reelection, the reformers announced their opposition. Hinky Dink sighed with relief. "Good," he said. "I'd lose my ward if they supported me."

The Bath briefly became a national figure. As the Democratic Party looked toward the presidential campaign of 1900, the party regulars plotted to withhold the nomination from William Jennings Bryan, the loser of 1896 and an outsider they rightly distrusted as not their kind. In the summer of 1899, Richard Croker summoned the big bosses of the party to Saratoga, New York. John Coughlin represented the Democratic machine of Chicago.

Amid the Vanderbilts and Drexels and the rest of Eastern high society, Bathhouse John—who visited several watering spots besides Saratoga on his grand tour of the East—cut quite a figure. "I'll show them a thing or two in dress reform for the masculine gender," he told a reporter before leaving Chicago. "I want to be strictly original. I think that the Prince of Wales is a lobster anyway in his tastes. He may be all right playing baccarat and putting his coins on the right horses at the races, but when it comes to mapping out style for well-dressed Americans, he's simply a faded two-spot in the big deck of fashion. People have been following his lead because no other guy has the nerve to challenge him for the championship. But I'm out now for first place, and you'll see his percentage drop." (The reporter returned to the offices of the *Times-Herald* and published the conversation under the multiple headline: "Dudes' New King! Hon. John Coughlin to Become a Sartorial Fashion Plate. Buys Elegant Wardrobe. Going to Seaside Resorts to Startle the Eastern Men with His Magnificence." The reporter included his own prediction: "He will pluck a few laurels in the field of fashion and become a 'lily of the valet.' ")

On arrival in the East, Coughlin seemed to devote less time to conferring with his fellow Democratic leaders than to consulting tailors. The newsmen who followed him around recorded each day's dress in detail. "The waistcoat worn by Bathhouse was yellow, with orange spots," one paper related after Coughlin spent an afternoon at a race track. "Miniature conch shells acted as buttons, and to heighten the effect the waistcoat was ballasted with a massive watch chain. The trousers worn with this were a sort of check, somewhat quieter than the coat. However, the alderman might walk up and down the Bay Ridge front on Dewey day and no one would notice the absence of cannon." Coughlin's jacket was described as having sky blue lapels and lining, with vertical stripes "somewhat larger and wider apart than the bars of the Cook County jail." When asked where he stood on the critical issues of the day, Bathhouse replied, "I'm agin' two things. One of them is three studs with full-dress evening suits, and the other is pink shirts with the same. I'm a quiet man, but three studs is worse than heel-and-toeing the last ace out of the box. Two is the limit."

Although Hinky Dink Kenna had long tolerated Coughlin's swellish excesses, upon reading the bulletins from New York he began to think his partner's dazzle might be blinding Croker and the other bosses and distracting them from the political matters at hand. Kenna hopped an eastbound train in order to add his own voice to the caucus.

He got there too late. With the Bath still astonishing reporters, Croker suddenly announced that the bosses could live with Bryan. What kind of deal had been cut, neither side would say. "I have decided that Mr. Bryan would be the best man," Croker declared matter-of-factly. Bryan, when questioned about the matter, stated, "Mr. Croker is a fine man. He never asked me for anything, and I never promised him anything."

IX

Following the caucus, Coughlin and Kenna returned to Chicago, where they lived and prospered for many more years. Too many, in the opinion of the muckrakers who made it their business to uncover the details of the boodlers' business, not only in Chicago but in various other American big cities. Beginning in 1902, *McClure's* carried a series of articles by Lincoln Steffens, later gathered into book form as *The Shame of the Cities*, detailing the activities of the machines run by men like Bathhouse John Coughlin, Hinky Dink Kenna, George Washington Plunkitt, and Richard Croker, as well as the pressure applied by the Charles Yerkeses who existed symbiotically wherever the bosses did.

The revelations of the muckrakers made the bosses a prime target of Progressive reformers. In many cities the Progressives succeeded in ousting the bosses, electing mayors pledged to refrain from even the "honest" graft extolled by Plunkitt, and to clean up the other forms of corruption on which the bosses grew powerful. In several locales the reformers went beyond throwing the rascals out to dismantling the machinery of municipal government that provided the bosses their opportunities for boodling. After a devastating hurricane ripped Galveston, Texas, in the summer of 1900, citizens of that community became disgusted with the inability of the city government to respond effectively and decided to place power in the hands of a commission charged with administering municipal affairs as efficiently as possible. The idea caught on, and during the first two decades of the twentieth century hundreds of other cities adopted this and related new forms of government.

But the Progressive reforms didn't always stick. As Richard Croker had explained to William Stead, the machines arose and persisted because they served a purpose. Life in the big cities was hard, especially for recent immigrants—Jacob Riis's readers knew that. The cities in the 1890s were caught between two eras of American life. They were neither the villages and small towns where people all knew and took care of one another, though many Americans wished they were, nor were they the models of rationality and efficiency the Progressives were trying to make them into. To use another analogy, the cities were a new ecological niche, a tidal zone between past and future. As in biology, where new forms of life flourish in boundary regions, so in the evolution of societies: the urban machines were a societal species peculiarly adapted to the region between the low tide of the preindustrial past and the high tide of the machine age. On this analogy—and on the experience of the 1890s and after—the machines wouldn't simply go away. Where they disappeared, they would have to be replaced by something else.

Chapter 4

BLOOD ON THE WATER

I

While the muckrakers and Progressives identified the city bosses as a principal source of the troubles that afflicted American society during the 1890s, many of the workers who lived in America's cities and towns placed primary responsibility elsewhere—and the responsibility they placed involved crimes considerably more heinous than the misappropriation of public funds. During the summer of 1892, steelworkers in Homestead on the outskirts of Pittsburgh fought a pitched battle against the hired guns of the Carnegie corporation; the fighting left a dozen dead and scores wounded. For years, workers in America's expanding industries had felt increasingly vulnerable to the power wielded by massive corporations like Carnegie's, and as those corporations took advantage of their power during the 1890s the workers resisted, often forcibly.

It wasn't by chance that the decade's first major armed conflict between workers and management happened at Homestead. If Carnegie meant steel in America, Homestead meant Carnegie. The land in the area of the town had originally been granted to Revolutionary War veterans by a cash-strapped but real estate–rich federal government in the 1780s. At the turn of the nineteenth century the two most prominent landowning families in the neighborhood were the Lowreys and the McClures. The latter called their farm the "Homestead," and when subdividing began a few decades later the name stuck.

In 1850, Abdiel McClure sold 150 acres to the city of Pittsburgh for a "poor farm" where able-bodied unfortunates could live and earn their keep while waiting for the local economy to perk up and their chances of finding real work to improve. By 1876, the farm sheltered over two hundred men and one hundred women and brought the city $6,500 from the sale of crops and livestock, in addition to a minor amount of income from clothing the women made.

In 1871, McClure parted with some more of his inheritance. McClure and a neighbor surveyed and divided 230 acres of their property into half-acre and smaller lots; within a short time they unloaded nearly 500 of them. What made the parcels attractive was the imminent arrival of the Pittsburgh, Virginia & Charleston Railroad, which brought Homestead to within thirty minutes of downtown Pittsburgh. The rapid growth of the larger city and of its concentration of smoke-billowing steel mills was driving up property prices and driving out many middle-class residents. Prices in Homestead—around $400 per lot—were considerably more affordable than in Pittsburgh; the air was cleaner and life less harried. By 1873, more than two hundred families had built houses in McClure's subdivision.

Homestead might have gone the way of hundreds of other bedroom communities built during the second half of the nineteenth century if not for the financial crash of 1873. The crash sent real estate prices into free fall, and the hopes of promoters like McClure plummeted with them. For five years, lots in Homestead grew weeds instead of houses.

But McClure's bust was other people's opportunity—the other people in this case being Pittsburgh factory owners who were looking for low-cost land for expansion. In 1872, McClure had rejected the idea of selling lots to industrialists; the whole point of his project (aside from the obvious one of making money) was to provide an alternative to dingy, smelly Pittsburgh. But by the middle of the decade he was far less fastidious about the uses to which his land was put. First came a planing mill, then a brickworks, then a glass factory. By the mid-1880s, the character of Homestead had changed completely. Once a rural getaway from industrialized Pittsburgh, it was fast becoming a smaller replica of the big city. The 1880 census, taken in the year Homestead officially incorporated, tallied slightly less than 600 residents; by the end of the following year, the town's population had tripled; by 1882, it totaled some 3,000. In 1890, Homestead would boast nearly 8,000 souls.

The two biggest employers in Homestead were the Pittsburgh Bessemer Steel Company, which operated a rail mill on the eastern edge of town, and the Bryce Higbee glassworks. At first skilled workmen dominated the Homestead labor landscape. The Bryce Higbee works required a large number of well-trained and experienced glass blowers and pressers. Pittsburgh Bessemer relied less heavily on master craftsmen who had worked their way up the ladder from apprentice and journeyman, but even at the rail mill the men responsible for heating and rolling the rails brought skills to their jobs that couldn't easily be replaced. Consequently workers enjoyed a status in Homestead not too far removed from that of workers in preindustrial communities where guilds constituted a kind of aristocracy of labor.

Yet times were changing, especially in the steel business. New methods of producing and processing steel relied more heavily on technology and less on human expertise. The introduction of the new methods increased worker productivity, in the long run allowing an increase in worker incomes. But the new methods eroded the position of individual workers, erasing the importance of experience and making workers as interchangeable as the steel plates, bars, and rails the modern technology produced. Interchangeable parts came cheap, whether plates or people.

No one introduced new technology more swiftly than Andrew Carnegie, and when Carnegie bought up Pittsburgh Bessemer in 1883, the new technology soon arrived in Homestead. Carnegie shifted the emphasis of the Homestead plant from steel rails to structural steel and armor plate—to meet the demands of growing cities and the U.S. Navy, which was completing its conversion from wooden ships to steel. To boost production and cut costs, Carnegie outfitted Homestead with the latest open-hearth furnaces.

The new furnaces continued the erosion of the status of skilled workers in Homestead, represented chiefly by the Amalgamated Association of Iron and Steel Workers. The Amalgamated had established a chapter in Homestead two years before Carnegie bought in to the community. Initially the union served as much a social as an economic purpose: the lodge halls hosted dances, dinners, weddings, and wakes, and provided members an outlet for those energies left over from the course of workaday life (which weren't all that many or great: steelworkers normally put in an 84-hour week).

But during the 1880s the Amalgamated increasingly focused on pocketbook issues of wages and conditions of work. The same imperatives of competition and personal ambition that drove Carnegie to introduce more-efficient equipment caused him to cut workers' pay and, more important, to undercut the union. The Amalgamated had gone out on strike once before Carnegie bought the Homestead plant; in 1882, Amalgamated workers led a walkout against an effort by the management of Pittsburgh Bessemer to enforce anti-union restrictions as a condition of employment. Strikers picketed the Homestead works and protested the introduction of strikebreakers. When management hired guards to protect the strikebreakers, strikers assaulted the guards, who assaulted back. Within a couple of weeks management gave in, agreeing to forgo the restrictive clauses and accept the union.

Carnegie was tougher than the management of Pittsburgh Bessemer. He was determined to slash costs, and he had no intention of sharing power with his employees. In 1889, he proposed to reduce workers' pay by 25 percent; at the same time he refused to negotiate with the union collectively, offering only individual contracts to workers.

Carnegie was tough but not utterly inflexible. When the union rejected his proposal, he compromised—slightly. He consented to collective bargaining, accepting a three-year extension of the existing contract. And instead of an across-the-board pay cut he allowed wages to be pegged to market conditions. This let workers share in the benefits of bull markets; it also made them share the pain of bear markets.

As matters turned out, the 1889 pact was a truce rather than a treaty. As the 1892 expiration of the contract approached, Carnegie made it clear that his flexibility had limits. Carnegie's second-in-command, Henry Frick, opened talks with the union but soon indicated he wouldn't be disappointed if the talks failed. Frick made an offer that specified sharp cuts in wages; he informed the union representatives they could accept the offer or go to work elsewhere. If they refused the offer, the company would de-recognize the union and deal solely with individual workers.

By the time the June 30 deadline arrived, Carnegie had left the United States on his annual holiday, traveling to his native Scotland. He delegated authority to Frick, although he kept in touch by telegraph. Frick fully shared Carnegie's passion for efficiency; he also shared, not quite as fully, Carnegie's proprietary interest in the outcome of the Homestead negotiations. At the time the confrontation with the Amalgamated union was coming to a head, Frick was working out the details of a merger between two Carnegie businesses that would produce Carnegie Steel Company Ltd. The new firm would be capitalized at $25 million, with Carnegie himself owning just over half the stock, and Frick and Henry Phipps, a Carnegie partner in one of the merging firms, each owning 11 percent. The merger would take effect July 1, 1892, the day after the Homestead contract with Amalgamated expired. It would be a double feather in the cap for Frick, the chairman of the combined corporation, to engineer the merger and to break the union, thereby starting the new company in business unfettered by collective bargaining obligations. Moreover, breaking the union would materially enhance Frick's personal ability to run the new company.

The people of Homestead caught wind of Frick's intentions during the spring of 1892 when he hired carpenters to build a twelve-foot-high fence around three sides of the Homestead plant (the fourth side fronted the Monongahela River). Barbed wire topped the fence and steel gates secured the entrances. Holes periodically broke the solid wall of the fence; they were at about eye level—or, viewed more ominously, about the level of a rifleman's shoulder. Combined with the frowning demeanor of the plant's turreted brick buildings, the fence gave the place the appearance of a fortress. Homestead residents soon named it "Fort Frick."

Frick's fence didn't improve the atmosphere for negotiations; neither did a public rally at which increasingly frustrated workers hanged Frick in effigy. Frick met with workers one last time on June 23. They refused to accept his offer, causing him to break off talks. He announced that the plant would close July 1 and reopen July 6. Individual workers who agreed to the company's terms would be welcome to come back; the union would not be welcome.

For a week an ominous calm blanketed Homestead. Workers watched—and helped—the company increase its already large inventories, knowing that this was ammunition that would be used against them. They hoarded what pay they could, uncertain when they might be paid again. The Amalgamated union hastily signed up as many new members as possible; it doubled its rolls, albeit to only about a fifth of the Carnegie workforce at Homestead.

The distinction between members and nonmembers largely disappeared when the nonunion steelworkers chose overwhelmingly to support the union in a walkout. The strikers elected a committee to coordinate their boycott as well as to keep order and serve as what amounted to de facto government in a nascent workers' commonwealth. As one of its first actions, the committee issued a statement announcing the formation of a militia consisting of the entire striking workforce and devoted to the task of "watching the plant." The force of four thousand was to be organized into three divisions, which would be responsible for three daily eight-hour watches. The three division commanders each would be assisted by eight captains drawn from the eight local lodges of the Amalgamated union. The captains would report half-hourly to strike headquarters and would assume personal responsibility for the key locations around the plant and town: the plant gates, the railway stations, the water pumps, and the riverfront. A network of messengers would allow rapid communication between strike headquarters and the guard units; no point in the community or surrounding area would be more than ten minutes from headquarters. In addition to the militia of the regular workers, an auxiliary force of several hundred day laborers would be held in reserve.

II

Henry Frick was ready for the kind of difficulties his announcement portended, or he thought he was. On June 25, following the suspension of talks with the union representatives, Frick had finalized arrangements with Robert Pinkerton of the well-known—and already notorious—detective agency, calling for the employment of three hundred guards. The guards, in the words of Frick's letter to Pinkerton, would be "for service at our Homestead mills as a measure of precaution against interference with our plan to start operation of the works on July 6th, 1892." Frick downplayed—optimistically or disingenuously—the chances that the Pinkerton men would encounter violence. The only difficulty he anticipated, he said, was an attempt to prevent replacement workers from going to work, and "possibly some demonstration of violence upon the part of those whose places have been filled, or most likely by an element which usually is attracted to such scenes for the purpose of stirring up trouble." Frick said he didn't desire for the Pinkertons to come armed, although he allowed that circumstances might later dictate passing out weapons "for the protection of our employees or property."

The preparations for battle deepened the philosophical rift that separated management from labor. From Frick's point of view, the fundamental question at issue was who owned the Homestead plant. Naturally he thought he and the other shareholders in Carnegie Steel did. As owners they had the right to contract with whomever they chose to work there, on whatever conditions were mutually acceptable to ownership and workers. The conditions specified by the old contract with Amalgamated were no longer acceptable to the company; the company's new conditions were evidently unacceptable to the union. So the company and the union were parting ways. Frick denied charges of a lockout, saying that union members were voluntarily severing their connection with the company. As to the Pinkertons, they were coming simply to protect company property and the rights of workmen who accepted the company's new conditions. Frick placed no faith in the ability or willingness of local law enforcement authorities to safeguard either the plant or the new workers against mobs of strikers. Frick later explained his thinking to a congressional commission: "From past experience, not only with the present sheriff but with all others, we have found that he has been unable to furnish us with a sufficient number of deputies to guard our property and protect the men who were anxious to work on our terms."

The strikers looked on the situation quite differently. They—especially the skilled members of the Amalgamated union—tended to believe that their work at Homestead had given them a certain ownership interest in their jobs. They definitely rejected the notion that Carnegie Steel could summarily dismiss them and replace them with new workers. Carnegie and Frick and the other shareholders might hold legal title to the Homestead plant, but they themselves, having invested much of their lives working there, held a kind of moral title. The legal owners of Carnegie Steel were wealthy men who had property and interests beyond Homestead and in most cases far beyond their needs; the workers at Carnegie Steel had only their jobs. In defending their jobs against the company and against strikebreakers, the workers were defending their way of life. Strikebreakers weren't merely new employees; they were life-stealers. Pinkertons weren't security guards; they were mercenary troops enlisted to abet the thieves.

Like most mercenaries, the Pinkertons were less concerned with the merits of either side's argument than with seeing that they remained in one piece to collect their paychecks. They had no desire to become either heroes or villains. With that negative goal in mind, they intended to approach Homestead behind a veil of secrecy. Frick fully shared their intention. He later explained how the company tried to introduce the watchmen "as quietly as possible." He added, "We hoped to have them enter our works without any interference whatever and without meeting anybody."

It was a vain hope, violently dashed. Robert Pinkerton transported his three hundred men to Ashtabula, Ohio; from there they traveled to Bellevue, Pennsylvania, a few miles downstream from Homestead, arriving on July 5. That evening the men—an assortment of laid-off workers, college students on summer break, criminals between prison stretches, and mercenary regulars—boarded two barges owned by Carnegie Steel and recently outfitted by Frick to accommodate people rather than coal or other bulk products. Curious locals had observed the conversion of the two barges— the *Iron Mountain* and the *Monongahela*—with interest piqued by the knowledge of the impending showdown between the company and the workers. Their interest was piqued further when the trainload of Pinkertons appeared. The strikers' communications network functioned perfectly: the Pinkertons had scarcely detrained in Bellevue before the strike headquarters in Homestead knew where they were and easily guessed where they were headed.

The Carnegie barges put out into the current at midnight, towed behind a pair of tugboats, the *Tide* and the *Little Bill*. A summer fog enveloped the rivers, darkening further an already dark night. About a mile from Homestead, one of the towboats—the *Tide*—developed engine trouble. Its captain transferred his load to the *Little Bill*. Doubly laden, the *Little Bill* struggled against the current, slower than before. Frick had hoped to beat the dawn in landing the Pinkertons at the Homestead works, but the sky already bore bright streaks when the tug and the two barges pulled within sight of the company docks, still most of a mile away.

Union lookouts spotted the flotilla. The chairman of the strike commit-tee, Hugh O'Donnell, gave the warning by sounding a steam whistle. In the early morning grayness the town leaped to life. The worker militia mobilized; women cooked breakfast and enough other food for a day on the barricades; children tagged along to take in the action. Riflemen ran to the riverbank below the town to give the Pinkertons a rousing greeting.

Even before the slow-moving tug and barges were within range, the strik-ers opened fire. Their buckshot fell short; their bullets mostly ricocheted harmlessly off the steel sides of the barges, although a few bullets knocked out some glass in the windows of the tug. The greatest damage was to the spirits of the Pinkertons. Not many of the agents were avid newspaper readers; most had possessed only a vague notion of what they were getting into when they signed on for the Homestead operation. Pinkerton and his subordinates hadn't gone out of their way to enlighten them. Some stray shots earlier had hinted at trouble; now the constant heavy fire from the shore confirmed it. The night had been warm and the barges were stuffy, but to approach a porthole or to venture onto the deck was to provide the strikers an irresistible target. Most chose to sweat it out below.

Until this point the Pinkertons had not been individually armed, although the detective agency transported along with the men a considerable quan-tity of crated rifles and handguns. The orders from Robert Pinkerton were to refrain from any act of aggression and not to resort to weapons unless lives were in danger. With the shots of the strikers rattling the sides of the barges and the enraged shouts of the townspeople echoing across the water, the leaders of the Pinkerton group decided the time had come to break out the firearms.

Not all the agents wanted them. Their view of the shore was limited by their confined situation, but the auditory evidence alone indicated they were vastly outnumbered. Some decided that surrendering and resigning from Pinkerton employ afforded the highest probability of living to earn another paycheck, if perhaps not with that same agency. By contrast, others wanted to be able to shoot back at their persecutors, not wishing to throw them-selves on the mercy of a crowd that sounded singularly short of that quality.

As often in such situations, the predominant mood was confusion. The Pinkertons didn't know how many people the crowd included, how well they were armed, or what their ultimate intentions were. They had hoped that once past the place where the Frick fence touched the river, they would be safe. But the mob had trampled the fence and now occupied the steelworks, thronging the landing site and destroying that hope.

For their part, the strikers didn't know exactly who was on the barges. There were Pinkertons, surely, but there might also be scabs. Scabs might be appealed to as fellow workers and made to see the light of labor solidarity. Than Pinkertons, on the other hand, there was no lower form of life.

One group of the Pinkertons decided to attempt to get off the barges. The captain of the *Little Bill* drove the barges stern-first onto the beach, and a handful of the more intrepid or claustrophobic of the agents threw a gangplank ashore. The leader of the Pinkertons, Frederick Heinde, bravely addressed the crowd, declaring that he and his men were taking control of the steelworks and urging the strikers to leave the premises and go home. The crowd replied with jeers, rocks, and warnings to stay on the barge.

Heinde nonetheless proceeded down the gangplank, backed by half a dozen Pinkertons. A striker physically tried to block his way; when Heinde attempted to push past the striker, the man pulled a revolver and shot Heinde in the thigh. The shot triggered a hail of gunfire from the shore. One bullet caught Heinde again, in the shoulder. Another bullet hit one of Heinde's men in the head, killing him instantly. Four other Pinkertons fell wounded.

From loyalty to their fellows or from a disinclination to be murdered where they sat, several more Pinkertons emerged from the barges and commenced firing into the crowd. At close range and with so many targets, they couldn't miss. Two dozen strikers were hit, two fatally.

With this exchange the situation careened entirely out of control. Strikers blasted the barges with indiscriminate gunfire, causing the Pinkertons who had started to head for the gangplank to scurry back below. Rifle bullets raked the deck and wheelhouse of the *Little Bill*; its captain was reduced to steering the vessel while lying nearly flat on his stomach. The tug took aboard some of the wounded Pinkertons along with the body of one of the dead. Then the captain pulled away from the barges and headed toward Pittsburgh.

This left the rest of the Pinkertons trapped aboard the barges, facing a crowd inflamed by the killing and wounding of their brethren. Opinions on how to treat Frick's hired guns varied from hanging their leaders to roasting them all alive. Cooler heads realized that a massacre wouldn't speak well for the morality of the strikers' claims, but whether cooler heads or hotter would prevail was an open question.

The cooler heads tried to parley with the Pinkertons. Hugh O'Donnell told Charles Nordrum, Heinde's second-in-command, that he was having a hard time holding the strikers back; unless the Pinkertons surrendered at once, a bloodbath might ensue. Nordrum, a Pinkerton veteran, tried to bluff his way out. He announced that the strikers must vacate the company's property at once. Otherwise he and his men would be required to take forcible action. "If your men don't withdraw," he warned, "we will mow every one of you down." The strikers laughed. Nordrum grunted huffily and went back to his barge.

Inside the barges, the level of fear rose with the sun. The almost three hundred agents had little food or water and hardly more air. As the sun grew hotter that July day, the shortage of these necessities became an increasing burden. A group of Pinkertons tried to dash for the bank; rifle bullets felled three at once, then a fourth. The unhit returned to the barge. A few who could swim slipped into the river from the side of the barges away from the strikers and managed to escape to the other bank.

When the captain of the *Little Bill* had grounded the two barges, the *Monongahela* had been closer to shore and more exposed to the workers' fire. As time passed, the Pinkertons aboard found their way to the *Iron Mountain*. This strategy lessened their immediate danger, but it exacerbated the conditions of heat and crowding that were making the agents' situation intolerable.

The workers did their best to make it still worse. By midmorning, news of the fight at Homestead had spread all around the area; armed men from nearby communities joined the Homestead strikers in protest of management's highhandedness. Some of the workers commandeered small boats and harassed the Pinkertons from the water, at the same time interdicting the swimmers' line of retreat. Others found dynamite and lobbed sticks at the *Iron Mountain*. Those bits of explosive that hit the sides of the vessel did little damage; those that landed on the deck did more. All wreaked havoc on the now nearly nonexistent morale of the Pinkertons. Defiance vanished; the agents wanted only to get off whole and not bleeding too badly.

The mob on the shore wanted no such thing. Relatives and friends of those killed or wounded by Pinkerton bullets demanded revenge; many sought to make an example of the mercenaries as a means of deterring others from following their lead. Once during the morning some of the Pinkertons showed a white flag; it merely provoked a renewed salvo of gunfire. A desperate agent dove into the river when the strikers on the boats weren't watching and struck out for the north bank; either because he wasn't a strong swimmer to begin with or because the trials of the night and day had weakened him, he drowned midstream.

About noon a group of workers brought up a cannon, liberated from the G.A.R. hall in the neighboring community of Braddock. Some artillery officers who fondly remembered their days in Lincoln's army loaded and fired the gun. One shot punctured the deck of the *Iron Mountain*, but others bounced more or less harmlessly off the sides of the barge. The cannoneers kept up their fire until a wild shot decapitated a striker; then they called it off.

Another group of strikers tried to fry the Pinkertons. Operating a hand pump upstream from the barges, they poured hundreds of gallons of oil onto the water. As the oil drifted down in the direction of the Pinkertons, the workers attempted to set it afire. But the slick wouldn't catch, and the effort merely created a huge mess in the river.

Then the strikers seized a raft, intending to convert it into a blazing ram. They piled it high with oil-soaked combustibles, torched it, and pushed it toward the *Iron Mountain*. This time the current was what frustrated the arson. The roaring raft approached the barge but just missed, burning itself out as it disappeared downstream.

Next the strikers tried a land-based version of the same idea. They loaded a railcar with whatever they could find that was intensely flammable and started it down a siding in the direction of the barges. The Pinkertons— those who had the nerve to look—watched with horror as this infernal vehicle gained speed in its approach. The burning car hurtled off the end of the track and flew through the air—only to fall short of the Pinkertons' redoubt and come to a sucking halt in the soft, wet earth of the riverbank.

For the strikers and their supporters, the effort to destroy the barges had taken on the atmosphere of a circus. (The better educated of the Pinkertons might have thought of a Roman circus with themselves as Christians and the strikers as the lions.) Each new idea for destroying the invaders elicited cheers, each failure groans. Loud applause greeted an attempt to blow up the barges with a cloud of natural gas. The strikers opened a valve that shot the gas in the direction of the barges; then, dipping into a stockpile left over from Independence Day celebrations, they fired incendiary rockets into the cloud. The gas ignited with a roar, but there wasn't enough and what there was wasn't sufficiently close to the barges to accomplish any major damage. For the Pinkertons, however, a hellish fate seemed that much closer.

This assault exhausted the ingenuity of the strikers for a time; anyway they were getting hungry, and it was time to break for the midday meal. Women and children brought food to those on the front lines. All picnicked while they plotted what to do next. The Pinkertons continued to stew inside the barges.

In the early afternoon, the Pinkertons' hopes rose momentarily. The tug *Little Bill* was spotted moving slowly up the river; if it could reach the *Iron Mountain*, it might pull the agents to safety. But the sight of the tug simply spurred the strikers to renewed efforts. As the captain testified afterward, "We were met with heavy volleys from both sides of the river, particularly the Homestead side, and from behind entrenchments. The firing was so heavy the pilot and engineer were compelled to stop the boat, which drifted around at the mercy of the mob, which continued firing." The boat floated out of range of most of the riflemen, allowing those on board to raise their heads and look around. The sight was terrifying, as the captain related. "The shore was lined with thousands on the Homestead side, and a good number on the opposite side, all of whom seemed bent on destroying our lives." The captain found particularly distressing the strikers' continued fire at men already hit. "I have never heard or read of any such inhuman action as that of this mob, or a part of it, in shooting at wounded men and doing it with fiendish delight."

The delight, such as it was, gradually diminished. By mid-afternoon, everyone could see that the Pinkertons posed no threat to the strikers; the only question was whether the strikers would let them surrender or insist on their blood. A few militants still wanted blood; these advocated storming the barges. But July's afternoon torpor was setting in and people were beginning to wander back to their houses. Most were willing to call the day a victory.

For the first time, Hugh O'Donnell and the strike committee believed they could recommend moderation and not lose control of the situation to hard-liners and what O'Donnell himself afterward characterized as "the rabble." The strike chairman walked from headquarters to the waterfront to address the crowd still milling around there. Arguing that the workers must not let the newspapers portray the situation in Homestead as anarchy, he declared that the Pinkertons must be allowed to surrender in peace. Too many lives had been lost already.

O'Donnell's plea came a bit too soon. From several directions voices insisted that no quarter be given. The blood of the slain workers called out for vengeance. O'Donnell, afraid to press his case lest the strike committee deplete its credibility, retired to headquarters.

An hour or so later, the strike chairman received reinforcements in the persons of the regular elected leadership of the Amalgamated union. The reinforcements helped, but not a lot. President William Weihe rose to speak to an open air meeting of a thousand workers; hard-liners hollered him down. President-elect William Garland tried next. Climbing atop some machinery in the yard of one of the plant buildings, Garland sympathized with the workers who had lost loved ones to the Pinkertons or been hit themselves. "These men have killed your comrades," he said. "But it can do no good to kill more of them." The crowd ignored him. "For God's sake, be reasonable," he implored; the reaction was the same.

Amalgamated vice president G. N. McEvoy offered another argument for moderation. "This day you have won a victory such as was never before known in the history of struggles between capital and labor," McEvoy said. "But if you do not let these men go the militia will be sent here and you will lose all you have gained." Some of the workers thought McEvoy might have a point; while they could deal with Pinkertons, they would have a much harder time against trained soldiers. Yet somebody shouted a scurrilous epithet and the incipient moderation evaporated. McEvoy was forced to sit down; the crowd coagulated into clots of angry fist-shakers.

The strike committee and the union officials then tried another approach. Recruiting like-minded men, they circulated among the workers and reasoned with them quietly. The Pinkertons and the owners had learned a lesson, they said. The American people had been alerted to the plight—and the courage—of the steelworkers. (By now afternoon papers all over the eastern half of the country were carrying accounts of the Battle of Homestead.) This positive sentiment would vanish if the retribution handed out to the Pinkertons exceeded what most people thought they deserved. Determination and magnanimity made a powerful combination; having demonstrated their determination, the workers now must show their magnanimity.

Gradually these arguments took effect. After about an hour, O'Donnell was sufficiently encouraged to try them out on the crowd as a whole. He proposed a cease-fire and a promise of safe conduct out of town for the Pinkertons. He said he would carry these terms to the barges under a flag of truce.

Some workers still resisted, saying the Pinkertons ought to come to the strikers under a truce flag rather than the other way around. One person urged that the Pinkertons be handed over to the sheriff and charged with murder; others remarked in response that the law wasn't likely to take sides against management in a labor dispute.

While O'Donnell was trying to figure out how to deal with this lingering stubbornness, the Pinkertons solved his problem. Most had been ready to surrender for several hours, but some of the leaders had opposed the idea. Now almost all wanted off the barges and off Pinkerton's payroll. With O'Donnell fumbling for a riposte to the latest hard-line objections, the Pinkertons once more waved a white flag. This time no one shot up the flag, which seemed a positive sign. O'Donnell hurried down the slope and across the gangplank. He spoke to a captain of the agents and discussed terms of surrender. The captain wanted assurances that his men wouldn't be molested and, speaking for his employer, requested permission to collect the Winchester rifles the men had been issued. These would be recrated and sent back to Pinkerton headquarters. O'Donnell accepted the terms and relayed them to the strikers.

Initially it was unclear whether the deal would hold. Scores of well-armed strikers pushed onto the barges and surrounded the Pinkertons. One by one the agents emerged on deck and turned over their handguns. Though most tried to put on brave faces, it was a daunting scene that confronted them: more than a thousand angry strikers and supporters who until an hour before had been cheering efforts aimed at the gruesome destruction of the Pinkertons. At least then the Pinkertons had been armed and sheltered inside the barge; now they were unarmed and fully exposed. But for the moment the worst of their fears remained unrealized. Some received rude cuffs, yet all made it ashore without serious injury.

Once the barges were emptied of their prisoners, the crowd vented its anger on the vessels. An incendiary crew boarded, splashed oil all around, and struck a match. Within minutes the two barges were roaring infernos; in hardly more than an hour they had burned to the waterline. The fire spread to a pumphouse on the bank, causing brief concern that the whole steel plant would go up in flames. But the pumphouse burned itself out with no further extension of the conflagration.

The Pinkertons made their way a few hundred yards up the slope before the union officers lost their grip on the crowd. Blows from fists gave way to rocks and sticks. O'Donnell later admitted that the Pinkertons received "very inhuman treatment" as they struggled up the hill. Nearly all were beaten and kicked, some beyond consciousness. One young agent, seeing what was happening to those in the line ahead of him, decided to make a break for safety after a striker identified him—apparently inaccurately—as the triggerman in the deaths of two strikers earlier in the day. He described his attempt to get free: "I ran down a side street and ran through a yard. I ran about half a mile, I suppose, but was rather weak and had had nothing to eat or drink. My legs gave out. I couldn't run any further. Some man got hold of me by the back of my coat, and about twenty or thirty men came up and kicked me and pounded me with stones. I had no control of myself then. I thought I was about gone and commenced to scream." Luckily, some of the strikers O'Donnell and the committee had designated to keep order came to the young man's rescue.

At least two men died as a result of the ordeal; dozens required hospitalization; scores were battered and bruised. The Pinkertons gained a temporary refuge in the town theater where O'Donnell's men stood guard while awaiting a special train quickly hired by Frick to transport the Pinkertons to Pittsburgh. At times the theater seemed hardly safer than the barges had been; many workers still howled for the heads of all the agents. Moderates eventually quelled talk of mass summary executions, but they had greater difficulty dissuading those who wanted drumhead trials and exemplary hangings of at least a few of the Pinkertons. The argument raged on until well after dark.

By then, however, the strikers had been on full alert for eighteen hours, and they were getting tired. One by one they headed home. When the train Frick sent arrived just after midnight, no one seriously contested the Pinkertons' departure.

The day's toll of casualties included at least a dozen dead, about evenly divided between strikers and Pinkertons; sixty wounded by gunfire, more strikers than Pinkertons; and at least one hundred Pinkertons beaten.

The strikers claimed a moral and tactical victory. They had defended their right to work under reasonable conditions of dignity and security, and they had frustrated the efforts of the Carnegie management to make the mill safe for scab labor.

Strategically, though, the Battle of Homestead proved a defeat. The local sheriff had stood aside during the fighting, unwilling to provoke the strikers and unable to find deputies to step into the line of fire. But the Pennsylvania governor, Robert Pattison, felt required to act when the news of the conflict made the national papers. The *New York Times* castigated the strikers for vigilantism and "mob law"; editors elsewhere echoed the theme and called for a return to order. The chief justice of the Pennsylvania supreme court described the Homestead action as labor terrorism. "It was not a cry of 'bread or blood' from famished lips or an ebullition of angry passions from a sudden outrage or provocation. It was a deliberate attempt of men without a grievance to wrest from others their lawfully acquired property." The chief justice went on to say that the Homestead crowd was guilty of "treason"—specifically, of "levying war against the State."

Under enormous political pressure, not all of which was necessary, Pattison ordered units of the Pennsylvania militia to Homestead to impose and enforce order. The militia met almost no resistance from the strikers, since the union leadership wished to salvage what respectability it still retained and the unrulies didn't desire to take on the eight thousand trained soldiers who arrived on July 12. Pattison conspicuously leased a house near the Carnegie plant and pledged to live there as long as necessary to restore calm. In addition, he promised to empty the Pennsylvania treasury if such was required to keep the soldiers in Homestead until the workers learned to obey the laws of the state.

Some labor officials complained that Pennsylvania was coming down too hard on the workers. Samuel Gompers of the American Federation of Labor, of which the Amalgamated union was a part, challenged the governor's right to call out the militia under present circumstances.

But the Amalgamated leadership was relieved to let the soldiers carry the burden of preventing a revolution in the steelyards, and it was generally content to see the struggle against the Carnegie corporation contained within the normal channels of labor activism. The union organized sympathy walkouts at other Carnegie mills in Pittsburgh and down the Ohio River at Beaver Falls. An Amalgamated representative in Beaver Falls pledged that he and his fellows would stay off the job until Henry Frick consented to re-recognize Amalgamated as the bargaining agent of the workers at Homestead.

Frick flatly refused. Moreover, he threatened to use the sympathy strikes as a reason for breaking the union at the other plants. Meanwhile the company advertised for workers to fill the slots of the Homestead strikers. A company poster announced: "It is our desire to retain in our service all of our old employees whose past records are satisfactory and who did not take part in the attempts which have been made to interfere with our right to manage our business." The notice went on to say that employees who declined to return to work by the evening of July 21 would be considered as having no desire to reenter Carnegie employment. "The positions which they held will be given to other men."

Workers—a smattering of old hands, more new—slowly came in. By July 16, nearly two hundred were at work; more arrived daily. With justified confidence, Frick wrote to a friend at the Illinois Steel Company, "I am pretty well pleased with the situation." To another correspondent, he said, "You can rest assured that we propose to manage our own business as we think proper and right."

Frick's confidence, although not his physical well-being, strengthened further on July 23. That afternoon a young man posing as a representative of a New York employment agency entered Frick's office. The Carnegie chairman might ordinarily have referred the visitor to a subordinate, but at this time hiring for the Homestead plant was a priority. He instructed his office boy to show the young man in.

Had the visitor arrived a few minutes earlier he would have found Frick alone. As it was, the company chairman was speaking with his assistant, John Leishman. Frick started to rise as the visitor entered but stepped back when he saw the young man pull a pistol. The gunman fired once, with the bullet nicking Frick's left ear before entering his neck and passing down between his shoulders. As Frick fell, twisting, the intruder fired again, hitting the chairman in the right side of the neck.

Before the assassin could pull the trigger a third time, Leishman leaped at him and knocked the gun awry. The weapon went off, missing its target, and Leishman and the man grappled desperately. Frick pulled himself off the floor, bleeding badly, and helped Leishman wrestle the intruder down. Frick's effort aided Leishman but opened Frick to another attack: the man slipped a hidden dagger out of a pocket and stabbed Frick three times, once in the hip, once just above the kidney, and a third time in the leg. Despite the additional wounds, Frick helped Leishman pin the attacker to the carpet until clerks alarmed by the noise of the gunshots and the scuffling entered the room and overpowered the young man.

The attacker turned out to be a self-professed anarchist named Alexander Berkman. He had been born in Russia and emigrated to the United States at the age of nineteen in 1886. He found few friends, even among his fellow radicals, and he embarked on a lonely career of saving the world by means of the destruction of government and other institutions of power. Fortunately for the Amalgamated union and organized labor generally, no one could discover any connections between Berkman and labor unions; he simply seemed to be taking the opportunity, while Frick was in the news, to strike a blow against a leading figure of American capitalism.

Frick played the attack for all it was worth. With considerable strength of will yet also with an eye toward what kind of image he would project, he put on the stiffest of upper lips. He let it be known that while his loyal and outraged subordinates had been prepared to do the assailant in on the spot of the attack, he had insisted that the law be allowed to take its course. Even as the doctors were trying to stop his bleeding he arranged for his wife, ailing since a recent difficult childbirth (on the day of the Homestead battle), to be notified of the attack in a way that would minimize her distress. To his elderly mother, already immobilized by the news of the Homestead riot, he dictated a terse cable: "Was shot twice but not dangerously." To Andrew Carnegie in Scotland, he wired: "There is no necessity for you to come home. I am still in shape to fight the battle out." He refused anesthesia when the doctors probed for the bullets; he wished to assist in finding the lead.

Frick rested for an hour after the removal of the bullets, then returned to his desk to complete the day's work. Before being carried home by ambulance, he issued a statement to the press declaring that the attempted assassination would not change the attitude of Carnegie Steel. He added, "I do not think I shall die, but whether I do or not the Company will pursue the same policy and it will win." The next morning he put out another statement, this one to the new workers at Homestead, assuring them that "in no case and under no circumstances" would a single new hire be discharged to make room for an old worker. In other words: no quarter to the union, no amnesty for strikers.

On August 3, Frick suffered through the death of his newborn son, Henry Junior. The steel chairman took time to bury his namesake and comfort his wife; then, on August 5, he arose early, walked alone to the streetcar stop near his home, and rode unguarded to his office. Visibly back on his ordinary routine, he sat down at his desk promptly at eight and called for the mail.

The wheels of justice ground fairly quickly for Alexander Berkman, who was shortly tried, convicted, and sentenced to twenty-one years in the state penitentiary for assault with intent to kill, and one year in the state workhouse for carrying concealed weapons. After serving thirteen years in prison, Berkman was released in 1905. Some of Frick's friends worried that Berkman might again attempt to kill him, but Berkman showed no interest in such an endeavor and Frick showed no intention of fretting about the possibility. Yet Berkman remained on the minds of law enforcement authorities, and in the anti-radical roundup of 1919—the so-called Palmer raids, ordered by Attorney General A. Mitchell Palmer—Berkman was arrested and deported. One hour before his ship was to leave New York, he received word that Henry Frick had just died of natural causes. Berkman remarked, "Anyhow, he left the country before I did."

The Homestead strike probably would have ended the way it did even without Frick's heroics, although editors wouldn't have had such fun making double plays on the term "man of steel." With the Pennsylvania national guard protecting the Homestead strikebreakers, with a Republican administration keeping watch in Washington, and with the mood of the country—or at least those groups in the country most influential in shaping public policy—strongly set against labor violence, the Homestead strike gradually crumbled. The sympathy walkouts collapsed under the weight of Frick's reprisal threat and slack employment prospects in the steel belt, and with each passing week additional hands signed on at Homestead. By the end of August nearly two thousand workers were manning the works there.

Apparent sabotage—and murder—failed to prevent the strikebreakers from taking employment at Homestead. In August a man named Hugh Dempsey, an officer in the radical Knights of Labor, paid some accomplices to put poison in soup and coffee served to workers in the Homestead plant. That, at any rate, was what Dempsey was subsequently charged with and convicted of. The poison—said to be arsenic and antimony mixed with croton oil—was the evident cause of several sudden deaths and numerous illnesses suffered by employees at the plant.

As with the Berkman assassination attempt, nothing linked the poisonings to the Amalgamated union, but these too provoked a conservative reaction that made the union's efforts at public education more difficult. By the end of September, operations at the Homestead plant were almost back to normal, and the threat of violence had so dissipated that Governor Pattison felt able to recall the militia. The last troops left in mid-October. A month later, the local leadership of the union conceded defeat and released members from their obligation to honor the strike.

To the Carnegie Company's way of thinking, the strike had been costly but worth the expense. Frick wrote Carnegie, "I never want to go through another such fight"; he added, "We had to teach our employees a lesson, and we have taught them one that they will never forget."

Nor did the company forget. It blacklisted the members of the union's strike committee and effectively barred them from work in the steel industry for the rest of their lives. Hugh O'Donnell eventually had to leave Homestead to try to find other employment; for a while he managed an itinerant vaudeville company, then drifted into other ventures. Frank Bell, one of the leaders of the first group attacking the Pinkerton barges, stayed in Homestead but went into barbering. John McLuckie, who was charged with murder in the assault on the Pinkertons, won acquittal yet might as well have been convicted, for all the good the verdict did in clearing his name in Pennsylvania. Unable to find steady work as far as the writ of Carnegie ran, McLuckie wandered south and west, ultimately winding up in Mexico, where he found a new wife and a new life.

The backfiring effects of the strike went beyond the principals. Carnegie Steel used the Homestead affair as the occasion for a concerted campaign of union-busting; from the summer of 1892 it adopted an unstated but effective policy of hiring only nonunion workers. Carnegie's competitors followed suit. Within a year the Amalgamated union had lost ten thousand members throughout the iron and steel industry. Membership declined further during the depression of the 1890s. Occasionally workers banded together to voice grievances; the typical consequence of such temerity was summary dismissal. As one despondent worker told a public opinion surveyor a few years later, "If a man wants to talk in Homestead, he talks to himself."

IV

The Homestead strike taught a number of lessons to those willing to extract edification from its failure; of these a primary one was that unions enrolling only the skilled workers in an industry would often lack the heft necessary to offset the enormous and still-growing size and power of the largest corporations. Two philosophies of organization informed the labor movement in America (and in other industrial nations), and gave rise to two different kinds of unions. Trade unions were relatively small and exclusive; they drew their membership from a well-paid and hard-to-replace elite of the working class. They tended to be relatively conservative, accepting the division of society into workers and owners, and concentrated chiefly on bettering the already comparatively good condition of their members. They resisted agitation designed to exacerbate class struggles, and their members often felt almost as far removed from the unskilled workers who formed the bulk of the industrial labor force as the owners and managers did. The foremost institutional proponent and prime beneficiary of the trade union philosophy of labor organization was the American Federation of Labor.

Industrial unions, by contrast, embraced all workers within an industry regardless of skills or job descriptions. Industrial unions were big and often rowdy, drawing from the bottom as well as the top of the labor pool. The agendas of the industrial unions were as political as they were economic, and their politics were usually radical. They refused to accept the status quo in property relations as immutable. Workers were workers and capitalists were capitalists—for now. As the class struggle intensified, things might change. During the late nineteenth century, various organizations waved the banner of industrial unionism. The Knights of Labor was most prominent in the late 1870s and 1880s before declining after the Haymarket riot of 1886; the United Mine Workers was established in Ohio in 1890 and quickly spread throughout the coal fields of the East and Midwest. But the depression of the 1890s dealt industrial unionism a series of crippling blows, and the movement never really recovered until the emergence of the Congress of Industrial Organizations in the 1930s.

Industrial unionism's lack of success during the 1890s wasn't for want of trying, and no industry saw greater efforts by the industrial unionists than the railroads. In 1893, a group of railway workers met at Chicago to establish the American Railway Union. As a deliberate contrast to several preexisting railway brotherhoods, which embodied the trade union principle, the A.R.U. opened its rolls to all white employees of railroad companies who weren't part of management. (The color bar set limits on the inclusiveness of even industrial unions.) To join the A.R.U., workers didn't actually have to work on trains; longshoremen and coal miners who worked for railroad companies qualified. So did employees of companies that operated railroads as a sideline.

The guiding light of the A.R.U. was Eugene Debs. Thirty-eight years old at the time of the A.R.U.'s founding, Debs had been born and raised in Indiana. He quit school at fourteen to take a job as a railroad-car cleaner, then as a car painter, and eventually as a locomotive fireman. Subsequently he left railway work and went into state politics. But he found politics in the age of Grant disgusting, and he turned to union organizing instead. He became a charter member of the Brotherhood of Locomotive Firemen and editor of the group's journal. Though he remained active in the brotherhood for more than a decade, he grew increasingly impatient with the narrowness of its concerns and the fact that its leadership spent more time worrying about what the other brotherhoods were doing than about the welfare of railway laborers generally. It was this impatience that led Debs to break from the brotherhood and help found the A.R.U.

Debs was a striking individual, although physically unimposing. His hair left him early, as did sharp eyesight. But neither his baldness nor his myopia prevented people who encountered him from appreciating the strength and warmth of his character. Clarence Darrow, the labor lawyer, later remarked of Debs, "He was the bravest man that I ever knew. He never felt fear." Darrow added, "There may have lived some time, somewhere, a kindlier, gentler, more generous man that Eugene Debs, but I have never known him."

Under Debs's direction, the A.R.U. got off to a fast start. Despite the opposition of the railroad brotherhoods, it quickly began enrolling members by the thousands. The A.R.U. received some unintentional assistance from the Great Northern Railroad just ten months after the union's founding. Great Northern president James Hill, like many corporate chief executives, responded to the onset of the depression in the 1890s by slashing wages. Hill's workers, led by A.R.U. members, resisted the cuts and walked off the job. For eighteen days the strikers stayed out; with the A.R.U. enforcing good order and discipline, the strike remained peaceful. Following unsuccessful negotiations with management, Debs and the union consented to submit their grievances to arbitration. A panel consisting chiefly of businessmen from Minneapolis and St. Paul agreed that the workers were getting a rotten deal; the panel ordered Hill and Great Northern to boost pay a total of more than $145,000 per month. This stunning success for the new union caused membership to soar faster than ever. During the year after its founding it enrolled more than 150,000 members.

The victory in the Great Northern strike spawned imitation. In the spring of 1894, workers at the Pullman Palace Car Company called for Debs to lead them off the job. The town of Pullman adjoined the southern edge of Chicago; it had been founded by George Pullman in 1880 as the site for the manufacture of his special railroad sleeping cars. Prior to Pullman, overnight travelers on trains had had to make do with their ordinary coach seats or with rough bunks built as an afterthought into coach cars. This hadn't been a huge hardship in the early days of American railroading when tracks didn't extend very far and journeys of more than twenty-four hours were uncommon. But by the final third of the nineteenth century, as railroads stretched into the vast reaches of the West, passengers became increasingly appreciative of better accommodations.

Pullman produced his first cars in 1858; they met indifferent success and he became discouraged. But following a fling with gold mining during the rush to Pike's Peak, he tried again. His new model, the Pioneer, was wider and taller than his first—so much so, in fact, that it didn't fit bridges and station platforms then in use. Yet it was the latest in luxury, and Pullman was convinced the world would beat a path to his door—or at least would widen and raise railway bridges and platforms.

Pullman got his big break when John Wilkes Booth shot Abraham Lincoln and the Chicago & Alton Railroad determined to carry the body back to Illinois in finest style. This meant the Pullman Pioneer. The railroad hurriedly made the changes necessary to accommodate the car along the funeral route. Other railroads didn't desire to be seen as lacking concern for the comfort and safety of their riders; when General Grant traveled home to Galena after the Civil War, the Michigan Central Railroad made similar provisions along its line for Grant's Pullman. Before long all the major roads did likewise.

Pullman rapidly expanded production to meet rising demand. In the process the company acquired other companies, some of which not only built or modified cars but also owned and operated railroad lines. As the expansion progressed, the Pullman Company found itself operating production and repair facilities scattered about the Middle West; in order to consolidate affairs, Pullman decided to build a new plant from scratch in the suburbs of Chicago. To provide housing for the plant's workers, the company decided to build a town to go with it.

The town of Pullman was patterned after industrial model towns in Europe, including the Krupp community at Essen in Germany and Sir Titus Salt's Saltaire in England. As the Pullman Company described the new town in literature distributed to visitors, Pullman was adorned with "bright beds of flowers and green velvety stretches of lawn"; it was "shaded with trees and dotted with parks and pretty water vistas and glimpses here and there of artistic sweeps of landscape gardening." It was a place "where all that is ugly and discordant and demoralizing is eliminated, and all that inspires to self-respect is generously provided." Pullman illustrated the best in modern industrial relations: "the helpful combination of Capital and Labor without strife or stratification, upon the lines of mutual recognition."

The reality of Pullman was something else. The company owned all the land and buildings in the town; it was at once employer and landlord for five thousand workers and their families. The company collected rent, provided water and gas and sewage disposal, and ran a subscription library. The green lawns and tree-shaded gardens were for impressing visitors; workers lived in tenements much like those found in ordinary industrial towns across the country. Several families commonly shared a single toilet and water faucet; high rents required families to accept lodgers, crowding things further.

But life was hard for workers everywhere, and until 1893 those at Pullman didn't complain more than most. In the year the big depression began, however, the Pullman Company curtailed production and slashed wages. Pay cuts between September 1893 and May 1894 averaged 25 to 40 percent. Workers noted bitterly that during this period the company did not decrease dividends or the salaries of management. In fact, during the year from August 1, 1893, to July 31, 1894, though wages fell from $7.2 million to $4.5 million, dividends actually rose from $2.5 million to $2.9 million.

What hurt still more was that the company refused to reduce rents even as it cut wages. Management held that the company's actions as employer were distinct from those as landlord—despite the fact that the company gave preference in hiring to its own tenants, with the result that workers couldn't move out of company housing without jeopardizing their jobs. During slack periods such as the winter of 1893–94, it wasn't unusual for deductions for rent and utilities to leave workers with mere pennies at the end of each month. To feed and clothe a family on the leftovers was impossible.

By the spring of 1894, the workers had had enough. They formed a grievance committee, which demanded restoration of wage scales to those of the previous summer, and they requested a meeting with George Pullman. Pullman agreed to the meeting, which took place on May 9, but he didn't agree to the rollback of wage reductions. Pullman pleaded low prices and lack of work as an explanation of the wage cuts; he avowed that the company was losing money on production even as matters stood. He went on to say he was insisting on keeping the shops open, despite the company's losses, lest the workers lose their paychecks and their families suffer. The grievance committee expressed skepticism at this claim of unselfishness. The skepticism increased the next day when Pullman laid off three members of the committee.

These layoffs, which violated a pledge Pullman had made not to retaliate against committee members, unleashed months and years of pent-up resentment. Delegates from each of the nineteen local chapters of the A.R.U. met in an emergency secret session on the night of Thursday, May 10; the angry conference lasted until dawn, with the delegates voting unanimously to lead their locals out on strike on Saturday.

A management spy tipped Pullman off to the plan. He responded by deciding to preempt the strikers; he would send them home at noon Friday and lock the plant gates. A union spy in turn tipped off the strike leaders to the impending lockout; they passed word on the shop floors that the strike would begin immediately. It did, and by the time the lockout was set to begin, the shops were already empty and quiet. The union notified Pullman of the workers' demands: reinstatement of the three committeemen, reduction of rents, and restoration of wages.

After the experience of Homestead, the Pullman strikers recognized that while violence might be momentarily satisfying, it would prove counterproductive in the long run. The strike committee conducted daily meetings with workers and their families, stressing the need to maintain peace and order. The workers themselves posted guards around the Pullman plant to prevent damage to company buildings or equipment. For one week, then two, then a month, then two months, the town was tense but quiet.

Meanwhile strike relief committees collected and distributed food and clothing to the hardest-hit families. The A.R.U.'s general membership supported the Pullman strikers by a three-cent-per-day levy on each employed worker. Sympathetic bystanders helped as well, donating money and food.

Even some businessmen gave food, and the *Chicago Daily News* allowed the use of part of its warehouse for storing strike relief supplies.

Like the strikers, George Pullman also tried to avert violence. The company chose to leave its plant idle rather than bring in strikebreakers—a relatively painless decision in light of the depression-induced lack of orders for Pullman cars. Management saw no need to provoke a confrontation; it relied on hunger and destitution to wear the strikers down.

The strike elicited a flurry of national attention at first, but as the weeks passed without violence it gradually faded from the news. Attention revived, however, when the A.R.U. held its annual convention in Chicago in June. Militants among the delegates from the 465 locals advocated strong action against Pullman. Debs, a pacifist by nature (a nature that would earn him a prison term during World War I) and a tactical moderate, cautioned against aggravating the situation. In light of the fact that the national press was mostly conservative, anything approaching violence would jeopardize public support for the union. Better to let Pullman damn himself by his intransigence than let the press damn the union for tossing a few rocks. Besides, the A.R.U. was young and inexperienced. To take on more than it could handle would help neither the Pullman strikers nor railway workers at large. Debs recommended arbitration, and the A.R.U. membership went along.

George Pullman refused the union's overtures, saying he couldn't in conscience submit the affairs of the Pullman Company to outside arbitration. "Arbitration always implies acquiescence in the decision of the arbitrator, whether favorable or adverse," he declared. "How could I, as president of the Pullman company, consent to agree that if any body of men not concerned with the interests of the company's shareholders should, as arbitrators, for any reason seeming good to them so decree, I would open the shops, employ workmen at wages greater than their work could be sold for, and continue this ruinous policy indefinitely; or be accused of a breach of faith?"

Pullman's refusal to arbitrate, if only as a public relations measure, struck even some of his fellow Republican capitalists as foolish. Mark Hanna of Ohio, already grooming William McKinley for the presidency, sent McKinley's brother to Chicago to try to talk sense into Pullman. When the mission failed and Pullman still refused, Hanna burst out, "The damned idiot ought to arbitrate, arbitrate, arbitrate! What for God's sake does he think he is doing?" Hanna went on to say, "A man who won't meet his men halfway is a God-damned fool."

Yet Pullman's refusal to arbitrate also undercut Debs and added cogency to the arguments of the militants in the union. On June 21, the A.R.U. as a body voted to give Pullman an ultimatum: Meet with employees and talk or face a nationwide boycott of Pullman cars.

This ultimatum represented a signal escalation in the Pullman battle. Until now the quarrel had produced only a local stoppage; by threatening action against Pullman across the country, the A.R.U. raised the prospect of a broad-gauged disruption of America's transportation system.

Just as the other A.R.U. locals had come to the aid of their Pullman brothers, so did George Pullman's fellow railroad managers rally to his defense. The General Managers' Association had been founded in 1886 as the capitalists' counterpart to the railway unions; with headquarters in Chicago, the G.M.A. embraced as members the leaders of the twenty-four lines operating out of that city. The companies affiliated with the G.M.A. ran 40,000 miles of road, employed 220,000 workers, and had assets of over $2 billion. The association functioned as a lobby for railroad interests, seeking to secure passage of favorable legislation; but above all it served as a vehicle for opposing the influence of railway unions.

In the Pullman case, the G.M.A. took charge of the fight against the A.R.U. The day before the union's boycott of Pullman cars was scheduled to go into effect, the association declared its intention to resist the boycott, and it ordered the firing of any employee who refused to handle Pullman cars. This quickly converted the boycott into a strike, since whenever a company dismissed a switchman, for instance, for cutting out Pullman cars, the switchman's co-workers walked off the job in solidarity.

Within hours rail traffic out of Chicago slowed to a standstill; within days the paralysis spread across the West and South. Debs appealed to railwaymen throughout the nation to support their comrades at Pullman. "The struggle with the Pullman Company has developed into a contest between the producing classes and the money power of the country," Debs declared. "We stand upon the ground that the workingmen are entitled to a just proportion of the proceeds of their labor. This the Pullman company denied them." Debs decried the way in which the company had reduced workers' pay until they were hopelessly in debt to the heartless corporation. Now the G.M.A. had sided with the company's chief and pledged to "stand by him in his devilish work of starving his employees to death." The A.R.U. would not retreat. "The American Railway Union accepted the gage of war, and thus the contest is now on between the railway corporations united solidly upon the one hand and the labor forces upon the other."

Debs overstated the case. Although A.R.U. members throughout the country supported the strike and boycott, some other unions didn't. Debs issued special pleas for assistance to the major railway brotherhoods, to the American Federation of Labor, and to the United Mine Workers. Only the mineworkers promised full cooperation. The rest ignored the pleas, mumbled evasions, or flatly rejected Debs's request.

Other groups looked even less favorably on the rail stoppage. Many newpaper editors adopted the view that the Pullman workers had legitimate grievances against the Pullman management but that Debs and the A.R.U. had gone too far in trying to paralyze the nation's rail system. "While the boycott is ostensibly declared as a demonstration of sympathy in behalf of the strikers in the Pullman shops," the *New York Times* said, "it in reality will be a struggle between the greatest and most powerful railroad labor organization and the entire railroad capital." In such a major battle the interests of the country as a whole would run a sorry second. *Harper's Weekly* depicted the boycott in blunter language: "The brigand who demands ransom for his prisoner, with mutilation or death as the alternative; the police captain who sells for money his power to arrest the dealers in vice and crime; the news-monger who gathers scandal in order that he may be paid for suppressing it—these are the types of blackmailers whom all the world loathes. The boycott ordered by the railway union is morally no better than any of these acts. It is an attempt at blackmail on the largest scale."

V

With the opinion of the proper classes on its side, the managers' association sought the aid of the federal government. The association hired a battery of high-powered lawyers to figure out what laws the A.R.U. and its members might be breaking; the lawyers filed an appeal with the U.S. Justice Department charging the union with interference with interstate commerce and delivery of the mails.

The G.M.A. didn't have to ask twice for help. President Cleveland's attorney general, Richard Olney, was a corporation lawyer with thirty-five years' experience advising management clients. Railroads were Olney's specialty; as well as having advised and defended rail corporations, he sat on the boards of directors of several, including the Atchison; the Chicago, Burlington & Quincy; and the New York Central. By inclination and association, Olney saw the world much as the railroad managers did, and he viewed the A.R.U. boycott as the opening wedge of anarchy. He determined to crush the boycott—and, if necessary or even merely possible, the A.R.U.

The union tried to avoid giving Olney and the government an excuse for intervention, knowing that if the contest became one between the union and the federal government, the union would certainly lose. The American public might—or might not—sympathize with workers against owners; it would almost assuredly not sympathize with workers against the duly constituted forces of law and order. The A.R.U. declared its desire to prevent disruption of mail deliveries, going so far as to offer to operate special trains to carry the mail.

But neither the managers nor Olney especially wanted the mail delivered; they wanted to break the union. The railroad managers went out of their way to ensure that the mails were disrupted, deliberately attaching mailcars to the ends of trains carrying Pullman cars. When the workers sidetracked the Pullman cars, the mails necessarily were delayed. Olney thereupon authorized the U.S. marshal in Chicago, John Arnold, to swear in as many deputies as he required to forcibly forestall any further disruption of mail service. By July 1, Arnold had signed up four hundred special deputies; within a few additional days he enrolled three thousand more. Most of the special deputies were vetted by the managers' association and paid by the railroads. Many were regular employees of the railroads who continued to fulfill their ordinary tasks while adding badges to their work uniforms.

The introduction of the federal officers sparked a storm of protest among those partial to the strikers—and even some complaints among the impartial. The *Chicago Herald* called the deputies "a very low, contemptible set of men"; a reporter for the *Chicago Record* who closely followed the strike stated, "I must say that I saw more deputy sheriffs and deputy marshals drunk than I saw strikers drunk." As the strike continued, the *Record's* correspondent added, "They became aggressive, ran around and made arrests on all sorts of provocations."

The introduction of the federal officers also touched off the first serious violence of the strike. While the deputies were being deployed, someone set fire to a number of freight cars in Chicago. The flames lit the night sky and the smoke drifted across the city, lending plausibility to the managers' charges that anarchy was afoot. The managers naturally blamed the strikers; the union rejected the allegation, asserting the companies had hired the arsonists in order to make the union look bad.

Wherever the blame rested, the destruction of property contributed to an atmosphere conducive to still stronger anti-union measures. The managers requested the federal circuit court in Chicago to issue an injunction prohibiting all persons from interfering with rail traffic, saying that such interference blocked the prompt delivery of mail and unlawfully restrained commerce. The court, with the hearty approval of the Cleveland administration, issued the injunction.

For the A.R.U. to have obeyed the injunction would have amounted to abandoning the strike, which the union had no intention of doing. When Marshal Arnold read the injunction to a crowd of workers outside Chicago, he was hooted down and his deputies jostled. Arnold magnified the incident into incipient revolution and demanded the dispatch of regular army troops. Recounting the affair in a telegram to Olney, the marshal said, "I am unable to disperse the mob, clear the tracks, or arrest the men who are engaged in the acts named, and believe that no force less than the regular troops can procure the passage of the mail trains or enforce the orders of the court." Arnold concluded, "It is my judgment that the troops should be here at the earliest moment."

This message was just what Olney was waiting for. The attorney general relayed the report and recommendation to President Cleveland, who concurred that the time had come to send in the soldiers. On the afternoon of July 3 the president ordered the commander of nearby Fort Sheridan to move all his troops into Chicago.

There was a major difference between this deployment of troops and that which took place during the Homestead strike. In the Homestead case, the troops belonged to the state militia and were ordered into action by the governor. In the Chicago case, they were federal army soldiers dispatched by the president. There was good reason for the difference: Illinois

Governor Altgeld vehemently objected to the use of force against the strikers.

Unlike Governor Pattison of Pennsylvania, Altgeld was no great friend of big business. On the contrary, among business circles Altgeld possessed a reputation as a flaming radical. His 1893 decision to pardon the surviving individuals convicted—wrongly, he believed—in the Haymarket bombing of 1886 convinced many conservatives he was in cahoots with the anarchists. Altgeld consistently took the side of labor in industrial quarrels, which rendered him still more suspect. His objection to Cleveland's deployment of federal troops in the Pullman strike seemed thoroughly in character.

Altgeld challenged both the constitutionality and the prudence of Cleveland's decision. In ordering the troops to Chicago, the president implied that the state government of Illinois was either unable or unwilling to ensure compliance with the law within its borders. Altgeld bridled at the mere thought and told Cleveland as much. "Waiving all questions of courtesy," he wrote the president, "I will say that the State of Illinois is not only ready to take care of itself, but it stands ready to furnish the Federal government any assistance it may need elsewhere. Our military force is ample, and consists of as good soldiers as can be found in the country." The Cleveland administration was acting under a misapprehension in proceeding as though the situation in Chicago or the surrounding area was slipping out of control. Altgeld conceded that the trains weren't running, but this was because the railroad companies couldn't get men to run them, not because they were being obstructed. Newspaper accounts had been wildly exaggerated, in some cases fabricated entire. The Cleveland administration was following the advice of men who had "political and selfish motives for wanting to ignore the State government." Altgeld didn't dispute the supremacy of the federal government, but he reminded Cleveland of the cherished American principle of local self-government. "Federal supremacy and local self-government must go hand in hand," he said, "and to ignore the latter is to do violence to the Constitution." The governor concluded by urging immediate withdrawal of the troops.

Altgeld's protest unleashed a torrent of abuse. The *Chicago Tribune* denounced him violently. "This lying, hypocritical, demagogical, sniveling Governor of Illinois does not want the laws enforced," the *Tribune* asserted. "He is a sympathizer with riot, with violence, with lawlessness and with anarchy. He should be impeached." The *Philadelphia Telegraph* chimed in from a distance: "A sausage-maker from Wurttemberg or some other locality"—Nieder Selters, in fact—"permitted by the strange folly of the people of Illinois to be made governor of that State, has had the insolence to offer a gross and outrageous affront to the President of the United States—an affront more abominable than any indignity since the degradations submitted to by James Buchanan at the hands of the Southern secession." *The Nation* of New York described Altgeld as "boorish, impudent, and ignorant," and added, "It should surprise nobody that

Governor Altgeld of Illinois came to the rescue of Debs and his fellow law-breakers by protesting against the efforts of the federal authorities to restore order in Chicago. He is the executive who pardoned the anarchists out of prison, and it is only natural that he should sympathize with anarchists who have not yet been sent to prison."

Olney and Cleveland ignored Altgeld's protest, and the troops continued to move in. Their arrival triggered an escalation of the violence. With Chicago looking like an armed camp, people began to act as though in a war zone. Since the Panic of 1893, Chicago had become a gathering ground for thousands of homeless, jobless, hopeless individuals. Many had arrived for the Columbian Exposition seeking honest or dishonest work and been stuck there when the sightseers went home. The confrontation between strikers and soldiers promised excitement at least and quite possibly loot.

The excitement initially took the form of Independence Day celebrations that went wild. Large crowds roamed the streets of Chicago on the night of July 4, overturning railroad cars and smashing windows. The goings-on brought out more people the next day; hundreds swarmed over the tracks of the Rock Island Railroad to topple cars and set them afire. A mob of perhaps ten thousand filled the Union Stock Yards and confronted federal troops there. Bayonets were unsheathed and mounted soldiers charged the crowd, fortunately producing only minor injuries. On the evening of July 5 a small fire, apparently deliberately set, grew into a huge conflagration on the grounds of the Columbian Exposition. There was no evidence that strikers had anything to do with the fire, but it was easy for federal officials and the railroad managers to portray the fire as the result of a general condition of chaos the strike had created.

The destruction grew worse the next day. Arsonists used torches to set fire to railcars in the yard of the Illinois Central; water was short and the wind was strong, and the closely grouped cars burned hot and fast. When a company agent shot two rioters, the crowd grew crazier still. As dusk fell, a mob moved into the neighborhood of the Panhandle yards in South Chicago, threatening wholesale havoc. An eyewitness described the event: "From this moving mass of shouting rioters, squads of a dozen or two departed, running toward the yards with fire brands in their hands. They looked in the gloaming like specters, their lighted torches bobbing about like will-o'-the-wisps. Soon from all parts of the yard flames shot up and billows of fire rolled over the cars, covering them with the red glow of destruction. The spectacle was a grand one. . . . Before the cars were fired, those filled with any cargoes were looted. . . . The people were bold, shameless, and eager in their robbery. . . . It was pandemonium let loose, the fire leaping for miles and the men and women dancing with frenzy. It was a mad scene where riot became wanton and men and women became drunk on their excesses."

With the beginning of this real violence—as opposed to the earlier incidents exaggerated by the railroad managers and the Cleveland administration—Altgeld ordered the Illinois state militia to Chicago. On July 7, the state troops tangled with a crowd determined to prevent the clearing of the tracks of the Grand Trunk line near Loomis Street. A special repair train accompanied by the militia was surrounded by thousands of angry rioters, many throwing rocks, a few firing guns. The commander of the state troops ordered the crowd to disperse; when it didn't, he directed his men to load their weapons. Further stoning provoked a bayonet charge, which in turn further enraged the crowd. Several militiamen went down, including one officer. The commander thereupon ordered his soldiers to fire on the crowd. Before they ceased their fire, four rioters lay dead and a score wounded.

The violence and the introduction of military force strained the strike, but still it held. A majority of the twenty-four railroads operating out of Chicago were shut down entirely; the rest ran only a small portion of their normal traffic. Sympathy strikes hampered railroad operations as far away as California. Though the railroad brotherhoods as such refused to aid the A.R.U.—the Brotherhood of Locomotive Firemen went so far as to expel members who took part in the Pullman boycott—many individual brothers backed the strike. Some brotherhood lodges even chose to defect and join the A.R.U.

This support encouraged Debs to raise the stakes. After meeting with officials of other unions in the Chicago area, the A.R.U. leader announced a general strike in the city, to begin July 11 if Pullman still refused to arbitrate.

Pullman did still refuse, but as the day of the general strike approached, a federal grand jury in Chicago indicted Debs and other A.R.U. officers on charges of conspiracy. Just hours before the general strike was to begin, Debs was arrested. Similar indictments, granted on the basis of the July 2 injunction against interfering with the mails and interstate commerce, led to hundreds of arrests across the country. Though Debs was released on $10,000 bond, most of those arrested didn't have access to that kind of money and stayed behind bars. In any case, Debs's freedom was fleeting. Because he refused to desist from strike-related activities, he was arrested again several days later.

The scheduled general strike in Chicago failed to materialize. Debs's arrest deprived the strike of its leader; equally damaging was the refusal of the local trade unions to join the strike. Debs personally asked Samuel Gompers of the American Federation of Labor to cooperate, but Gompers refused. Gompers called the proposed strike "unwise and inexpedient" and encouraged A.R.U. members to go back to work.

With the power of both the army and the court system arrayed against them, and in the absence of solidarity on the part of labor, the strikers wavered. A nationwide strike such as the A.R.U. was attempting required painstaking coordination; Debs had been sending telegrams by the hundreds to locals and supporters in more than half the states. His arrest and the arrests of other union officials shattered this coordination. And with federal and state troops occupying the railyards, guarding strikebreakers, and intimidating strikers, the rank and file found it very difficult to hold out. Gradually workers began to filter back to their jobs, and the trains began to move again. As they did, the morale and solidarity of the strikers slipped further, allowing yet more trains to move.

Debs realized he had lost. He gave up hope of achieving the original goals of the boycott and concentrated on preventing a rout. Using the mayor of Chicago as an emissary, he offered to drop the boycott in exchange for a promise from the managers' association that the strikers wouldn't lose their jobs.

The managers refused. Heady with the power of the federal government on their side, they chose to press their advantage and drive the A.R.U. to the wall. They declared that there would be no amnesty for strikers—not now, not ever.

Debs gamely tried to keep the strike going, looking westward for the strength that was waning in Chicago. "We will win our fight in the West," Debs declared. "There is brawn and energy in the West. Men there are loyal, fraternal and true. When they believe they are right, they all go out and stay out until the fight is over."

The West did hang on longer against the managers and the government than the rest of the country, but the West couldn't sustain the union. Shortly after the managers' latest refusal to talk, Debs was arrested for the second time. Once again the court set bail at $10,000. Although Debs might have raised the money, he recognized that he would probably keep getting arrested as long as he tried to lead the strike, and he decided to stay in jail and press for a speedy trial to test the government's case.

Arrests of other A.R.U. leaders followed, making a continuation of the strike almost impossible. By its liberal—or rather, reactionary—use of the injunction, the government had rendered illegal many acts that formerly had been an accepted part of the give and take of labor-management relations. Simply by advocating that workers leave their jobs, union officials found themselves liable to criminal prosecution. Some unionists complained that it would have been more straightforward to outlaw strikes altogether—but that would have required the approval of Congress, which despite the conservatism in the air wasn't willing to go quite so far. The Cleveland administration's approach had the advantage for conservatives of not requiring the assent of the people's representatives.

After Debs's second arrest, the Pullman Company felt confident enough about the outcome of the contest to unlock the plant gates and resume operations. On July 18, the company advertised for workers. Hiring the requisite number took several days, but by the first part of August the company had its equipment up and running again.

Debs finally decided to give in. From his jail cell he called a convention of the A.R.U. With much of the union's leadership behind bars, only fifty-three delegates answered the call. On August 5, the union announced the end of the rail strike. The strike at Pullman remained technically in effect until September 6, but the company had no difficulty ignoring it.

VI

Debs's trial in federal court began the day before the Pullman strike finally ended. He faced two charges: conspiracy to obstruct interstate commerce and the mail, and contempt of court in violating the injunction against the strike. The contempt hearing started first, with the prosecution contending that while Debs and the A.R.U. leadership might not have physically obstructed trains themselves, they encouraged others to do so, which amounted to the same thing. The defense didn't deny that Debs had directed the strike, but it challenged the right of the court to issue the injunction in the first place. The defense also asserted that the contempt hearing and the conspiracy trial amounted to double jeopardy, since Debs and the others were in effect being tried twice for the same offense. Finally, because the outcome of the contempt hearing was to be decided by a judge and not a jury, the defendants were being deprived of their constitutional right to trial by jury.

The court found the A.R.U. leaders guilty of contempt, which didn't surprise very many people. The judge, William Woods, was known to be conservative; throughout the hearing he showed himself supportive of the prosecution, upholding the government on every point of substance. He sentenced Debs to six months in jail and the other A.R.U. officials to three.

Debs appealed the case, which went to the United States Supreme Court. While the appeal was pending, though, Debs had to begin his sentence; by the time the high court took up the case at the end of March 1895, his term was nearly half over.

Debs's defense team included S. S. Gregory, who had represented the A.R.U. throughout the strike; Lyman Trumbull, an octogenarian liberal who had been a law partner and friend of Abraham Lincoln and later an Illinois supreme court justice and a U.S. senator; and Clarence Darrow, who was on his way to becoming the most celebrated legal advocate of radical causes in America. Until this time Darrow had managed to keep one foot in the world of corporate America, acting as general counsel for the Chicago & Northwestern Railway, but the Pullman strike forced him to choose, and he chose Debs and labor over the Chicago & Northwestern and management.

The defense hammered on what it saw as the capriciousness and unconstitutionality of the anti-strike injunction. Gregory characterized the use of injunctions as subversive of the democratic process and the Bill of Rights. "No more tyrannous and arbitrary government can be devised than the administration of criminal law by a single judge by means of injunction and proceedings in contempt," Gregory declared. "To extend this power generally to criminal cases would be absolutely destructive to liberty and intolerable to a free people. It would be worse than ex post facto legislation. No man could be safe; no limits could be prescribed to the acts which might be forbidden nor the punishment to be inflicted."

Lyman Trumbull denied that Debs and the others had done anything wrong. All they had done, he said, was attempt to persuade the Pullman Company to adopt a reasonable policy toward its employees. The means of persuasion they utilized was entirely legal. "Refusing to work for a railroad is no crime," Trumbull asserted. "And though such action may incidentally delay the mails or interfere with interstate commerce, it being a lawful act and not done for the purpose, it is no offense."

Clarence Darrow disputed prosecution claims that the activities of Debs and the A.R.U. were the cause of the violence and destruction that accompanied the strike. Violence and destruction had occurred; no one could assert otherwise. But the A.R.U. leaders had remained well within the bounds of the law and had not been responsible. "If men could not do lawful acts because violence might possibly or reasonably result, then the most innocent deeds might be crimes," Darrow said. "To make men responsible for the remote consequences of their acts would be to destroy individual liberty and make men slaves." Strikes were deplorable, Darrow conceded. So were the causes of strikes. Until the causes of strikes were eliminated, government must not forcibly preclude strikes, which were a justified form of cooperation by workingmen. "They are not justified because men love social strife and industrial war, but because in the present system of industrial evolution to deprive workingmen of this power would be to strip and bind them and leave them helpless as the prey of the great and strong."

Opposing Debs, Darrow, and the defense was the government's counsel, led by Richard Olney himself. The attorney general considered this case to be of gravest importance both because it involved the legality of injunctions as measures to prevent or end strikes and because it involved Debs, whom Olney judged to be one of the most dangerous men in America. Nothing the courts might mete out, Olney held, would be sufficient to the crimes Debs had committed. "No punishment he is likely to get, if he is convicted and sentenced on all the pending indictments, will be commensurate with his offense," Olney declared. The attorney general argued that the government possessed triple authority to issue the injunction: first from the Sherman Antitrust Act, which outlawed conspiracies in restraint of trade; second from the government's property interest in the mailbags and related equipment; third from the U.S. Constitution's grant of control over interstate commerce to the federal government. If Debs and the others hadn't personally set fire to boxcars, Olney said, their advocacy of the strike made them responsible for the destruction the strike produced—unless it were the case "that a man can wantonly touch the match to powder and yet be blameless because not rightly realizing the ensuing devastation."

The Supreme Court rendered its decision at the end of May 1895. It found in favor of the government, unanimously upholding the decision of the lower court. The federal government, the high court ruled, did indeed possess the authority to prevent interference with the mails and with interstate commerce, and injunctions were an acceptable means of exercising this authority.

The court's decision heartened the American business classes and discouraged the supporters of labor. The chairman of the legal committee of the railroad managers' association wrote Olney a letter of thanks, saying, "I congratulate you with all my heart on the Debs decision. The Supreme Court seems to agree with you that 'the soil of Illinois is the soil of the United States.'" Governor Altgeld decried the advantage the Supreme Court's decision awarded to management in industrial disputes. The decision, Altgeld said, gave legitimacy to something new in American history: "government by injunction." Unprecedented power now resided with the courts, sometimes with a single judge. "He issues a ukase which he calls an injunction, forbidding whatever he pleases and what the law does not forbid, and thus legislates for himself without limitation and makes things penal which the law does not make penal, makes other things punishable by imprisonment which at law are only punishable by fine, and he deprives men of the right of trial by jury when the law guarantees this right, and he then enforces this ukase in a summary and arbitrary manner by imprisonment, throwing men into prison, not for violating a law, but for being guilty of contempt of court in disregarding one of these injunctions."

Past experience—including a Supreme Court ruling just the previous week overturning a federal income tax—demonstrated that the courts saw eye to eye with American capitalists. "The corrupt money power has its withering finger on every pulse in the land," Altgeld said, "and is destroying the rugged manhood and love of liberty which alone can carry people through a great crisis." Forty years earlier, the slave power had predominated in Washington; now it was the money power. Quoting an antebellum critic of slavery, Altgeld declared of capitalism: "It sits in the White House and legislates in the capitol. Courts of justice are its ministers and legislatures are its lackeys. And the whole machinery of fashionable society is its handmaid."

One of the chief complaints of Altgeld and other critics of government-by-injunction was that it allowed the courts to imprison people juries wouldn't; the other Debs trial, the one on the conspiracy charges, appeared to prove this point. The conspiracy trial opened while the contempt case was still on appeal. Darrow and Gregory managed the defense; Debs was their chief witness. Calmly the A.R.U. leader recounted his role in the boycott and strike, endeavoring to demonstrate that there was nothing conspiratorial about his actions. Far more gripping than Debs's testimony were copies of minutes of meetings of the managers' association that Darrow had obtained by means he wouldn't disclose and which showed that if anyone had been conspiring, it was the managers. So skillfully did Darrow and Gregory conduct the defense and so strong was the case they constructed that George Pullman refused to testify even after being subpoenaed. The judge let this show of contempt pass unchallenged.

Early in February 1895, one of the jurors became ill. Darrow and the defense were eager to push on with the case, convinced they would gain acquittal. The judge, however, suspended the trial, and the district attorney, after a few face-saving delays, quietly dropped the case.

This legal victory for Debs was followed by a more resounding popular triumph that took place upon his release from jail in November 1895. Debs traveled by special train to Chicago, where a crowd of 100,000 cheered him wildly. Debs had entered prison a moderate unionist; he emerged from prison, after heavy reading and reflection, an incipient socialist. He told the gathered crowd that the future of American liberty lay in the hands of American workers, and he called on his listeners to help create a "cooperative commonwealth." He castigated the "money power" that permeated every aspect of American life: the churches, the schools, the state and federal legislatures, the courts. The courts in particular had been corrupted. "If not this," he asserted, "I challenge the world to assign a reason why a judge, under the solemn obligation of an oath to obey the Constitution, should in a temple dedicated to justice, stab the Magna Charta of American liberty to death in the interest of corporations, that labor might be disrobed of its inalienable rights and those who advocated its claim to justice imprisoned as if they were felons." Debs took courage from the overwhelming enthusiasm that greeted his return to free society, for it signified that redemption was nearer at hand than before. "It means that American lovers of liberty are setting in operation forces to rescue their constitutional liberties from the grasp of monopoly and its mercenary hirelings. It means that the people are aroused in view of impending perils and that agitation, organization and unification are to be the future battle cries of men who will not part with their birthrights."

VII

The strikes staged by the Homestead steelmen and Debs's railway workers were one sort of dramatic labor action during the 1890s; another was a march on Washington orchestrated by Jacob Coxey during the spring of 1894. Coxey was thirty-nine years old in 1894 and a native of central Pennsylvania. His father had been an engineer in an iron-rolling mill; the son joined the father in the mill at the age of sixteen. Jake was a bright, enterprising lad, and he worked his way quickly up the ranks, himself becoming an engineer (that is, an operator of steam engines) by the age of twenty-four.

But Coxey preferred managing his own business to working for someone else, and when an uncle offered him a chance to become a partner in a scrap metal firm, he took it. A business trip carried him to Massillon, Ohio, in 1881; he was so smitten by the region that he decided to relocate. A month later he bought a farm near Massillon and a small and hitherto not very profitable sandstone quarry. Coxey improved the quarry, added a crushing works, and soon began producing specialty sands for the steel, pottery, and glass industries. An engaging individual and a persuasive salesman, he expanded operations throughout the upper Ohio Valley. By the mid-1880s he had achieved a comfortable standard of living; by 1890 a small fortune. He enlarged his house; he built stables; he purchased several racehorses. The horses ran on tracks across the country, and though they didn't always make Coxey money, neither did they cost him more than he could afford.

But crushing stone and racing horses occupied only part of Coxey's mind, and not the more inquisitive, philosophical part. From his early years he had sampled different religions; he found none that met his needs, yet he never became so discouraged as to cease searching. He was still looking during the summer of 1893 when he met a man in Chicago who changed his life. Coxey had gone to Chicago to see the Columbian Exposition and to attend a meeting of free silver supporters, among which he included himself. Silverites from all over America were there. The South and Rocky Mountains were most heavily represented, but the person who created the greatest sensation was Carl Browne, a tall, broad-shouldered Californian. Browne stepped off the train wearing a buckskin suit and a sombrero cocked low on the right side of his head. "Coming, as I do, from the western frontier," he declaimed, "I wear the garb of the frontiersman." He also spoke the language of the frontiersman—or his best imitation thereof. Browne had had plenty of practice imitating one thing and another. An Illinoisan by birth, he had been a painter, a sculptor, a rancher, a farmer, a journalist, a politician, a cartoonist, and a patent medicine salesman. For the last couple of years he had been touring the country promoting free silver. His voice rivaled that of William Jennings Bryan for power and stamina; one afternoon in Nebraska he spoke for three hours outdoors in the teeth of a howling windstorm. In Chicago the weather was less challenging and on his best day there he held forth for five hours.

Browne's advertised topic was silver, but what really interested Jacob Coxey was the thinking of the Californian on reincarnation. Browne was a Theosophist, and Coxey soon converted. Coxey afterward described his conversion: "I felt within a craving and a longing on the subject of religion which the churches seemed entirely unable to satisfy. There were many undefined beliefs in my mind which I was unable to concentrate into any concrete form, and when Carl Browne explained to me his theories of reincarnation, I knew in a flash that it was what I had been searching for."

Browne immediately gained a power over Coxey that alarmed many of the latter's acquaintances. "Browne is a deep-dyed villain," charged Coxey's former wife—who happened to hold the second mortgage on Coxey's quarry. "He is working for Coxey's money and nothing more." Coxey shrugged off allegations that he had been pulled in by an unscrupulous schemer, likewise dismissing comments that he was a bit daft on reincarnation and related subjects. "It doesn't hurt me to be called a lunatic," he said cheerfully.

Soon Coxey's lunacy, if such it was, took a specific form. For years he had traveled the Midwest on roads that froze in the winter, dissolved into mud during the spring and fall, and disappeared amid clouds of dust in the summer. He believed that America couldn't grow and prosper unless it improved its roads, and he began to agitate quietly for measures designed to effect just such improvement. After the Panic of 1893, his agitation grew louder, for now his road construction ideas offered the bonus of providing jobs for thousands of out-of-work men. In December 1893, he issued *Bulletin No. 1* of his newly established Good Roads Association; this initial number contained a proposal that Congress should appropriate $500 million for road improvement projects. He sent copies of the bulletin to the congressman from his home district in Ohio and to Populist Senator William Peffer of Kansas. Each legislator introduced Coxey's proposal in his respective chamber; in neither the House of Representatives nor the Senate did the bill get anywhere.

One reason for the lack of enthusiasm on Capitol Hill was an inability to figure out where the $500 million would come from. Coxey solved the problem—to his satisfaction at any rate—on New Year's Eve. That night he had a dream, and in the dream he hit upon the idea of issuing non–interest-bearing bonds to finance the roadbuilding. Under this plan the federal government would lend money to the states and localities, which would use the funds to build roads, bridges, schools, libraries, and the like. The program would have two aims: to build what needed building, and to put the unemployed back to work. It was visionary, anticipating what the administration of Franklin Roosevelt would do during the next great depression. But Coxey's contemporaries found it a bit too visionary. Coxey didn't adequately explain who would buy the non-interest bonds or whatever fiscal instruments were used to support them, and the financial markets classed his plan with his views on reincarnation as the product of a warped mind. Because Coxey didn't disguise the fact that the idea came to him in a New Year's dream, more than a few people suggested he go back to bed and sleep it off.

Coxey had kept in touch with Carl Browne since the previous summer, and between the two of them they decided to publicize Coxey's program by a protest march to Washington. *Bulletin No. 3* of the Good Roads Association, issued early in 1894, contained a map of the proposed route from Coxey's farm in Massillon to Washington and announced the starting date as Easter Sunday, March 25. The group would travel under the name "Commonweal of Christ" and would arrive in Washington by May 1.

The march might have consisted solely of Coxey and Browne if a bored reporter for the *Massillon Independent* hadn't seen in the scheme the basis for some colorful copy. The wire services picked up his story, which was repeated in newspapers all across the country. Several of those newspapers then sent their own correspondents to cover the Coxey affair, giving the protest far more publicity than the bulletins of Coxey's Good Roads Association ever could have provided.

As the word spread of what Coxey was up to, letters of support and inquiries for information began flowing in. Some of the letterwriters said they would be at Massillon for the start of the march; others said they would join on the way; still others said they would meet Coxey in Washington. Many indicated that they would bring their friends—lots of friends. One man said he would bring 67 from Indiana; a second promised 1,200 from Chicago; a third 1,500 from Pittsburgh; a fourth 1,000 from Woonsocket, South Dakota (which was more than the population of that town). A Chicagoan named H. B. Clark offered to come with one hundred and fifty baseball players who would raise money by playing exhibitions in communities along the road. Another Chicagoan, Patrick Prendergast, wrote to say he wished he could accompany the marchers, but circumstances prevented it. Prendergast had recently been convicted of the murder of Chicago Mayor Carter Harrison (the father of the associate of Bathhouse John Coughlin and Hinky Dink Kenna); he had an engagement with the gallows he couldn't get out of.

Coxey's neighbors weren't thrilled at the thought of hordes of the unemployed descending on Massillon, but since it seemed that these people were determined to come, they hoped for the success of the march or at least of its start, lest the vagrants hang around. As things happened, only one hundred and twenty-two marchers arrived in time for the Easter departure, and some of these included undercover agents sent by the chief of Pittsburgh's police, anxious to learn about this army that appeared headed his direction.

More important than the number of marchers was the number of journalists. When Coxey's army hit the road, it was accompanied by forty-four representatives of the press: one for every three marchers. If an army marches on its stomach (and Coxey's, like all others, did), its press auxiliary forces march on the news copy they file. From the start, the correspondent camp followers wrote and sent reams of copy, as much as 100,000 words per day. When the army was in the field far from the nearest telegraph office, Western Union would tap into its lines and create a temporary office. At other times, the reporters would crowd the regular telegraph stations and shove their stories into the faces of the operators. One day the army was on the bank of a river opposite a telegraph station; spying a ferry, a group of reporters clambered aboard and asked to be taken across. "Ain't no use going over," the ferryman said. Why not? the reporters asked. "I was up to the telegraph station an hour or two ago," the boatman replied, "when the man got the message saying you fellows was coming and wanted him to telegraph something like 150,000 words." So? the reporters demanded. What did he do? "He went to bed," the ferryman answered, "and told me to tell you'se all he was dying."

This particular press season was otherwise slow, and the reporters' editors called for stories on the dramatic and unusual aspects of the Coxey protest. Participants in the march, especially Carl Browne, helped the reporters oblige. While Coxey provided from his own pocket most of the money for the march, Browne directed its day-to-day management. Browne made himself a center of reporters' attention. He gave countless interviews in which he explained his theology as well as his politics; he told reporters how he considered himself a partial reincarnation of Jesus Christ. (Coxey, perhaps because of his subordinate position as Browne's student in matters of reincarnation, was less ambitious, settling for being a reincarnation of Andrew Jackson.) He held Sunday reincarnation services designed to help people get in touch with their previous selves. On other days he gave army members and inhabitants of the neighborhoods the army passed through instruction regarding the finer points of the currency controversy. Browne turned charge of the army's medical treatment over to one "Cyclone" Kirkland of Pittsburgh, reputed to be a doctor and indisputably an eccentric. Kirkland claimed to be the reincarnation of an Indian chief named Cyclone; besides ministering to the medical needs of the Coxeyites, he served as the army's chief astrologer. He daily passed along signs from the heavens concerning the fate of Coxey's Commonweal army. In nearly all cases the signs were good.

Browne's most eye-catching public relations ploy involved the Great Unknown. The Unknown was a man who had arrived in camp from parts undetermined several days before the army left Massillon. He appeared to be in his mid-thirties, and by his bearing and horsemanship evidently had a military background. Adding to this impression was a limp, presumably the result of a war wound, that made it difficult for him to get around on foot. He spoke with a minor accent—just what kind was hard to tell—and he favored a double-breasted blue overcoat and patent leather boots. When he was named Browne's lieutenant and started to exercise considerable authority in camp, and especially when he began lecturing marchers on the need for the poor to rise up and smite the rich, reporters clamored to learn more about his background. "I am the Great Unknown," he replied, "and the Great Unknown I must remain."

Intensifying the enigma of the Unknown and giving reporters an additional hook to hang stories on was the presence nearby of a mysterious veiled woman. Persons who caught a glimpse beneath the veil said she was a beautiful brunette about thirty years old. Someone claimed to have seen a bruise on her face. Was she the wife of the Great Unknown? He denied it vigorously—too vigorously, some thought.

A further factor contributed to the puzzle of the Great Unknown. Ray Stannard Baker, then a new reporter working out of Chicago, one day surreptitiously saw the Unknown burst into hysterical laughter. The fit didn't last long, and the normally grave Unknown quickly resumed his sober demeanor. Baker wondered what it meant. Was the Unknown playing a huge joke on everyone, perhaps including the trusting Coxey? Baker couldn't say, but he included the incident in his daily dispatch from the line of march.

The conditions of travel during the march's first weeks were difficult though not unfriendly. The spring rains had softened the roads so that the Coxeyites walked ankle-deep in mud. Snow occasionally mixed with the rain to thoroughly chill the marchers, most of whom lacked foul-weather gear. Yet the natives were generally supportive. In Beaver Valley, just across the state line into western Pennsylvania, thirty thousand residents came out on a Sunday to cheer. They also brought fresh provisions, which were even more appreciated than the good wishes.

Some of the friendliness dissipated as the Coxeyites neared Pittsburgh. The steel city still bore bad memories of the Homestead strike, memories the depression had only intensified, and the town fathers looked disapprovingly on the approach of an army of agitators. In the Pittsburgh suburb of Allegheny City, the town constables prevented the marchers from walking through working-class neighborhoods. Later the police arrested two dozen Coxeyites for vagrancy and sentenced them to thirty days in the local workhouse. Within a short time, however, the judge reconsidered; not wishing to incur the expense of feeding the jailed Coxeyites for a month nor desiring to give the rest of the army any excuse to loiter, the judge ordered the convicted released and sent on their way.

Despite the official unwelcome, the common people of Pittsburgh and its vicinity came out in a show of enthusiastic support. Four hundred members of the Iron Moulders' Union marched ahead of the Coxeyites; then came one hundred bicyclists shouting praise for the man who wanted to pave America's roads. Representatives of other labor organizations joined the parade; a band played pieces specially composed for the occasion; bakers sold cookies carrying the message "Coxey" in icing on top.

From Pittsburgh, the army made its way up the Monongahela Valley and into the Allegheny Mountains. The weather turned colder; snow covered the road and an icy wind scoured the passes. Tempers grew short along with the rations. When Coxey absented himself on business, mutinous murmurs were heard among the foot soldiers. A Pittsburgh newspaper printed a story alleging that the Great Unknown was a Pinkerton spy. He denied the charge, but many of the rank and file asked themselves why he was so secretive. What was he hiding? Carl Browne worried that suspicious moonshiners in the hollows on either side of the road would take pot shots at his men. Browne also worried about rumors that the Unknown was plotting a rebellion to overthrow him. For some time the men had grumbled about the fact that Browne helped himself to better rations and softer beds than the rest; the grumbling now turned more serious.

Tension between Browne and the Unknown reached a critical point just across the line into Maryland. While the army was trudging up the flank of Big Savage Mountain, the Unknown rode back to the commissary wagon for a bite to eat. This infuriated Browne, who gave him a tongue-lashing for eating between rest stops while the men had to march hungry. "Don't let me see such a thing again," Browne warned.

The Unknown said nothing at the time and continued eating. A short while later, after muttering to himself over the rebuke, he returned and confronted Browne. "See here, Browne, you fat-faced fake," he said. "This is my bark today; next time I'll bite. Just get it through your head that if you ever try to make another grandstand play around me I'll make a punching bag out of your face." Grabbing Browne by the lapels, he shouted from a distance of six inches: "Confound you! I found you on your uppers in Chicago. I picked you out of the mud. I've the greatest mind to pull you out and show you up before the men right now."

Browne decided to call the Unknown's bluff. He galloped to the head of the line, raised his arm, and commanded, "Commonweal, halt!"

The Unknown accepted the challenge. "Forward, march!" he yelled.

The marchers hesitated between their two leaders. The Unknown, who for the sake of convenience was going by the name of Smith, seized the moment of their hesitation. "Men of the Commonweal!" he called. "You and I have roughed it together. We have fought it out with the winter weather from the Ohio to the Alleghenies, and we have won. You know how I have been with you, working for your comfort, while others were enjoying their ease and you were tired, hungry, wet and cold. It is for you to say, men, who shall command you. I have nothing more to offer. Will you have Smith, who has brought order out of chaos and made the army what it is, or will you follow this leather-coated polecat?"

The challenge hung on the misty air for several seconds. Then a man near the front of the line took off his hat and hurled it into the air. "Hurrah for Smith!" he shouted. Immediately cries of "Smith! Smith! Give us the Unknown!" echoed through the mountain pass.

Smith stood in his saddle. "If you say Smith is to command you, then Smith is to command you," he declared. "Commonweal, attention! Forward!"

Browne spluttered with rage. "This is mutiny!" he screamed. "What do you fellows mean by taking up with this hireling Pinkerton? This man has been written up as one, and I believe it. He's a Pinkerton!"

The Unknown retorted, "That is a falsehood spoken by a coward, and not one of our people will believe it."

Browne countered, "You may lead these men astray if you wish, but I control the commissary wagons, and I shall not proceed."

The Unknown ignored Browne's bluster and ordered a group of men to commandeer the wagons. Since no one listened to Browne, he could only stand by and steam. As the column moved off up the road, Browne headed in the opposite direction, bound for the nearest telegraph office where he intended to cable Coxey the news of the rebellion.

Browne's message reached Coxey at Cumberland, Maryland. Coxey at once hired a carriage and began racing toward Frostburg, the site of the marchers' camp that night. After several hours on the road, he arrived at the camp just at sunrise.

Coxey spoke to the opposing parties in the dispute. Browne told his version of the story; then the Unknown did likewise. Then Coxey talked to his eighteen-year-old son Jesse, who had backed the Unknown. Finally Coxey pulled a box to the center of the Frostburg opera house, which served as overnight headquarters, and called for a vote. All those in favor of the Unknown, he said, should stand up. One hundred fifty-eight men arose, leaving only four men opposed. The Unknown beamed with pride and the confidence of victory. Browne scowled darkly, vowing vengeance.

To everyone's amazement, Coxey declared, "I cast 154 votes for Brother Browne." This knotted the vote, leaving Browne in command. After letting the shock sink in, Coxey added, "I further order that Mr. Smith, the Unknown, be forever expelled from the army."

Before the Unknown could rally the men behind him, Coxey demanded that the Commonweal confirm his decision. Chastened and uncertain who else would feed them, the members of the army did so and voted for the Unknown's ouster. Some complained that if the Unknown had to leave, so should Jesse Coxey for lending the air of his father's authority to the Unknown's coup.

Coxey considered the point for a minute, then agreed. "All right, if Jesse was wrong, he will have to go too."

By this time the Unknown had recovered from his surprise. In a field across the street from the opera house, he denounced Browne once more. "I have been deposed by a patent medicine shark, a greasy-coated hypocrite, a seeker for personal advancement."

Browne, feeling more self-assured now, charged across the street, intending to fight. But Coxey intervened. He pulled Browne back and ordered the Unknown to leave. If he didn't leave, Coxey said, he'd have him arrested.

The Unknown chose to retreat. With a small group of followers, including Jesse Coxey, he left the camp and rode out of town.

To consolidate his victory, Browne held a press conference that evening and revealed the secret of the Unknown's identity. According to Browne's testimony, as augmented by reporters' digging, "Smith" was in fact A. P. B. Bozarro, a patent medicine salesman, an occultist, and the "Wizardo Supreme" of an outfit calling itself the American Patriots, of which he was also the founder. Browne had met him in Chicago, where he had been dressed like an Indian and wore his hair down to his shoulders. Browne and Bozarro had formed a partnership, with the former lecturing on silver and the tariff and reincarnation and the latter hawking a potion to "purify" the blood. After Browne had hooked up with Coxey, he decided to bring Bozarro along to help with the logistics of the march and to keep the reporters interested. (In fact, some of the reporters on the trip had figured out who the Unknown was but declined to leak the story lest their readers lose interest.)

VIII

While Coxey's army was making its way down the Maryland side of the Alleghenies into the Potomac Valley, other contingents of the unemployed, spurred by Coxey's message and example, were moving toward Washington as well. California, the home state of Carl Browne, organized two columns—not including the "Heaven at Hand" army of San Francisco, whose members considered it their divinely ordained duty to topple the Cleveland administration and the rest of the government in Washington. "It is part of our religion to seize the government of the United States," said "General" Stephen Maybell. "It is my intention to march straight to Washington and demand a government for the people and by the people. If we don't get it, we will eject Congress and behead Cleveland." Maybell's proposal was a bit extreme, even for California, and the Heaven-at-Hands never got out of the Bay area.

Another group did. At the beginning of April a crowd of one thousand five hundred unemployed men gathered in San Francisco, determined to travel across the country and meet Coxey's army in Washington for May Day. Obviously they couldn't walk, as Coxey's army was doing; that left the railroads as the only feasible means of transport. The city authorities in San Francisco and Oakland urged the directors of the Southern Pacific to give the group passage out of the region and out of their hair. At first the railroad wanted to charge regular rates, but this was far more than the men could afford. Eventually the company sharply reduced its fare, and the men piled into the cars and headed east.

Trouble developed, however, at the end of the Southern Pacific line in Utah. The Union Pacific, the connecting line, wanted to charge the full coach fare. A standoff ensued. The Union Pacific refused to transport the Coxeyites east; the Southern Pacific refused to take them back west. Meanwhile the government of Utah began to panic, fearing they would stay. Impatiently the men started walking east from Ogden toward the Wyoming line. After several days of bad publicity, the Union Pacific, under pressure from Utah officials, relented and let the Coxeyites ride some empty boxcars at a cut rate.

This time they got to Council Bluffs, Iowa, where the Union Pacific line ended, before they had to figure out their next move. Although most Iowans expressed sympathy for the plight and objectives of the marchers, the managers of the connecting rail lines stood firm against any concessions. The railroad companies had been laid low by the depression and could hardly afford to do any favors; besides, they didn't want to set a pernicious precedent. For a while it appeared that the marchers would be stranded in Council Bluffs. Marchers and supporters from the area held meetings to decide what to do; at one meeting during which denunciations of the arrogant railroad companies were especially vitriolic, a handful of sympathizers having railroad experience talked themselves into stealing a train. They went first to the yards of the Milwaukee and Rock Island line, only to find them locked and empty. While they were scratching their heads, a Union Pacific train pulled in from Omaha. The train-stealers swarmed aboard. First into the cab was a Knights of Labor man, a railroad engineer. He discovered that the engineer driving the train was his father. Father and son stared at each other for a moment; the son broke the silence by saying, "Pop, you are our prisoner." The father cursed the son for stupidity and unfilial disrespect, but turned over control of the train and stomped off.

The new crew drove the train to the camp of the Coxeyites, where they were greeted with loud cheers. However, Charles Kelley, the de facto leader of the marchers, worried that the hijacking would jeopardize the favorable public image of the marchers and provoke government officials into action against the army. After congratulating the hijackers for good intentions, Kelley requested that they take the train back to where they had stolen it. To provide the hijackers an additional reason for honoring his request, he asked that they give rides to several marchers who needed medical attention. The hijackers agreed, though some wondered at Kelley's scruples and questioned how he thought he would guide this army of down-and-outers across the continent if he was going to be so finicky.

A third wing of Coxeyites had no such problems of conscience. Word of Coxey's protest had spread swiftly through the mining towns of the Mountain States, where thousands of men sat idle near the mouths of closed mines. In Butte, Montana, two hundred laid-off miners gathered and decided to join the forces descending on Washington. Direct, no-nonsense types, they responded to a refusal by the Northern Pacific to offer reduced rail rates by heading straight for the Northern Pacific yards on the outskirts of Butte; there they seized and occupied several boxcars. Butte's business leaders pleaded with the Northern Pacific to reconsider and transport this unruly crowd out of Butte and out of Montana. The company refused. The protesters then broke into a roundhouse in the dead of night and stole a locomotive. They headed east at full throttle; by daybreak they had put a hundred miles behind them.

When the Northern Pacific management realized it was missing a train, it placed another one on the track, loaded with a federal marshal and a posse of sixty-five deputies. The chase began. The posse pulled out of Butte while the hijacked train was stopping in Bozeman to refuel and take aboard food furnished by supporters in the town. During their Bozeman stop, the hijackers intercepted a telegraphed report that a landslide had closed the eastern entrance to the Bozeman tunnel, a dozen miles away. Some among them scented a railroad trick; others argued that the line might really be closed. The engineer and crew of the outlaw train pulled slowly toward the tunnel, where they discovered that the reports were accurate. The protesters hefted picks and shovels and fell to the task of removing the mud and rocks. Recent rains had triggered the slide, and the debris that covered the rails still had the consistency of porridge. The more mud they dug, the more oozed down from the mountain. Meanwhile, with each minute that they spent digging, the train carrying the posse closed in on them.

Finally the hijacking engineer could bear the delay no longer. Warning the shovelers to stand aside, he backed the train away from the mud and debris. He got up a head of steam and then came tearing down the track, slamming into the slide and sending rocks and mud flying in all directions. The locomotive's cowcatcher bent violently on impact, but the train plowed forward. When it was halfway through the blockage, the drive wheels of the locomotive began to slip. The engineer pulled the lever that spilled sand onto the rails; with this added purchase the train slithered through. The shovelers clambered aboard, and all continued their race to the east.

When the posse learned that their quarry had escaped the landslide, they connived to create another. The Northern Pacific's division superintendent, J. D. Finn, wired ahead to a work gang, ordering it to dynamite a bluff that overhung the track. The gang did so, but to little effect. When the runaways arrived, they quickly cleared the small amount of dirt and stones from the track and continued on. Finn then directed his men to throw all switches that would force the train onto sidings and to spike the switches so they couldn't be thrown back. He also told his crews to drain all the water tanks along the route; without water, the steam locomotive of the stolen train would be forced to halt.

The tank-draining produced results first. As its water supply ran short, the hijacked train had to slow down. Periodically the protesters were able to replenish the supply from ponds and streams, but each stop to replenish cost precious time.

Just as the train started moving after one such stop, lookouts on the last car spotted a headlamp on the track behind. The posse train had closed to less than a mile and was gaining ground fast. A quick-thinking hijacker spied a bridge ahead and told the engineer to stop when the tail of his train was halfway across. If the posse wanted to make arrests, they'd have to fight their way onto the bridges with the icy Yellowstone River roiling below.

The engineer followed the advice: moments after the hijackers halted, the posse train stopped at the water's edge. Several of the deputies emerged from the cars and aimed rifles at the hijackers. The federal marshal called to the hijackers to surrender or his men would open fire.

The hijackers responded by draping a United States flag and the banner of the Butte Miners' Union over the back of their train. "Fire if you dare!" they taunted.

The deputies had to think this one over. Most had been deputized specially for the chase; they lived in Butte on the same streets as many of the hijackers. Already some were being branded as Pinkertons and mercenaries merely for pursuing the hijackers. If they shed blood and spattered the union flag and Old Glory in the process, they could forget about returning to their homes. Caution got the better of them; they lowered their weapons and returned to their cars.

The hijackers whooped in triumph. They too climbed aboard their cars, and the stolen train moved on. Still short of water, it had to continue to go slowly. The posse train followed at the same speed, keeping a circumspect distance.

The hijackers rolled into Billings, where they were greeted by a delegation of town officials and several hundred well-wishers. The people were in a holiday mood; they invited the Coxeyites to join them for a feast. Famished from the long day's excitement, the hijackers readily assented.

While wolfing down the food the townsfolk provided, the hijackers momentarily grew complacent. The deputies stopped their train on the out-skirts of town and quietly mingled with the crowd. Suddenly two deputies leaped aboard the hijackers' locomotive, sticking the barrels of their hand-guns in the ribs of the hijackers who were supposed to be on guard. One of the latter swore at them: "Shoot and be damned!" When the people in the crowd heard the commotion, everyone began shouting and many started racing toward the engine. The deputies on the ground, seeing their comrades—and themselves—threatened, opened fire. One man was killed; several others were wounded.

The shooting outraged the crowd. Men and women seized rocks, sticks, pipes, and anything else they thought they could crack a head with, and advanced on the deputies. The deputies realized they were in danger of being massacred and raced for cover, most of them heading for a Northern Pacific roundhouse nearby. There they barricaded themselves in while hun-dreds of townsfolk and hijackers milled outside, cursing them loudly and promising to rip them to pieces.

With their pursuers incapacitated for the moment, the Coxeyites steamed up and continued east. They still faced the problem of empty water tanks along the way, but in Billings they had picked up a hose and a pump, which they used to pull water from streams they crossed. With a full water supply and with coal stores replenished in Billings, they flew down the tracks toward the Dakota line.

By now the news of the great railroad chase in Montana had hit the Eastern papers. "Blood Flows from Coxeyism," blared the headline in the *New York Times*; the subhead added, "Battle between Law and Anarchy." Officials of the Cleveland administration, especially Attorney General Ol-ney, considered the safety of the Republic to be at risk. On Olney's urging, Cleveland called out federal troops to intercept the Coxeyite hijackers. The Northern Pacific was more than willing to help; Superintendent Finn sent a special train to Miles City to pick up five hundred soldiers from nearby Fort Keogh.

The troops met the hijackers at Forsyth, Montana, where the latter were refueling and searching for some necessary spare parts. The troop train stopped outside the town, and in the midnight darkness the soldiers crept up and surrounded the hijacked train. They unsheathed their bayonets, and just as the Coxeyites were preparing to pull away, they closed the ring. The hijackers surrendered without a fight. The workers had been willing to tangle with part-time deputies but didn't desire to shoot it out with fully armed regular troops.

The legal authorities now faced the problem of what to do with the prisoners. As far as most observers could tell, the hijackers hadn't violated any federal laws, train-stealing not being a federal offense. Montana offi-cials didn't especially want to hold several hundred men who, in taking on the Northern Pacific, had become instant folk heroes to many Montanans. Besides, the local jails lacked the capacity to handle the hijackers. After the federal judge for Montana conferred with lawyers for the Northern Pacific and proposed to detain the hijackers at least temporarily in a prison in Helena, one Montana editor remarked wryly, "It appears that his disposition of the men is in accordance with the instructions of Northern Pacific attorneys in New York, who, living within easy reach of the Tombs and Blackwell's Island and Sing Sing, evidently have a very high opinion of Helena's prison facilities." It didn't help the Montana government's problem that not long after the hijackers surrendered, a hundred more Coxeyites who had missed the train after an earlier emergency stop arrived at Forsyth and demanded to share their comrades' fate.

Almost as vexing as the question of the prisoners was the question of the deputies. After the anger of the crowd in Billings had cooled, most of the deputies managed to slink out of town. They boarded their train and followed the hijackers east, maintaining a safe separation. When the federal troops surrounded the hijackers, the deputies hurried forward to claim a share of the credit for the capture. But after the Coxeyites were taken into custody, the deputies began to consider how they would effect their reamalgamation into civilian life. Fearing for their safety, they pleaded with the soldiers to guard their train on its way back to Butte. The soldiers, many of whom had reservations of their own about the whole affair, scorned the deputies, as did much of the Montana press. "Seventy-five armed men were never more struck with terror than these deputies are," the *Helena Independent* noted derisively. The soldiers left the deputies to fend for themselves.

IX

The wild events in Montana, together with the troubles of the California Coxeyites in Iowa, provided a backdrop for the final approach of the main column of Coxey's army toward Washington. During the last days of April 1894, the Ohio Coxeyites descended the Potomac Valley to the District of Columbia. On the 29th, they pitched camp at Brightwood Riding Park, approximately seven miles from the Capitol. Finding a campsite hadn't been easy; no one knew how long the unemployed vagabonds would stay, and no one wanted to make an open-ended commitment. The owner of Brightwood park let the protesters pitch camp on his property only as a complaint against the local police, whom he suspected of corruption and who were trying to prevent the Coxeyites from finding quarters.

With but forty-eight hours to go until the time when Jacob Coxey had vowed to speak from the Capitol steps, the Washington press corps, the district's law enforcement officers, and assorted area notables were all in a tizzy. Reporters jammed the camp, wanting to know from Coxey and Carl Browne what their intentions were, and from the rank and file what the highlights and lowlights of the march had been. Police laid plans for stopping what they worried was an incipient revolution. On the door of a district police office hung a sign: "Fe, Fi, Fo, Fight; We Smell the Blood of a Coxeyite." Elected and appointed officials, including senators, congress-men, and members of the Cleveland administration, visited the camp, some to lend moral support, some to register scorn, some simply to gawk. For-eign diplomats, including two members of the Chinese legation in satin robes and braided queues, joined the parade. Although some Populist Party leaders had early distanced themselves from Coxey—Nebraska Senator William Allen called Coxey a man "who, if not a knave, is crazy" and labeled the Coxey movement "absurd and useless"—both Allen and Pop-ulist Senator Peffer of Kansas came out to the camp to offer the marchers their best regards.

The Cleveland administration joined the police in preparing for trouble. Orders went out to the U.S. arsenal at Springfield, Massachusetts, to rush hundreds of new weapons to Washington and to prepare thousands more for shipment. Army troops at the Washington Barracks and Fort Myer were placed on alert; troops in other locations along the East Coast were readied for dispatch to the capital if necessary. At the Navy Yard and the Marine Barracks, sailors and marines drilled with unusual intensity in exercises designed to mimic close-quarters combat.

As the great day approached, the Coxeyites in camp grew restive. Last-minute preparations, not to mention the head-turning effect of all the pub-licity, distracted Coxey and Browne from the daily necessity of feeding the hungry campaigners. On April 30, the marchers went without breakfast and dinner; the only thing that quieted the inevitable grumblings was the late-afternoon arrival of Browne driving a wagon filled with bread.

The next morning shortly, after ten o'clock—and after a soul-strengthening breakfast of eggs, bread, and coffee—Coxey's army began its final march on the Capitol. No one knew what to expect. Coxey had attempted to gain congressional permission to speak from the Capitol steps, to no avail. The police refused to grant a permit to march and indicated their intention to arrest Coxey if the protest leader insisted.

Coxey did insist. He argued that it was his constitutional right to speak and that the Capitol steps were public property. He and his men had marched four hundred miles to carry their message to the legislature; they wouldn't be stopped four miles from their goal.

Coxey slowly led his column into the central part of Washington, moving south along 14th Street. At Pennsylvania Avenue the marchers turned southeast and brought the Capitol into view for the first time. Crowds of bystanders thickened as they approached Capitol Hill. Officials of the Treasury Department who feared a massed attack on the government's supplies of coin and bullion had ordered out special guards; these swarmed around the Treasury building as the Coxeyites passed. Twenty thousand people had gathered at the Capitol to witness what at the least would be a curious spectacle, at the most a bloody battle. Either way it would be worth seeing.

At the head of the procession was Jacob Coxey, riding a carriage with his wife and their small son, Legal Tender Coxey (his real name). Coxey's seventeen-year-old daughter, who, with her mother and brother had traveled from Ohio by train, rode a white charger beside them; the girl was costumed as "the Goddess of Peace." Carl Browne came just behind, on his own horse.

As the column, numbering about four hundred, arrived at the east entrance to the Capitol, Browne called a halt. He and Coxey conferred for a moment, then made their way on foot toward the Capitol steps. A mounted policeman cut them off and told them they couldn't pass. Coxey and Browne dodged the officer, leaped over the low stone wall separating the street from the Capitol grounds, and ran through the crowd toward the steps. Police followed in hot pursuit.

Browne made the easier target, his bulky frame and buckskin outfit standing out among the throng. Yet he was swift for his size, and he darted in and out of the trees and shrubbery. Eventually several policemen hauled him to earth near the southeast corner of the Capitol, trampling the landscaping in the process. Browne resisted arrest with a will—and with the help of a score of spectators who attacked the officers. The police responded by laying all about them with billy clubs. They pummeled Browne and dozens of onlookers, including some women and children, before they succeeded in forcing Browne into a paddy wagon.

During this diversion—evidently planned as such—Coxey slipped through the crowd and onto the Capitol steps. He ascended halfway to the top before a pair of officers darted in front of him and prevented his passage. They asked him his business. He said he wished to make a speech. They said he couldn't. He turned to address the crowd anyway, and the officers began pushing him down the steps. On his way down he threw a written copy of what he would have said to a reporter. The police roughly hustled him back toward his carriage.

The crowd began to chant, "Coxey! Coxey! Coxey!" He climbed onto his carriage and waved acknowledgment of the popular support. After a few brief words, mostly drowned out by the din, he directed his army to retreat. The column marched down from Capitol Hill toward a new campsite a mile away.

The riot at the Capitol had lasted only several minutes. It ended with Carl Browne and one other marcher, a man named Christopher Columbus Jones, in police custody, most of the rest of the army having stood quietly by during the melee. The law enforcement authorities in the federal district unknit their brows, relieved that nothing more serious had happened. Two sympathizers—Elizabeth Haines, a Washington merchant, and Emily Edson Briggs, a major property owner in the capital—posted bond for Browne and Jones. Browne rejoined the army at its new location, a former dump, and received a rousing show of support. For the time being, previous causes of dissatisfaction with Browne were forgotten.

The next morning Coxey accompanied Browne and Jones to police court. There, to his surprise, he was arrested. Along with the two others, he was charged with violating an 1882 statute governing use of the Capitol grounds; in effect, they were being accused of unauthorized parading on the grass.

The actions of the police the day before had elicited ridicule from many observers; now the charge brought against Coxey, Browne, and Jones provoked snorts of scorn. A number of Populist legislators volunteered to assist in the defense of the Coxeyites. When the trial nonetheless went forward and the jury found the trio guilty, the scorn only intensified. The *Omaha World-Herald* caught a common feeling with a blistering editorial: "Every detail of the proceedings was stamped with the effort on the part of the prosecutor to make a mountain out of a mole hill. The crime: Carrying banners on the Capitol grounds! Trespassing on the Grass! Great Caesar— if the several kinds of fools who are managing the anti-Coxey crusade at the national capital were in the employ of Coxey, they could not do him better service than they are doing him today."

A more adept agitator than Coxey might have turned the verdict to his account. Coxey tried to, proclaiming, "This country is like a big bunch of straw, and all that is necessary to start it into a roaring blaze is the torch. Do you dream that in court today the torch was applied?"

It wasn't. Coxey and the two others went to jail, where they stayed for twenty days. The marchers were exhausted after six weeks on the road. Their goal had been to reach Washington, and they had reached it. They had never known what they would do afterward, and still didn't.

More significant, the nation had grown weary of the Coxey story. For a while the Coxey march had offered editors a readymade human interest feature. But after six weeks Coxeyism was old news. "Drop Coxey tonight," Ray Stannard Baker's Chicago editor ordered on the morning after the riot. "Report in Chicago Monday noon." Baker was happy enough to comply. "I bade a joyful farewell to Coxey's army," he remarked later. "I was terribly tired of the whole infernal business. I wrote in all about 75,000 words, a big book, on the subject, and I didn't have much more to say."

The loose ends to the Coxey story required a little longer to tie off. Thousands of Coxeyites were still on the road in the West and Midwest on May 1 when the Washington affair took place. The members of the San Francisco contingent stuck in Iowa had decided that if they couldn't get a train east they would take boats. They hammered together a flotilla of one hundred and forty rude vessels and set sail down the Des Moines River. After a dozen days they reached the Mississippi, where they lashed the small boats into a large raft. With the assistance of friendly tugboat captains, they floated the Mississippi to its junction with the Ohio, then began a tow-ride east up the Ohio. They got past Cincinnati before fatigue, illness, and lack of funds frustrated their efforts. After a journey of more than two thousand miles, the San Francisco column melted away.

In Helena, the Montana wing of Coxey's army was being released from behind bars about this time; the citizens of Montana saw no good reason to pay for the protesters' room and board. The residents of Helena went their state one better—to prevent the area from being burdened with hundreds more jobless, the city purchased a load of lumber and hired a boatbuilder to fashion a fleet to get the Coxeyites out of town. After a week of construction the army set off down the swirling Missouri. The river produced a hair-raising ride but, astonishingly, no casualties. The boats reached St. Louis at the end of July. By this time nearly all the wind had gone out of the Coxeyite sails; happy to be back on solid ground, the Montanans chose to give up their quest.

Other, smaller Coxeyite contingents likewise met discouraging fates. A group of a few hundred stole a train from Portland and barreled east through the Columbia Gorge before being captured on the desert of eastern Oregon. Some Colorado Coxeyites tried floating down the Platte River only to meet disaster in the rushing, spring-swollen waters. At least six drowned. The toll may in fact have been higher, but, Coxeyites being the hard-luckers they were, no one kept very good records. A column from Southern California arrived in Washington in June after a heroic cross-continent trek, only to find the Coxeyites there disbanding.

Carl Browne, following his release from jail, tried to revive interest by announcing a march on Wall Street. Cynics saw this as an attempt to reclaim the limelight—which it surely was. Browne and a few others made it to Manhattan, but no one there paid them any attention.

Coxey returned home to Ohio to run for Congress. If he won, he figured, he could do all the speaking he wanted from the Capitol steps and from inside the building as well. (He lost.) His parting advice to his followers—to get themselves arrested and let the government feed and house them—didn't go down very well. Some of those left behind remained in Washington for want of anything better to do; most gradually gravitated back toward their homes.

Chapter 5

THE MATTER WITH KANSAS

I

While labor unionists and the unemployed were sometimes more violent than others in expressing their dissatisfaction with the American status quo in the 1890s, they were hardly alone in their discontent. Farmers were just as upset. Even before the depression of the 1890s set in, a leading farm journal editor wrote, "There is something radically wrong in our industrial system. There is a screw loose. The wheels have dropped out of balance." This editor continued: "The railroads have never been so prosperous, and yet agriculture languishes. The banks have never done a better or more profitable business, and yet agriculture languishes. Manufacturing enterprises never made more money or were in a more flourishing condition, and yet agriculture languishes. Towns and cities flourish and 'boom' and grow and 'boom,' and yet agriculture languishes. Salaries and fees were never so temptingly high and desirable, and yet agriculture languishes."

Why did agriculture languish? The editor, observing affairs from upland North Carolina, spoke for most farmers when he blamed the "industrial system." For a century farmers had been told by politicians, preachers, and other keepers of the nation's conscience that they were the backbone of the Republic, the salt of the American earth. Thomas Jefferson, gentleman planter, had made a cult figure out of the yeoman farmer. In Jefferson's view, political liberty would survive only as long as the family farm. Land provided men an independent livelihood, rendering them impervious to the dictation of other men; once a man owed his living to another man, the latter could readily command the political actions of the former.

Farmers might have suspected Jefferson of insincerity, of telling farmers what they wanted to hear in exchange for their votes. Most sweat-stained sons of the soil had difficulty identifying with the master of Monticello. Yet Jefferson in fact did more for American farmers than any other president, by acquiring title to Louisiana, thereby doubling the national domain and securing land for the sons and grandsons and great-grandsons of the farmers who cast their ballots for him in 1800 and 1804.

Or maybe it was Abraham Lincoln who did the most for the farmers. Lincoln lifted the blight of slavery from the land, confirmed the dignity of labor, and prevented the development of a permanent Southern aristocracy. White small farmers in the South hadn't cheered Lincoln during the 1860s; they had taken up weapons to oppose the armies he sent to subdue the secessionists. But the defeat of the slaveholders gave the Southern white farmers of modest means a better chance at political and economic power than they had ever had before. Black farmers in the South didn't need to be told of their debt to Lincoln. Farmers in the North had been less concerned about slavery than about the viability of the Union and the availability of land; Lincoln pleased them by holding the Union together and signing into law the Homestead Act, which allowed millions of American families to experience the frontier of open land Frederick Jackson Turner would make so much of.

But about the time of Lincoln's death, farmers began noticing a decline in the respect the country paid them. The new Republicans had always been the party of business more than the party of (Northern) farmers, and as the country tore headlong into the industrial era, businessmen seemed to monopolize America's attention. Everywhere one turned, one read of the latest railroad construction, the latest oil discovery, the latest steel merger, the latest Wall Street corner, the latest electrical invention. The captains of industry and their lieutenants infiltrated the government, delivering money and other favors in exchange for special consideration in the lawmaking process. Wealth became concentrated in the cities, which exerted an irresistible attraction upon the children of the farmers. The tillers of the land, once so honored, now found themselves caught in a cultural backwater.

Nor were the farmers' complaints merely a matter of perceptions. The world really was tilting against them. The most obvious indication of the tilt was the relentless decline of commodity prices in the years after the Civil War. In 1870, wheat sold for $1.06 per bushel; by 1890, it was down to 71 cents; by the mid-1890s, it had dipped below 65 cents. In 1870, corn was 43 cents per bushel; it was 42 cents in 1890 and 30 cents in 1895. Cotton brought 15 cents per pound in 1870, 8 cents in 1890, and 6 cents in 1895.

The falling prices spawned unusual behavior. Corn farmers in Kansas burned their crops for fuel, corn being cheaper than coal. Wheat was left standing in Dakota fields; the cost merely of hauling it to market exceeded the price it would bring there. Hog raisers in Nebraska shot their animals and threw the carcasses into ditches. Regularly farmers' investment in crops was greater than the returns the crops commanded, yet because the farmers needed cash to live on they continued to invest and produce. In doing so they dug themselves deeper into debt.

Farmers complained of the mixed signals they received from government leaders and other figures of authority. Hard work was supposed to be the American way, the path to prosperity, the answer to their problems. But what had hard work brought the farmers? "We were told two years ago to go to work and raise a big crop, that was all we needed," one dissatisfied farmer grumbled. "We went to work and plowed and planted; the rains fell, the sun shone, nature smiled, and we raised the big crop that they told us to; and what came of it? Eight cent corn, ten cent oats, two cent beef, and no price at all for butter and eggs—that's what came of it."

This farmer's remarks indicated one underlying cause of the distress on the land. During the three decades after the Civil War, American farmers raised crops and livestock in unprecedented quantities. The opening of the Great Plains to settlement brought millions of new acres under cultivation; at the same time, the mechanization of American agriculture made farms already in operation far more productive than before. Though the American population also increased during this period as a result of both immigration and a post–Civil War baby boom, the population increased much more slowly than agricultural production. Consequently the nation's commodity markets were buried beneath mountains of wheat, corn, and cotton. American farmers partially alleviated the pain of overproduction by shipping some of their surplus overseas, but similar influences were at work in other parts of the world. By the 1890s, world markets in major commodities groaned under the weight of unrelieved excesses.

Individual farmers were caught in a bind. Agriculture was a highly competitive business; hundreds of thousands of farmers grew wheat for market, hundreds of thousands corn and cotton. No individual farmer exercised more than the most minuscule influence over price levels; as a result, the only way for any one farmer to increase revenues was to increase production. But lots of other farmers had the same idea, with the effect that all the extra production simply drove prices still lower, so that farmers often wound up making less money than before. It was no wonder that farmers spoke of screws loose in the system.

Falling prices were a particular problem for farmers because agriculture was a business that ran on debt. Farmers borrowed money to buy land; they borrowed money to purchase machinery and seed and fertilizer; they borrowed money to pay the laborers who helped with plowing and planting and harvesting. Only after the farmers had borrowed all this money and gathered their crops did they receive any return—namely, the price their crops brought.

As Brooks Adams explained, debtors detested falling prices: falling prices made the debtors work harder to earn the dollars they needed to pay off their debts. Absent the question of debt, farmers during the late nineteenth century had no special cause for complaint about falling prices for the goods they sold, since prices of the goods they purchased were falling even faster. These were the years when Rockefeller and Carnegie were constantly increasing the efficiency of their enterprises, continually driving prices down. As a result, despite the fall in crop prices, the purchasing power of farmers was in fact *increasing*. But the debt question overrode all others, washing out whatever gains the farmers were making relative to the rest of the American people.

Besides, it was easy for farmers to keep track of the price of the one or two crops their livelihoods depended on; it was much harder for them to monitor the prices of the many less consequential goods they purchased in their day-to-day routines. They lived and breathed the price of corn or wheat or cotton; they paid less attention to the price of salt and kerosene and gingham and glass and writing paper.

Other complaints helped convince farmers that the deck of life was stacked against them. Farmers couldn't gather around the stove at the general store or mingle in the churchyard after services on Sunday without cursing the railroads. Most of rural America, especially that portion settled after about 1850, depended on railroads for its existence. The railroads made possible the settlement of huge tracts that had been economically inaccessible before. Farmers were independent-minded folk, and they didn't like to be dependent on others, especially faceless corporations such as the railroads. Neither did they like feeling gouged, and they certainly felt that the railroads were gouging them. Farm commodities traveled to market by rail; in most cases, particularly in the West, a single rail line served any individual community. Farmers either paid the rates the railroad charged or watched their crops rot.

Farmers had little sympathy for the railroads' claims of competitive exigency, and they certainly didn't accept that cutthroat cut-rating in the East justified jacking up rates in the West. When the railroads pointed out that traffic in the West, especially during harvest season, flowed almost entirely one way, and that for every wheat hopper that traveled full from Fargo to Chicago, another had to travel empty from Chicago to Fargo, the farmers dismissed the reasoning as lawyerly sophistry. The farmers asked why they had to pay the entire rate to Chicago even if their cargo was being unloaded at Minneapolis, and why rail rates went up during the winter, coincidentally at the time when ice closed the Great Lakes harbors and eliminated an alternative means of transport.

The sometimes spectacular corruption that characterized railroad operations during the post–Civil War period further confirmed farmers in their belief that the railroad managers were thieves and brigands. Farmers replayed the Crédit Mobilier scandal endlessly, like Civil War veterans waving the bloody shirt, to discredit railroads generally. They cited stock-watering schemes as evidence that the railroads were pulling in far more profits than they were admitting. They pointed to the profligate dispensation of free passes to state and federal legislators, newspaper editors, lawyers, ministers, and judges as proof of the railroads' subversion of the democratic process. "Do they not own the newspapers?" the *Progressive Farmer* of Raleigh, North Carolina, demanded. "Are not all the politicians their dependents? Has not every Judge in the State a free pass in his pocket? Do they not control the best legal talent of the State?"

The identity of the chief corporate villains varied from place to place. In Nebraska, the Burlington and the Union Pacific predominated; in Kansas, it was the Santa Fe. In certain other states, several roads seemed a malign monolith. While the roads fought each other for control of lucrative markets in the East, in the West, where local monopoly was the rule, they presented a common front, most notably against unfriendly regulation (and of course against labor union action). They stood for the sanctity of property rights against legislative meddling, although they didn't object when Congress and the state legislatures voted to subsidize railroad construction. On the contrary, the railroads—both East and West—exercised impressive ingenuity and a mastery of the lobbying arts in squeezing every last nickel from Washington, the state capitals, and local communities hopeful of attracting rail service. They conned towns into entering bidding wars against each other; the losers resented the railroads for their loss, the winners for the tax bills victories produced.

If the railroads protested their devotion to property rights too much, it may have been because they had too much property. So it seemed, at any rate, to millions of farmers who had counted on the Homestead Act and its subsequent corollaries to enable them to acquire free land. The railroads, by virtue of the terms of their construction contracts—these in turn by virtue of their political pull—had become the largest landowners in most of the Western states. Their land was located close to their tracks, which made it the most valuable kind. The railroads were busy trying to sell their land, to convert it to cash. But prospective homesteaders, having been inspired by a vision of free land, objected to being required to *buy* land, certainly at prices dictated by the railroads. A Nebraska editor complained, "Only a little while ago, the people owned this princely domain. Now they are starving for land, starving for an opportunity to labor, starving for the right to create from the soil a subsistence for their wives and little children." The enormous excitement that greeted the opening of Oklahoma attested to this hunger; in Oklahoma, people could still get good land *free*. In most of the rest of the West they had to pay for it, sometimes dearly.

Almost as unpopular as the railroads were the operators of grain elevators and other storage and distribution facilities. The elevator operators were even more dependent on the railroads than the farmers were. Their facilities were usually located on railroad land, and they relied entirely on the railroads for their business. For their own protection, the elevators often formed business alliances with the railroads and stood by them against the assaults of the farmers. Though the elevator companies in theory might have provided the farmers an alternative outlet for their produce, in practice they didn't.

The elevator companies engaged in many of the same monopoly tactics the railroads employed, and they added a few of their own. One standard technique involved the grading of grain. An easy way to lower the price paid out to farmers was to de-grade the wheat the farmers brought in. Grading wheat was a subjective process, and since agents of the elevators did the grading, judgment calls usually went against the farmers. Farmers noticed that graders raised their standards when supplies of wheat were largest; Charles Pillsbury, a leading elevator owner, admitted as much. Pillsbury explained that grading was most liberal at the beginning of the harvest when supplies were tight. Later, as more wheat entered the market and the elevators had greater quantities to select from, grading became more rigorous.

The railroads and the elevators were the large businesses farmers had closest contact with, but the rural view of big business didn't improve with distance. Farmers constantly complained that they were victimized by the trusts that were coming to dominate numerous industries. Cattle ranchers decried the beef trust; cotton farmers excoriated the cottonseed oil trust; corn growers (among others) blasted the fertilizer trust; farmers at large (and many nonfarmers) lambasted the money trust. In some cases the trusts identified were figments of fevered imaginations: an Iowa editor wrote of 400 trusts menacing the American people—about 380 more than had any meaningful existence. Yet it was indeed true that farmers (and other consumers) were coming up short in their dealings with the sizable number of corporations that had succeeded by one means or other in shielding their operations from competition.

Farmers also complained about the protective tariff. Again, they shared their grievance with other consumers; yet the farmers, among all consumers, took particular umbrage at the tariff. In the first place, although some urban workers—those in protected industries—benefited from a high tariff, almost no farmers did. Second, farmers found it especially onerous to buy what they had to buy on a protected and therefore noncompetitive market while being forced to sell what they had to sell on an unprotected and consequently competitive market. As *The Nation*—hardly a mouthpiece of the farmers' movement—put it, farmers were "the victims of a system of free-trade selling and protected purchasing."

Added atop all the farmers' other complaints was the currency question. Being debtors, farmers suffered from the deflation that was the result of the American economy growing faster than the American money supply. Farmers desired, and increasingly demanded, various measures to reflate the currency, including the issuing of more paper money and especially the remonetization of silver. But control of the money supply remained in the hands of the Eastern establishments that dominated each major political party, and those Eastern establishments remained wedded to gold. While gold served the interests of bankers and other creditors, it was crushing farmers; yet farmers weren't able to do anything to ease their pain.

The problems the farmers complained of weren't new in the 1890s. Some—the problem of the trusts, for instance—were more acute than before, but most of the problems had been around for a decade or longer. Prior to the 1890s, however, farmers could always take comfort in the fact that if things got *really* bad they could pick up stakes and move west, there to start over again. Now, with the passing of the frontier, that option was quickly vanishing. Retreat was becoming impossible; if farmers were to survive, they would have to stand and fight.

II

Among some precocious farmers the fight had already started. Two years after the end of the Civil War, a Minnesotan named Oliver Kelley organized the National Grange of the Patrons of Husbandry. Initially stressing social and educational matters—square dances, barn raisings, lectures—the Grangers soon began branching out into economic and political affairs. They set up cooperative purchasing and marketing organizations and lobbied for regulation of railroads and grain elevators. The cooperatives achieved modest success, and the lobbying efforts paid off in Midwestern state laws that set maximum railroad and elevator rates. Though bitterly attacked by the railroads, elevators, and businesses generally, the Granger laws received the definitive seal of approval when the Supreme Court in the 1877 case of *Munn* v. *Illinois* upheld the principle that states could regulate private businesses invested with a significant public interest.

The Grangers gave rise to the Farmers' Alliance, a more overtly political organization. The Farmers' Alliance was actually several alliances, of which the two most important were the National Farmers' Alliance and the National Farmers' Alliance and Industrial Union. The former was based in the upper Mississippi Valley and was commonly called the Northern Alliance; the latter was strongest in the South and was called the Southern Alliance.

The Northern Alliance got its start in the late 1870s in either Kansas or upstate New York, depending on whether Kansans or New Yorkers were to be believed. The rival claims notwithstanding, the Northern Alliance didn't pick up momentum until the early 1880s when the editor of a Chicago farm journal, the *Western Rural*, took a personal interest in the organization. The editor, Milton George, declared, "The railroads are literally starving some of our farmers to death," and decided to do something about it. George called a meeting of like-minded agriculturalists; they gathered at Chicago in the autumn of 1880 and denounced the current political and economic system as giving power and wealth to the few undeserving while denying same to the many worthy.

George utilized the pages of the *Western Rural* to urge farmers in the various states to form Alliance chapters for the purpose of bringing pressure for change to bear on the two major political parties. Although some other farm journals were distinctly cool to the idea—a number of editors thought George was using the Alliance chiefly to boost circulation of his paper—farmers rallied to the cause in great numbers. By the time a second convention was held in 1881, the Alliance boasted nearly 25,000 members; by 1882, membership had topped 100,000.

The Southern Alliance originated in the efforts of Texas ranchers to catch horse thieves and round up strays. The Texas organization also attempted to counterbalance the excessive—at least in the minds of its members—influence of large landowners in Texas state politics. Partly for this reason the Southern Alliance started as a secret organization. But despite the secrecy, it too caught on quickly; by the mid-1880s, it had some 50,000 members.

The early success of the alliances, however, gave way later in the 1880s to a period of decline. For independent-minded farmers (these being almost the only kind), joining a mass movement like one of the alliances cut against the grain. They did so only under strong pressure, such as that produced by the drought that seared the upper Midwest during the first part of the 1880s. It wasn't coincidental that the Northern Alliance drew its greatest membership in precisely those states where the drought was most severe. Conversely, the return of prosperity during the mid-1880s caused farmers to drift away from the Alliance. Interest was already waning at the time of the annual meeting of the Northern Alliance in late 1883; the Alliance didn't bother to call a meeting the following year. Even Milton George got discouraged, and for a couple of years the *Western Rural* said hardly a word about the Alliance.

Good times always end eventually. Overproduction caused crop prices to fall in 1884 and 1885, and the winter of 1886–87 was the harshest on record. Largely as a consequence, farmers again turned to each other and to the Alliance for mutual support. Farmers signed up once more; by 1890, members were enrolling at the rate of one thousand per week. Milton George regained the faith; the *Western Rural* crowed, "The people are aroused at last. Never in our history has there been such a union of action among farmers as now."

"Union of action" was the essential concept. While farmers watched the corporations with which they did business get larger and more consolidated, they increasingly felt the need to consolidate in self-defense. An individual farmer had no leverage in dealing with the railroads or the grain elevators or the fertilizer manufacturers, but a hundred farmers banded together might, and a thousand farmers would have still more. The purchasing and marketing cooperatives farmers had formed had demonstrated the strength that lay in numbers. Further, farmers increasingly understood that many of their problems could be addressed only through the political process. To cap railroad rates and insist on fair grading practices at the elevators would most likely require changes in state and federal laws. The railroads and the other big corporations exercised influence in the state capitals and Washington by means of their great financial resources; the farmers didn't swing such financial clout, so they would have to rely on their united votes.

A desire to increase the farmers' political strength prompted some leaders of the Northern Alliance to seek a merger with the Southern Alliance. Although the Supreme Court in the *Munn* case had allowed the states to regulate commerce within their borders, really effective action would require regulating interstate commerce, which fell within the exclusive purview of Congress. Passing federal laws required organization at the national level.

To this end, the leaders of the Northern and Southern Alliances agreed to hold concurrent annual meetings in St. Louis in December 1889. The Southern Alliance sent some two hundred official delegates to St. Louis; the Northern Alliance authorized about seventy-five. The two groups began their sessions separately, with the Southerners gathering in the Exposition Building and the Northerners in the Planters' House. But fusion proponents expected that once old business had been disposed of, the smaller Northern contingent would join the Southern group.

Making the marriage wasn't as simple as moving in together, though. The Northerners objected to the secrecy the Southerners practiced; more important, they disliked the racially exclusionist policies the Southerners insisted on. The Southern Alliance barred blacks, who had formed an organization of their own, the Colored Farmers' National Alliance and Cooperative Union. Many Southern Alliance members appreciated the wisdom of encouraging blacks to form a union that could work in tandem with their own, but few wished to allow the blacks equal status in the Southern Alliance. The Northern Alliance, by contrast to the Southern, encouraged blacks to join, although not many did, there being relatively few black farmers in the North. To most of the Northern Alliance members, the exclusion of blacks seemed a vestige of the days of slavery. Tens of thousands of members of the Northern Alliance were Union veterans of the Civil War—just as tens of thousands of members of the Southern Alliance had fought for the Confederacy. Old wounds healed slowly; old memories died hard.

In the end, the hopes for amalgamation foundered on the rock of this surviving sectionalism. Northerners and Southerners still eyed each other warily, and on the matters that separated the two alliances neither would concede to the other. To a certain extent, the two groups saw different issues as being the most pressing. Northerners wanted more than anything else to rein in the railroads; to Southerners, the currency question was paramount.

The leaders of the two alliances decided to keep their organizations separate while working for the same goals. The platforms devised by the two groups at St. Louis were quite similar; such differences as existed were mostly matters of emphasis. Both groups demanded regulation of railroads, expansion of the currency, and readier access to land by small farmers. Though the St. Louis meetings dealt a setback to those who desired a near-term merger, this coincidence of views afforded encouragement to those who sought to promote farmers' interests. The St. Louis delegates returned home eager to get to work electing candidates to office; with the election of 1890 just months away, they had plenty to do.

In some states the farmers chose to work through the existing political parties. This was especially true in the South, where the Democratic Party wasn't merely a political organization but also a continuing instrument of white solidarity against the North and against blacks. Alliance politics in the South consisted of efforts to capture the state Democratic parties and to elect candidates pledged to support Alliance interests.

In the North, Alliance members often broke with the existing parties and created new ones of their own. In Kansas, for example, a group of Alliance leaders joined forces with representatives of the Knights of Labor, the Grange, and a few smaller fringe organizations, and formed the Kansas People's Party. The new party held a convention in August 1890 and nominated a full ticket of candidates for offices. Similar coalitions formed in other states. Nebraska's new party took the name People's Independent Party; South Dakota's, Independent; Colorado's, Independent Fusion; Indiana's, People's.

An evangelical sense of righteousness imbued the new parties; this as much as their policy positions distanced them from the Republicans and Democrats, who were typically seen as apathetic and corrupt (and often were). Neither of the major parties had speakers to match those who preached the Alliance gospel. Mary E. Lease created a stir by telling Kansas farmers to raise "less corn and more Hell." (The middle "E." was for Elizabeth, but critics changed it to Ellen so they could call her "Mary Yellin.'") Mrs. Lease talked about much more than corn and hell. A thirty-seven-year-old mother of four who nonetheless had found the energy to study law and gain admission to the Kansas bar, Lease gave one hundred and sixty speeches on behalf of Alliance candidates in 1890. Her theme was the perversion of American democracy by the money power of the East. "Wall Street owns the country," she declared. "It is no longer a government of the people, by the people and for the people, but a government of Wall Street, by Wall Street and for Wall Street. The great common people of this country are slaves, and monopoly is the master. The West and South are bound and prostrate before the manufacturing East. Money rules."

Lease ridiculed the notion that farmers had brought their woes on themselves through overproduction. "The parties lie to us and the political speakers mislead us," she insisted. Overproduction was a myth designed to deflect blame from where it properly belonged. "Overproduction!—when 10,000 little children, so statistics tell us, starve to death every year in the United States, and over 100,000 shop-girls in New York are forced to sell their virtue for the bread their niggardly wages deny them!" The problem wasn't too much production by the common people; it was too much greed by the rich. "There are thirty men in the United States whose aggregate wealth is over one and one-half billion dollars. There are half a million looking for work!"

The wealthy had better be warned. The people knew what they wanted and were determined to get it. "We want money, land and transportation. We want the abolition of the National Banks, and we want the power to make loans direct from the government. We want the accursed foreclosure system wiped out." The people had had enough of the old way of doing things. "We will stand by our homes and stay by our firesides by force if necessary, and we will not pay our debts to the loan-shark companies until the Government pays its debts to us. The people are at bay; let the bloodhounds of money who have dogged us thus far beware."

Where Mary Lease castigated the creditor class, Jeremiah Simpson focused his fire on the railroads and the big grain companies. Simpson had arrived on the Kansas frontier in the late 1870s and been active in radical politics since. In 1890, he ran for a congressional seat from Kansas's seventh district. One of his opponents was a well-heeled Republican named James Hallowell, whom Simpson derided as "Prince Hal." To score points with rural voters, Simpson claimed that Hallowell wore silk stockings. A Hallowell backer retorted that Simpson wore no stockings at all—which led to Simpson's being called "Sockless Jerry."

Simpson charged the railroads and grain brokerages with arrogance and misuse of power. The railroads had watered their stock and now expected their users to pay rates based on their grossly inflated valuation. "We who use the roads," Simpson declared, "are really paying interest on $600 million instead of on $100 million as we ought to." The grain brokers were no better, buying farmers' crops when the price was low and selling when the price was high. Furthermore, the "grain gamblers" had corrupted government, making it an instrument for squeezing profits out of farmers. "If the government had protected the farmers as it protects the gamblers, this could not have happened," Simpson argued. The time had come for farmers to claim their own.

North of Lease and Simpson, in Minnesota, the person who most readily roused the masses was Ignatius Donnelly. Like Lease, Donnelly was of Irish descent; like her, he had studied law and tried his hand at the bar but become bored. Donnelly had arrived in Minnesota in the 1850s and founded the city of Nininger on the banks of the Mississippi. Donnelly's dream was for Nininger to become the great western metropolis, the gateway to the upper Mississippi Valley. For some time he employed his considerable rhetorical talents promoting his dream, but the financial panic of 1857 snuffed it out—for everyone else, that is. Donnelly refused to quit dreaming, and for a while lived alone in the city he had brought to life.

Donnelly learned two things from his ill-fated venture: that real estate promotion was risky business, and that when he opened his mouth to speak, people listened. He turned to politics, gaining election first as lieutenant governor of Minnesota and then as a congressman. From the start, Donnelly showed a reformist streak. He joined the Republican Party in the 1850s when opposition to the expansion of slavery was the glue that held the Republicans together; after the Grant administration succumbed to the temptations of power, Donnelly left the party for more radical causes. He stood with the Grangers against the railroads and with the Greenbackers against gold.

Donnelly also indulged a penchant for eccentric intellectual pursuits. In 1882, he published a study of the lost continent of Atlantis, claiming that it really had existed just as Herodotus said. The following year he produced *Ragnorak: The Age of Fire and Gravel,* in which he asserted that a long-ago collision between the earth and a comet accounted for such tall tales of antiquity as Noah's flood. Turning his historical sleuthing in a different direction, he concluded in his *The Great Cryptogram* that Francis Bacon had really written the plays and poems attributed to William Shakespeare. In 1891, he published his biggest seller, *Caesar's Column*. This book described a society in which moneylending for interest was forbidden, in which no person could own more than a fixed amount of land or other property, in which money was paper and expanded freely to match the growth of the economy, and in which government served the interests of the many instead of the few.

Donnelly's images in *Caesar's Column* were more powerful than his prescriptions. The most telling likened the gold standard to an iron waistband: "Take a child a few years old; let a blacksmith weld around his waist an iron band. At first it causes him little inconvenience. He plays. As he grows older it becomes tighter; it causes him pain; he scarcely knows what ails him. He still grows. All his internal organs are cramped and displaced. He grows still larger; he has the head, shoulders and limbs of a man and the waist of a child. He is a monstrosity. He dies." So it was, Connelly said, with the gold standard, which had made a monstrosity out of American society and would kill it if not hacked off soon.

In another section, Donnelly compared the small class of the very wealthy to ravenous beasts: "If a community were to send to India and import a lot of man-eating tigers, and turn them loose on the streets, to prey on men, women and children, they would not inflict a tithe of the misery that is caused by a like number of millionaires. And there would be this further disadvantage: the inhabitants of the city could turn out and kill the tigers, but the human destroyers are protected by the benevolent laws of the very people they are immolating on the altars of wretchedness and vice."

Given Donnelly's background and talents, it was no surprise that he became a leading figure in Alliance politics in Minnesota. It would have been far more surprising if he hadn't; as the *New York Sun* remarked, a protest movement in Minnesota without Donnelly would have been "like catfish without waffles in Philadelphia." (Presumably the *Sun's* East Coast readers knew about catfish and waffles in Philadelphia, even if Minnesotans didn't.) Donnelly dearly hoped to be elected governor of the state. In 1888, he came within a catfish's whisker of getting the Union Laborite gubernatorial nomination; in 1890, he angled to be named the Alliance candidate. Once again he was disappointed, but he didn't let personal disappointment dampen his enthusiasm for the hustings.

Donnelly traveled up and down and across the state, lecturing and exhorting large crowds everywhere he went. In a movement that lived on blood-pumping oratory, Donnelly was commonly considered the best of the bunch. He skewered the wealthy with satire; he hurled thunderbolts of indignation at the powerful; he adduced evidence to support his views from the most obscure corners of human knowledge. People would have come out to listen to Ignatius Donnelly no matter what subject he was declaiming on; the fact that he told them what many of them wanted to hear only enhanced his appeal.

Less flamboyant but more substantial than Donnelly was James Weaver of Iowa. Unlike Donnelly and Lease, Weaver had actually practiced law for several years, starting in Ohio prior to the Civil War. During the war he attained the rank of colonel in the Union army; he used the title for the rest of his life. After Appomattox, Weaver moved to Iowa, where he resumed law practice and gained minor success in politics as a Republican. Like Donnelly, Weaver grew disenchanted with the party of Grant and James Blaine; he joined the Greenback Party and was elected to Congress in 1878. Two years later, the Greenbackers nominated him for president. He didn't come anywhere near getting elected but he carried the message of the virtues of an expanded money supply to almost the whole country, campaigning from the Midwest to the Atlantic and from the Gulf of Mexico to Lake Michigan. During the 1880s, Weaver was returned to Congress. There he was the best known of those who threw their lot in with the Alliance and the only one with national stature.

Alliance candidates and spokesmen in the South were at least as strikingly idiosyncratic as those in the North. For several years, "Pitchfork" Ben Tillman had been waging political war against the white aristocracy of South Carolina on behalf of the lower-class whites of the backcountry. An affinity for violence ran in the Tillman family. Of Ben's five brothers, one was killed in the Civil War, two were murdered, and another—George—himself murdered a man. This last incident, the consequence of a dispute at cards, didn't hurt George's career; he ran for Congress and won. His South Carolina constituents evidently liked a man who wouldn't walk away from a fight. Younger brother Ben took note.

Ben lost his vision in one eye while fighting for the Confederacy during the Civil War. The events of the Reconstruction years further embittered him against Republicans—and added freedmen to his enemies list. With many of his race and class, he rode nights to terrorize Republicans and blacks into withdrawing from South Carolina politics. Largely successful in this endeavor, he next turned his attention to the Bourbons who still controlled state politics. His activities dovetailed neatly with those of the Farmers' Alliance, and by 1890 he was the most prominent Allianceman in South Carolina.

Because the South remained a one-party region, the fight for control of South Carolina politics took place within the Democratic Party. Tillman embodied the forces of rural protest; party conservatives threw their support to James Earle. The fight split South Carolina whites along class lines, with hard-handed, poorly educated, backcountry small farmers rooting for Tillman, and well-born, well-educated, well-to-do gentry and city dwellers cheering for Earle. Tillman made the most of the difference between his background and Earle's. He used the earthy, direct language of poor whites and described his own difficult life in terms they could appreciate. They shouted in reply, "Give us the one-eyed plowboy." He told how he had fought the carpetbaggers during Reconstruction, how he had worked his farm through good years and lean, how he had begun to listen to the siren song of creditors. That was when his troubles really started, he said. "The devil tempted me to buy a steam engine and other machinery, amounting to two thousand dollars, all on credit." He succumbed to the temptation, to his eternal regret. Drought withered his crops; he was unable to make his payments; he was forced to sell his land.

The experience—one most of his listeners shared at least in part—convinced Tillman there was something criminally wrong with the system. Being a fighter, he said, he had determined to fight the system. Now he wanted the people's help. They were three quarters of the South Carolina population; together they could beat the system.

Thomas Watson of Georgia couldn't claim the long list of troubles Tillman did, if only because Watson was but thirty-four years old in 1890. Yet his life too had been one of struggle. From a poor family, he had had to work day and night to gain an education. He attended college for two years before taking a job teaching school. Subsequently he read law and won admission to the bar. His flamboyant courtroom style and combative nature brought him many cases if not many friends. But because he championed the little man beaten down by the big corporations, voters responded to his message. In 1890, Watson challenged an incumbent Democratic congressman, unleashing the full Alliance arsenal of anti-gold, anti-monopoly, anti-tariff complaints and demands. He charged his opponent with being "a soured outlaw who is so accustomed to abusing everything and everybody that the restraints of truth have no power over him." Watson's opponent took offense and called for a duel. Watson responded that he would make himself available on the streets of Atlanta during the state fair. His opponent, apparently reconsidering, chose to skip the fair.

Watson was noteworthy—but not unique—among Southerners for his insistence on uniting the white and black races in the struggle against the common foe. Though Watson later would change his mind, during the early 1890s he spoke loudly in favor of cooperation between poor whites and poor blacks. He accused Democratic and Republican leaders alike of cynically manipulating bad feeling between the races to their own selfish ends. "Both the parties have done this thing until they have constructed as perfect a 'slot machine' as the world ever saw," he declared. "Drop the old, worn nickel of the party slogan into the slot, and the machine does the rest. You might beseech a Southern white tenant to listen to you upon questions of finance, taxation, and transportation; you might demonstrate with mathematical precision that herein lay his way out of poverty into comfort; you might have him almost persuaded to the truth, but if the merchant who furnished his farm supplies (at tremendous usury) or the town politician (who never spoke to him excepting at election times) came along and cried 'Negro rule!' the entire fabric of reason and common sense which you had patiently constructed would fall, and the poor tenant would joyously hug the chains of an actual wretchedness rather than do any experimenting on a question of mere sentiment." This part was the Democrats' doing; the Republicans applied analogous treatment to blacks. The result, Watson said, was "a solid black vote against the solid white."

Watson warned that the present hostility between white and black could not persist without grave danger to both. For this reason, citizens of sober sense and honest judgment must adopt a policy designed to "allay the passions and prejudices of race conflict." The adoption of such a policy could come about only by abandoning the two major parties. "The white people of the South will never support the Republican Party. This much is certain. The black people of the South will never support the Democratic Party. This is equally certain." Only a break with the established parties would allow a break with the past. "The two races can never act together permanently, harmoniously, beneficially, till each race demonstrates to the other a readiness to leave old party affiliations and to form new ones, based upon the profound conviction that, in acting together, both races are seeking new laws which will benefit both."

Watson, Tillman, Weaver, Donnelly, Lease, and scores of other Alliance candidates and speakers pounded away at their opponents through the summer and early autumn of 1890, and after the election results were tallied they claimed a remarkable victory, especially in the South. Alliance candidates won the governorships in South Carolina (Tillman), Georgia, and Tennessee, and a friendly non-Alliance man triumphed in Texas. Eight Southern states—Alabama, Florida, Georgia, Missouri, Mississippi, North Carolina, South Carolina, Tennessee—elected legislatures controlled by the Alliance. More than forty Alliance candidates gained congressional seats from the South; three U.S. senators (at that time still chosen by the state legislatures) expressed strong Alliance leanings.

In the North and West, the Alliance did less well but still showed substantial strength. Alliance candidates won a clear majority in the lower house of the Kansas legislature; these legislators then ousted the incumbent U.S. senator and replaced him with an Allianceman. Five congressional representatives-elect prepared to carry the Alliance banner from Kansas to Washington. In Nebraska, the Alliance captured control of both houses of the state legislature and elected one congressman. In South Dakota, the Alliance held the balance of power in the legislature; the Alliance legislators then parlayed their votes into victory for a sympathetic candidate for federal senator. In Minnesota, the Alliance held a similar swing position in the legislature.

So strong was the showing of the radicals in the 1890 elections that the leaders of the farmers' movement immediately began laying the foundation for a national party of protest. When the representatives of the Southern Alliance gathered at Ocala, Florida, in December 1890, they talked about little else—except how nice it was to be in Florida in December and how accommodating their Florida hosts were. The farmers' representatives received red carpet treatment, including free railroad tickets, free hotel rooms, and all the oranges, grapefruit, and lemonade they could eat and drink. Florida had yet to gain a reputation as a winter convention site, but it was working hard to do so.

Although many Southerners were still reluctant to leave the Democratic Party, the brilliant victories of the Alliance-backed candidates in the South suggested that the Democrats might need the Alliance more than the Alliance needed the Democrats. Some Alliance members believed that a third party could fairly quickly supplant the Democrats as the majority party of the South; others less sanguine were willing to go along with the formation of a third party on the reasoning that only such a move would cause the Democratic Party to change its hidebound ways. Besides, Alliance leaders in the North were champing at the third-party bit; if the South didn't join them, Southern interests might get short shrift.

The proponents of a third party couldn't muster quite enough support at Ocala to accomplish their goal on the spot, but they did get the Southern Alliance to declare the sense of the convention as being in favor of calling another convention specifically to consider the question of a third party in time for the next round of elections. As the approved motion stated, "If the people by delegates coming direct from them agree that a third party move is necessary, it need not be feared."

Many members of the Northern Alliance wanted to organize the third party right away. At the spring meeting of the Northern Alliance in Cincinnati, Ignatius Donnelly led a faction that demanded immediate creation of a third party. James Weaver and some less impatient radicals wanted to delay. In the end, the two sides compromised. The convention voted to create a third party—named the People's Party—but put off substantive party business until 1892.

In the interim, the farmers continued their barrage against the status quo; they also attempted to broaden their political base to include urban workers and other downtrodden folks. From Kansas, the central committee of the state People's Party issued a manifesto summarizing the conditions that made a third party necessary:

> Every branch of business is depressed. The merchant fails for want of trade, and the banker from depreciation of values. Labor is unemployed and inadequately paid. Our cities are the abode of poverty and want and consequent crime, while the country is overrun with tramps. Starvation stalks abroad amid an overproduction of food, and illy-clad men and women and helpless children are freezing amid an overproduction of clothing.
>
> We hold that these conditions are the legitimate result of vicious legislation in the interests of the favored classes and adverse to the masses of American citizens; and we appeal to the great body of the

people, irrespective of occupation or calling, to rise above the partisan prejudices engendered by political contests, and calmly and dispassionately examine the facts which we are prepared to submit in support of our claims. We appeal to reason and not to prejudice, and if the facts and arguments we present can be refuted we neither ask nor expect your support.

In Washington, Alliance congressmen caucused to determine how best to put their program into effect. Most were Southerners and still nominally Democrats; the question was whether they would accept party discipline. Some did, but others followed Sockless Jerry Simpson of Kansas and Tom Watson of Georgia into rebellion. They declared their independence of the Democratic leadership, and to symbolize their independence they nominated Watson for speaker of the House of Representatives. Leaders of the farmers' groups meanwhile contacted officials of labor unions and other agitators against the status quo to assess the practicability of a united front against the big bankers and the captains of industry.

After much talk and a couple of ground-clearing meetings, the long-awaited national convention of the new third party took place in Omaha in July 1892. More than one thousand three hundred delegates arrived, despite the refusal of several of the railroads to grant the convention-goers the usual convention discount. Although the great majority of the delegates represented farmers, there was a sizable admixture of Knights of Labor, prohibitionists, and single-taxers. The convention had two orders of business: to nominate candidates for president and vice president and to write a platform.

Choosing candidates required balancing the claims of North and South as well as of the different groups that made up the new party. A frontrunner for the leading spot on the ticket had been Leonidas Polk of North Carolina, the president of the Southern Alliance. Polk carried the baggage of being a former Confederate officer, and it seemed likely that many Northerners would hesitate to help him haul that burden to the White House; yet a Polk nomination would assist considerably in pulling Southerners away from the Democrats, and recently Polk had made statements aimed at increasing his attractiveness to Northern voters. He had gone so far as to say that his support of the Confederacy had been reluctant, that he had really favored the preservation of the Union. This statement didn't endear him to his fellow Southerners, but it did assuage Northern concerns somewhat. Unfortunately, Polk died all of a sudden just before the convention.

Polk's death shifted the attention of many delegates to Walter Gresham of Indiana. Gresham was a federal judge in Chicago who had shown sympathy for farmers and other railroad customers in various decisions. He was also—at least until he started flirting with the new party—a well-respected Democrat. Precisely for this reason he appealed to a certain segment among the delegates: those anxious to demonstrate that the new party wasn't merely a fringe movement. On the other hand, a substantial portion of the delegates thought the nomination ought to go to someone who had been with the movement all along. As one opponent of outsider nominations, the editor of the *Great West* of St. Paul, wrote, "We do not believe in going outside the ranks of the workers-in-the-vineyard to find men who ought to be of us and are not, to execute our will." For his part, Gresham seemed intrigued by the possibility of a run for the presidency. He conspicuously declined numerous opportunities to disavow interest. Until the very end, that is—evidently convinced by friends that he would be keeping bad company, he cabled the convention asking that he not be considered.

A few other candidates flashed in the pan more briefly. California Senator Leland Stanford had talked favorably about free silver; for some at the convention this Western railroad baron possessed the same kind of appeal as Gresham. Yet the California delegation vetoed Stanford, branding him a monopolist and an oppressor of the people. Some delegates touted Ignatius Donnelly. Yet though all agreed that a Donnelly candidacy would be entertaining, only a minority thought it would be fruitful.

The nomination finally went to James Weaver. To most of the delegates, Weaver was the safe choice. He was well known, and if he lacked flair, neither would he invite the ridicule some other candidates might. Besides, not even the most starry-eyed delegate thought the new party's candidate had a genuine chance of winning in 1892; the point of the campaign was to gain respectability. Weaver would be better at this than Donnelly or any number of others.

Moreover, it was the platform rather than the candidate that mattered most to the delegates. They were sick and tired of the politics of personal preferment, of politics as the mere quest for office. Theirs was to be a campaign of issues. Above everything they wanted to carry their message of protest to the country as a whole. By all evidence, if Republicans and Democrats had to choose between enacting policies and holding office, they would choose office. (In fact, some observers thought the situation had degenerated beyond even this abysmal condition. Often neither side evinced much confidence in its own candidates, but merely seemed to want to prevent the other from winning. One contemporary observer described the situation between Republicans and Democrats in 1892: "Each side would have been glad to defeat the other if it could do so without electing its own candidate.") But the new party of the people, if it had to choose between policies and office, would choose policies.

For this reason, Ignatius Donnelly consoled himself that he had got the better half of the bargain. Weaver won the nomination, yet Donnelly guided the drafting of the platform. "We meet in the midst of a nation brought to the verge of moral, political, and material ruin," the preamble intoned. "Corruption dominates the ballot-box, the Legislatures, the Congress, and touches even the ermine of the bench. The people are demoralized; most of the States have been compelled to isolate the voters at the polling places to prevent universal intimidation and bribery. The newspapers are largely subsidized or muzzled, public opinion silenced, business prostrated, homes covered with mortgages, labor impoverished, and the land concentrated in the hands of the capitalists."

There was more along these lines; then the platform got down to particulars.

1. We demand free and unlimited coinage of silver and gold at the present legal ratio of 16 to 1.

2. We demand that the amount of circulating medium be speedily increased to not less than $50 per capita.

3. We demand a graduated income tax.

4. We believe that the money of the country should be kept as much as possible in the hands of the people, and hence we demand that all State and national revenues shall be limited to the necessary expenses of the government, economically and honestly administered.

5. We demand that postal savings banks be established by the government for the safe deposit of the earnings of the people and to facilitate exchange.

These demands formed the centerpiece of the party's platform, reflecting the delegates' preoccupation with currency and related questions. The platform additionally insisted on public ownership of the railroads ("The time has come when either the railroad corporations will own the people or the people must own the railroads") and on reversion to the people of lands owned by railroads and other corporations in excess of use ("The land, including all the natural sources of wealth, is the heritage of the people, and should not be monopolized for speculative purposes"). The platform also called for the creation of a "subtreasury" system of government lending, by which farmers' crops would serve as collateral for loans, allowing the expansion of credit without subjecting farmers to further manipulation by the big bankers.

To these basic platform planks were added a number of "sentiments" designed to appeal to particular groups, especially organized labor. The convention endorsed the eight-hour day, immigration restriction, and the banning of Pinkertons and other private detectives employed to help break strikes. Further, it called for a sympathy boycott of some clothing manufacturers currently being struck by the Knights of Labor, and it condemned the recent use of federal law enforcement officers, operating in conjunction with "the hired assassins of plutocracy," in a miners' strike in Wyoming Territory. To the advocates of good-government political reforms it offered backing for the secret ballot, the initiative, and the referendum; to Union veterans it promised liberal pensions.

The convention endorsed the platform with tremendous enthusiasm. An astonished Eastern journalist, describing the reaction of the delegates to the reading of the platform, told of men and women who "leaped upon tables and chairs in the ecstasy of their delirium," and of "the cheers and yells which rose like a tornado from four thousand throats and raged without cessation for thirty-four minutes, during which women shrieked and wept, men embraced and kissed their neighbors." The journalist added in somber summary: "Over all the city during that summer week brooded the spectres of Nationalism, Socialism and general discontent."

The new party named itself the People's Party, but its members were equally often called Populists, and under the Populist banner the delegates fanned forth to spread their message across the country. Tactically, it helped their cause during the months leading up to the 1892 elections that the Democrats made no effort to appease them. The Democratic presidential nomination went to Grover Cleveland, a man as sound on gold as the staunchest Republican and otherwise opposed to everything important the Populists stood for. A South Carolina Populist described Cleveland's nomination as "a prostitution of the principles of Democracy, a repudiation of the demands of the Farmers' Alliance, which embody the true principles of Democracy, and a surrender of the rights of the people to the financial kings of the country." Mary Lease called Cleveland "the agent of Jewish bankers and British gold." The Republicans, who renominated President Benjamin Harrison, were even less disposed than the Democrats to give the radicals what they wanted. Consequently the Populists offered a clear choice to those who thought the country was going in a fundamentally wrong direction.

To most observers it appeared that the key to whatever substantial success the Populists would achieve lay in the South. There the Populists would have to convince voters to abandon the Democrats and embrace the new party. They had their work cut out for them, for though many of the leaders of the Southern Alliance had taken the Populist pledge, most of the rank and file remained leery. Tom Watson put his finger on the crucial issue when he said, "The argument against the independent political movement in the South can be boiled down into one word—*nigger*." As Watson had predicted, Democratic spokesmen accused Watson and other Populists who advocated cooperation across racial lines of "nigger-loving." It didn't help matters that candidate James Weaver was a former Union officer. Weaver's life was threatened when he campaigned in Tennessee, where many of the residents remembered him personally from the war years. Southerners were equally uncomfortable with Mary Lease, who likewise made a swing through the old Confederacy. One Southern editor characterized the sight of a woman traveling across the country giving political speeches as "simply disgusting"; this writer added, "Southern manhood revolts at the idea of degrading womanhood to the level of politics."

The Populists' efforts in the South were unavailing. On election day not a single Southern state went for Weaver, and only Alabama gave him as much as 30 percent of the popular vote. Elsewhere in the region the Populist tally ranged from 24 percent in Texas to less than 4 percent in South Carolina.

The Populists' best showing proved to be on the Great Plains and in the

Mountain West. The silver states of Nevada, Colorado, and Idaho awarded Weaver his highest percentages (and his only clear majorities); he also carried Kansas and fell just shy of half the vote in North Dakota.

After the high hopes of 1890, the election of 1892 came as a distinct disappointment. The radical farmers and their allies discovered that cracking the duopoly of the Republicans and Democrats was harder than they had expected. Optimists among them had hoped to follow the path of the Republicans, who had seized the presidency in 1860 on only their second try. The 1892 election didn't shatter these hopes, but it suggested to those who held them that they needed to find both their irrepressible conflict and their Lincoln.

IV

To many of the Populists, the irrepressible conflict was obvious. Most Populists perceived a wide and nearly unbridgeable gap between the people (meaning themselves) and the plutocrats (the big bankers, industrialists, and others who made the people's lives miserable). This division of American society into two classes was described with greater or less accuracy in various ways: debtor versus creditor, producer versus expropriator, worker versus manager, labor versus capital. No matter how they described the conflict, the farmers and their supporters were convinced their cause embodied justice and right and their opponents' cause injustice and wrong. Jerry Simpson declared, "It is a struggle between the robbers and the robbed." A widely read Populist manifesto asserted, "There are but two sides in the conflict that is being waged in this country today. On the one side are the allied hosts of monopolies, the money power, great trusts and railroad corporations, who seek the enactment of laws to benefit them and impoverish the people. On the other are the farmers, laborers, merchants, and all other people who produce wealth and bear the burdens of taxation." The manifesto concluded, "Between these two there is no middle ground." William Jennings Bryan, who remained within the Democratic Party but showed decidedly Populist leanings, denounced the Cleveland administration's efforts to repeal the Sherman Silver Purchase Act in similarly dichotomous terms. "On the one side," Bryan proclaimed, "stand the corporate interests of the United States, the moneyed interests, aggregated wealth and capital, imperious, arrogant, compassionless. . . . On the other side stand an unnumbered throng, those who gave to the Democratic party a name and for whom it has assumed to speak." (Needless to say, the Populists differed with Bryan on who currently spoke for the "unnumbered throng.")

Since there were more people than plutocrats, and since the United States was at least nominally a democracy, Populist leaders had to explain how it was that the plutocrats so often prevailed. Their explanation invoked the time-honored device of conspiracy. Everywhere they looked, the Populists saw conspiracies. The preamble to the Populist platform of 1892 put the issue directly: "A vast conspiracy against mankind has been organized on two continents, and it is rapidly taking possession of the world. If not met and overthrown at once, it forbodes terrible social convulsions, the destruction of civilization, or the establishment of an absolute despotism." A Populist campaign broadside asserted flatly, "As early as 1865–66 a conspiracy was entered into between the gold gamblers of Europe and America." The conspirators threw the dust of distraction into the eyes of the people while they pursued their self-interested purpose of maintaining the gold standard. They did so still. "Every device of treachery, every resource of statecraft, and every artifice known to the secret cabals of the gold ring are being made use of to deal a blow to the prosperity of the people and the financial and commercial independence of the country."

Because the conspirators were said to include European financiers, there developed in Populism a strong strain of xenophobia and nativism, and because European financiers were assumed to be principally Jews, the xenophobia and nativism tended toward anti-Semitism. Tom Watson denounced immigration as destructive of American values. "We have become the world's melting pot," Watson declared disapprovingly. "The scum of creation has been dumped on us. Some of our principal cities are more foreign than American. The most dangerous and corrupting hordes of the Old World have invaded us. The vice and crime which they have planted in our midst are sickening and terrifying." The main character in one of Ignatius Donnelly's lesser-known books asserted that, on account of immigration, America was "united by a ligament to a corpse—Europe." Two of the more despicable villains in Donnelly's *Caesar's Column* were Jews, one of them a Russian exile who intended to "revive the ancient splendors of the Jewish race in the midst of the ruins of the world." Mary Lease identified Grover Cleveland as "the agent of Jewish bankers and British gold." A Populist document that gained wide readership alleged a secret transaction between Hugh McCulloch, the treasury secretary under Lincoln and Andrew Johnson, and British banker James Rothschild. "The most direful part of this business between Rothschild and the United States Treasury," the document explained, "was not the loss of money, even by hundreds of millions. It was the resignation of the country itself INTO THE HANDS OF ENGLAND, as England had long been resigned into the hands of HER JEWS."

The conspiracy theory of history served the politically valuable purpose of personifying the enemy. The forces arrayed against the farmers in the 1890s were mostly impersonal forces: industrialization, urbanization, deflation, the decreasing availability of land. But it was often difficult to explain such forces, let alone rally the faithful against them. It was far easier, conceptually and politically, to deal in more concrete terms: the railroads, the trusts, the international financiers. These were enemies a person could fight. How could one fight industrialization? How could one turn back the clock on urbanization?

Moreover, farmers were engaged in a kind of collective self-deception. They clung to the received vision of America's past even as they helped make real the arriving vision of America's future. Farmers liked to think of themselves as independent yeomen, the tamers of the frontier who stood largely outside the net of commerce and industry that was coming to dominate the American economy and American society. In fact they were businessmen (and businesswomen), fully as dependent on the vicissitudes of market economics as anyone else. And while they complained against persons who bought land for speculation, many of them were speculators themselves. As far back as the 1830s—during what farmers took to be their golden age—the French observer Alexis de Tocqueville had described the farmers' activities: "Almost all the farmers of the United States combine some trade with agriculture; most of them make agriculture itself a trade. It seldom happens that an American farmer settles for good upon the land which he occupies; especially in the districts of the far West he brings land into tillage in order to sell it again, and not to farm it; he builds a farmhouse on the speculation that, as the state of the country will soon be changed by the increase of population, a good price will be gotten for it." Frontier folk were not simply those who had failed farther east; they were often those who had succeeded by settling land that subsequently appreciated and who had sold out intending to repeat the process to the west.

But this reality didn't fit comfortably with farmers' preferred view of themselves, and, as people do, they found it easier to blame their troubles on someone else than on themselves. The more specific that someone else was, the easier it was to pin blame. No one had forced farmers in North Dakota to bet on a bonanza in wheat and thereby place themselves at the mercy of the railroads; they had done so of their own volition. Yet now that they were suffering the consequences of their action, they sought to restrict what the railroads could charge. No one had forced farmers in Kansas to borrow money to buy the latest farm equipment, knowing (at least they should have known) that prices might fall as well as rise; they themselves had chosen to do so. Yet now that the money was due, they wanted to change the value of the currency.

The currency question more than any other lent itself to a conspiracy interpretation of history. As the Populists and their allies saw things, America's money troubles dated to the "Crime of '73," the most heinous act of the country's most dastardly and cunning conspiracy. So ingenious was the conspiracy that produced this offense that not even all of those who committed the crime realized what they had done. The misdeed referred to was the Coinage Act of 1873, which attempted to straighten out the mess the nation's currency system had fallen into during the Civil War and Reconstruction. The act specified which coins would continue to be minted and which not. Among the coins dropped from the list was the silver dollar.

At the time, no one thought much of exclusion of the silver dollar, since very few silver dollars had been minted for a generation. From the establishment of the federal government in 1789, the United States had committed itself in principle to bimetallism: the coinage and circulation of both gold and silver. Maintaining bimetallism in practice, however, was another matter, since the two metals fluctuated in value relative to each other. As one became more valuable, people stopped paying their debts in the valuable one, instead hoarding it or selling it for other uses and giving their creditors the less valuable one. In consequence, the more valuable metal tended to disappear from circulation while the less valuable one carried the major burden of currency transactions.

From the 1790s until the early 1830s, gold was relatively more valuable than silver, and therefore gold gradually vanished from circulation. Thus for the first forty years of its national existence America was effectively on a silver standard. Partly because of congressional efforts to rectify this imbalance, and partly because of big gold strikes in California and Nevada and Australia in the 1840s and 1850s, the pendulum subsequently shifted in the other direction. Gold became relatively plentiful and consequently relatively cheap; silver became relatively scarce and expensive. Before long the silver in a silver dollar rose in market value to $1.03, and silver producers stopped delivering silver to the U.S. mint (where they received only $1.00); they sold it on the open market instead. So did coin collectors and ordinary people who liked the idea of selling $10 worth of silver coins and receiving $10.30 (minus the dealer's commission perhaps) in exchange.

As a result of this series of developments, by 1873 silver dollars had been essentially out of circulation for twenty years. Plenty of Americans at that time had never even seen a silver dollar. When Congress dropped the silver dollar from the approved list, the legislators were simply codifying an existing state of affairs. Almost no one batted an eye; no one at the time complained.

Events that followed, however, soon cast the Coinage Act of 1873 in a decidedly different light. In that same year the new German empire, having recently adopted the gold standard, melted down its silver coins and dumped the resulting bullion on the world market. Largely as a result, several other European countries, including France, Belgium, Switzerland, Italy, and Greece, severely curtailed the minting of silver coins. Sweden, Norway, and Holland went off silver entirely, likewise adding to the available supply of silver. At almost the same time, new silver mines opened in the American West, contributing still further to the silver glut. The consequence of this confluence of events was a sharp fall in the price of silver relative to gold.

Under previous circumstances, such a shift in relative values would have caused silver dollars to replace gold dollars, just as gold dollars had replaced silver dollars a generation earlier. But now the U.S. mint was no longer stamping silver dollars. The American money supply was artificially crimped—artificially, that is, by historical standards.

The period of crimping coincided with the big post–Civil War expansion of the American economy. American industrial and farm output grew rapidly in the 1870s and 1880s; but because the money supply was constrained and prevented from increasing at an equal pace, prices fell. Debtors' burdens grew, and the various other side effects of deflation set in.

Debt-burdened Americans now looked back to the Coinage Act of 1873 with an eye to assigning blame for their current troubles. The conspiracy-minded among them found it convenient to ascribe malevolent intentions to those who had pushed to delete silver dollars from the list of approved coins. Clearly creditors were benefiting from the fall in prices; clearly the government's refusal to mint silver dollars was contributing to the fall. The international aspects of the money situation suggested an international dimension to the conspiracy, making it all the more exotic, seductive, and undisprovable. If the culprits couldn't be definitively identified in America, they must be hiding out overseas—in the London offices of the Rothschilds, probably.

The folklore that grew up around the silver issue helped make it the most explosive political topic of the 1890s. Silverites demanded a return to bimetallism; anti-silverites adamantly defended the gold standard, for all the reasons the silverites didn't. Pamphlets propagandized both sides of the issue; magazine articles explained the virtues of a silver standard, and its vices; books delineated the causes and consequences of the Crime of '73, and the nonsense that the very label entailed; stump speakers exhorted listeners to demand the "dollar of our daddies" (silver), and to abjure silver as theft. Like arguments about religion, arguments about silver and gold often passed beyond the realm of reason, ultimately turning on matters of faith. Few people managed to hold to a middle ground between silver and gold. Silverites regularly impugned the motives of gold-bugs, marking them as minions of the international bankers' conspiracy. Backers of gold dismissed the sanity of the silverites, despairing that democracy required granting the vote to persons with such malfunctioning minds.

V

Of all the articles, pamphlets, and books the silver movement spawned, none generated a greater impact than a slim volume authored and published in Chicago by William Harvey. Forty-two years old when the Panic of 1893 hit, Harvey had grown up in western New York. After completing the equivalent of high school in Buffalo, he briefly attended a teachers' college before deciding to become a lawyer. He read law and was admitted to the bar at the tender but not unheard of age of nineteen, whereupon he transplanted to West Virginia to practice law in a town named for railroad tycoon Collis Huntington. In the mid-1870s he moved again, to the Cleveland of John Rockefeller. After three years there the wanderlust hit him once more, and he headed for Chicago. He stayed in Chicago only a short while before returning to Ohio. His family was growing—he had three children now—but the additional responsibility did little to soothe his itchy feet.

Silver first started to fascinate William Harvey in 1883 when he traveled to Colorado on business. Few people ever fell so hard; he returned to Ohio, packed up his wife and children, recruited ten young men whose imaginations and greed he fired with visions of immense wealth waiting to be taken from the ground, and headed for the Rockies. He installed his family in a rough-and-ready cabin on a mountainside where he and his crew dug and blasted and sifted and hauled from earliest spring until the snows of autumn closed the mine entrance. Harvey's tireless efforts produced a fair amount of silver, but they didn't yield much wealth, for the world silver glut had depressed prices, forcing marginal operations over the brink into bankruptcy and requiring the rest to compete frantically for the markets that remained. Even less insightful men than Harvey could see that the silver business would remain in the doldrums until some new demand for the metal appeared.

Harvey dropped out of mining and out of the mountains, moving down-slope to Pueblo, Colorado. There he practiced law again, sold real estate, peddled a tonic called the "Elixir of Life," and promoted an exhibition housed in a "Mineral Palace" and displaying the gems and minerals of the Rockies and other regions. Although the elixir didn't bring Harvey's luck to life, the Mineral Palace did well for a time after its opening in 1890. Yet it didn't do well enough to keep Harvey from looking for bigger opportunities. He relocated to Denver, then to Ogden. For some reason he purchased a mile-long frontage on the Great Salt Lake. Local tradition has it that he intended to establish an annual festival patterned on the New Orleans Mardi Gras. Only afterward did he appreciate the fact of the over-whelming Mormon presence in the Utah area and understand why a Bourbon Street on the lake wasn't a good bet. His education in the matter cost him a sizable part of his savings.

In May 1893, Harvey and his family joined the hundreds of thousands of other Westerners heading for Chicago and the Columbian Exposition. The fair had the effect on Harvey that Daniel Burnham and the other pro-moters hoped it would have on many visitors, and he decided to stay in Chicago and establish a new business. In Harvey's case, the business was publishing. His publishing house would dedicate itself to economic af-fairs—in particular to the currency question.

Harvey's first publication appeared just over a year later. The events of that intervening year made it seem much longer, especially for anyone in-terested in the nation's finances. The Panic of 1893 produced its tsunami of liquidations, foreclosures, and bank failures; these helped trigger the run on the government's gold reserve and the fevered efforts by the Cleveland administration to plug the dike. Cleveland's special summons of Congress to repeal the Sherman Silver Act convinced the silverites that the president was a stooge of the bankers; the success of the repeal effort indicated that the selling of the American people into permanent bondage to the bankers was dreadfully near. The arguments of the most powerful orators among the silver forces had failed to prevent this financial putsch; even the volleys of William Jennings Bryan had merely glanced off the sides of the gold juggernaut.

Into the breach strode William Harvey. More precisely, into the breach strode Harvey's fictional alter ego, a young financier named Coin, proprietor and professor of *Coin's Financial School*. Much like the young Jesus in the Temple, who had instructed the supposedly learned men of his day regarding matters of religion, Coin instructed the supposedly learned men of the 1890s regarding matters of finance. "My object," Harvey had Coin tell his auditors on the first day of Coin's seminar, "will be to teach you the A, B, C of the questions about money that are now a matter of everyday conversation."

Beginning at the beginning, Coin explained that just as in arithmetic there had to be a single unit of measurement (namely, the number 1), so there had to be a single unit in finance. By the power granted it under the Constitution, the first Congress had chosen the dollar as the unit of measurement and defined it to consist of 371 and ¼ grains of pure silver. "This was in 1792," Coin remarked meaningfully, "in the days of Washington and Jefferson and our revolutionary forefathers, who had a hatred of England and an intimate knowledge of her designs on this country."

Coin went on to stress repeatedly how the silver dollar of 371 and ¼ grains was the fundamental unit of currency, and how all other units, including the gold dollar, were defined in terms of silver. This was the law from the earliest years of the American republic. "This continued to be the law up to 1873," Coin said, touching another base with the conspiracy theorists. "During that long period, the unit of values was never changed and always contained 371 and ¼ grains of pure silver. While that was the law, it was impossible for anyone to say that the silver in a silver dollar was only worth 47 cents, or any other number of cents less than 100 cents, or a dollar. For it was itself the unit of values. While that was the law, it would have been as absurd to say that the silver in a silver dollar was only worth 47 cents as it would be to say that this figure 1 which I have drawn on the blackboard"—illustrated in Harvey's text—"is only forty-seven one-hundredths of one." Coin said that the silver in a silver dollar might sell for *more* than one dollar, due to increased demand for silver in industry or the arts or as money in other countries. "But it could never be worth less than a dollar—less than itself."

Coin went on to describe silver as the money of the people, as contrasted to gold, the money of the rich. The founding fathers had adopted silver because it enjoyed great popularity, because it was "more reliable" than gold, and because, being more plentiful and widely scattered, it was less liable to be cornered by unscrupulously designing men. While the rich handled gold regularly, the poor handled it rarely and the very poor almost never; silver was far more democratic.

After this introductory exposition, Coin entertained a question from a cub reporter in the audience evidently bent on refuting the lecturer. The question proved to be a trivial one, though, hardly meriting Coin's attention. He handled it easily. The narrator of Harvey's story described the questioner's chagrin: "The young journalist turned red in the face and hung his head."

Another questioner then stood up to challenge Coin. He raised a point that required an intimate knowledge of the statutes governing the establishment of the American currency system. His cleverness greatly pleased himself. "He sat down looking as proud as a cannoneer who has just fired a shot that has had deadly effect in the enemy's ranks."

Coin parried the attack by citing the relevant passages chapter and verse from the statute books and offering a detailed exegesis from the text. This questioner too was forced to beat a hasty retreat.

Coin proceeded to discuss in rather more heated language the infamous Coinage Act of 1873. That act, he said, while "purporting to be a revision of the coinage laws," was in reality far more. It destroyed the monetary system that had undergirded the Republic for eighty years, by depriving the people of their right to silver. The deed was accomplished with great stealth; the measure slipped through Congress—here Coin quoted a too-late-wise lawmaker—with "the silent tread of a cat." Many legislators had no idea what they were passing; President Grant signed the bill into law without recognizing that it demonetized silver. Coin summarized: "An army of a half million of men invading our shores, the warships of the world bombarding our coasts, could not have made us surrender the money of the people and substitute in its place the money of the rich. A few words embraced in fifteen pages of statutes put through Congress in the rush of bills did it. The pen was mightier than the sword."

An interlocutor objected that in 1873 silver had been so relatively scarce that no one was bringing it to the mint; the Coinage Act slipped through Congress not by a conspiracy but by lack of interest.

Coin quickly blocked this thrust, calling it after-the-fact sophistry—as were the other objections to silver currently being raised. Speaking collectively of such arguments, he declared, "They are all the bastard children of the crime of 1873." There could be no question what had happened to silver. "It was demonetized secretly, and since then a powerful money trust has used deception and misrepresentations that have led tens of thousands of honest minds astray."

On this emphatic note, the first day of lectures at Coin's Financial School closed. Word soon circulated throughout Chicago, where Harvey located Coin's school, about the precocious young man who was spreading the silver gospel. The *Chicago Tribune*, rumored (in Harvey's book and other Populist circles) to be secretly controlled by British investors, editorially abused the upstart. The other pillars of the banking community seconded the *Tribune*'s sentiment.

Consequently when Coin convened his class at the beginning of the second day, he found the hall filled with middle-aged and older men who apparently intended to embarrass the speaker. "Knotty questions would be hurled at him—perplexing queries and abstruse propositions. They would harass him, worry him, and tangle him, laugh at his dilemma and then say: 'We told you so.' This was the programme."

But Coin bearded the lions. He had hardly opened his mouth when the most fearsome member of the pride, Lyman Gage, the (real-life) chairman of the First National Bank of Chicago (and later William McKinley's treasury secretary), interposed an objection. Harvey had Coin's listeners on the edges of their seats as Gage rose to confront the upstart. "All eyes were on him," Harvey's narrator said. "He had been watching for an opening, and now he thought he had it, where he could deliver a telling, and follow it up with a knock-out, blow."

Leaving his readers hanging for a moment, Harvey digressed to get in a few blows of his own: against people like Gage who specialized in making money off the work of other people, and against the cities that produced such unproductive persons. "Cities do not breed statesmen," Harvey wrote. "They breed the specialist. A specialist favors what will tend to promote his business though it may injure the business of others." The people who produced the wealth and property of the world, not those parasites who lived off the labor of the people, should be the ones who determined public policy. "The men who handle this property after it is produced have little regard for the interests of the producers. Their selfishness and greed blind them."

Returning to the matter at hand, Harvey had Gage ask Coin how the government could hope to hold two different metals of varying quantity at a fixed ratio to each other.

Coin accepted the challenge. He explained that Gage's objection held true in the case of ordinary commodities operating under the ordinary rules of supply and demand; but precious metals weren't ordinary commodities, and when the government threw open the doors of the mint and pledged to coin all the silver and gold delivered to its doorstep, it created a situation of "unlimited demand." This had the effect of allowing the government to set the price of silver or gold more or less as it chose.

To illustrate his point, Coin drew a picture on the blackboard behind him. (Harvey's book reproduced the picture for his readers.) The picture showed two hands each holding a rope that suspended one end of a plank. The hands represented the government's demand for silver and gold respectively. As long as the government kept a firm grip on the ropes, the plank, representing the overall price level and the country's financial health generally, remained stable. But when government let go of one of the ropes—as the American government had let go in 1873 by demonetizing silver—the plank fell crashingly askew.

Coin's illustration impressed his audience. Even Gage, the bank chairman, was at a loss for a retort. He sat down and paid close attention to what Coin had further to say.

The young schoolmaster drove home his argument with another illustration. This time he drew a picture showing two large vessels of water. Above each was a spigot pouring water into its vessel. The two vessels were connected at their bottoms by a pipe. As Coin explained things, the two vessels represented silver and gold. The water pouring into each represented the supplies of the metals delivered to the mint. The pipe connecting the two vessels signified the free coinage of both metals. As long as the pipe remained open, the water level in both vessels rose at the same rate and the economy remained in equilibrium. But as soon as the pipe was closed—as it had been in 1873—the economy was thrown into chaos.

This second illustration convinced even many of the skeptics. "Coin had been listened to with rapt attention. A pin could almost have been heard to drop at any moment. No sound was heard except the voice of the young speaker, whose pleasant style of address had a charm about it that did not wear away. . . . There was a fascination in Coin's manner of delivery that had caused every word he uttered to be heard and understood. They had listened critically, expecting to detect errors in his facts or reasoning. There were none. They were amazed."

Coin's school continued through the rest of the week. Each day the financial wunderkind gained new converts to the cause of silver. During the course of the lectures, he added new illustrations to reinforce his lessons. As a demonstration of how confining gold was as a sole standard of money, Coin had assistants measure off the dimensions of a cube 22 feet on a side. A cube of this size, he said, could hold all the gold ever mined and available for use as money. ("A buzz of conversation went around the room with expressions of disbelief—such as 'impossible,' 'it cannot be.' ") He likened a currency dependent on only one metal to a bird trying to fly with one wing or a man trying to walk on one leg. He depicted the American economy as a cow fed by the farmers of the West but milked by the bankers of the East. Prosperity was shown as a maiden about to be ravished by a banker wearing a top hat labeled "England" while nearby the hero Silver was chained to the pillars of the temple of finance. An octopus identified as "Rothschilds" stretched its tentacles across a map of the world; the caption declared, "The English Octopus: It Feeds on Nothing but Gold!"

By the sixth and last day of lectures, Coin was the toast of the city. Everywhere people talked of this "little financier of the people," who had refuted conventional wisdom and made the genuine wisdom of free silver utterly transparent and irresistible. When the doors of the lecture hall opened on the morning of the sixth day, long lines had already formed; thousands had to be turned away.

Coin had saved to the last the vexing—to ordinary economists—issue of whether the United States could unilaterally remonetize silver when most of the other countries of the world had abandoned it. The entire audience wanted to hear what he had to say on the subject. He didn't disappoint them.

"In the midst of plenty, we are in want," he began. "Helpless children and the best womanhood and manhood of America appeal to us for release from a bondage that is destructive of life and liberty. All the nations of the Western Hemisphere turn to their great sister republic for assistance in the emancipation of the people of at least one-half the world. The Orient, with its teeming millions of people, and France, the cradle of science and liberty in Europe, look to the United States to lead in the struggle to roll back the accumulated disasters of the last twenty-one years. What shall our answer be?"

The audience waited, hushed, for Coin to tell them.

He kept them in suspense momentarily, then continued, "If it is claimed we must adopt for our money the metal England selects, and can have no independent choice in the matter, let us make the test and find out if it is true. It is not American to give up without trying." Coin didn't think the claim was true; indeed, he was prepared to demonstrate logically that it couldn't be true. But if it was, patriotic Americans would know what to do. "Let us attach England to the United States and blot her name out from among the nations of the earth!"

The audience roared its approval, forcing Coin to stop. When the tumult eventually diminished, he went on, "A war with England would be the most popular war ever waged on the face of the earth!"

More loud applause, forcing another halt.

"If it is true that she can dictate the money of the world, and thereby create world-wide misery, it would be the most just war ever waged by man!"

Applause still more deafening than before.

Coin allowed the audience to vent its emotions. He wished to proceed in a different direction. "Fortunately, this is not necessary." It was true, he said, that England, uncoerced, would never voluntarily accept silver as a monetary standard. England was the world's great creditor, and creditors loved gold, which drove prices down and the value of their credits up. Nor would the Eastern bankers in the United States ever voluntarily remonetize silver, for they were in the same position vis-à-vis the masses of the American people that England was in vis-à-vis the world.

Yet if the American people would refuse to let the English and their American collaborators dictate currency policy, and if they would take America's destiny into their own hands, they could reclaim the power that gold gave to these enemies of the public welfare. By remonetizing silver, the American government would unlock an American agricultural and industrial treasure trove. In a matter of just a few years, America would leave England far behind.

"The gold standard will give England the commerce and wealth of the world," Coin asserted. "The bimetallic standard will make the United States the most prosperous nation on the globe."

Applause.

"To avoid the struggle means a surrender to England. It means more— it means a tomb raised to the memory of the republic. Delay is dangerous. At any moment, an internecine war may break out among us. Wrongs and outrages will not be continuously endured. The people will strike at the laws that inflict them."

Americans needn't stand helplessly by while revolution tore their country to shreds. The people must realize that they had been frightened by illusions—illusions conjured by persons whose self-interest dictated making those illusions as fearsome as possible.

Americans wouldn't be alone in their struggle to break the grip of England on the commerce of the world. France would join the United States in support of silver. So would Mexico, the countries of Central and South America, and several Asian nations. Soon the forces of gold would be outnumbered and outproduced.

Americans had no choice if they cherished their liberty. At present England was engaged in the quiet conquest of America. "What she failed to do with shot and shell in the eighteenth century, she is doing with the gold standard in the nineteenth century."

Applause.

"The conservative monied interest furnished the Tory friends of England then, and it furnishes her friends now."

More applause.

"The business men of New York City passed strong resolutions against the Declaration of Independence in 1776, and they are passing strong resolutions against an American policy now."

Still more applause.

"Citizens! The integrity of the government has been violated. A Financial Trust has control of your money, and with it, is robbing you of your property. Vampires feed upon your commercial blood. The money in the banks is subject to the check of the money lenders. They expect you to quietly submit, and leave your fellow citizens at their mercy. Through the instrumentality of law they have committed a crime that overshadows all other crimes. And yet they appeal to law for their protection. If the starving workingman commits the crime of trespass, they appeal to the law they have contaminated, for his punishment. Drive these moneychangers from your temples. Let them discover by your aspect their masters—the people!"

Tremendous applause.

"This is a struggle for humanity. For our homes and firesides. For the purity and integrity of our government." Americans who understood the gravity of the challenge to democracy must alert their fellow citizens. "Go among the people and awake them to the situation of peril in which they are placed. Awake them as you would with startling cries at the coming of flood and fires. Arouse them as did Paul Revere as he rode through the streets shouting: 'The British are on our shores!' To let England dictate to us was not once the spirit of Americans!"

With his audience on the verge of an explosion, Coin paused and held them there. He related a story about Benjamin Franklin in London, at a state dinner. Toasts were offered to the countries represented, by the ranking officials at table. The English prime minister offered, "To England, the sun that gives light to the world." The French minister responded, "To France, the moon that controls the tides of the world." All eyes then turned to Franklin. What could the commissioner from the fledgling American republic say? How would he represent the United States? Very deliberately, gazing slowly around the table, Franklin replied, "To the United States, the Joshua that commanded the sun and moon to *stand still*, and they *stood still*."

Coin's audience bellowed its hearty approval—of Franklin and of Coin. Not waiting this time for the clamor to die down, Coin raised his voice above the din. "If we had an administration and Congress now that would say to England, 'Stand still!,' one glad shout would be heard in this country from sea to sea and Lakes to Gulf, proclaiming the second independence of the United States!"

The crowd poured into the aisles and climbed onto the chairs; hundreds yelled at the top of their lungs for Coin. They surrounded him on the stage, pumping his hand and slapping his back. After several minutes of this demonstration, one convert to the cause called for attention. It was J. L. Caldwell, a noted banker. "I am the president of a national bank," he declared, "and I want to first say to you people that all national bankers do not regard selfish personal interest as paramount to love of country and the interests of the whole people. A few of us have stood out against this gold standard system, and are in favor of immediate free coinage, 16 to 1 or 15 and 1/2 to 1, independent of England!"

Applause and shouts of support.

"I now propose *three cheers for Coin!*"

The crowd approved deliriously. "Hip! Hip! Hurrah!" The echoes rolled out the windows of the meeting hall and through the streets of Chicago.

With Coin utterly victorious, William Harvey concluded his story. "Thus ended the school. Chicago has had its lesson on bimetallism. How will this contest end? No one can tell. In the struggle of might against right, the former has generally triumphed. Will it win in the United States?" On the page below this question, Harvey printed a drawing of a crypt. Skulls and loose bones littered the entrance; a skeleton hung in the shadows inside. Over the door was a sign, "Gold Standard." Beneath was the legend, "All ye who enter here, leave hope behind."

VI

Harvey's Professor Coin became an overnight sensation, and not just in Harvey's fictionalized Chicago. In the two years between the 1894 publication of *Coin's Financial School* and the 1896 elections, the book sold nearly a million copies. During some stretches of that period, several thousand copies were going out the door of Harvey's publishing plant every day. Coin's fame spread by word of mouth to millions who didn't read the book; many of those who knew him only by reputation thought he was a real person and really had got the best of the country's financial panjandrums.

Harvey's book spawned imitations. Ignatius Donnelly tried his hand at the currency question in *The American People's Money,* a tale in which a banker and a farmer find themselves sharing a railway coach on a trip across the country. The banker attempts to educate the farmer about money, but the farmer is the one who has the right answers and he educates the banker.

The defenders of gold came out in force to rebut Harvey, Donnelly, and the other silver authors. Titles in the anti-silver genre included *Coin's Financial Fool, or The Artful Dodger Exposed; The Mistakes of Coin; A Freak in Finance; Cash vs. Coin; Coin's Financial School Exposed and Closed; Real Bi-Metallism, or True Coin versus False Coin;* and *Farmer Hayseed in Town, or The Closing Days of Coin's Financial School.* The critics pointed out Coin's (Harvey's) errors in history and logic. America's founding fathers had not made the silver dollar the fundamental unit of currency; rather, they had made the dollar the unit of currency and allowed it to be issued as gold or silver. (Coin's argument was plausible due to the fact that the Coinage Act of 1792 had not provided for a gold *dollar* coin. Gold coins came in sizes of $10, $5 and $2.50; the only *dollar* coin was the silver dollar.) The bimetallic system had never operated as smoothly before 1873 as Coin claimed; one metal had predominated for a time, then the other. The Coinage Act of 1873 wasn't the result of any conspiracy; it actually did follow from a general lack of interest in silver.

But most of the silverites didn't read Coin's critics, whose total sales didn't approach Harvey's. And even if they had, they probably would have dismissed the critics' arguments as apologetics for the plutocracy. The silver case was sufficiently credible that people who wanted it to be true could believe that it was.

Different people wanted it to be true for different reasons. Colorado silver miners wanted it to be true so that the government would buy more silver (as the government had done between the passage of the Sherman Silver Act in 1890 and its repeal in 1893). Kansas farmers wanted it to be true in order for the government to expand the currency and thereby ease their debts. Merchants in depressed regions wanted it to be true to revive business activity. Many ordinary people in the West and South (and some in the East) wanted it to be true so that the big bankers would be knocked down a couple of pegs.

Because the silver case was as much a matter of faith as of logic, its adherents were often judged to be cranks and lunatics. Some of them were. William Harvey took part of the royalties from *Coin's Financial School* and subsequent books and began construction of a large concrete pyramid, a modern American equivalent of the pyramids of Egypt. This monument was to be 130 feet high; it would contain copies of Harvey's books explaining how the gold standard and related evils were producing the decline of Western civilization, as well as copies of the Bible and a few other works; it would last for a million years. Atop the pyramid, high enough to protrude from the rubble and dust of future centuries, would be a plaque carrying the message,

"When this can be read, go below and find the cause of death of a former civilization." Unfortunately for Harvey—and future civilizations, presumably—the money ran out before the project got very far.

The eccentricities of the few were often stretched by critics to cover the activities of the many. While the defenders of gold were working over Harvey and Coin, other conservatives castigated other aspects of the Populist program. The *New York Times* branded the Populists' subtreasury scheme "one of the wildest and most fantastic projects ever seriously proposed by sober man." The *Atlanta Constitution* warned of the "anarchy and communism" being preached by Populists like Tom Watson. When a group of Watson's supporters rallied to the defense of a black man threatened with lynching, the *Augusta Chronicle* declared flatly, "Watson has gone mad." The *Daily States* of New Orleans asserted that an anti-lynching plank in the platform of a Populist gubernatorial candidate indicated that the party "inferentially approved" of white women being raped by black men. E. L. Godkin, the longtime editor of *The Nation*, accounted Populism "the vague dissatisfaction which is always felt by the incompetent and lazy and shiftless when they contemplate those who have got on better in the world." Godkin proceeded to explain to his mostly Eastern readers, regarding the Midwest, that "a large body of farmers of that region are now really peasants fresh from Europe, with all the prejudices and all the liability to deception of their class."

The anti-Populist diatribe that garnered the greatest attention came not from the East but from deep in the heart of Populist country. William Allen White, the young owner and editor of the *Emporia Gazette* of Kansas, disliked Populism on grounds both philosophical and personal. When the other paper in Emporia, the *Republican,* spoke out in favor of silver, the Populists in the area flocked to it and declared a boycott of White's paper, which hadn't. Adding insult, they heckled and harassed White on the streets of the town. On one August day in 1896, White was walking from his newspaper office to the post office when he was surrounded by a crowd of Populist types. White had the well-fed look of the stereotypical conservative Republican, and on this day he happened to be wearing his best summer suit. As he later recalled the incident, having mellowed somewhat in the meantime: "I probably looked like a large white egg as I waddled down the street to the post office, and came back with my arms full of newspaper exchanges. A block from the office a crowd of Populists tackled me. I was impatient and wanted to be on the way. They surrounded me. They were older men—men in their forties and fifties and sixties—and I was twenty-eight. They were shabbily dressed, and it was no pose with them. They were struggling with poverty, and I was rather spick-and-span, particularly offensive in the gaudy neckties for which I have had an unfortunate weakness. Anyway, they ganged me—hooting, jeering, nagging me about some editorial utterances I had made. I was froggy in the meadow and couldn't get out, and they were taking a little stick and poking me about. And my wrath must have flamed through my face."

White eventually escaped, but the experience infuriated him. As soon as he made it safely to his office, he sat down, mopped his brow, and slashed off an editorial entitled "What's the Matter with Kansas?" White began by noting a recent report from the Kansas department of agriculture saying that the population of Kansas had increased by less than two thousand persons during the past year. Ten thousand babies had been born in the state, but eight thousand people had moved out. At a time when the rest of the country was growing by leaps and bounds, Kansas was stagnating. "In five years, ten million people have been added to the national population, yet instead of gaining a share of this—say, half a million—Kansas has apparently been a plague spot, and, in the very garden of the world, has lost population by ten thousands every year."

That wasn't all Kansas had lost. Money was flowing away with the people who were going. "Every moneyed man in the state who could get out without loss has gone. Every month in every community sees someone who has a little money pack up and leave the state. . . . In towns where ten years ago there were three or four or half-a-dozen money-lending concerns, stimulating industry by furnishing capital, there is now none, or one or two that are looking after the interests and principal already outstanding."

Kansas's neighbors were prospering. Missouri had gained 2 million in population; Nebraska was filling in nicely; Colorado was expanding by the day. But not Kansas.

"What's the matter with Kansas?" demanded White.

"Go east and you hear them laugh at Kansas; go west and they sneer at her; go south and they 'cuss' her; go north and they have forgotten her. Go into any crowd of intelligent people gathered anywhere on the globe, and you will find the Kansas man on the defensive. The newspaper columns and magazines once devoted to praise of her, to boastful facts and startling figures concerning her resources, are now filled with cartoons, jibes and [Senator William] Pefferian speeches. Kansas just naturally isn't in it. She has traded places with Arkansas and Timbuctoo."

"What's the matter with Kansas?" demanded White again.

Answering his own question, he decried the character of the political leadership of the state. The 1896 elections were approaching, and the candidates were a sorry lot: "an old mossback Jacksonian who snorts and howls because there is a bathtub in the State House"; a "shabby, wild-eyed, rattle-brained fanatic who has said openly in a dozen speeches that 'the rights of the user are paramount to the rights of the owner' "; "an old human hoop-skirt who has failed as a businessman, who has failed as an editor, who has failed as a preacher"; and "a kid without a law practice"—this last unworthy running for attorney general. To add to the uplifting tone of the campaign, Kansans had "decided to send three or four harpies out lecturing, telling the people that Kansas is raising hell and letting the corn go to weed."

White's pen spewed sarcasm as he specified the remedy to the problems of Kansas. "What we need is not more money, but less capital, fewer white shirts and brains, fewer men with business judgment, and more of those fellows who boast that they are 'just ordinary clodhoppers but they know more in a minute about finance than John Sherman' "—the senator of the Silver Purchase Act. "We need more men who are 'posted' [foreclosed on], who can bellow about the crime of '73, who hate prosperity, and who think, because a man believes in national honor, he is a tool of Wall Street. We have had a few of them—some hundred fifty thousand—but we need more."

By now White was thoroughly hot to his subject. "We need several thousand gibbering idiots to scream about the 'Great Red Dragon' of Lombard Street [the London financial community]. We don't need population, we don't need wealth, we don't need well-dressed men on the streets, we don't need cities on the fertile prairies; you bet we don't! What we are after is the money power. Because we have become poorer and ornerier and meaner than a spavined, distempered mule, we, the people of Kansas, propose to kick; we don't care to build up, we wish to tear down."

White lambasted those who argued that prosperity percolated upward from the masses through society, that government could legislate good times by taking money from the rich and handing it out to the poor. "That's the stuff! Give the prosperous man the dickens! Legislate the thriftless man into ease, whack the stuffing out of the creditors, and tell the debtors who borrowed the money five years ago when money 'per capita' was greater than it is now, that the contraction of currency gives him a right to repudiate. Whoop it up for the ragged trousers; put the lazy, greasy fizzle, who can't pay his debts, on the altar, and bow down and worship him. Let the state ideal be high. What we need is not the respect of our fellow men, but the chance to get something for nothing."

White had a full head of steam by now. "Oh, yes, Kansas is a great state. Here are people fleeing from it by the score every day, capital going out of the state by the hundreds of dollars; and every industry but farming paralyzed, and that crippled, because its products have to go across the ocean before they can find a laboring man at work who can afford to buy them. Let's don't stop this year. Let's drive all the decent, self-respecting men out of the state. Let's keep the old clodhoppers who know it all. Let's encourage the man who is 'posted.' He can talk, and what we need is not mill hands to eat our meat, nor factory hands to eat our wheat, nor cities to oppress the farmer by consuming his butter and eggs and chickens and produce. What Kansas needs is men who can talk, who have large leisure to argue the currency question while their wives wait at home for that nickel's worth of bluing.

"What's the matter with Kansas?"

Nothing at all, except that she was losing everything worth having in life—population, wealth, respect. "She has started in to raise hell, as Mrs. Lease advised, and she seems to have an overproduction. But that doesn't matter. Kansas never did believe in diversified crops."

VII

William White's anti-Populist diatribe won him immediate national recognition. The big Eastern papers picked up and reprinted his editorial, which was deemed especially significant in light of its geographical origin. Before long White had been elevated to the position of respected spokesman for the voice of reason in middle America.

The Eastern enthusiasm for White suggested that the forces of respectability in America might be getting scared. They had some reason to be. Although the Populist Party wasn't making quite the headway its more optimistic members hoped for, the Populists' agenda continued to gain ground. The movement's orators certainly spoke with as much conviction as ever. "We now have two parties arrayed against each other, Aristocracy against Commonality," Ignatius Donnelly thundered. "Thirty thousand families own one-half the wealth of the country, and they have no part in producing it. They have stolen it from the labor and toil that has produced the nation." A widely circulated Populist cartoon showed Uncle Sam wearing a crown of thorns, with each bloody spike bearing the label of some malevolent trust or some diabolically reactionary doctrine such as monometallism.

Yet there was also reason for thinking Populism as a separate movement might have peaked. The political arithmetic of the 1892 elections, especially as it pertained to the presidency, convinced many people of Populist persuasion that they would do better boring from within the Democrats (especially) and the Republicans than hammering from without. On the silver issue, for example, they might most quickly achieve remonetization by capturing one of the major parties and propelling it to victory.

For this and other reasons that varied from district to district and state to state, the Populists slipped in 1894. The Republicans were the big winners in the upper Midwest and the Mountain states; in the South the Democrats siphoned off many Populist votes (sometimes by fraud and force). After the 1894 elections, only four senators and four congressmen openly affiliated themselves with the Populist Party; most Populist-leaning legislators preferred to maintain affiliation with one of the major parties.

But if the 1894 elections indicated that the Populist Party couldn't crack the condominium of the Republicans and Democrats, it also indicated that the major parties would have to pay greater attention to Populist concerns. Conservative Democrats joined conservative Republicans in branding free silver a heresy and a hallucination; all the same, silver generated excitement like no issue either established party brought forward. This excitement was what kept the Populists going. As long as the silver issue was theirs, they would have to be reckoned with.

Chapter 6

PLESSY V. CROW

I

As the experience of Populists like Tom Watson demonstrated, and as the investigations of Jacob Riis in the slums of New York indicated, few issues in American life during the 1890s could be considered without considering race. Racial suspicions prevented white farmers and black farmers in the South from making common cause against their common oppressors; racial tensions aggravated the poverty and violence that vexed America's big cities. The race question—how the white majority and the black minority should deal with each other—was one that America had wrestled with for centuries. The framers of the Constitution hadn't answered it, merely deferred it. The debaters over states' rights during the first half of the nineteenth century hadn't answered it, only inflamed it. Lincoln and the Union army in the Civil War hadn't answered it, although they made more progress in less time than any who had gone before. The Reconstruction Congresses hadn't answered it, though they laid the constitutional basis for an answer—by means of the Thirteenth, Fourteenth, and Fifteenth amendments—before becoming weary and throwing the question back to the South in the Compromise of 1877.

During the 1890s, the race question in America was as open as it had ever been. Old institutions had crumbled; new ones had yet to take their places. Prior to the Civil War, the institution of slavery had regulated relations between most African-Americans and the European-Americans with whom they came into contact. The large majority of blacks were slaves, which by definition made them subordinate to their masters, the overwhelming majority of whom were white. There were some anomalies in this system, including the few African-Americans who owned slaves and the greater number of African-Americans who were *not* slaves. But the anomalies weren't sufficient to cause the system to break down, and the equating of African-American with slave afforded a fair approximation to reality.

The chief preoccupations of the slaveholders were two: to extract labor from the slaves and to prevent slave insurrections. Both of these required close contact between the two races, or at least between certain segments of them. White overseers directed gangs of black plantation field hands; inside the plantation houses, slaves participated in the daily lives of their masters. On the more plentiful small farms, slaves and masters regularly rubbed shoulders, often literally. Slaveholders did their best to prevent the slaves from gathering on their own, out of white view. Whites feared that such gatherings would be the preludes to rebellion, as they in fact occasionally were.

In antebellum Southern cities, blacks and whites mingled constantly. New Orleans, for example, continually surprised visitors by the casualness with which the two races mixed in saloons, gaming halls, and brothels, not to mention in places of daytime business. Some visitors attributed New Orleans's racial openness to the Crescent City's French heritage, but similar conditions pertained in other Southern cities.

The fact of the matter was that segregation under a regime of slavery was both impractical and unnecessary. To separate the races would have made both the extraction of labor and the monitoring of the behavior of African-Americans inordinately difficult. Nor was separation necessary to remind blacks of their place in American society. Slavery made clear the relative status of the races.

Emancipation changed the situation dramatically. The end of slavery overturned the system of coerced labor; equally important, it undermined the status structure of the South. No longer could whites readily dictate what individual African-Americans must do on a daily basis: where they must live, with whom they could or could not associate. Further, the end of slavery and the ratification of the Reconstruction amendments created a psychological need in many whites for a new way of marking the distinction between the races. Under slavery there was never any doubt that whites were superior; under the newly amended Constitution there was serious doubt. In the eyes of the supreme law of the land, blacks were now the equals of whites. For whites—particularly for lower-class whites whose position on the social ladder was tenuous and uncertain—reaffirming white superiority became a pressing problem.

One possible answer to the problem was the Jim Crow system of racial segregation; but it wasn't the only conceivable answer. During the quarter century after Reconstruction, various persons and groups in the South proposed different models of race relations. George Washington Cable, author of the 1885 book, *The Silent South,* denied that one race had to be socially superior to the other. Speaking as a native of Louisiana, an officer of the Confederacy and, as he said, "a lover of my home, my city, and my State, as well as of my country," Cable declared that progress for the South required the advancement of both races, black as well as white. Cable rejected a familiar argument of the "Redeemers"—the upper-class whites who regained power in the South after Reconstruction—that progress for blacks had to await the restoration of law and order and honest government. Enforced inequality for blacks, Cable asserted, by its very nature corrupted government. The South would never have honest and good government until it had government that represented all the groups residing there. It should live up to its hopes rather than down to its fears. "A hundred years we have been fearing to do entirely right lest something wrong should come of it; fearing to give the black man an equal chance with us in the race of life lest we might have to grapple with the vast, vague afrite of Amalgamation." The time had come for a new approach.

Lewis Blair made much the same argument in 1889 in a book entitled *The Prosperity of the South Dependent upon the Elevation of the Negro.* Blair condemned measures that consigned blacks to inferior status, especially measures involving segregation. "The Negro must be allowed free access to all hotels and other places of public entertainment," Blair wrote. "He must be allowed free admittance to all theaters and other places of public amusement; he must be allowed free entrance to all churches, and in all public and official receptions of the president, governor, mayor, etc.; he must not be excluded by a hostile caste sentiment." To so exclude him would damage whites as well as blacks and retard the development of the South as a whole. "In his descent he drags us down with him," Blair said.

The arguments of Cable and Blair for black equality didn't persuade many white people in the South; the notion of white superiority was too firmly entrenched. Other opponents of the Jim Crow system took this assumption of white superiority as their point of departure. So transparent, in fact, was white superiority to them that they saw no need to reinforce it by artificial programs like segregation. "The Negro race is under us; he is in our power," said Governor Thomas Jones, the leading spokesman of Democratic conservatives in Alabama during the 1890s. "We are his custodians." This being the case, whites should treat the Negro fairly and with consideration. "We should extend to him, as far as possible, all the civil rights that will fit him to be a decent and self-respecting, law-abiding and intelligent citizen." As caretakers of society, whites could do no less. Treating blacks decently was not just the requirement of noblesse oblige; it was in whites' self-interest. Echoing Cable and Blair in this regard, Jones declared of blacks: "If we do not lift them up, they will drag us down."

Obviously it was easier for white aristocrats to take such a position than it was for lower-class whites. The aristocrats didn't need their status in society reinforced; their wealth and power sufficed. By contrast, lower-class whites often did feel the need for the kind of reinforcement segregation provided. Yet even among the lower classes there existed support for alternatives to a policy of separation. Tom Watson and the Populists argued for class solidarity across racial lines. In the Populist view, segregation and other forms of enforced inequality served chiefly to keep the rich in power and the poor in line. A Texas Populist put the case for white-black cooperation succinctly: "They are in the ditch just like we are." Climbing out would require the efforts of both races working together.

For a while, Southern practice partially reflected these alternative views. Until the 1890s, visitors to the South noted a hodgepodge of policies existing side by side. Segregation typified some areas of life; racial mixing marked others. In 1885, an African-American journalist, T. McCants Stewart, left Boston to tour the South. He was prepared to detect the slightest evidence of discrimination against blacks. "I put a chip on my shoulder," he wrote afterward, "and inwardly dared any man to knock it off." Stewart did indeed discover evidence of discrimination, but he also observed a much greater degree of equality than he had anticipated. One day in Virginia he found himself seated in a railroad car that was becoming crowded. Late-arriving white passengers were forced to sit on their luggage. "I fairly foamed at the mouth, imagining that the conductor would order me into a seat occupied by a colored lady so as to make room for a white passenger," Stewart recounted. No such demand occurred. He continued his journey into South Carolina. From Columbia, he wrote, "I feel about as safe here as in Providence, R.I. I can ride in first-class cars on the railroads and in the streets. I can go into saloons and get refreshments even as in New York. I can stop in and drink a glass of soda and be more politely waited upon than in some parts of New England."

Another traveler in the South, Charles Dudley Warner, visited New Orleans for the International Exposition of 1885. Warner later recalled, "White and colored people mingled freely, talking and looking at what was of common interest." On "Louisiana Day" at the fair, blacks were as well represented as whites. "The colored citizens took their full share of the parade and the honors. Their societies marched with the others, and the races mingled in the grounds in unconscious equality of privileges."

But the mingling didn't last forever. Hopes for a future of racial equality gave way to fears of the same thing, and a system of legalized castes gradually emerged. During the late 1880s and especially the 1890s, several Southern states passed Jim Crow laws. In doing so, they looked to precedents established, ironically, in the North. Slavery had largely vanished in the North a half century before it disappeared in the South, and although the North never had the large numbers of blacks the South had, Northern whites had to deal with some of the same issues of status Southern whites would encounter after the Civil War. Thus Northerners adopted many of the features of segregation that would later become the hallmark of Southern race relations. Northern blacks were required to use separate railway cars and stagecoaches and separate cabins on steamboats; they were forced into separate sections of theaters and churches; they were excluded from the best restaurants and hotels. They had to live in separate neighborhoods; they had to send their children to separate schools, their sick to separate hospitals, their dead to separate cemeteries. The Northern system of segregation wasn't uniformly rigorous. Massachusetts was more tolerant than most Northern states; the Midwestern and Western states were less tolerant. Yet in the North as much as in the South it was completely respectable to consider whites superior to blacks. Northern attitudes toward race relations were summarized by no less a figure than Abraham Lincoln two years prior to his first election as president. Lincoln declared, "There is a physical difference between the black and white races which I believe will for ever forbid the two races living together on terms of social and political equality. And inasmuch as they cannot so live, while they do remain together"—Lincoln flirted with the idea of sending American blacks to Africa—"there must be the position of superior and inferior; and I as much as any other man am in favor of having the superior position assigned to the white race."

II

The first Jim Crow laws passed in most Southern states pertained to transportation, particularly aboard trains. There were two reasons for singling out rail travel. First, it involved close contact among passengers, frequently including women, for many hours and often overnight. On this account, opponents of race mingling found integrated railcars particularly offensive. Second, trains almost always had more than one car, so that railroad companies could easily segregate passengers with little expense or lost ridership.

Florida led the way by mandating separation of the races on trains in 1887. Mississippi mimicked Florida in 1888, Texas in 1889. Louisiana passed a Jim Crow train law in 1890, followed by Alabama, Arkansas, Georgia, and Tennessee the next year, and Kentucky in 1892. North Carolina, South Carolina, and Virginia held out for several years, not ordering the segregation of railroads until almost the beginning of the twentieth century.

The Carolinas and Virginia delayed as long as they did partly because they wanted to see whether the Jim Crow laws would withstand constitutional challenge. Since the Compromise of 1877—the arrangement whereby the South and the Democrats conceded the contested presidential election of 1876 to Rutherford Hayes and the Republicans in exchange for a tacit agreement by the Republicans to pull the last federal troops out of the South—African-Americans had watched the equality apparently guaranteed to them under the amended Constitution get chipped away, right by right. A Supreme Court decision in the 1883 *Civil Rights Cases* declared that the Constitution afforded no protection against discrimination by private individuals or private businesses. If the managers of hotels or restaurants or music halls or railroads decided on their own to restrict or bar black patrons, that was their own affair. Some did discriminate, but most, not wishing to lose business to competitors, awaited action by the state legislatures. The Jim Crow laws of the late 1880s and 1890s were just what they were waiting for.

To African-Americans, the shift from private Jim Crowism to public Jim Crowism was significant and ominous. The shift appeared to portend a large increase in the practice of discrimination; many more activities than heretofore would now be off limits to blacks. Additionally and far more important, the governmental sanctioning of segregation placed the seal of public approval on anti-black discrimination. The law had never been able to prevent private ugliness; probably most people doubted that it could or maybe even should. But democratic governments were not supposed to act in a deliberately discriminatory fashion toward any honest and peaceful segment of their populations.

Hoping to stem the tide of segregation, a group of African-Americans from Louisiana decided to challenge the constitutionality of the state's Jim Crow railroad law. Their challenge was a continuation of an earlier fight to block passage of the law—as well as other discriminatory measures—in the Louisiana legislature. The anti-discrimination forces succeeded in sidetracking efforts to disenfranchise blacks, but despite the presence of sixteen African-American lawmakers in the general assembly in Baton Rouge, and despite petitions from black citizens' groups, they failed to stop the Jim Crow railroad law.

The preamble to the law stated its purpose as being "to promote the comfort of passengers on railway trains." It didn't have to be spelled out *which* passengers' comfort was being promoted. The next clause contained the essence of the measure: all railway companies offering passenger service in Louisiana were required "to provide equal but separate accommodations for the white and colored races, by providing separate coaches or compartments so as to secure separate accommodations."

Following passage of the measure, the Louisiana African-American community considered its options. "The Bill is now a law," editorialized the *New Orleans Crusader*. "The next thing is what we are going to do." Some persons suggested a boycott of the railroads, but the *Crusader*'s editor, L. A. Martinet, urged a response through the legal system. "We'll make a case, a test case, and bring it before the Federal Courts," Martinet wrote. With the *Crusader*'s encouragement, several of New Orleans's most prominent African-Americans formed a "Citizens' Committee to Test the Constitutionality of the Separate Car Law."

The first order of committee business was raising money; the second was finding suitable circumstances for testing the law. The money flowed in at a modest pace while the committee looked for a good lawyer and a promising defendant. The lawyer was the more easily found. Martinet wrote to Albion Winegar Tourgée, a former carpetbagger currently living in upstate New York. Tourgée was an Ohio native and a former Union officer who had moved to North Carolina in 1865 to practice law and help the Radical Republicans reconstruct North Carolina; subsequently he served with some distinction on the North Carolina superior court. What really set Tourgée apart from hundreds of other carpetbaggers, though, was the literary mileage he had got out of his experience. Beginning in the late 1870s, he published several novels based on what he had encountered and endured in the postwar South. Though his efforts with the pen never gained him a great deal of money or a lasting reputation as an author, they kept him in the public eye. "We know we have a friend in you," the New Orleans committee wrote, adding, "We know your ability is beyond question." When the committee asked Tourgée to serve as lead counsel in an effort to overturn the Louisiana Jim Crow law, he accepted.

Tourgée recommended that the committee choose for the person to test the law an individual, perhaps a woman, who was "nearly white." Presumably this would underline the arbitrariness of the ban. Martinet doubted that such a plan would work, since a very light-skinned African-American, especially a woman, probably would be allowed to pass for white. "It would be quite difficult to have a lady *too* nearly white refused admission to a 'white' car," Martinet wrote Tourgée. "There are the strangest white people you ever saw here. Walking up and down our principal thoroughfare—Canal Street—you would be surprised to have persons pointed out to you, some as white and others as colored, and if you were not informed you would be sure to pick out the white for colored and the colored for white. Besides, people of tolerably fair complexion, even if unmistakably colored, enjoy here a large degree of immunity from the accursed prejudice. In this respect New Orleans differs greatly from the interior towns, in this state or Mississippi." Yet despite his reservations, Martinet was willing to go along with Tourgée's advice. "We will try to do the best we can."

Members of the African-American citizens' committee then approached the railroads. Several of the companies opposed the law, partly because of the trouble of policing it, partly because of the risk of alienating blacks, who formed an important portion of their clientele, and partly because of the expense, albeit relatively small, of running extra cars in the cases where extra cars were needed. The first company Martinet and his associates contacted said it didn't enforce the law. It posted the requisite signs but instructed its personnel not to bother blacks who ignored them. Two other companies said they didn't like the law and hoped to see it overturned, yet they desired to talk with their lawyers before getting involved in what might be a costly court fight.

Eventually, Tourgée, Martinet, and the committee worked out a plan with a line that consented to cooperate. A black man—rather than a woman: Martinet's objection wasn't without effect—would buy a train ticket and take a seat in a white car. A white passenger in the car, who would have volunteered for the task, would complain to the conductor. The conductor, also acting according to instructions, would tell the black man to move to the Jim Crow car. The black man would refuse. The white person would file a complaint.

All went as planned on February 24, 1892, when Daniel Desdunes, the twenty-one-year-old son of a founding member of the citizens' committee, boarded a train in New Orleans bound for Mobile, Alabama. Desdunes sat in the white car, was asked to move, refused, and was complained against. He was arrested, released on bond, and scheduled for trial in New Orleans district court.

Preparing for the trial, the two top lawyers for the defense, Tourgée and associate counsel James Walker, had a disagreement regarding the strategy they ought to pursue. Walker recommended attacking the Jim Crow law as a violation of the interstate commerce clause of the Constitution. Tourgée granted that such an approach might succeed in voiding this particular statute, perhaps even an entire class of laws pertaining to transportation; but it wouldn't get to the heart of the matter, which was whether states could pass laws mandating segregation of blacks in any business whatever.

Tourgée and Walker were saved the trouble of resolving their difference by the Louisiana supreme court. In May 1892, the state's high court ruled in a separate case brought by the Pullman Company that the Louisiana Jim Crow law did in fact infringe the interstate commerce clause and therefore was void as it related to interstate passengers. Because Desdunes had purchased a ticket for a destination in Alabama, the case against him collapsed.

Some members of the New Orleans black community applauded the court's decision as a signal victory. "The Jim Crow car is ditched and will remain in the ditch," declared Martinet's *Crusader*. "Reactionists may foam at the mouth, and Bourbon organs may squirm, but Jim Crow is dead as a door nail."

Others, including Tourgée and most of the citizens' committee, remained unsatisfied. The Jim Crow law still applied to travel within Louisiana; more important, the principle of state-ordered segregation stood intact. Even James Walker agreed that the assault on the law must continue.

Accordingly a new test was arranged. Early in June, Homer Plessy bought a ticket from New Orleans to Covington, Louisiana, on the East Louisiana Railroad. Although some of the details of the affair are unclear, the citizens' committee evidently had apprised the railroad company of its plan, as it had done in the previous test, for otherwise Plessy would probably not have been noticed. He had very light skin—he described himself as seven-eighths Caucasian and one-eighth African—and he customarily passed for white in New Orleans. Plessy took a seat in the white coach. A conductor asked him to move; he refused. A detective arrested him, and trial was scheduled.

When Plessy came to trial before the criminal court of the parish of New Orleans, Tourgée and Walker presented a plea specifying fourteen objections to the Jim Crow statute. The essence of the plea was that the statute established "an invidious distinction and discrimination between citizens of the United States based on race which is obnoxious to the fundamental principles of National Citizenship, perpetuates involuntary servitude as regards Citizens of the Colored Race under the merest pretense of promoting the comfort of passengers on railway trains, and in further respects abridges the privileges and immunities of Citizens of the United States and the rights secured by the XIIIth and XIVth Amendments to the Federal Constitution."

The trial judge praised the defense counsel on its "great research, learning and ability," but indicated that he didn't think much of the defense's arguments. The court found the Jim Crow law constitutional and Plessy guilty.

The court's decision elicited applause from leading organs of the white community in New Orleans. The editor of the *Times-Democrat* congratulated the court for upholding the separate-car law and thus putting "a quietus to the efforts of some negro agitators to disobey it and sweep it aside." The *Times-Democrat* reminded readers that the paper had supported passage of the Jim Crow law when it was before the legislature; indeed, the paper had urged more far-reaching segregationist measures. "The law, however, was a move in the right direction, framed in the interest of the traveling public and intended to show the negroes that while they lived side by side with the whites the line of distinction and separation between the races was to be forever kept up." The paper hoped the recent court decision would cause the "silly negroes" who were fighting the law to cease and desist. "The sooner they drop their so-called 'crusade' against 'the Jim Crow car,' and stop wasting their money in combatting so well-established a principle—the right to separate the races in cars and elsewhere—the better for them."

But the "silly negroes" had no intention of calling off their fight. No sooner had the New Orleans court handed down its decision than Tourgée and Walker appealed to the Louisiana supreme court. The two attorneys weren't encouraged by the fact that the chief justice of the court was former governor Francis Nichols, who in 1890 had signed the Jim Crow bill into law, but they pressed ahead. Their efforts were rewarded when the court accepted the case for review.

The Louisiana high court conducted its review with dispatch and soon delivered its judgment. After clearing away some procedural clutter, the court declared, "We thus reach the sole question involved in this case, which is, whether a statute requiring railroads to furnish separate, but equal, accommodations for the two races, and requiring domestic passengers to confine themselves to the accommodations provided for the race to which they belong, violates the XIV Amendment." On this point the court cited precedents from other states. Not coincidentally, two of these precedents came from the North, the birthplace of Jim Crow. An 1849 case from Massachusetts upheld the principle of segregation in schools. The Massachusetts supreme court had answered objections by declaring, "It is urged that this maintenance of separate schools tends to deepen and perpetuate the odious distinction of caste founded in a deep-rooted prejudice in public opinion. This prejudice, if it exists, is not created by law and cannot be changed by law." The Massachusetts court went on to say that prejudice would be as likely to increase as to decrease, as the result of mixing schoolchildren.

The second case came from Pennsylvania. The supreme court there upheld a law quite similar to the Louisiana law, mandating separate accommodations in rail travel. The Pennsylvania court reasoned, "To assert separateness is not to declare inferiority in either. It is simply to say that following the order of Divine Providence, human authority ought not to compel these widely separated races to intermix." The Pennsylvania court continued, "Law and custom having sanctioned a separation of races, it is not the province of the judiciary to legislate it away."

The Louisiana court chose to be guided by these precedents. The court asserted that the challenged law applied with "perfect fairness and equality" between the races. In support of this point, the court noted that the charge against Plessy didn't specify whether he was black or white, merely that he insisted on sitting in a coach "to which by race he did not belong." The court added, "Obviously, if the fact charged be proved, the penalty would be the same whether the accused were white or colored." The court professed to be mystified that blacks were making such a fuss about placing themselves where they clearly weren't welcome. "Even if it were true that the statute is prompted by a prejudice on the part of one race to be thrown in such contact with the other, one would suppose that to be a sufficient reason why the pride and self-respect of the other race should equally prompt it to avoid such contact." Moreover, the "unreasonable insistence upon thrusting the company of one race upon the other" would merely "foster and intensify repulsion between them, rather than to extinguish it." The court denied Plessy's appeal.

The next step was the United States Supreme Court, which had been the objective of the New Orleans citizens' committee all along. It didn't take long for Tourgée and Walker to file the necessary papers, nor for the Supreme Court to consent to hear the appeal. But it *did* take a long time for the case actually to come before the federal high court. The delay owed partly to a backlog of cases on the court's docket and partly to a decision by Tourgée not to press for quick action. Tourgée examined the makeup of the court and wrote to Martinet, "Of the whole number of Justices, there is but one who is known to favor the view we must stand upon. One is inclined to be with us legally, but his political bias is strong the other way. There are two who may be brought over by the argument. There are five who are against us. Of these, one may be reached, I think, if he 'hears from the country' soon enough. The others will probably stay where they are until Gabriel blows his horn." Tourgée declared that the Supreme Court had "always been the foe of liberty until forced to move on by public opinion." He hoped public opinion would force the court to modify what evidently was its position in this case, but that might take some time. In any event, Tourgée believed, delay could only help the Plessy side. The moderate oppositionists might change their minds; they or some of the hard-core four might retire or die and be replaced by more liberal successors. Tourgée deemed delay far preferable to defeat. "It is of the utmost consequence that we should not have a decision against us, as it is a matter of boast with the court that it has never reversed itself on a constitutional question."

Though Tourgée wasn't quite accurate in this last claim (or perhaps the boasters he had heard were wrong), his basic point was right. The Supreme Court generally tried to adhere to the principle of *stare decisis*, meaning that it was guided by previous decisions. It would be better for the cause of equal rights to have no decision at all than to have one that favored segregation.

Tourgée recognized that popular opinion in the United States wasn't exactly overwhelming in its support for equal rights. If anything, the tide of opinion appeared to be moving in the opposite direction. Yet the situation wasn't hopeless. There were plenty of people in the country who supported equality between the races; they might be mobilized by an energetic campaign of education. "There are millions of the white people of the United States," Tourgée told Martinet, "who believe in justice and equal right for the colored man, who desire for him all that they would wish and pray for were they in his conditions. You know this is true. There are thousands who have attested it, by faithful service. Think of the millions of dollars they have freely given for the uplifting of the race! Think of that wonderful army of white-souled saints who went out of our Northern homes to face ostracism and ignominy to teach the way of life and self-respectful civilization!" Even while praising carpetbaggers like himself, Tourgée conceded that their efforts had left something to be desired. "All has not been wisely done. The people of the North did not know your conditions and could not then provide effective remedies." But the carpetbaggers' hearts had mostly been in the right place, and the spirit of equality that motivated them might again be called forth. "The will, the purpose, the means exist, and may be reached and united." Spokesmen for the black race, people like Martinet, must make the effort. "The appeal, and in some sense the initiative, must come from your people. You must unite in making appeal to, and in demanding of the American people and of American Christians, *Justice.*" White Americans of good faith must then echo this appeal. "In union there is strength, and without it weakness."

As things turned out, efforts by Martinet and others to galvanize public opinion against segregation proved unavailing, and when the Supreme Court heard the Plessy case the atmosphere was, if anything, less conducive than earlier to equalitarian arguments. By this time, the case had become *Plessy v. Ferguson.* The second name was that of John Ferguson, the judge of the New Orleans criminal court that initially heard the case and whose decision Tourgée and Walker were appealing on Plessy's behalf.

In their brief, Tourgée and Walker described several deficiencies in the Louisiana Jim Crow law and the reasoning employed to uphold it. "The Statute," they wrote, "imports a badge of servitude imposed by State law, and perpetuates the distinction of race and caste among citizens of the United States of both races, and observances of a servile character coincident with the institution of Slavery, heretofore exacted by the white race and compulsorily submitted to by the colored race." In doing so the statute discriminated between white citizens and black citizens, abridging the rights, privileges, and immunities of the latter.

In addition, the statute contained no provisions to guarantee that the separate accommodations it called for would be equal. Indeed, given human nature and the social and political conditions in the United States, it was impossible that the accommodations would be equal. "The court will take notice of a fact inseparable from human nature," Tourgée wrote, "that when the law distinguishes between the civil rights or privileges of two classes, it always is and always must be to the detriment of the weaker class or race. A dominant race or class does not demand or enact class-distinctions for the sake of the weaker, but for their own pleasure or enjoyment. This is not an act to secure *equal* privileges; these were already enjoyed under the law as it previously existed. The object of such a law is simply to debase and distinguish against the inferior race."

Moreover, the statute failed to define "colored race" and "persons of color." "There is no law of the United States, or of the State of Louisiana, defining the limits of race—who are white and who are 'colored.' By what rule then shall any tribunal be guided in determining racial character? It may be said that all those should be classed as colored in whom appears a visible admixture of colored blood. By what law? With what justice? Why not count everyone as white in whom is visible any trace of white blood?" Where would the court draw the line? "Will the court hold that a single drop of African blood is sufficient to color a whole ocean of Caucasian whiteness?" Tourgée asserted that in the absence of legal guidelines defining racial membership, decisions were left to employees of the railroads. These decisions would be made in an arbitrary and—on the evidence of the case at hand—unfair fashion.

Tourgée went on to say that in allowing the railroads—rather than the courts—to decide who should ride in white-only cars, the statute deprived blacks of their property without due process of law. He contended that "in any mixed community, the reputation of belonging to the dominant race, in this instance the white race, is *property*, in the same sense that a right of action or of inheritance is property." Tourgée asked: "How much would it be worth to a young man entering on the practice of law to be regarded as a white man rather than a colored one?" He noted that six sevenths of the population of the United States was white, that nineteen twentieths of the property in the country belonged to whites, that ninety-nine one-hundredths of the business opportunities were in the control of whites. Even assuming perfect harmony between the races, a black man embarking on a career was at a severe disadvantage compared to a white man. In light of the antagonism that often actually existed, the disadvantage was far greater. So great was the disadvantage, Tourgée suggested, that most white persons would prefer to die rather than live as blacks. "Under these conditions, is it possible to conclude that the reputation of being white is not property? Indeed, is it not the most valuable sort of property, being the master-key that unlocks the golden door of opportunity?" The Jim Crow law, by allowing railroad employees to determine who was white and who was black, deprived blacks of this property without due process of law—a clear violation of the Fourteenth Amendment.

The law was also unjust in that it exempted certain classes of people—for example, nurses attending children of the other race—from its provisions; it thereby compounded its racial unfairness with class inequities. Besides, though this clause contained no explicit racially discriminatory language, it operated in a racially discriminatory fashion. If there existed a case of a white nurse attending the children of black parents, no one in Louisiana had ever seen it. What, then, was the effect of this provision? Simply to allow white parents to take blacks into the white coaches when the blacks were "in a menial relation" to the whites. This demonstrated that the framers of the statute didn't intend to prevent whites and blacks from mingling, but only from doing so on a basis of equality. "In other words, the act is simply intended to promote the comfort and sense of exclusiveness and superiority of the white race. They do not object to the colored person in an inferior or menial capacity—as a servant or dependent, ministering to the comfort of the white race—but only when as a man and a citizen he seeks to claim equal right and privilege on a public highway with the white citizens of the state."

The statute invaded the sanctity of marriage and the family by requiring individuals and offspring of mixed-race unions to travel in separate cars. "A man may be white and his wife colored; a wife may be white and her children colored. Has the State the right to compel the husband to ride in one car and the wife in another? . . . Has a State the right to order the mother to ride in one car and her young daughter, because her cheek may have a darker tinge, to ride in another?" Tourgée contended that the states did not.

Finally, the law forced railroads chartered as common carriers to violate the terms of their charters. Common carriers were required to accept the patronage of all customers on an equal basis. Distinguishing between whites and blacks inevitably led to favoring whites over blacks: blacks were thus treated unequally. Tourgée argued that the plain purpose and effect of the Jim Crow law was "to provide the white passenger with an exclusive first class coach without requiring him to pay an extra fare for it."

The plaintiff's brief contained other objections, but the sum of them all was that states must not be allowed to draw distinctions between citizens on the basis of race. "If the State has a right to distinguish between citizens according to race in the enjoyment of public privilege, by compelling them to ride in separate coaches, what is to prevent the application of the same principle to other relations? Why may it not require all red-headed people to ride in a separate car? Why not require all colored people to walk on one side of the street and the whites on the other? Why may it not require every white man's house to be painted white and every colored man's black?" Arguments that turned on the equality of the accommodations afforded the two races missed the point. "The question is not as to the equality of the privileges enjoyed, but *the right of the State to label one citizen as white and another as colored* in the common enjoyment of a public highway." In a single sentence that encapsulated the argument for

Plessy's side, Tourgée declared, "Justice is pictured blind, and her daughter, the Law, ought at least to be color-blind."

On the other side of the case, the attorney general of Louisiana, Milton Cunningham, and associate counsel Alexander Morse argued for Judge Ferguson. Cunningham and Morse made three points primarily. First, they said that the Louisiana separate-car law did not violate the rights of members of any race, since it did not legislate inequality. On the contrary, it mandated that facilities for the two races should be equal. Sorting individuals by race—as, for example, to reduce the "danger of friction from too intimate contact"—was a legitimate exercise of the state's police power.

Second, the claims of the Plessy side notwithstanding, the Louisiana law did not contradict the Fourteenth Amendment guarantee of due process. The law did not exempt railway companies or their employees from liability for civil damages if they incorrectly assigned passengers; a person assigned to a wrong car could sue and presumably win. Nor did the law specify criminal penalties for the failure of a passenger to comply with a wrongful assignment. In no way, therefore, did the law transfer judicial authority from the courts to the railway companies.

Third, the argument of the Plessy side that determinations of race were difficult if not impossible was fatuous. People made such determinations daily with no great problem. Ferguson's counsel cited several precedents that they said demonstrated that "every man must know the difference between a negro and a white man" and that "the exercise of judgment is not necessary to determine the question." In those rare instances where it really was difficult to decide which race a person belonged to, individuals wrongly assigned could sue for damages. This fact alone would deter railway officials from capricious decisions.

Cunningham and Morse filled out their briefs with further contentions, but the crux of their argument was the opposite of that of Plessy's side. The state *did* have the right to distinguish between individuals on the basis of race so long as it did not do so for the purpose of legislating inequality. The Louisiana law did not legislate inequality; therefore the state's distinguishing between whites and blacks was constitutional.

IV

On May 18, 1896, the Supreme Court rendered its decision in the Plessy case. By a vote of 7–1, the court affirmed the decision of the Louisiana courts and found the separate-car law to be constitutional. Associate Justice Henry Billings Brown wrote the decision for the majority. One by one, Justice Brown dismissed the objections of the counsel for Plessy. Brown denied that the Louisiana law had anything to do with slavery. "It would be running the slavery argument into the ground," he wrote, quoting the court's decision in the *Civil Rights Cases,* "to make it apply to every act of discrimination which a person may see fit to make as to the guests he will entertain, or as to the people he will take into his coach or cab or car, or admit to his concert or theatre, or deal with in other matters of intercourse or business." Speaking in his own voice, Brown added, "A statute which implies merely a legal distinction between the white and colored races—a distinction which is founded in the color of the two races, and which must always exist as long as white men are distinguished from the other race by color—has no tendency to destroy the legal equality of the two races, or to reestablish a state of involuntary servitude."

Brown conceded that the purpose of the Fourteenth Amendment was to enforce the "absolute equality" of the two races before the law, but he rejected the notion that it had been designed to abolish distinctions based on race. Neither had it been designed to enforce social equality, as contrasted to political equality, nor to impose a commingling of the races on terms unsatisfactory to either. For years courts had allowed school boards to distinguish between white and black children in assigning pupils to schools. The United States Congress had registered its concurrence with this practice by allowing the segregation of schools in the District of Columbia.

Brown rejected Tourgée's contention that the Jim Crow car law deprived African-Americans of property rights. The associate justice didn't deny that property issues were involved, but he accepted the arguments of the Louisiana side that a person wrongly assigned—and therefore wrongly deprived of the property in his reputation—could seek damages in the civil courts.

Brown likewise dismissed the argument that allowing states to pass Jim Crow car laws would lead to all manner of absurd and abitrary segregationist measures. Inherent in the police power of the states was the stricture that this power be used in a reasonable manner, in good faith and for the public welfare rather than the annoyance or oppression of a particular class. The legislation at issue was reasonable, certainly as reasonable as the acts of Congress mandating separation of schoolchildren by race in the District of Columbia.

Brown didn't consider the problem of determining who was black and who white to be insuperable; neither did he consider it to be a matter for the Supreme Court to worry about, at least not in the present case. The states should establish their own guidelines. If these guidelines proved to be unsatisfactory, they might become an issue in later cases. Plessy might have grounds for complaining that he was white rather than black, but he wasn't so arguing, and any such complaint had no bearing on the constitutionality of the law at hand.

The fundamental problem with the argument of the Plessy side, Brown explained, and the reason the court was rejecting Plessy's suit, had to do with the alleged implications of racial distinctions. Brown denied that mere distinction between the white and black races implied the subordination of the latter to the former. "We consider the underlying fallacy of the plaintiff's argument to consist in the assumption that the enforced separation of the two races stamps the colored race with a badge of inferiority. If this be so, it is not by reason of anything found in the act, but solely because the colored race chooses to put that construction upon it." Brown pointed out that during Reconstruction, when blacks and their allies had passed legislation most Louisiana whites didn't like, none of those whites for a moment had thought that such legislation meant the white race was inferior to the black race.

The plaintiff's argument placed entirely too much importance on legislation as social engineering, Brown said. The argument assumed "that social prejudices may be overcome by legislation, and that equal rights cannot be secured to the negro except by a forced commingling of the two races." Brown rejected this proposition. "If the two races are to meet upon terms of social equality, it must be the result of natural affinities, a mutual appreciation of each other's merits and a voluntary consent of individuals." Concluding his decision, Brown wrote: "Legislation is powerless to eradicate racial instincts or to abolish distinctions based upon physical differences, and the attempt to do so can only result in accentuating the difficulties of the present situation. If the civil and political rights of both races be equal, one cannot be inferior to the other civilly or politically. If one race be inferior to the other socially, the Constitution of the United States cannot put them upon the same plane."

Although Justice Brown spoke for the court, he didn't speak for all the justices. Associate Justice John Marshall Harlan vehemently disapproved of the court's decision and delivered a blistering rebuke to the majority in a vigorously phrased dissent. Where Brown had contended that the slavery issue was not germane to the Plessy case, Harlan declared that slavery was absolutely germane. The Thirteenth Amendment, he said, "not only struck down the institution of slavery as previously existing in the United States, but it prevents the imposition of any burdens or disabilities that constitute badges of slavery or servitude." To strengthen the Thirteenth Amendment, Congress and the people of the states had approved the Fourteenth Amendment; together, the two amendments "removed the race line from our governmental systems." Quoting an earlier decision involving the scope of the Fourteenth Amendment, Harlan explained that the Supreme Court had declared "that the law in the States shall be the same for the black as for the white; that all persons, whether colored or white, shall stand equal before the law of the States, and, in regard to the colored race, for whose protection the amendment was primarily designed, that no discrimination shall be made against them by law because of their color."

Harlan dismissed as disingenuous the argument by the attorneys for the Ferguson side that the Louisiana law did not discriminate, but treated blacks and whites equally. "Everyone knows that the statute in question had its origin in the purpose, not so much to exclude white persons from railroad cars occupied by blacks, as to exclude colored people from coaches occupied by or assigned to white persons." Harlan continued, "The thing to accomplish was, under the guise of giving equal accommodation for white and blacks, to compel the latter to keep to themselves while travelling in railroad passenger coaches. No one would be so wanting in candor as to assert the contrary."

Harlan likewise dismissed the contention that the assignment of the two races to separate cars was merely an exercise of the state's police power and that the use of this power would be confined to reasonable purposes. He thought the same logic that would allow a state to segregate passengers on railcars would allow states to segregate passengers on streetcars, to segregate visitors to legislative assembly halls, or to segregate voters convening to discuss political issues of the day. Further, there was no clear reason why segregation had to be restricted to racial classification. "Why may not the State require the separation in railroad coaches of native and natural-ized citizens of the United States, or of Protestants and Roman Catholics?"

Defenders of segregation said that such measures wouldn't be "reason-able." Harlan thought reasonableness entirely too slippery a standard, for it got the courts into matters of policy and expediency as they related to legislation. "I do not understand that the courts have anything to do with the policy or expediency of legislation." Taking a position that, ironically, would be adopted by defenders of segregation half a century later, Harlan decried the "dangerous tendency in these latter days to enlarge the func-tions of the courts" until the courts encroached on the prerogatives of the legislature. "Our institutions have the distinguishing characteristic that the three departments of government are coordinate and separate. Each must keep within the limits defined by the Constitution. And the courts best discharge their duty by executing the will of the lawmaking power, con-stitutionally expressed, leaving the results of legislation to be dealt with by the people through their representatives."

The white race considered itself dominant in America, Harlan went on; and so it was by any objective measure of social status, achievements, ed-ucation, wealth, or power. But this was all the more reason for guarantee-ing legal equality between blacks and whites. "In view of the Constitution, in the eye of the law, there is in this country no superior, dominant, ruling class of citizens. There is no caste here. Our Constitution is color-blind, and neither knows nor tolerates classes among citizens. In respect of civil rights, all citizens are equal before the law. The humblest is the peer of the most powerful. The law regards man as man."

Yet the decision of the court in the Plessy case tended in precisely the opposite direction. "The judgement this day rendered," Harlan predicted, "will in time prove to be quite as pernicious as the decision made by this tribunal in the *Dred Scott* case"—the notorious 1857 case regarding slavery and black citizenship that did much to bring on the Civil War. "The present decision, it may well be apprehended, will not only stimulate aggressions, more or less brutal and irritating, upon the admitted rights of colored cit-izens, but will encourage the belief that it is possible, by means of state enactments, to defeat the beneficent purposes which the people of the United States had in view when they adopted the recent amendments of the Constitution." The 60 million whites living in America were under no threat whatsoever from the 8 million blacks; if anything, the threat lay the other way. More to the point, the destinies of whites and blacks were indissolubly joined, and the interests of both groups dictated that the seeds of race hate not be planted under the sanction of law. "What can more certainly arouse race hate, what more certainly create and perpetuate a feeling of distrust between these races, than state enactments, which, in fact, proceed on the ground that colored citizens are so inferior and degraded that they cannot be allowed to sit in public coaches occupied by white citizens?"

Harlan closed with a grim warning. "If evils will result from the commingling of the two races upon public highways established for the benefit of all, they will be infinitely less than those that will surely come from state legislation regulating the employment of civil rights upon the basis of race. We boast of the freedom enjoyed by our people above all other peoples. But it is difficult to reconcile that boast with a state of the law which, practically, puts the brand of servitude and degradation upon a large class of our fellow-citizens, our equals before the law. The thin disguise of 'equal' accommodations for passengers in railroad coaches will not mislead any one, nor atone for the wrong this day done."

V

The Supreme Court's affirmation of the Louisiana Jim Crow railroad law was a disheartening setback to Tourgée, Martinet, and other advocates of equal rights between the races. In hoping that procrastination would help swing public and judicial opinion around to the anti-segregationist side, Tourgée had made a grave tactical error. In fact, procrastination had had precisely the opposite effect. Public attitudes were *more* favorable to segregation in 1896 than they had been when Homer Plessy boarded the train in New Orleans in 1892, rather than less. In 1892, Tourgée, Martinet, and the others had felt they were fighting an uphill battle; during the subsequent four years the hill only got steeper.

Unexpectedly, it was an African-American who probably did more than any other single individual to render segregation acceptable to the American public. By the 1890s, Booker T. Washington was the most prominent black person in the country. Washington had been born in Virginia, most likely in the spring of 1856. His mother was a slave belonging to James Burroughs, a rough-living farmer of the Virginia hill country who had more in common with his slaves than with the tidewater aristocracy of slaveholders. Washington never learned who his father was; Washington's appearance indicated that the father was a white man, but of more than that he couldn't be sure. If his mother knew who the father was, she didn't say. "Whoever he was," Washington wrote later, "I never heard of his taking the least interest in me or in providing in any way for my rearing."

Washington's mother cooked for the Burroughs family as well as for the other slaves on the farm. The cabin Booker grew up in was constantly lit and heated—overheated, during the summer—by the cooking fire. The cabin had one room and was built of split oak logs; it had openings for windows but no glass in them. The floor was hard-packed dirt. In the middle was a pit where Burroughs stored his sweet potatoes after the harvest. The family cat lived in the house; a hole at the base of one wall allowed the pet to leave and return during the night. The cat-hole also allowed winter winds to enter, as did numerous cracks where the chinking had fallen out.

Booker grew up barefoot. Not until he was eight did he wear shoes, even in winter. His chief item of apparel was a stiff, scratchy shirt made of homespun flax, prized by Burroughs for its cheapness, certainly not for the comfort it didn't afford the slaves. Booker recalled that his brother John had once done him a great favor by breaking in a new flax shirt, wearing it until the harsh fibers had grown somewhat softer and more pliant.

Booker accompanied his mother to the master's table when she served food. There he had the job of fanning flies away from the food and the diners. He operated a new invention that connected several paper fans to ropes and pulleys; by tugging energetically on a single rope, he could ventilate the whole room. The young boy overheard much conversation at his task, and if the company wasn't especially refined, at least the experience broadened his horizons beyond those that circumscribed the lives of most slave boys. "Much of the conversation of the white people turned upon the subject of freedom and the war," he recalled, speaking of the period of the Civil War. "I absorbed a good deal of it."

Booker was only nine years old when the Union's victory brought an end to slavery in Virginia, but for the rest of his life he retained memories of life under the threat of the lash. And not only the threat: one vivid recollection was of a time his uncle was stripped naked, tied to a tree, and whipped by a member of the Burroughs family with a strap of cowhide. Such whippings may not have been common on the Burroughs farm— descendants of James Burroughs denied he had ever so mistreated his slaves—but even one was enough to etch the scene unerasably on Booker's mind.

Perhaps as important as his memory of the whipping were his recollections of occasions when slaves outsmarted the masters. A black man named Jerome McWade once appeared in the neighborhood attired in a fancy red velvet waistcoat, which happened to be the same waistcoat his master had worn on his wedding day and since misplaced. When confronted by the master and accused of stealing the vest, McWade explained that he had purchased it from another man, evidently the thief who *had* purloined it. The master said this was no excuse; purchasing stolen property was just as criminal as doing the stealing directly. McWade objected that such couldn't be true. "You wouldn't receive stolen goods yourself, if it was bad," he told his master. "You bought and paid for me the same as I bought and paid for that red velvet waistcoat. Well, wasn't I stolen, same as the waist-coat was? Wasn't I stolen out of Africa?"

Other memories were those held by any child who grew up on a Virginia farm in the middle of the nineteenth century. Of the butchering of the hogs in early December, Washington wrote, "I recall the great blazing of fire flaring up in the darkness of the night, and grown men and women moving about in the flickering shadows. I remember with what feelings of mingled horror and hungry anticipation I looked at the long rows of hogs hung on the fence-rail, preparatory to being cut up and salted away for the year." Christmas came soon after the butchering. "Looking back to those days, when Christmas, for me, was a much more momentous event than it is now"—Washington was fifty-one years old at the writing—"it seems to me that there was a certain charm about that Virginia Christmas time, a peculiar fragrance in the atmosphere, a something which I cannot define, and which does not exist elsewhere in the same degree, where it has been my privilege to spend the Christmas season." On Christmas Day the slaves typically received gifts from the masters, often utilitarian items that the masters would have been required to furnish anyway, but sometimes special treats. Washington recollected the last Christmas he spent as a slave, when he was eight years old. "I awoke at four o'clock in the morning in my mother's cabin, and, creeping over to the chimney, I found my stocking well filled with pieces of red candy and nearly half a dozen ginger-cakes. In addition to these were the little wooden shoes with the leather tops"—the first pair of shoes he ever owned.

Washington may have had something of a selective memory, or perhaps as a child in the Virginia foothills he escaped the worst aspects of the slave system; in either case he never developed the deep-seated resentment against whites that marked many others who survived slavery. This lack of resentment would have an important effect on the attitudes he displayed and the policies he promoted as an adult.

Washington's experiences after slavery contributed to his relatively benign view of whites. In the summer of 1865, he traveled with his mother and two brothers to Malden, West Virginia, where his stepfather had taken work at a salt distillery. Young Booker joined his stepfather shoveling salt into barrels. The workday sometimes started as early as four o'clock in the morning and continued until dark, and the work was heavy for a full-grown man, let alone a boy not even ten. Fortunately it wasn't long before he found other employment as a house servant in the home of General Lewis Ruffner.

Washington's new position placed him in contact with the patrician class of old Virginians. General Ruffner's ancestors had come to America from Switzerland during the eighteenth century and had settled in the Shenandoah Valley before moving farther west. Lewis Ruffner himself had been a slaveowner; in 1860, he owned twenty-six slaves. But he opposed secession and assisted in the formation of the state of West Virginia. He fought in the Civil War on the Union side, rising to the rank of major general of militia.

The general's wife, Viola Knapp Ruffner, was a Vermonter. She had come to West Virginia to be governess to the general's children following the death of his first wife. They fell in love and married. The children didn't like the idea of someone taking the place of their departed mother—and a Yankee to boot. Their hostility made the new Mrs. Ruffner's life difficult and often lonely.

Booker Washington helped relieve the loneliness. He never became quite a son to her, but he did become something of a protégé. A strict taskmaster in the tradition of New England Puritanism, Viola Ruffner demanded punctuality, perseverance, and above all cleanliness. She also showed affection, in her reserved, proper way. Washington thrived on the attention and before long developed habits of work he would later pound into his students at Tuskegee. "The difference in social conditions," he afterward remarked, "is principally the result of intelligent energy." Washington also developed a respect for the "better class" of whites, people who didn't feel threatened by blacks nor by their efforts to advance themselves.

No one tried harder to advance himself than Booker Washington. When he gained his freedom in 1865, Washington was totally illiterate. His first acquaintance with the mysteries of written language came at the Malden salt works where he learned to recognize and write the number 18, the mark that distinguished his barrels from those of other workers. He subsequently managed to acquire a spelling primer and for a while puzzled through it by himself. His big chance arrived in the autumn of 1865, when a young man from Ohio opened a school in Malden. Booker began attending classes at night after work; later he switched to daytime classes, working from four in the morning until nine, attending school, then returning to work for a few more hours shoveling salt. The move to the Ruffner home eased this strenuous schedule somewhat, but he still found himself studying at odd hours. "I used to sit up nearly all night burning dear old Mrs. Ruffner's oil," Washington recalled.

Washington's ceaseless ambition—Mrs. Ruffner later remembered that the question he constantly asked himself was, "Am I getting on?"—prompted him to leave Malden and the Ruffners' employ for the Hampton Normal and Agricultural Institute. Washington traveled to Hampton, Virginia, by train, stagecoach, and foot, being reduced to the humbler modes of transport as his money ran out. He arrived on the doorstep of the new college for blacks penniless, exhausted, and hungry. He had been on the road for weeks; during that time he had neither bathed nor shaved.

Fortunately for Washington, the principal of the college recognized in this scruffy young man something worth cultivating. As an entrance examination Miss Mary Mackie—who was almost a cultural clone of Mrs. Ruffner—required Washington to sweep a classroom. He did so, applying himself with the thoroughness Mrs. Ruffner had insisted on, so that after he had swept the floor four times and dusted it three it fairly glistened.

Miss Mackie tested the corners, window sills, and other crannies where dirt might hide; finding none, she said, "I guess we will try you as a student."

Washington responded to Miss Mackie as eagerly as he had to Mrs. Ruffner, but his most important model at Hampton was General Samuel Armstrong, the founder and headmaster of the school. Armstrong was the son of Presbyterian missionaries to Hawaii; during the Civil War he had displayed conspicuous talent and courage, rising rapidly through the officer ranks and being named a general while still in his twenties. After the war he had stayed in the South to try to complete the job the fighting had begun. He took the lead in establishing Hampton and quickly became the idol of many of the students. Washington described Armstrong as "more than a father," "the most perfect specimen of man, physically, mentally and spiritually" he had ever known, "a great man—the noblest, rarest human being that it has ever been my privilege to meet." Washington's initial encounter with Armstrong set the tone for their subsequent relationship. "I shall always remember that the first time I went into his presence he made the impression upon me of being a perfect man; I was made to feel that there was something about him that was superhuman."

Armstrong's philosophy of self-responsibility and quiet fortitude informed the curriculum at Hampton. Armstrong summarized his thoughts in some advice he offered students and former students in an 1877 issue of the Hampton school magazine. "Be thrifty and industrious," Armstrong wrote. "Command the respect of your neighbors by a good record and a good character. Own your own houses. Educate your children. Make the best of your difficulties. Live down prejudice. Cultivate peaceful relations with all. As a voter, act as you think and not as you are told. Remember that you have seen marvellous changes in sixteen years. In view of that, be patient—thank God and take courage."

The regimen Armstrong established at Hampton strongly influenced Washington's character development, as well as his later philosophy of education. Students rose at 5:00 A.M., groomed themselves for inspection at 5:45, breakfasted at 6:00, said prayers at 6:30, prepared their rooms for inspection at 8:00, attended classes from 8:30 until 3:00 with a break for the midday meal, performed military drills from 4:00 until supper at 6:00, prayed at 6:45, studied until 9:00, and retired at 9:30.

Studies focused on industrial education, on fitting former slaves for life in a world of economic competition, and on developing teachers to do the fitting. Much emphasis was placed on the acquisition of skills; even more was placed on the acquisition of a temperament conducive to success in the work world. Industriousness, thrift, diligence—the same qualities Mrs. Ruffner had stressed—were endlessly reinforced by General Armstrong.

Washington spent three years at Hampton. He always afterward considered them the most significant years of his life. "At Hampton I found an opportunity for class-room education and for practical training in industrial life, opportunity to learn thrift, economy and push," he wrote. "Amid Christian influences I was surrounded by an atmosphere of business, and a spirit of self-help that seemed to awaken every faculty in me and cause me for the first time to realize what it means to be a man instead of a piece of property."

Following graduation from Hampton, Washington took a job teaching school not far from his former home in Malden. His approach to pedagogy reflected the influence of both Mrs. Ruffner and Armstrong. Washington put great store in cleanliness. "In all my teaching I have watched carefully the influence of the tooth-brush," he explained later in a widely recounted remark, "and I am convinced that there are few single agencies of civilization that are more far-reaching." He insisted on good grooming. As he informed friends back at Hampton, "I require all to keep their clothes neat and clean, and their hair combed every morning, and the boys to keep their boots cleaned. To see that this is done, I have a morning inspection, as we did at Hampton."

Washington initially contracted to teach daytime classes, but in his ambition and zeal he soon opened a night school as well. Although the double load left him little time for sleep, his enthusiasm carried him forward. His day classes expanded to almost one hundred students; his night classes were nearly as large. With energy still to spare, he established a lending library and a debating society.

Washington probably wished that the outside world would leave him alone to educate his students undistracted, but it didn't. Although life in West Virginia during the 1870s wasn't as violent as life in certain other former slave states at this time, it was fraught with plenty of tension— some interracial, some not. On Christmas Eve of 1875, two white men from the community, Rufus Estep and John Dawson, murdered another white man in shockingly brutal fashion. Although Estep and Dawson were arrested, tried, and imprisoned for the crime, relatives and friends of the victim believed that the murderers deserved to die. They convinced others and organized a lynch mob. The local sheriff foiled the lynchers and spirited Estep and Dawson to another county, but a second mob gathered a few weeks later, determined not to be frustrated again. The crowd surrounded the jail where the murderers were being held and prepared to drag the prisoners outside to vigilante justice.

At this point their objectives paralleled those of a second mob. An Irishman named Hines, said to be enamored of the wife of an African-American man, had slit the throat of the husband, who died shortly afterward. Hines was soon arrested. Black members of the community were outraged at the murder, and they applauded the arrest, but they feared that the white-controlled legal system would let Hines off leniently. They prepared to take the law into their own hands. A black crowd of some fifty persons marched on the jail, where they collided with the much larger crowd of whites seeking Estep and Dawson. The combined force of more than five hundred had no difficulty seizing the three jailed and now thoroughly terrified men.

The integrated mob began to segregate itself while preparing the prospective victims for execution. The whites conducted Estep and Dawson to the bridge where they had committed their murder; they strung ropes over the railings and around the necks of the convicted pair. The blacks found a tall, strong locust tree nearby and uncoiled a rope of their own.

By this time, some of the whites were beginning to have second thoughts—not about hanging Estep and Dawson, but about allowing a crowd of blacks to hang Hines, a white man, albeit one who was good for nothing. As an eyewitness remarked, "Even in their great excitement, it was seen that the hanging of a white man by negroes must be productive of the most awful consequences."

The blacks weren't picky about who did the hanging; they just wanted it done. Some among their leaders offered to let the whites have the honor if that would make the whites feel better. A few of the whites liked this idea, but others objected that they had nothing against Hines. He was the blacks' problem.

After further give and take, the two hanging parties agreed on the original division of labor: the whites would string up Estep and Dawson; the blacks would dispatch Hines.

Now it was Estep and Dawson's turn to complain. They declared that it would be a disgrace to themselves personally and to the white race as a whole for them to be hanged in front of a crowd of blacks. This argument touched a chord of racial solidarity among the whites. They removed the ropes from the necks of the two and from the bridge. In a group they moved away, leaving the blacks alone. They then found a tree from which they duly hanged Estep and Dawson. Meanwhile the blacks hanged Hines from his own tree.

Though the violence in this case showed no particular anti-black character, it reminded Washington how great was the potential for mob action in the South. Earlier, when he was living with the Ruffners, he had witnessed an incident sparked by a fistfight between a black man and a white. A local auxiliary of the Ku Klux Klan, called Gideon's Band, vowed to avenge the insult to the white race by punishing the black pugilist. This led to a confrontation between a large crowd of whites and a smaller group of blacks on the street just outside the Ruffner home. General Ruffner, hearing the commotion, ran out and tried to intervene. A brick flew from some unseen assailant's hand and hit the general in the back of the head. He went down, unconscious. For several days he lay in critical condition, and he never fully recovered. Yet the general's intervention helped the besieged blacks make their escape without serious injury.

While the general hovered between life and death, the ranks of the Gideons swelled to some two hundred. They terrorized the blacks involved in the incident, along with many who hadn't been involved, and succeeded in running them all out of Malden. Washington, who had followed General Ruffner into the street, recalled afterward, "It seemed to me as I watched this struggle between the members of the two races that there was no hope for our people in this country." Washington's despair dissipated—he being of a congenitally optimistic nature—but he never forgot the precariousness of the African-American condition in a world dominated by whites. Nor did he forget the heroic actions of General Ruffner, and he came to believe that if blacks were to find any allies in the white world, such allies would have to come from the educated and well-off classes.

General Armstrong reinforced this belief, not least by his personal support of Washington as the younger man started his teaching career. In 1879, Armstrong invited his twenty-three-year-old former student to join the faculty at his alma mater. Where Hampton's faculty originally had been entirely white, it was now beginning to add black instructors, mostly its own graduates. And just as it was diversifying its faculty, so the school was diversifying its student body. Armstrong appointed Washington to take charge of the school's new Indian dormitory, which housed Kiowa and Cheyenne Indians captured as prisoners of war in recent battles on the Great Plains and who now were Hampton students. Armstrong had a particular purpose in appointing Washington to supervise the Indians. Hampton's objective was to instill in its students the values and skills that would fit them for life in a white-dominated society. A white role model might have served, but Washington served still better. Washington had overcome the handicap of slavery and the other disabilities that went with his dark skin, and he had mastered the values that were so important for success among whites. If Booker Washington could do it, so might Indians—and of course other blacks.

Washington fulfilled Armstrong's expectations, and taught for two productive years at Hampton. Then, in the spring of 1881, Armstrong received a letter from the directors of a new normal school for blacks in Tuskegee, Alabama. The directors were looking for a principal, and they asked Armstrong to recommend one of his faculty or some other white man. Armstrong replied, "The only man I can suggest is one Mr. Booker Washington, a graduate of this institution, a very competent, capable mulatto, clear-headed, modest, sensible, polite, and a thorough teacher and superior man. The best man we ever had here." After asking some questions about the job, Armstrong concluded with another pitch for Washington: "I am confident he would not disappoint you. I know of no white man who could do better." A week later came the answer from Tuskegee: "Booker Washington will suit us. Send him at once."

Washington seized the opportunity. He packed his few belongings and left for Tuskegee. As he neared his destination, he paid close attention to the conditions of life of his new neighbors. The vast majority of these worked as sharecroppers on land owned by whites. Cotton was the primary crop, in most cases the only crop. At the insistence of the owners, who wanted to generate the maximum amount of cash from their properties, the tenants planted cotton everywhere, from fencerow to fencerow and right up to the steps of the ramshackle cabins the tenants called home. Many sharecropper families didn't have even a vegetable garden; many kept no chickens or pigs. They purchased their food—cornmeal and fatback pork, mostly—from grocery stores just as city dwellers did. They were caught in a cycle of debt: they couldn't terminate their contracts with the landlords since they had no money to settle their obligations and no resources with which to relocate, but the longer they stayed the deeper in debt they sank.

Washington soon got to know the people of Macon County, where Tuskegee was located. In order to cultivate community support for the institute, he spent almost every weekend touring the countryside—usually in a borrowed buggy, living off the charity of the people of the county. The more he saw, the more he grew convinced that the vocational model of education practiced at Hampton was what was needed at Tuskegee. Sixteen years after the end of slavery, African-Americans remained almost as disadvantaged as they been in servitude. They had more legal and political rights than before, but economically they were as oppressed as ever. Political advancement was a fine thing, but without economic advancement it was a weak reed for a people to rely on. What the white majority had given, the white majority might take away. Only when blacks gained the respect of their white neighbors would their rights be really secure. And only through self-improvement could blacks gain that respect.

Washington had been improving himself for most of his twenty-five years, and he began improving the Tuskegee Institute the moment he arrived. As the school had no adequate source of revenue—the tuition-paying capacity of the students being limited—Washington immediately started developing one. He learned that a defunct plantation a mile outside of town would be going up for sale. He investigated the matter, borrowed the down payment from a friend back at Hampton, and negotiated the purchase. Before long, students were reconstructing the abandoned buildings, restoring fences, chopping weeds and saplings, and putting fields back into production.

This manual labor didn't initially go over well with the students. Many of them were older than Washington; many were teachers who thought they had grubbed their last stump and dug their last well. Almost all had enrolled in the school on the assumption that education was their ticket out of the world of manual labor. Now Washington was leading them right back in. About the only thing that prevented an outright mutiny was the fact that he was indeed *leading* them. Whenever the students were turned out for a "chopping bee" or other edifyingly backbreaking task, Washington set the pace. He worked harder and faster and longer than anyone else; though many grumbled, most adopted the attitude that if Mr. Washington could do it, they could too.

To the extent possible, Washington recreated the conditions he had so appreciated at Hampton. The Tuskegee schedule closely followed that of Hampton, from the 5:00 A.M. wakeup to the 9:30 lights out. Washington conducted military-style inspections; a stained shirt, muddy shoes, or a missing collar brought a reprimand and firm though not harsh punishment. Sessions in the field complemented lessons in the classroom—an approach designed to fill the students' minds and hearts with an appreciation of the nobility of honest labor, and fill their stomachs with the produce they grew. Over several years Washington added various other enterprises to the vocational curriculum. Certain clay found on the farm was suited to making bricks, some of which were used in new buildings at the school, others sold to the neighboring public. The public sales of bricks—and later lumber, furniture, wagons, tools, clothing, and various additional items—had the bonus benefit of bringing visitors to Tuskegee who otherwise never would have seen the place. The typical white customer came to pick up a load of bricks and left admiring the hundreds of industrious black men and women who were molding themselves into models of social responsibility. The brick buyer went home and told his friends, who spread the word farther. In this manner Washington and Tuskegee gained a wide and almost uniformly positive reputation.

To spread the word still farther—and more important, to solicit money to expand and improve the school—Washington began taking longer journeys on Tuskegee's behalf. In 1882, he crossed the Mason-Dixon line for the first time, traveling to New York and New England to acquaint potential friends and benefactors with the work he and his associates were doing at Tuskegee. The reception was cool at first, but gradually Washington's earnestness and perseverance—aided by some door-opening efforts by General Armstrong—paid off. Donations began trickling in, slowly increasing to a steady stream. Most givers supplied money; others contributed books, clothing, or other necessities of school life. During his first two years, Washington raised $11,000; during the third year, he raised $10,000 more.

By bringing Tuskegee to the attention of a national public, Washington also brought himself to public attention. During the 1880s, he served three terms as president of the Alabama State Teachers' Association; in 1884, he gave an address before the National Education Association at its annual convention in Madison, Wisconsin. In 1893, *Outlook* magazine ran a story on America's most prominent educators: Washington's profile appeared alongside those of the presidents of Harvard, Yale, and Princeton.

At first, influential groups in the North were more interested in hearing what Washington had to say than comparable groups in the South were. Conscience still tugged at Northern white liberals, who opened their auditoriums and their pocketbooks to him. Southern blacks also listened to Washington, for different reasons. But until the mid-1890s, Washington had almost no opportunity to speak directly to large audiences of Southern whites. Many well-meaning Southern whites doubted that an ex-slave had anything worthwhile to say; others simply refused to grant an African-American the respect a prominent forum implied.

The situation changed in 1895. In that year, Atlanta hosted the Cotton States and International Exposition, a fair inspired by Chicago's Columbian Exposition. For some time, Atlanta's city fathers had engaged in a campaign to drum up money to underwrite the exposition. As they prepared to travel to Washington to make their pitch to Congress, they got the bright idea of bringing along a few prominent blacks. Northerners dominated

Congress, especially the House of Representatives where any bill supporting the Atlanta exposition would have to originate. Many Northerners still judged the South to be a backward and blighted region trapped in delusions of the Lost Cause. The aim of the exposition was to show the North and the rest of the world that this stereotype was inaccurate and that the South was as progressive as any part of the United States. What better demonstration of this fact than the inclusion of some well-spoken representatives of the black race in a delegation to Washington?

Booker Washington joined two other African-Americans, both bishops, in the two-dozen strong contingent that traveled by (segregated) train to the national capital. The whites filled most of the time the House committee allotted to the Atlanta presentation; only fifteen minutes were left to the blacks. Washington spoke last. He briefly described what he was trying to accomplish at Tuskegee; these remarks did little to rouse the sleepy committee members. But when he declared that he had followed a consistent policy of staying out of politics and encouraging his students to do likewise, telling them to concentrate instead on making themselves productive farmers and artisans, everyone in the hearing room took note. And none took more careful note than Washington's fellow delegates from Atlanta, particularly the white ones, who crowded around him after the hearing and congratulated him on his wisdom and forthrightness. It only heightened their good feeling that the committee voted unanimously to approve the appropriation the Atlantans requested. Congress as a whole accepted the committee's recommendation, giving the exposition organizers $200,000.

As the organizers spent the money, they also devised a program for the exposition. Those who had heard Washington testify on Capitol Hill urged that he be invited to address the exposition. From the perspective of the white ruling classes in the South, Booker Washington was a dream come true. He was the modest, hardworking black whom the patricians saw as the ideal example for the rest of his race. He didn't upset the status quo; his agenda for the improvement of African-Americans was unthreateningly patient and incremental.

Washington duly received an invitation to speak at the opening ceremonies of the exposition, scheduled for the middle of September 1895. The invitation elicited notice from newspaper editors and other observers all around the country. The *New York Tribune* suggested that Southern leaders were making "a bid for Northern commendation." The *Philadelphia Telegram* commented, "Had any one predicted twenty-five years ago that the South would so honor a Negro, he would have been looked upon as a madman." A letterwriter to the *New York Sun* suggested that the South had stolen a march on the North: "When has the North recognized the negro in a way that the Atlanta Exposition directors have done?" T. McCants Stewart, the black journalist and lawyer in New York, exclaimed, "Surely, what hath God wrought!"

Washington himself grew nervous as the appointed day approached. He realized the great responsibility that was being placed on his shoulders as a spokesman for his race, and he worried that he might not live up to it. His difficulty was summarized by a white neighbor who lived near Tuskegee. "Washington," this farmer said, "you have spoken with success before Northern white audiences, and before Negroes in the South. But in Atlanta you will have to speak before Northern white people, Southern white people and Negroes altogether. I fear they have got you in a pretty tight place."

The place didn't get any less tight as Washington boarded the (Jim Crow) train for Atlanta. His warm sendoff from Tuskegee was followed by an even warmer welcome in Atlanta. A committee from the African-American community met him at the station and escorted him to his (Jim Crow) hotel. Atlanta was teeming with visitors who wanted to be present at the opening of the exposition. Just as the Columbian Exposition had served to demonstrate Chicago's revival after the 1871 fire and that city's coming of age as the metropolis of the new West, so the Atlanta exposition served to mark Atlanta's revival after the destruction of the Civil War and its coming of age as the metropolis of the new South.

Washington didn't sleep much the night before his address. When dawn lightened his hotel room, he reviewed for the hundredth time what he would say that afternoon. "I also kneeled down and asked God's blessing upon my effort," he said afterward. This was an indication of the pressure Washington felt; he wasn't an especially religious person.

A few hours later a reception committee came to Washington's hotel and guided him to his place in the opening-day parade. Washington joined other African-American dignitaries: ministers, bishops, industrialists, merchants, and professionals. Although it seemed to Washington that the white marshals overseeing the parade were taking pains to treat blacks with respect, the black contingent was assigned a position at the rear.

The parade lasted three hours, winding through Atlanta under a hot September sun. By the time the final marchers arrived at the exposition site, Washington was exhausted. "When we reached the grounds," he wrote, "the heat, together with my nervous anxiety, made me feel as if I were about ready to collapse, and to feel that my address was not going to be a success."

The auditorium was packed. Whites filled the best seats; blacks took those less well situated. Hundreds of persons of both races who hadn't been able to get tickets crowded the walkways outside. The parade had lasted longer than anticipated; the speakers were over an hour late taking their spots on the platform. The audience was hot and restless, and the noise level grew by the minute. But when Washington mounted the stage, a hush fell over the whole building. This was a curiosity the likes of which Atlanta had never seen. Everyone wondered what this black man would have to say. Would he speak wisely or make a fool of himself? The audience was divided as to which outcome to hope for.

A former governor of Georgia, Rufus Bullock, addressed the audience first. He was followed by various other white notables who described the great strides the South had made in the last generation and the brilliant future that lay before it. A band afforded relief from the rhetorical monotony. The musicians struck up "The Star-Spangled Banner," segueing into "Dixie" and then "Yankee Doodle." When the closing notes of the last tune died away, Governor Bullock introduced the next speaker. "We shall now be favored with an address by a great Southern educator," he said. The crowd applauded automatically, many not knowing what Southern educator the governor was referring to. When Washington stepped forward, the applause from the white section of the auditorium ceased. "We have with us today a representative of Negro enterprise and Negro civilization," Bullock continued. The black section cheered heartily; the whites gave a polite smattering.

A reporter sent by the *New York World* to cover the speech described the impression Washington made as he stood before the audience. He was, the reporter wrote, "a remarkable figure, tall, bony, straight as a Sioux chief, high forehead, straight nose, heavy jaws and strong, determined mouth, with big white teeth, piercing eyes and a commanding manner." Perhaps Washington seemed so from below the rostrum; in fact, he was of middling height and not especially straight or bony. The reporter went on, "The sinews stood out on his bronzed neck, and his muscular right arm swung high in the air with a lead pencil grasped in the clenched brown fist"—this pencil being Washington's constant stage prop when speaking. "His feet were planted squarely, with the heels together and the toes turned out."

Washington began by thanking the organizers of the exposition for affording Negroes the opportunity to participate and for providing himself the opportunity to speak. He suggested that the exposition would go far toward promoting amicable and profitable relations between the races.

Washington conceded that relations had not always been amicable, and he accepted some blame for that fact on behalf of African-Americans. In the aftermath of emancipation, blacks had made errors. "Ignorant and inexperienced, it is not strange that in the first years of our new life we began at the top instead of at the bottom; that a seat in Congress or the state legislature was more sought than real estate or industrial skill; that the political convention or stump speaking had more attractions than starting a dairy farm or truck garden." The South and the country as a whole had suffered as a result of these mistakes, but no group had suffered more than the blacks themselves. Some blacks were advocating emigration schemes, as to Africa. Others were relying on Northerners to lift them up. These efforts, while perhaps well intentioned, were misguided, Washington said.

He told a story to illustrate his point. A ship had been lost at sea for many days; supplies of fresh water ran short, then ran out. The crew and passengers began to perish from dehydration. Suddenly they spotted another vessel on the horizon. "Water! Water! We die of thirst!" the stricken vessel signaled. The answer came back, "Cast down your bucket where you are." The captain of the first vessel thought he must have been misunderstood. "We die of thirst!" he repeated. Again came the reply, "Cast down your bucket where you are!" A third time the distressed ship asked for water. A third time the reply was returned, "Cast down your bucket where you are!" Finally the captain heeded the advice and ordered a bucket put down. When it was drawn up, it contained fresh, sweet water. All the while that the ship's passengers and crew had been suffering and dying from thirst, the vessel had been in the broad mouth of the Amazon River.

Highlighting the moral, Washington stated: "To those of my race who depend on bettering their condition in a foreign land, or who underestimate the importance of cultivating friendly relations with the Southern white man, I would say: 'Cast down your bucket where you are!'—cast it down in making friends in every manly way of the people of all races by whom we are surrounded."

The white race might also heed the moral of the story. Some Southerners were looking to foreign immigrants for the labor needed to build up the region. "I would repeat what I say to my own race," Washington declared. "Cast down your bucket among these people who have, without strikes and labor wars, tilled your fields, cleared your forests, builded your railroads and cities." By casting down their bucket among their black neighbors, Southern whites would assure themselves of the cooperation of "the most patient, faithful, law-abiding and unresentful people the world has seen." Blacks had proved their loyalty in past generations, nursing the babies of the whites, tending to the sick and aged. Blacks were ready to prove their loyalty again. "In the future, in our humble way, we shall stand by you with a devotion that no foreigner can approach, ready to lay down our lives, if need be, in defense of yours, interlacing our industrial, commercial, civil and religious life with yours in a way that shall make the interests of both races one."

Through most of his address, Washington avoided large gestures of hands or arms. But as he arrived at the sentence that summarized his message, employing a metaphor that subsequently came to represent his entire approach to race relations, he raised his right arm straight up in the air, fingers outstretched at first, then clenched tightly into a fist. "In all things that are purely social, we can be as separate as the fingers, yet one as the hand in all things essential to mutual progress."

Speaking still to the white South, Washington continued, "Nearly sixteen millions of hands will aid you in pulling the load upward, or they will pull against you." Blacks constituted one third of the population of the South. "We shall constitute one-third and more of the ignorance and crime of the South, or one-third its intelligence and progress; we shall contribute one-third to the business and industrial prosperity of the South, or we shall prove a veritable body of death, stagnating, depressing, retarding every effort to advance the body politic." Washington cautioned whites not to expect too much too soon from his race. Only thirty years distanced his people from slavery. An immense amount of work remained to be done in fitting them to take their place in a prosperous new South. But with the help of the white race, the black race would accomplish that goal.

Speaking now to his fellow blacks, Washington urged them to set their sights on the attainable. "Our greatest danger is that in the leap from slavery to freedom we may overlook the fact that the masses of us are to live by the production of our hands, that we shall prosper in proportion as we learn to glorify common labor and put brains and skill into the common occupations of life; shall prosper in proportion as we learn to draw the line between the superficial and the substantial." This was the fundamental lesson that blacks had sometimes forgotten. "No race can prosper till it learns that there is as much dignity in tilling a field as in writing a poem. It is at the bottom of life we must begin, and not at the top. Nor should we permit our grievances to overshadow our opportunities."

Washington rarely discussed politics, but now, in the spotlight, and at a time when Jim Crow laws were spreading across the South, he addressed himself to the issue of segregation. What he said offered no encouragement to those who were fighting against Jim Crow. "The wisest among my race," he said, "understand that the agitation of questions of social equality is the extremest folly, and that progress in the enjoyment of all the privileges that will come to us must be the result of severe and constant struggle rather than of artificial forcing." Blacks must demonstrate that they were worthy of an equal place in society. If they did so, they had nothing to fear. "No race that has anything to contribute to the markets of the world is long in any degree ostracized. It is important and right that all privileges of law be ours, but it is vastly more important that we be prepared for the exercise of these privileges. The opportunity to earn a dollar in a factory just now is worth infinitely more than the opportunity to spend a dollar in an opera house." Political agitation tended to divide the two races, one from the other. What the South needed at this stage in its history was unity and cooperation. If the two races worked together, each offering "patient, sympathetic help" to the other, they could create a prosperity that would bring "into our beloved South a new heaven and a new earth."

When Washington finished, applause resounded from all parts of the auditorium. Most whites presumably cheered him for his message of modest conciliation; many blacks cheered him for his mere presence and the fact that the whites were honoring him. Governor Bullock strode across the stage to pump Washington's hand enthusiastically. White women threw flowers down from the balconies. Well-wishers flocked to the platform, making it difficult for the program to continue, which, anticlimactically, it eventually did.

The praise only increased during the days after the Atlanta speech. "Your address is glorious, beyond all words glorious!" wrote Mary Stearns, the widow of an abolitionist who had helped John Brown carry out his famous raid. "The Dawn is at hand; and this second 'Washington' is its Heaven-appointed herald." Atlanta newspaperman Clark Howell described the speech as "a platform on which the whites and blacks can stand with full justice to each race," and predicted that it would trigger "a moral revolution in America." Tuskegee benefactor William Baldwin called the address "tip-top," "gilt-edged," "super-extra." President Grover Cleveland characterized Washington's message as the basis for "new hope" for Negroes. From Wilberforce University, a recent Harvard Ph.D. named W. E. B. Du Bois wrote Washington, "Let me heartily congratulate you upon your phenomenal success at Atlanta—it was a word fitly spoken." A short while later, Du Bois amplified his approval in a letter to the *New York Age*. "Here might be the basis of a real settlement between whites and blacks in the South, if the South opened to the Negroes the doors of economic opportunity, and the Negroes co-operated with the white South in political sympathy."

VI

Du Bois wouldn't always be so enamored of Washington's views. One reason was that his background could hardly have been more different than Washington's. Du Bois (who pronounced his name Du Boyce) was born in Massachusetts three generations after that state had outlawed slavery and three years after the Union victory in the Civil War had ended slavery throughout the country. He grew up in the town of Great Barrington, where African-Americans numbered perhaps fifty out of a population of five thousand. Partly because the black community in the area was so small and therefore nonthreatening, and partly because of Massachusetts's long-standing tradition of comparative liberalism on matters of race, Du Bois encountered little discrimination as a youth. His mother encouraged him to make the most of himself, saying that if he had enough ambition, nothing could stop him. He took her words to heart and began ascending the academic ladder. It helped that Massachusetts's public schools were among the best in the United States; enrolling in the standard curriculum for the college-bound, he took four years of Latin and three of Greek. It helped too that his high school principal was a broad-minded man who encouraged the young Du Bois, both verbally and financially, to set his sights high. (In later life Du Bois asked himself what would have become of him had this principal been "born with no faith in 'darkies.' ") It also helped that Du Bois was brilliant. In a community that placed strong emphasis on academic success, Du Bois was a star. Consistently at the top of his class, he was a gifted debater and a fluent writer; at fifteen, he wrote a regular column for the *New York Globe*. It was a situation that bred self-confidence. So certain was Du Bois that he was destined for great things that he began saving and annotating his personal papers for future biographers while still in high school.

Du Bois attended college at Fisk University in Nashville. It was his first experience mingling with large numbers of his fellow African-Americans and his first stay in the South. Both aspects of the situation had important effects on his intellectual development. His classmates were the best and brightest of their generation of blacks, drawn from all across the country. Yet, as in Massachusetts, Du Bois stood at the head of his class. He raced through Fisk in three years, slowing down just long enough to exhort his fellows—"ye destined leaders of a noble people"—to assume their rightful place in world affairs. "I am a Negro," he declared. "And I glory in the name! I am proud of the black blood that flows in my veins."

These college years in the South, however, also brought Du Bois face to face with the fact that the vast majority of African-Americans were not like him. Most members of his race were poor and ignorant. Most—certainly of those who lived in the South—constantly confronted personal and institutional discrimination. Describing his arrival in the South, Du Bois wrote, "I suddenly came to a region where the world was split into white and black halves, and where the darker half was held back by race prejudice and legal bonds, as well as by deep ignorance and dire poverty." Du Bois's experience in Tennessee didn't diminish his confidence in himself, but it caused him to recognize the depth of the rift between the races. He left Fisk, he recalled later, convinced of the "absolute division of the universe into black and white."

From Fisk, Du Bois went to Harvard. The reason he chose Harvard, as he attempted to explain on his application, was simple: "I have very little money and think I can get more aid there than elsewhere." Perhaps fortunately for him, one of his mentors at Fisk revised this frank statement before it got to Harvard, and he was admitted. Fitting into the life of a public high school in Great Barrington had been one thing; fitting into the life of Harvard, where social connections still mattered more than intellectual accomplishment, was something else. Du Bois never did. Not that he made any particular effort: his pride was of the sort that wanted nothing to do with those who wanted nothing to do with him. He lived some distance from the campus and habitually spent his non-study time away from the university.

Du Bois's course of study at Harvard followed a winding path. At first he specialized in science, particularly chemistry and geology. Next he tried philosopy, investigating the European philosophers with George Santayana and the latest in psychological and pragmatic approaches under William James. But though philosophy held his attention longer than the natural sciences, he eventually decided to devote his energies to a field where answers were at least as important as questions. By 1890, he had determined that studying history and the social sciences was what he really wanted to do. In applying for a graduate fellowship, he stated that he wished to do research in the developing body of social science "with a view to the ultimate application of its principles to the social and economic rise of the Negro people." After completing course work, Du Bois wrote a thesis on the suppression of the African slave trade to the United States; it was published in 1896.

Between his arrival at Harvard and the conferral of his doctorate,

Du Bois took two years out to travel around Europe and attend classes at the University of Berlin. He found Europe in the early 1890s to be enormously stimulating both culturally and psychologically. "From the physical provincialism of America and the psychical provincialism of my rather narrow race problem into which I was born and which seemed to me the essence of life," he wrote, "I was transplanted and startled into a realization of the real centers of modern civilization and into at least a momentary escape from my own social problems and also into an introduction to new cultural patterns." Europe's intellectuals treated him as an equal, reinforcing his belief that education and cultural refinement tended to dissolve racial prejudice. The experience strengthened his self-confidence and his belief that he must strive for great things. "I am glad I am living," he commented to his diary on his twenty-fifth birthday in 1893. "I rejoice as a strong man to run a race, and I am strong—is it egotism or is it assurance?—or is it the silent call of the world spirit that makes me feel that I am royal and that beneath my sceptre a world of kings shall bow? The hot dark blood of that black forefather born king of men is beating at my heart, and I know that I am either a genius or a fool." He didn't actually entertain the latter proposition.

Du Bois returned to America in 1894 and received his degree from Harvard the following year. By now he had fairly concrete career plans which he outlined in a letter to the foundation that had sponsored his European study. He said he wanted to take a position on the faculty at a Negro university, with two objectives: "1. Scientifically to study the Negro question past and present with a view to its best solution. 2. To see how far Negro students are capable of further independent study and research in the best scientific work of the day." To these ends, Du Bois accepted a job offer from Wilberforce University in Ohio. He had just started there at the time of Booker Washington's Atlanta address.

As Du Bois's congratulatory letter to Washington demonstrated, there was some common ground between the two men's approaches to race relations. Du Bois concurred with Washington that African-Americans must strive to prepare themselves to participate in the American economy. Hard work and thrift would open many doors now closed. "The day the Negro race courts and marries the savings-bank will be the day of its salvation," Du Bois declared in 1898. Du Bois also recognized that for the vast majority of blacks the most appropriate education followed the vocational lines mapped out by Washington's Tuskegee Institute. He wrote Washington to express his "best sympathy for the Tuskegee work."

But Du Bois disagreed with Washington regarding the role of African-American leadership—what Du Bois called the "talented tenth." An elitist to the core, Du Bois believed that the Negro race would be uplifted by the achievements of its most gifted members. These few—teachers, ministers, doctors, lawyers, scientists, writers—would demonstrate by their example that blacks were fully capable of matching the achievements of whites. Vocational training was fine for the masses of African-Americans, but to consign all blacks, even the brightest, to farms and factories would be to deny the race as a whole the chance to prove its equality with whites. The victories of African-American intellectuals, by exploding the idea that blacks were fit for menial labor only, would be victories for all African-Americans.

Booker Washington didn't deny that it was necessary to educate the most gifted members of the black race beyond the level of agricultural and industrial skills. Nor did he dispute the value of this group in raising up the less gifted. Washington's own policy of hiring the best-educated blacks he could find for Tuskegee testified to his agreement with Du Bois on this point.

The difference between the two men consisted chiefly in emphasis. For Washington, the training of the masses took priority. Like an army general gathering his infantry for attack, Washington intended to overwhelm the fortifications of the Jim Crow system by an assault across a broad front. For Du Bois, the education of the elite demanded initial attention. "To attempt to establish any sort of system of common and industrial school training," he said, "without *first* (and I say *first* advisedly)—without *first* providing for the higher training of the very best teachers, is simply throwing your money to the winds." Du Bois envisioned the assault on the racial status quo as being spearheaded by commando units of the talented tenth. These commandos would breach the segregationist front by the force of their intellect and gifts of leadership, and they would thereby open the way for the rank and file to follow.

Du Bois didn't overlook the deficiencies his people brought to their task of self-improvement. "We must unflinchingly and bravely face the truth, not with apologies, but with solemn earnestness," he wrote in 1897. "Unless we conquer our present vices, they will conquer us. We are diseased, we are developing criminal tendencies, and an alarmingly large percentage of our men and women are sexually impure." Describing his vision of a "Negro Academy," which he characterized as "an intellectual clearing-house" for the products of the African-American mind, he asserted, "The Academy should seek to gather about it the talented, unselfish men, the pure and noble-minded women, to fight an army of devils that disgraces our manhood and our womanhood." He continued, "We believe that the first and greatest step toward the settlement of the present friction between the races—commonly called the Negro Problem—lies in the correction of the immorality, crime and laziness among the Negroes themselves, which still remains as a heritage from slavery. We believe that only earnest and long continued efforts on our own part can cure these social ills."

Present problems notwithstanding, Du Bois was completely convinced of the brilliant future that lay before his people. "We believe that the Negro people, as a race, have a contribution to make to civilization and humanity, which no other race can make." It was the special responsibility of the talented tenth to awaken Negroes to their potential for contribution and to blaze the trail in making that contribution. Du Bois offered as part of a

creed for the Negro Academy a statement of racial solidarity and betterment: "Firmly believing in our high destiny, we, as American Negroes, are
resolved to strive in every honorable way for the realization of the best and
highest aims, for the development of strong manhood and pure womanhood, and for the rearing of a race ideal in America and Africa, to the
glory of God and the uplifting of the Negro people."

VII

Appealing to black pride as he did, Du Bois couldn't help drawing distinctions between his approach and that of Washington, for whom one of the
cardinal virtues was African-American humility. During the last years of
the 1890s these differences grew more marked, partly because Du Bois
became increasingly willing to challenge Washington's leadership of the
African-American movement, but mostly because the methods of Washington's Atlanta Compromise didn't seem to be working. During the late
1890s and after, the Jim Crow system continued to proliferate. With the
apparent approval of the United States Supreme Court, as evidenced in the
Plessy case, Southern states instituted legal segregation throughout nearly
all areas of social life. Justice John Marshall Harlan's dissenting warning,
about how the notion of what constituted reasonable grounds for applying
the state's police power to racial issues would prove enormously elastic,
came true. Before long blacks couldn't eat, drink, sleep, pray, be educated,
be entertained, or do almost anything else without facing a government-
imposed color bar. Worst of all—because it largely eliminated hope for
reversing the segregationist trend peacefully—African-Americans lost the
right to vote. By various subterfuges, including poll taxes, literacy tests,
white primaries, and "grandfather clauses," the Southern states subverted
the Fifteenth Amendment and essentially removed blacks from political participation.

Du Bois's proud spirit would in any event have had difficulty accepting
the terms of Washington's implicit pact with the white aristocracy: dropping demands for social and political equality in exchange for support of
black efforts at economic self-help. But the consequences of the Plessy case
made such acceptance wholly out of the question. In the late 1890s, Du
Bois increasingly distanced himself from Washington's platform, as did
many other African-American leaders. During this period and into the first
part of the new century, an irreparable breach opened between the Washington camp and the Du Bois camp.

The breach was painfully evident in *The Souls of Black Folk*, Du Bois's
landmark portrayal of African-American life. The author summarized
Washington's program: "Mr. Washington distinctly asks that black people
give up, at least for the present, three things—first, political power; second,
insistence on civil rights; third, higher education of Negro youth—and concentrate all their energies on industrial education, the accumulation of

wealth, and the conciliation of the South." For a decade, Du Bois said, this program had been the basis for black political and economic efforts. What had it accomplished? "1. The disfranchisement of the Negro. 2. The legal creation of a distinct status of civil inferiority for the Negro. 3. The steady withdrawal of aid from institutions for the higher training of the Negro." Du Bois conceded that these evil consequences weren't entirely Washington's work. They had required the malice of whites as well. But Washington had facilitated the process. "His propaganda has, without a shadow of doubt, helped their speedier accomplishment."

Du Bois contended that Washington misunderstood the close connection between civil and political rights, on the one hand, and economic betterment, on the other. As a result of this misunderstanding, Washington was caught in a "triple paradox": "1. He is striving nobly to make Negro artisans business men and property-owners; but it is utterly impossible, under modern competitive methods, for workingmen and property-owners to defend their rights and exist without the right of suffrage. 2. He insists on thrift and self-respect, but at the same time counsels a silent submission to civic inferiority such as is bound to sap the manhood of any race in the long run. 3. He advocates common-school and industrial training, and depreciates institutions of higher learning; but neither the Negro common-schools, nor Tuskegee itself, could remain open a day were it not for teachers trained in Negro colleges, or trained by their graduates."

Du Bois pointed out that Washington's program was being rejected by increasing numbers of blacks. Some of the rejecters argued that blacks would never achieve equality so long as they remained in America. They advocated removal to Africa or somewhere else beyond American shores. Du Bois didn't debate the merits of this argument beyond remarking that recent developments in American foreign relations, in particular the annexation of the Philippines and Hawaii and the effective conquest of Cuba, demonstrated that soon possibly no place on earth would be beyond the reach of the segregationists and their allies. "Where in the world may we go and be safe from lying and brute force?"

Others who rejected Washington's message intended to stay in America and fight for what was legitimately theirs. These people would demand three things of American society (Du Bois liked things in threes): "1. The right to vote. 2. Civic equality. 3. The education of youth according to ability." Du Bois's sentiments lay with these stay-and-fighters (later he would reconsider). Persons of this persuasion could honor Washington for the work he had done at Tuskegee, and applaud his efforts at promoting reconciliation in the South, yet at the same "insist that the way to truth and right lies in straightforward honesty, not in indiscriminate flattery." These strivers understood that civic and political equality wouldn't come in a moment. "They do not expect to see the bias and prejudices of years disappear in the blast of a trumpet." But they knew that struggle rather than submission was the means to achieve equality. "They are absolutely certain that the way for a people to gain their reasonable rights is not by voluntarily throwing them away and insisting that they do not want them; that the way for a people to gain respect is not by continually belittling and ridiculing themselves; that, on the contrary, Negroes must insist continually, in season and out of season, that voting is necessary to modern manhood, that color discrimination is barbarism, and that black boys need education as well as white boys."

Moral obligation as well as efficacy dictated the correct course of action for black Americans—and white Americans too. "We have no right to sit silently by while the inevitable seeds are sown for a harvest of disaster to our children, black and white." When Washington preached thrift, patience, and industrial training for the masses, he should be supported. But when he apologized for injustice and excused the denial of rights, he must be opposed. A better text than Washington's Atlanta speech was one written by another Southerner—a white man—more than a century earlier: "We hold these truths to be self-evident: That all men are created equal; that they are endowed by their Creator with certain unalienable rights; that among these are life, liberty, and the pursuit of happiness."

Chapter 7

CROSS OF GOLD,

TONGUE OF SILVER

I

What Du Bois was saying in quoting the Declaration of Independence was that blacks in America needed to look out for themselves and not rely on the goodwill of whites in power—much as the American revolutionists of 1776 had taken the colonies' fate into American hands and not left it to the goodwill of the British. Jefferson's manifesto was likewise a favorite among the Populists of the 1890s, although where Du Bois saw the fundamental division of American society running along racial lines, the Populists perceived it in economic and class terms. And where Du Bois demanded racial equality, the Populists wanted economic equality. The pivotal single event in race relations during the 1890s was the Plessy case of 1896; the pivotal political event of the decade, for the Populists and for the two major parties as well, was the presidential election of the same year.

The election campaign of 1896 was essentially a continuation of the political struggle that had been going on since the beginning of the 1890s. After their setback in the 1894 elections, the Populists as an organized party weren't quite so threatening to the status quo as they had seemed earlier. Populist-minded individuals gradually acknowledged that the mechanisms of American partisan politics militated against the rise of third parties. The Republicans had accomplished the feat in the 1850s, but that accomplishment had largely been due to the sectional crisis associated with slavery. Sectionalism still existed, as the 1896 election would reconfirm, but not in the virulent form of the pre–Civil War era. Assessing the situation in the mid-1890s, many Populists decided to rejoin the major parties and press their demands as Democrats, or less frequently Republicans. Others who had been tempted to bolt the major parties for the Populists stayed put.

The invasion of the Democrats by lapsed Populists and by Populist ideas almost split the party of Jefferson and Jackson in two. This was hardly surprising given the passion the Populists brought to politics and the explosiveness of the ideas they espoused. As had been true since early in the decade, the most explosive issue of all was free silver. The depression was still deep and painful as 1896 began, and if banks didn't fail quite as fast now as they had in the immediate aftermath of the Panic of 1893, nor foreclosures occur so frequently in some areas, when the banks now did fail and the farms were seized they only broke more cruelly the hearts of those who had hung on this long. The depression had ruined the reputation of Grover Cleveland, who in any event had used up his allotted (by tradition rather than Constitution) two terms as president.

The depression had come close to ruining the reputation of the entire Democratic establishment. Incumbents almost never do well during depressions, but the carnage suffered by the Democrats in 1894 had been especially shocking. The Republican leader in the House of Representatives, Thomas Reed of Maine, had gleefully predicted during the summer before the balloting that "the Democratic mortality will be so great next fall that their dead will be buried in trenches and marked 'Unknown.' " The event fulfilled Reed's prediction, converting a Democratic advantage of 91 in the House into a Republican margin of 139, and delivering the Senate from the Democrats to the Republicans as well.

As a consequence of Cleveland's retirement and the Democratic congressional debacle of 1894, the Democrats scoured the country during the spring and summer of 1896 for a leader who could rally the troops and mount a counteroffensive. William Jennings Bryan thought he fit the description. Bryan was a native of Illinois, born in the year of Lincoln's first election as president. From his parents he inherited an attachment to the Democratic Party, an attachment he never seriously questioned, any more than he questioned the fundamentalist Protestantism he also inherited from them. Bryan attended Illinois College and Union Law School, and after a lackluster effort at developing a law practice decided to embark on a career in politics. Illinois, however, was thick with would-be Lincolns (and Douglases), and like many another young man in the nineteenth century he judged that he would have better luck in the West. He moved to Nebraska in 1887 and quickly set about establishing a name for himself. He joined the local Democratic Party, met all the important people in the vicinity of Lincoln, his new home, and sought out potential supporters. His efforts paid off when just three years after his arrival the voters of Lincoln and the surrounding area sent him to Washington as their congressman.

Bryan's 1890 election was due to his personal gifts of sincerity, shrewdness, and fluency on the hustings; it was also a consequence of the dissatisfaction that was simultaneously giving birth to the Populist movement. Although Nebraska had long been Republican territory, the trials of the late 1880s had turned many Nebraskans against Republicanism. The Democrats and particularly Bryan reaped the harvest of this discontent. The voters in Bryan's district sent a message to Washington via the election of 1890; the message was that things had better change and fast.

Bryan proved to be an admirable messenger. He was a hard worker and a solid student of political and economic issues, even if he wasn't an original or profound thinker. He was also a firm believer in representative democracy, which meant that he kept a moistened finger to the breeze of popular sentiments. Initially he took up the tariff question as one that was crucial to master. For months he studied the issue, confirming his previous judgment that the tariff constituted a means for enriching the elites from the pockets of the people. After extensive preparation, Bryan rose in the Congress for his first major address. He railed against the tariff and vituperated especially against the version recently approved under the name of William McKinley. His performance brought nods of approval from his colleagues but not the kind of enthusiastic outpouring he had hoped for. As he sat down after the speech a fellow Democrat, Joseph Bailer of Texas, explained why. The tariff, Bailey said, hurt farmers; no doubt about it. But what the farmers really resented was endlessly falling prices. The currency question was where the votes were.

Bryan heeded the advice. He threw himself now into an examination of the merits of silver as opposed to gold. He didn't require long to decide that right, truth, fairness, and most other virtues lay on the side of silver. Bryan campaigned successfully for reelection in 1892 on a silver platform, and during the subsequent session of Congress he led the Democrats who broke with the Cleveland administration over the repeal of the 1890 Silver Purchase Act. That the administration defeated the defectors and carried the day did little to lessen the reputation Bryan gained from his impassioned plea for silver. In the heat of the battle he threatened to lead a bolt from the Democratic Party; but as tempers cooled, he contented himself with accepting the leadership of the party's silver wing.

In 1894, Bryan attempted to translate his popularity among the silverites into elevation from the House of Representatives to the Senate. To do so, in that age before the direct election of senators, required courting the members of the Nebraska state legislature. Bryan worked diligently to swing the legislature's Populists behind his candidacy. He went so far as to help throw the support of Nebraska's Democratic organization to the Populist candidate in a close race for governor. But the Populists refused to return the favor, and instead of backing Bryan for the Senate endorsed their own candidate. With the reform vote split, the Republicans walked away with the Senate seat.

The experience cured Bryan of what minor inclination he had to jump the Democratic ship for the Populist bark. Instead he concentrated on winning the Democrats over to the cause of silver—and winning for himself a prize bigger than a place in the Senate. By any calculation Bryan was a long shot for the presidential nomination. He had served a scant two terms in the House. He hailed from a lightly populated state with little heft in national affairs. He wasn't even old enough to qualify for the presidency, although he would be by the 1896 election. But no one ever accused Bryan of lacking ambition or perseverance in the pursuit of something he set his mind on.

Bryan spent the two years after his defeat in the Senate race making himself better known around the country. He signed on as editorial writer for the *Omaha World-Herald* and churned out a steady flow of commentaries on issues of the day, especially money. He sent copies of his remarks to other editors across the continent, openly soliciting plagiarism. He traveled extensively through the farm communities of the West and South. He introduced himself to influential Democrats wherever he could find them. He spoke to large groups and small, in auditoriums, meeting halls, schoolhouses, tents, and living rooms. Handsome, with a broad forehead, erect bearing, piercing eyes, raven hair, and a winning smile, and wonderfully gifted with a mellifluous yet compelling voice that easily reached audiences ranging from ten to ten thousand, Bryan made a favorable impression on nearly all who met him. Most of his audiences were happy to hear what he was saying, but even those who disagreed with his views couldn't help liking this earnest, engaging young man. Although many scoffed when he let it be known that he was considering a run for the presidency, most of the scoffers were reassured by Bryan's pledge to back any candidate the Democratic Party put forward who was sound on the issues.

By the time the Democrats gathered in Chicago in July 1896, Bryan could claim a small army of acquaintances among the delegates to the convention. Whether they would become his supporters was one of the major questions for the convention to decide. The other was where the party would position itself on the money issue. The gold-bugs in the party were on the defensive, to be sure. Cleveland's liaisons with J. P. Morgan and the big bankers of the East had alienated most of the West and South, which had been leaning hard toward silver anyway. Yet Cleveland remained president and retained the patronage and pull of his office. When he spoke, personally or through his lieutenants, the convention would have to listen.

Or so the members of the party establishment thought before arriving in Chicago. Almost as soon as they stepped off their special trains from the East, they sensed that they were in hostile territory. Ben Tillman threw down a challenge to the old guard. "The silver men are running this affair," the fiery South Carolinian declared, "and they propose to do it in their own fashion. If the gold men don't like it, let them bolt. I hope they will." When his words drew hisses from the party regulars, Tillman spat back, "There are only three things in the world that can hiss: a goose, a serpent, and a man." A friend of William Whitney, a leader of the Cleveland forces in Chicago, was shocked by the animosity that hung like a storm cloud over the convention hall. "For the first time, I can understand the scenes of the French revolution," he said. Cleveland's former postmaster general, William Vilas, currently a senator from Wisconsin, asked, "Perhaps somewhere in this country there lurks a Robespierre; a Danton; a Marat?" From his tone, Vilas seemed to think such malevolent spirits might be lurking within the very convention hall in Chicago. Senator David Hill, a party regular from New York, was asked why he didn't smile and look pleasant for the cameras. "I never smile and look pleasant at a funeral," Hill replied.

It was a bad sign for the gold-bugs that Illinois Governor Altgeld, who had so stoutly objected to Cleveland's actions in the Pullman strike, served as an informal host and keynote speaker for the convention. A reporter for *Harper's Weekly*, rooting for the Cleveland wing of the party, labeled Altgeld "the most dangerous influence in the convention." This reporter went on to describe Altgeld as having "the stamp of the agitator who, when the bludgeon had failed of its work, would be ready with the poisoned knife, and who, in leading a victory-drunken mob, would not hesitate to follow pillage with the torch." Yet though the conservatives despised and distrusted him, a majority of the delegates cheered Altgeld, yelling his praises to the rafters. Many observers guessed that if Altgeld had been a natural-born rather than naturalized American citizen (and therefore eligible for the presidency), he might easily have been swept to the nomination.

But the delegates had to look elsewhere for their champion. Early on, the silverites seized control of the convention, just as Ben Tillman said they would. The seizure began with the debate over the platform. Tillman led off with a vitriolic speech condemning Cleveland and all those who supported the president's policies. "We of the South have burned our bridges behind us so far as the Eastern Democrats are concerned," Tillman proclaimed. "We denounce the administration of President Cleveland as undemocratic and tyrannical." Tillman applauded the draft platform, which included planks excoriating Cleveland's dealings with Morgan and the Morgan syndicate, as well as the administration's resort to court injunctions and federal troops during the Pullman strike. It all showed a pattern of undemocratic highhandedness, Tillman said, amounting to nothing less than an attempt to establish a "plutocratic despotism."

Tillman's attack didn't go unanswered. Hill of New York declared, "I am a Democrat, but I am not a revolutionist. My mission here today is to unite, not to divide—to build up, not to destroy." Hill contended that the proposed platform, which had been written largely along lines dictated by the radical Southern and Western wings of the party, would divide the Democrats deeply. "I speak more in sorrow than in anger," Hill said. "You know what this platform means to the East." Recalling the party's patron saints, Hill added, "We want the principles of Jefferson and Jackson."

Whatever Jefferson and Jackson might have said on the issues of 1896, the draft platform of the Democratic convention said silver. "We are unalterably opposed to monometallism, which has locked fast the prosperity of an industrial people in the paralysis of hard times," the proposed statement read. "We demand the free and unlimited coinage of both silver and gold at the present legal ratio of 16 to 1, without waiting for the aid or consent of any other nation."

The silverites had won an initial victory in having this silver plank included in the draft platform, but the showdown didn't occur until the convention voted to accept or reject the platform. Tillman and Hill established the boundaries of the debate; other speakers added their arguments for and against. The climax of the debate, and indeed the high point of the convention, came when William Jennings Bryan mounted the stage. He approached the lectern "two steps at a time," in the words of a reporter for the *New York World.* His reception was wildly enthusiastic. "Ear-splitting noises were heard," the correspondent recounted. "Waves of scarlet fans danced in the galleries." Bryan later called this opportunity an "unexpected stroke of luck." Luck it might have been, but it wasn't unexpected. Bryan had plotted and planned for it for months and now intended to make the most of it.

He began softly and modestly. He admitted his youth and conceded that many in the convention had longer experience and greater reputations than he. Yet more was at stake than youth or age, experience or reputation. His voice grew deeper with conviction though not much louder in volume as he declared, "The humblest citizen in all the land, when clad in the armor of a righteous cause, is stronger than all the hosts of error. I come to speak to you in defense of a cause as holy as the cause of liberty—the cause of humanity." Bryan paused, then continued, "The individual is but an atom; he is born, he acts, he dies; but principle is eternal. And this has been a contest over principle."

Bryan played the audience with a virtuosity that was partly intuitive and partly the result of close study and endless hours on the stump and in the meeting tent. He measured his sentences, giving his supporters ample time to voice their agreement with one idea before proceeding to the next. Recalling the actions of the crowd, Bryan later wrote, "At the close of a sentence, it would rise and shout, and when I began upon another sentence, the room was as still as a church." Bryan realized that he was the master of the situation. "I thought of a choir, as I noted how instantaneously and in unison they responded to each point made."

In the next part of his speech—delivered, as always with him, without notes—Bryan remarked that proponents of silver had been accused by the capitalists and their agents of disturbing the business interests of the country. This was a malicious slander and a gross deceit. "We reply that *you* have disturbed *our* business interests by your course. We say to you that *you* have made the definition of a business man too limited in its application. The man who is employed for wages is as much a business man as his employer; the attorney in a country town is as much a business man as the corporation counsel in a great metropolis; the merchant at the crossroads store is as much a business man as the merchant of New York; the farmer who goes forth in the morning and toils all day—who begins in the spring and toils all summer—and who by the application of brain and muscle to the natural resources of the country creates wealth, is as much a business man as the man who goes upon the board of trade and bets upon the price of grain." After adding others to his dichotomy, including the miners who descended into the bowels of the earth to pry loose precious metals, contrasted against the financial magnates who manipulated the price of those metals from the back rooms of the world's financial houses, Bryan concluded this line of reasoning with the assertion that he and his supporters spoke for "this broader class of business men."

Having divided the business classes of America into the sheep and goats, the producers and the parasites, Bryan expounded their opposing philosophies of political economy. "There are those who believe that, if you will only legislate to make the well-to-do prosperous, their prosperity will leak through on those below. The Democratic idea, however, has been that if you legislate to make the masses prosperous, their prosperity will find its way up through every class which rests upon them."

Bryan elaborated on this idea of national prosperity as dependent on the working classes of the country. In doing so he drew another distinction— the one that most appealed to his followers. "You come to us and tell us that the great cities are in favor of the gold standard. We reply that the great cities rest upon our broad and fertile prairies. Burn down your cities and leave our farms, and your cities will spring up again as if by magic. But destroy our farms, and the grass will grow in the streets of every city in the country!"

At this the convention erupted in a sustained outpouring of approval. The delegates leaped to their feet, cheering this young man from Nebraska who voiced the feelings so many of them felt, yet which none had expressed so well. Bryan let the tumult swell, continue, and start to diminish before he went on.

By now he had identified the forces that were arrayed in the arena of battle, and he commenced issuing the call to arms. "We have petitioned, and our petitions have been scorned," he asserted. "We have entreated, and our entreaties have been disregarded. We have begged, and they have mocked when our calamity came." Enough of supplication! Enough of deference! "We beg no longer. We entreat no more. We petition no more. *We defy them!*"

The crowd was beside itself. The din crashed back and forth across the floor of the convention hall and shook the walls and roof. The anti-Bryanists knew their cause was lost when they saw even many among their numbers carried away by the passion of the moment.

But there was more. Bryan let the furor diminish a bit, then launched into his peroration. His voice dropped, drawing the crowd closer. "It is the issue of 1776 over again. Our ancestors, when but three millions in number, had the courage to declare their political independence of every other nation. Shall we, their descendants, when we have grown to seventy millions, declare that we are less independent than our forefathers?" No, that would not be the verdict of the American people. Bryan's voice began to rise now as he warned the proponents of gold what they had got themselves in for. "If they dare to come out in the open field and defend the gold standard as a good thing, we will fight them to the uttermost. Having behind us the producing masses of this nation and the world, supported

by the commercial interests, the laboring interests and the toilers everywhere, we will answer their demand for a gold standard by saying to
them"—a pause for effect, followed by a dramatic and moving gesture of
the arms, first pulling both palms down toward his head from straight
above, then both arms stretched straight out to the sides—"*You shall not
press down upon the brow of labor this crown of thorns! You shall not
crucify mankind upon a cross of gold!*"

Bryan stood before the audience as though on a cross, head bowed, arms
wide, exhausted by his oratorical effort. The audience hesitated momentarily. Then, understanding that this was the end, it exploded once more.
With nothing to stop the riot this time, the shouting and applause continued for half an hour. Delirious silverites stood on their chairs, poured into
the hallways, marched round and round the auditorium, screaming for their
newfound hero, their peerless leader. Those members of the Eastern old
guard who resisted the enthusiasm looked on glumly, knowing they had
lost control of the party and probably lost all chance of the Democrats'
winning the election.

Had the presidential nomination taken place at that moment, Bryan
doubtless would have been selected by acclamation. But the rules committee
insisted on following the set procedure. First came the vote on the platform,
which, following Bryan's overwhelming speech, was carried easily by the
silverites. The selection of the candidate didn't occur until the next day. At
the time the convention had begun, Bryan had been given no better than
an outside chance to win the nomination. On the first three ballots of the
voting for nominee, he ran second to the far better known Richard Bland
of Missouri. "Silver Dick" Bland had a long record of support for silver in
Congress, and the backing that he had developed in the party during that
time helped him hold off Bryan's challenge for a few hours. He counted
among his supporters Altgeld of Illinois, who told Clarence Darrow, "It
takes more than speeches to win real victories. Applause lasts but a little
while. The road to justice is not a path of glory. It is stony and long and
lonely, filled with pain and martyrdom." Altgeld added, sourly, "I have
been thinking over Bryan's speech. What did he say, anyhow?"

But the eleventh-hour efforts of the stop-Bryanists failed. The Nebraska
spell-binder passed Bland on the fourth ballot, and on the fifth he gained
the deciding margin. Having stirred the convention to the bottom of its
collective soul the previous day, Bryan now acted nonchalant. He went to
a barber while the final voting took place, and he learned of his nomination
while lathered and under the razor. Aware of both the magnitude and
limitations of his accomplishment, he remarked, "I seem to have plenty of
friends now, but I remember when they were very few."

The last matter the convention had to deal with was the vice-presidential
nomination. This went to Arthur Sewall of Maine, an Eastern silverite who
could balance the ticket geographically—if not ideologically: there would
be no quarter given to gold. The gold Democrats, appreciating the depth
of their defeat, broke with custom in refusing to make Bryan's nomination

unanimous, and many talked of leaving the party. Their sullenness had a dampening influence on the last hours of the convention. But their bad humor couldn't quite silence the echoes that still reverberated for Bryan and silver.

II

Although the Democratic Convention was the headline political story of the summer of 1896, it was sandwiched between two other conventions that, if not quite so dramatic, were nonetheless essential to the saga of Bryan. The Republicans had met in St. Louis in June. After the trials the nation had been experiencing for the previous several years, and after their party's overwhelming victory in the congressional elections of 1894, the Republicans were fairly drooling at the thought of recapturing the presidency, with all that that prospect entailed in the way of spoils and the other prerogatives of power. The Republicans had every reason to be confident. The bitter battles that were tearing the Democrats apart resonated only faintly in the Republican Party, where silverites were a small and relatively repressed minority. The country certainly appeared to be in a mood to throw the current Democratic rascals out of the executive branch. The only question the Republican leadership had to deal with was whom the prize should be bestowed upon.

Thomas Reed thought he was the most deserving. In 1896, Tom Reed was one of the legends of American congressional politics. Even in an age when heft was fashionable for men of affairs, Reed loomed large. Six feet three inches tall, weighing some three hundred pounds, and possessing "the largest human face I ever saw," according to a colleague, Reed's presence overpowered many lesser mortals. But Reed's reputation rested far more on his quick and often biting intellect. The Maine congressman played partisan politics with a zest few in the House of Representatives could match. When a Democrat from Illinois grandiloquently proclaimed that he would rather be right than president, Reed interrupted, in the down-east drawl that his opponents learned to dread, saying that the gentleman needn't be disturbed: he would never be either. Another House member, noted for rambling remarks devoid of reflection, began a speech, "I was thinking, Mr. Speaker, I was thinking . . . ," causing Reed, then speaker of the House, to applaud "the gentleman's commendable innovation." Reed was heard to say of two of the less profound members of the House that "they never open their mouths without subtracting from the sum of human knowledge."

After he silenced, with typical sarcasm, an opponent who tried to break into one of his own speeches, Reed declared, "Having imbedded that fly in the liquid amber of my remarks, I will proceed." He sardonically reassured a Democratic representative from Texas that his seat was safe, since the public school system hadn't extended that far south yet. When he began another speech by asserting that Democrats could always be counted on to do some "mean, low-lived and contemptible thing," and certain Democrats present responded with catcalls, he said, "There, I told you so." Informed that an uncherished colleague had died, and asked by an obituary writer what he should say about the deceased, Reed answered, "Anything but the truth." Noting the general unreliability of human nature, Reed observed that one person, with God, was always a majority. "But," he added, "many a martyr has been burned at the stake while the votes were being counted." The Reed epigram that entered most lastingly into the lexicon of American politics was his definition of a statesman as a "dead politician."

Reed did much more than throw off wry remarks. Almost singlehandedly he revolutionized the conduct of American congressional affairs. Henry Cabot Lodge, a student of politics as well as one of the more able practitioners in American history, said of Reed that there had never existed "a more perfectly equipped leader in any parliamentary body at any period." As speaker of the House in 1890, Reed erased a longstanding tradition by which a minority of the House could block action by refusing to answer quorum calls. House rules permitted one fifth of the membership to demand a roll call to determine whether a quorum existed on a particular issue. The very members who demanded the roll call could then sit silent while the roll was called and thereby block a quorum, preventing consideration of the measure at hand. By this means a minority could often frustrate the will of the majority.

As speaker and leader of the majority in the House, Reed determined to put an end to what he called "this peculiar art of metaphysics which admits of corporeal presence and parliamentary absence." After the elections of 1888, the Republicans controlled the House by a bare eight votes, and the 168 Republican members amounted to a mere three more than the required quorum of 165. If four Republicans were ill, at home visiting their districts, detained at the dentist, or held away from the House chamber for any other reason, the Democrats could demand a quorum call, keep their mouths shut when their names were called, and paralyze the proceedings. Reed found this circumstance intolerable. He quoted the Koran: "Dost thou think, O Man, that we have created the heavens and the earth in jest?" He went on, "Are elections a farce, and is government by the people a juggle? Do we marshal our tens of millions at the polls for sport? If there be anything in popular government, it means that whenever the people have elected one party to take control of the House or the Senate, that party shall have both the power and the responsibility. If that is not the effect, what is the use of the election?"

For his test of strength, Reed chose the issue of some contested congressional elections that the House had to settle. The Democrats, being in the minority and likely to lose out, were expected to demand a quorum call and refuse to answer. They did, and the quorum failed by two votes.

Reed responded by taking matters into his own hands. Eyeing the Democrats who sat large as life in front of him but insisted on being counted absent, he intoned, "The Chair directs the Clerk to record the names of the following members present and refusing to vote." He commenced to identify the silent individuals.

As soon as he did so, the silent members abandoned their silence in favor of loud protests. "I appeal! I appeal the decision from the Chair!" shouted Charles Crisp of Georgia. "I deny the power of the Speaker and denounce it as revolutionary!" roared William Breckinridge of Kentucky. "I deny your right, Mr. Speaker, to count me as present!" hollered James Mc-Creary, also of Kentucky. Reed ceased his listing of the Democrats in the room to answer McCreary. "The Chair is making a statement of fact that the gentleman is present. Does he deny it?" McCreary had no effective response, and Reed continued to the end of the alphabet. When he finished, he announced that a quorum was present.

This announcement hardly settled the question. The House debated the legitimacy of Reed's action for four raucous days. The Democrats repeated their earlier effort to deny Reed and the Republicans a quorum, but each time Reed overruled them as before. On the fifth day they physically boycotted the proceedings, forcing Reed to change his tactics. To complete the Republican majority he had his aides scour the city and environs for missing Republican representatives. Two were carried from their sickrooms to the House chamber on cots. A third was hustled back from out of town, giving Reed just the margin he needed.

The Democrats weren't quite beaten yet. They challenged the legality of Reed's action, carrying their challenge all the way to the Supreme Court. There they lost. In 1892, the high court held that the speaker of the House could count as parliamentarily present all those physically present.

The decision was a great victory for Reed, who for his pains was tagged "Czar" Reed. In time Reed grew rather fond of the title. On one subsequent occasion, when a House member offended Reed's sense of decorum and feeling of respect for the House by hoisting his feet onto his desk in the chamber and revealing a particularly egregious pair of white socks, Reed sent him a note: "The Czar commands you to haul down those flags of truce."

Reed hoped his fame and effectiveness as leader of the Republicans in the House could be converted into support for his candidacy for president in 1896. Reed was sound on the money question—meaning, for Republicans, that he was firmly in the gold camp. And he generated enthusiasm among certain factions of the party. Theodore Roosevelt told Reed, after the latter delivered an especially withering assault on silver, "Oh Lord, what I would not give if you were our standard bearer."

But Reed's style was too abrasive for most Republicans, even while they applauded his actions in intimidating the Democrats. And the Republican establishment, convinced that the presidency was within easy reach, didn't want to risk turning Reed's sharp tongue loose in a national campaign. Instead, the party leaders looked to an individual who, while possessing fewer of the gifts that had made Reed such a formidable opponent, also possessed fewer of the liabilities that had made him so many opponents.

William McKinley had gained national prominence with the passage of the 1890 tariff that bore his name. The prominence soon became notoriety as the tariff produced a backlash that helped hand control of Congress to the Democrats and sweep many Republican veterans, including McKinley, out of office. (In McKinley's case, Democratic gerrymandering also played an important part in his ouster.) Yet the Republican bosses and their colleagues in the corporate sector remembered McKinley, and they rewarded his good service on their behalf with the nomination for the governorship of his home state of Ohio. McKinley won election, partly because of his amiable and unobjectionable personality and partly because of the support of Marcus Hanna, who was becoming the most influential of the Republican big bosses.

Mark Hanna was something of a hybrid in American politics. In an age of business, he was a great businessman. Though not in the class of Carnegie and Rockefeller, Hanna ranked just below them. His business interests were eclectic. After starting out in the grocery trade with his father in Ohio during the 1850s, he diversified into several other activities. By the 1890s he had a hand in shipping, in coal and steel, in banking, in publishing, in urban transit, and even in opera and the theater.

Yet where Carnegie and Rockefeller built their economic empires with only modest help from government, Hanna worked the levers of government almost from the first. Hanna saw nothing untoward in cooperation between big business and government. On the contrary, he thought that such cooperation mitigated waste and inefficiency. An elitist at heart, Hanna believed that a certain class of men were best suited to govern society. Governance included direction of both political and economic affairs. It only made sense that this dual direction be carefully coordinated—ideally, that it be accomplished by the same set of people. Naturally this set included himself.

Hanna once remarked that all questions of government in a democracy were "questions of money." This kind of unbuttoned language was one reason why he never held public office on his own account until being appointed to the Senate in 1897 to fill a vacancy. Hanna preferred to work behind the scenes: to help elect like-minded individuals who would listen to his advice. He contributed heavily to the campaign of James Garfield in 1880. Hanna's contributions were instrumental in providing the exceedingly narrow margin by which Garfield slipped into the White House, although the effort went largely for naught when the assassin Charles Guiteau murdered Garfield just months after his inauguration.

Hanna's promotion of Ohio Senator John Sherman (later McKinley's secretary of state) for the presidency in 1888 was unsuccessful, but the experience drew Hanna's attention to yet another Ohioan, William McKinley. Hanna had been impressed by the fact that when a deadlock developed at the Republican convention and a McKinley nomination was suggested as a device to break the deadlock, McKinley refused to put himself ahead of Sherman, his senior in the Ohio organization. "You could have been president!" Hanna was reported to have said to McKinley afterward, with amazement. This was something new to Hanna—a politician who placed loyalty before ambition—and it convinced him McKinley was worthy of future support.

Hanna gave McKinley just such support in the latter's run for the Ohio governorship in 1891. Money, liberally administered, constituted one aspect of Hanna's support, yet the shrewdness behind the money was more valuable. Hanna was in the process of making a science out of the art of political management. As carefully as did Carnegie or Rockefeller, Hanna chose the men who labored beneath him. He counted on these subordinates to know just how much money would be required to deliver a particular county to McKinley. He trusted their judgment, and they rarely failed him.

At the same time, Hanna enlarged the scale of operations of the political manager. In much the way that the great industrialists secured their markets and broadened their supply bases by expanding into adjacent regions and eventually across the country, so did Hanna. Even as he guided McKinley to election in Ohio, Hanna traveled neighboring states with a message that if Ohio fell to the forces of radicalism, Pennsylvania and Illinois and other states might fall too. In this fashion he forged a network that eventually spanned much of the nation. The network united, in a more orderly and effective way than before, the financial resources of American big business with the political resources of the Republican Party. It came together during the 1890s partly because of the same kinds of economies of scale and other centralizing forces that produced corporate consolidation under Carnegie, Rockefeller, and Morgan, but equally because of the decentralizing forces that were producing the Populist revolt, the great labor strikes of the decade, and the outcry for free silver. The industrial lords and their political allies felt the need to band together against the anarchic tendencies they saw abroad in the land. To achieve their vision of America's future, they had to beat down the forces that wanted to take America backward into a mythical past.

William McKinley was the first important beneficiary of the new political system. McKinley began as Hanna's project, but before long he became Hanna's close friend—not that he ceased to be Hanna's project. Where Hanna was clever to the point of cunning and made as many enemies as friends, McKinley was straightforward, even simple, and charmed nearly all who came into contact with him. He certainly charmed Hanna. Opposition newspapers commonly treated McKinley as Hanna's pawn, with the innocuously smiling McKinley being manipulated by "Dollar Mark," who was usually caricatured as a walking moneybags in a suit embroidered with dollar signs. The reality was far more complicated. Hanna realized that he possessed certain gifts McKinley didn't, including a greater quickness of mind and a capacity for detailed planning. McKinley realized this too and felt little embarrassment in deferring to Hanna on matters where such gifts were essential. On the other hand, Hanna conceded a kind of moral superiority to McKinley. Hanna most likely wouldn't have passed up the chance to be president in 1888 the way McKinley had, if he had been in McKinley's place, and he respected McKinley for doing so. People who knew both men noticed the esteem in which Hanna held McKinley. William Allen White, who was on his way from being merely the owner and editor of the *Emporia Gazette* to being a widely heeded commentator on national affairs, said of Hanna that he was "just a shade obsequious in McKinley's presence." Another newsman, Herman Kohlsaat of Chicago, described Hanna's attitude toward McKinley as "always that of a big, bashful boy toward the girl he loves." Hanna himself confessed to an affection toward McKinley he couldn't exactly explain.

The pair made a potent political team. The candidate was pleasant to all who came to call on him. He had few strong views, and these he had been astute enough to keep largely to himself. A survivor of many political battles in Congress, he understood that enemies were a luxury successful politicians—successful presidential contenders, at any rate—couldn't well afford. Hanna, by contrast, was frank, often blunt. A longtime student of Republican politics remarked of Hanna that "he was openly for you or against you." McKinley was reluctant to push himself to the forefront, but Hanna filled this deficiency by pushing McKinley harder than McKinley ever could have. Nor could McKinley have pushed so effectively as Hanna did. Theodore Roosevelt, who never had any qualms about self-promotion, was taken a bit aback by Hanna's efforts. "He has advertised McKinley as if he were a patent medicine," Roosevelt commented. But McKinley wasn't complaining, and neither were his supporters in 1896.

Though McKinley was the frontrunner entering the Republican convention in June 1896, largely due to Hanna's pre-convention work on his behalf, the nomination wasn't a sure thing. Tom Reed wanted the prize, and others for various reasons simply wanted to stop Hanna and McKinley. Nor was the platform on which the nominee would stand foreordained. Although most Republicans held firm for gold against silver, a minority in the party, especially from the silver-producing states of the Mountain West, wanted silver. Further, whoever the nominee turned out to be, he would have to say something in reply to the expected taunts of the silver Democrats, who seemed likely to engineer the nomination of one of their own for president. What was needed was a platform plank wide enough to allow the candidate some room to dance around, without being so wide that the candidate and the message got lost.

The drafters of the platform came under great pressure from the highest financial circles in the country to state unequivocally the party's enthusiastic adherence to the gold standard. While the Republican leaders were gathering for their convention in St. Louis, J. P. Morgan was preparing to testify before the Senate committee investigating the terms of his bailout of the government. Morgan was arrogant enough to think that the investigations wouldn't touch him personally, but he worried about their effect on bond values. He believed that a decisive affirmation of gold was essential. An agent of Hanna and McKinley sent to the East to survey the situation summarized: "There seems to be no doubt that the most conservative bankers are extremely apprehensive that any hesitation on our part to take the squarest sound money ground would bring a great and probably sudden depression in values." An early draft of the Republican plank on money spoke of the "existing standard" in an effort to avoid inflaming the silverites more than necessary. Morgan demanded in characteristically autocratic fashion that the plank explicitly mention gold. His colleagues in the American Bankers' Association raised a special fund of $85,000, which they forwarded to St. Louis with instructions that it be used to prepare a sound money statement.

The platform writers received plenty of other advice, although little they attended to as closely as Morgan's. Henry Cabot Lodge approached Hanna offering a draft he had composed. Lodge could be quite obnoxious, as he apparently was on this occasion. One observer of the meeting had Lodge, who fancied himself more conspicuous and influential than some others did, telling Hanna: "You'll put this in the platform or we'll rip you up the back!"

Hanna responded, "Who in hell are you?"

"Senator Henry Cabot Lodge, of Massachusetts."

"Well, Senator Henry Cabot Lodge, of Massachusetts, you can go plumb to hell. You have nothing to say about it."

Shaping the currency plank consumed the energies of the sharpest minds of the party at St. Louis. The outcome of their labors was political carpentry at its finest. "The Republican Party is unreservedly for sound money," the currency plank read. The Republican Party, it continued, had caused the enactment of the law requiring the resumption of specie payments in 1879, and the party was proud of the fact. "Since then every dollar has been as good as gold." The Republican Party remained unalterably opposed to every measure that might debase America's currency or impair the country's credit abroad. "We are therefore opposed to the free coinage of silver"—now came the wriggle-room—"except by international agreement with the leading commercial nations of the earth, which agreement we pledge ourselves to promote." Until such agreement could be obtained—in other words, considering the profound opposition to silver in Britain and elsewhere, until water ran uphill—"the existing gold standard must be preserved." The section concluded, "All our silver and paper currency must be maintained at parity with gold, and we favor all measures designed to maintain inviolably the obligations of the United States and all our money, whether coin or paper, at the present standard, the standard of the most enlightened nations of the earth."

Hanna and the McKinley faction called this a compromise, but the silver Republicans took it as a rebuff. One of the most melodramatic moments of the convention occurred when Senator Richard Teller of Colorado—a charter member of the Republican Party from the days before the Civil War—announced that he couldn't accept the party's position on this crucial issue. He declared he would have to leave the party. Hanna, an ungracious victor, demonstrated why he needed McKinley as a front man when he responded to Teller's tearful leavetaking by shouting, "Go! Go!"

(In the press gallery an Omaha editor watched the departure with immense interest. William Jennings Bryan pondered what this split might mean for the election in the fall. A fellow journalist recorded, "There was a gleam of joy in Bryan's eye, and the least smile of satisfaction flitted across his face.")

The remainder of the Republican convention proved anti-climactic. Republican speakers delighted in excoriating the Cleveland administration. Though their words were hardly harsher than those used by Cleveland's opponents within the Democratic Party, the criticism naturally caused no such bruised feelings among the Republicans as similar complaints did among the Democrats. McKinley won on the first ballot, his total fittingly pushed over the top by the 46 votes of the Ohio delegation. Back home in Canton, Ohio—in those days candidates didn't usually attend conventions, Bryan being an exception—McKinley followed the balloting by telephone. Over the sizzle and pop of the wires he could hear the cheering that greeted his victory. He didn't hear Hanna impulsively shout, "I love McKinley! He is the best man I ever knew." But he may have guessed what Hanna was feeling.

III

After the Republicans and Democrats had chosen their nominees and written their platforms, only the Populists were left. The third party met in St. Louis shortly after the Democrats had finished in Chicago, and its members found themselves in a quandary. The Democrats, by adopting silver, had grabbed their best issue. If the Populists joined forces with the Democrats and perhaps with Teller and the silver Republicans, they might garner enough votes to elect Bryan and enact his platform. It was a heady thought for a party of outsiders. On the other hand, Populism was about more than free silver. The People's Party had been established to pursue a broad-gauged agenda designed to regain for the common people of America the power they had lost to the bankers, the industrialists, and the plutocracy of the East. The Democrats were closer to the Populist vision than the Republicans were, to be sure; but the Democrats were too closely tied to the status quo to support other items on the Populist agenda such as government ownership of railroads and utilities, direct election of senators, and the subtreasury for marketing crops.

There was something else that bothered many Populists. With the emergence of free silver as the touchstone issue of national politics, the Populist Party had been invaded by agents of the silver-mining interests of the West. Many Populists found collusion with such silver barons as Marcus Daly difficult to swallow. The swallowing grew more difficult still when, in order to keep the financial support of these renegade capitalists, some elements of the Populist Party began to focus almost exclusively on the currency question at the expense of the broader reforms. Henry Demarest Lloyd complained bitterly at what seemed a selling of the party's soul. "The Free Silver movement is a fake," Lloyd wrote. "Free Silver is the cowbird of the Reform movement. It waited until the nest had been built by the sacrifices and labour of others, and then it laid its eggs in it." As he watched the agents of the silver monopolists descend on St. Louis, Lloyd asserted that it was ironic that "the new party, the Reform party, the People's party, should be more boss-ridden, gang-ruled, gang-gangrened than the two old parties of monopoly." As the convention proceeded, Lloyd grew more despondent. "The People's party has been betrayed," he lamented.

Other Populists thought things weren't so bad as Lloyd depicted them. If compromises had to be made in order to achieve success, this was simply the nature of democratic politics. Some of the original stalwarts of the Populist Party argued forcefully for fusion—at least temporary fusion—with the Democrats and the silver Republicans. Jerry Simpson asserted, "I care not for party names. It is the substance we are after, and we have it in William J. Bryan." Senator William Allen of Nebraska, chairman of the convention, declared that he didn't want it said that "the Populists have been advocates of reforms when they could not be accomplished, but when the first ray of light appeared and the people were looking with expectancy and anxiety for relief, the party was not equal to the occasion; that it was stupid; it was blind; it kept 'in the middle of the road' and missed the golden opportunity." James Weaver proclaimed the present situation a "new Pentecost," and said he wouldn't refuse the help of 3 million silver Democrats and 1 million silver Republicans "simply because they have shown the good sense to come with an organized army ready for battle." Weaver asserted that Bryan was being assailed by "the sleuth hounds of the money power of the world" and deserved the support of the Populists. The former Populist presidential candidate urged his comrades to provide that support.

They did, albeit not without misgivings. One anti-fusionist declared of Bryan, "We put him to school, and he wound up by stealing the school-books." Tom Watson of Georgia remarked drily that the Democratic idea of fusion was that "we play Jonah while they play whale." Notwithstanding the misgivings, the convention endorsed Bryan's candidacy for president.

It drew a line, however, at supporting Bryan's Democratic running mate, Arthur Sewall. Despite being a silverite, Sewall was also a banker and a railroad director, which was more than a majority of the Populist delegates could accept. In place of Sewall, the Populists placed their own Tom Watson—who remembered that the whale had been made to spit Jonah back out—in the slot for vice president. Bryan attempted to block this ticket-splitting by sending a telegram to the convention declaring that if the Populists wouldn't support his choice for vice president, then he must respectfully decline their nomination. This would have thrown the Populist convention into an even greater hubbub than it already was in had Chairman Allen not intercepted the telegram and exercised a pocket veto—literally. Happily ignorant of the wishes of the man of the hour, the convention forwarded the ticket of Bryan and Watson to the American people.

IV

By the end of July 1896, the contest for the presidency had come down to Bryan versus McKinley. The two sides adopted dramatically different strategies in the contest. McKinley, in keeping with his image as a modest, unassuming, and unambitious man, one who didn't really seek the presidency but would accept it out of respect for the people who wanted him to serve, conducted a low-key campaign. He stayed close to home in Canton, Ohio. In fact, between the date of his nomination in June and the election in November, McKinley ventured away from Canton only three times: twice to fulfill previous promises to speak, once for a weekend of relaxation. Benjamin Harrison had tried something like McKinley's front-porch campaign in 1892, unsuccessfully. But McKinley and Hanna put a new twist on the idea. If McKinley shouldn't go to the people, the people should come to McKinley. The Republican national committee, now conveniently headed by Hanna, orchestrated the constant arrival of delegations from all over the United States who wanted to see the man who would rescue the country from the radicals.

The pilgrimages to the McKinley house began as soon as McKinley received the Republican nomination. When word arrived from St. Louis, via telephone and telegraph, that the hometown boy had been chosen, the community burst into ecstatic celebration. Bells pealed out the wonderful news, competing with firecrackers, cannons, rifles, and pistols for deafening honors. Flags were quickly hoisted to the breeze and bunting was draped on buildings throughout the town. From the town square an army of partisans descended on the McKinley home. Bicyclists raced horsemen to be the first there, while thousands followed on foot. Ohio veterans of the Civil War marched to remember "the Major," as McKinley was locally known from his days as a Union officer. The candidate greeted the crowd warmly. He thanked one and all for their kind thoughts. He uttered some inconsequentialities about the issues confronting the country. Then he returned to his living room and his quiet routine.

But not for long. During the week after the nomination, trainloads of McKinley supporters poured into Canton from the surrounding communities. (The railroad companies were happy to offer special group discounts for such a worthy purpose as electing McKinley.) Akron sent four thousand. Massillon—whence Jacob Coxey and his army of unemployed had started out for Washington two years before—dispatched a smaller but equally enthusiastic delegation. Even more enthusiastic were the proud citizens of Niles, which claimed equal rights in McKinley with Canton, since McKinley had been born in Niles.

From morning until nightfall the crowds flooded Canton. They devastated the area around the McKinley house, trampling shrubs, grinding grass to powder, wrenching branches from trees. The house and associated structures began to sag beneath the weight of McKinley's popularity. An iron fence fell under the crush of the excitement, and a grape arbor was stripped as if by locusts. The railing and support beams of the porch were seriously compromised. Some observers feared that the roof would crash down and kill the candidate.

The various delegations left gifts: minor and not so minor tokens of their admiration. Everyone brought flowers, which soon littered the yard and gave it the appearance of a cemetery a week after Decoration Day. Farmers brought produce and baked goods—cheese, butter, melons, squashes, berries, cakes, muffins, pies, cobblers—far faster than the McKinley family could eat them. Much was given to neighbors; much just went bad. A sculptor contributed a marble bust of McKinley. A bedridden woman from Cleveland who couldn't make the trip sent a bouquet of artificial blossoms. Steelworkers donated a special walking cane fabricated of cold-drawn steel tubing. Other metalworkers delivered the largest plate of galvanized iron ever produced in America, an almost-as-large sheet of tin, and a tin banner etched with the candidate's name. A woodworker from Illinois managed to secure a piece of Abe Lincoln's log cabin (so he said) and carved it into a gavel. Several supporters sent live bald eagles. Five of the great birds actually survived the trip to Canton and, after receiving appropriately Republican names, were turned over to a nearby zoo.

Hard as the hoopla for McKinley was on the candidate's house and yard, it did wonders for Canton's economy. The merchants and innkeepers of the town loved all the customer traffic. Business had never been better, certainly not since the Panic of 1893. Souvenir shops sprang up. Vendors sold sandwiches and hot dogs to hungry visitors. School-aged youths cut classes and deferred summer sports in order to make money showing the guests around. If this was what Republican prosperity was all about, let there be no end to it.

The uninterrupted procession, which lasted from June through the beginning of November, had the appearance of a spontaneous swelling of support for McKinley. A considerable part of the appearance was indeed genuine. After three years of depression, millions of people across the country, especially in the industrial regions of the East and the Old Northwest, looked to McKinley and the Republicans to restore the country to prosperity. Nothing works like a malfunctioning economy to turn voters against the party holding the presidency, and never had the American economy malfunctioned so badly as during Cleveland's second term. McKinley didn't have to be a genius to understand that much of the cheering for him was simply the result of the fact that he wasn't Cleveland.

Yet for all the sincerity of those who came to Canton, McKinley's front-porch campaign was one of the most carefully prepared and thoroughly organized political operations in American history. The guiding genius, of course, was Mark Hanna. McKinley's manager had intended to go to Europe for a holiday, but the tremendous impact Bryan's Cross of Gold speech and his subsequent nomination had on the American popular psyche caused Hanna to cancel his European tour in order to get to work right away. "The Chicago convention has changed everything," Hanna wrote McKinley. "Quit blowing and saw wood." Hanna set up campaign offices in New York and Chicago. From the former location he could keep in close touch with the party angels who dwelt in the nether reaches of Manhattan; from the latter he could assess the enemy's strength in the Midwest and beyond.

At first Wall Street responded tepidly to Hanna's applications for support. This might have seemed odd, considering what was at stake in the November election. But in fact it was precisely a consequence of the large stakes. John Hay explained the situation to his friend Henry Adams. Bryan had thoroughly terrified the gold-bugs of the East, Hay said. "If he had scared them a little, they would have come down handsome to Hanna. But he has scared them so blue that they think they had better keep what they have got left in their pockets against the evil day." Perhaps more important, Hanna initially was an unfamiliar figure on Wall Street. His business connections had been mostly in the Midwest. To the financiers and industrialists of New York and the Eastern seaboard, he was relatively unknown. Frightened as they were, they weren't eager to hand over lots of money to someone they weren't sure they could trust.

Eventually, though, Hanna soothed their fears—about himself, not about Bryan. He played on the latter to convince the moneyed men to pull their wallets out of their pockets and contribute to the McKinley cause. Ever organized, Hanna devised a schedule of assessments of the big banks, insurance companies, and other corporations, adjusted according to size and profitability. Hanna wasn't so tactless as to attempt to enforce his schedule. He simply presented the idea of a contribution as a prudent investment. Most of those he contacted eventually agreed that it was.

Hanna also mended fences with McKinley's former rivals. He talked to Tom Reed's supporters and persuaded them to pony up $400,000. He courted Thomas Platt, the main Republican boss of New York state, and brought his people aboard. He introduced himself to railroader James Hill, who in turn introduced him to the big shots of New York City. Hanna impressed one and all with his seriousness and efficiency. After a slow start, he managed to build up a war chest of between $3 and $4 million, the largest in American history to that time. And this was only what Hanna reported. He actually collected and spent much more—perhaps three to five times as much.

Most of the money Hanna collected was spent on campaign propaganda. Paid Republican speakers lectured on the virtues of sound money and the perils and dishonesty of silver-induced inflation. Sympathetic editors across the country were furnished evidence for supportive editorials—even, for the harried or less industrious, completed copy and finished plates ready for the press. Pamphlets, posters, fliers, and buttons were printed by the tens of millions and shipped out in boxcars bound for doubtful districts and swing states. Post offices in the Midwest and elsewhere were buried under an avalanche of Republican literature; postal carriers groaned under the burden and prayed for the strength to survive until election day. One of the most effective Republican pamphlets, and one of the most widely circulated, reproduced William White's stinging "What's the Matter with Kansas?" diatribe. (As a result of the campaign White became almost as well known as McKinley.)

While Hanna beat the bushes and shook the money trees, McKinley handled himself in masterly fashion. The pro-Bryan boom that developed in the wake of the Chicago convention made Hanna very nervous; not only did he cancel his European trip but he reconsidered the campaign's front-porch strategy. Hanna told a colleague, "We have got to get McKinley out on the road to meet this thing." McKinley told Hanna to calm down. "Don't you remember that I announced that I would not under any circumstances go on a speechmaking tour? If I should go now, it would be an acknowledgement of weakness." Besides, McKinley argued, he could never compete with Bryan on the lecture circuit. "I might as well put up a trapeze on my front lawn and compete with some professional athlete as go out speaking against Bryan. I have to *think* when I speak." And no matter how McKinley tried to package himself on the road, Bryan would get the better of the bargain. "If I took a whole train, Bryan would take a sleeper; if I took a chair car, he would ride a freight train." Bryan would insist on playing the underdog and on making McKinley look like the tool of the corporations. So McKinley insisted on sitting tight.

He let himself be seen pursuing a quietly dignified routine. He cared tenderly for his invalid wife and shared his house with his elderly mother. Every Sunday—the one day of the week he received no visiting delegations—he and his mother attended the nearby First Methodist Church. On other days she often sat on the porch in her rocker, observing the spectacle of her son's fame.

McKinley made a point of addressing every delegation that came to visit (sometimes he spoke to several at a time, so great was the crush). Between the middle of June and the beginning of November, he spoke to some 750,000 people from 30 states. Most of what he said was entirely predictable. Inflation was bad. It robbed the thrifty to pay the dissolute, took from savers, pensioners, and others on fixed incomes to let those who had lived beyond their means off the hook of their folly. McKinley didn't deny that difficult times were abroad in the land, but prosperity would never return if it had to arrive at the expense of the honest, diligent millions who had made America what it was today. Yet such shenanigans were precisely what the Democrats were calling for. "Good money never made times hard," McKinley said over and over, until the phrase assumed the status of a slogan.

Early in the campaign McKinley tried to play up the tariff. The protective tariff, he said, rather than inflation, was the way to restore prosperity. American markets needed to be protected for American producers and their workers. One reason for McKinley's choice of emphasis was his own association with the tariff. Another was that the tariff went down well with the manufacturers whom Hanna was dunning for support and with the workers who were pounding a path to his porch.

Yet another reason for stressing the tariff was that McKinley was still trying, if only halfheartedly, to straddle the money issue. The Republican platform allowed him to say that he would support silver when the other major trading countries did. Such a statement was essentially a throwaway line, but it might serve to hold some of those marginal voters who otherwise would jump to Bryan's camp.

Gradually, though, McKinley grew more forthright on the currency question. The big bankers wanted reassurance—especially since Bryan was creating such a flurry with his zealous advocacy of silver. At the end of July, McKinley told a delegation from Knoxville, Pennsylvania, "That which we call money, my fellow citizens, and with which values are measured and settlements made, must be as true as the bushel which measures the grain of the farmer, and as honest as the hours of labor which the man who toils is required to give." Those members of the Knoxville group who were up on the arguments of the inflationists might at this point have thought McKinley was going to back an easing of the currency. Parity—a restoration of the prices of commodities to what they had formerly been—was what the inflationists' argument was all about. But McKinley went on, "Our currency today is good—all of it as good as gold—and it is the unfaltering determination of the Republican party to so keep and maintain it forever."

By letting the magic word "gold" pass his lips, McKinley indicated he would have no truck with debasing the American currency. Wall Street breathed a sigh of relief and loosened its purse strings to Hanna. The battle lines between McKinley and Bryan became better defined than ever.

During August, McKinley ventured as close as he would at any time during the campaign to issuing a definitive exposition of his views on gold versus silver. In his formal letter of acceptance of the Republican nomination, the candidate once again derided the purveyors of easy money. "No one suffers so much from cheap money as the farmers and laborers," he asserted. "They are the first to feel its bad effects and the last to recover from them." McKinley cautioned that the people were being misled regarding this chimera called "free silver." It wouldn't be free to those who saw their savings evaporate and their insurance policies melt away. It would be free principally to those wealthy silver magnates who would see the value of their assets nearly double overnight. Someday, with the cooperation of other nations, the United States might shift to a bimetallic standard. But until the other nations agreed, the United States would be reckless to do so. Business leaders and investors would lose confidence in the future and would withhold the funds that were required to make the economy grow and prosper. After the withering depression of the last three years, the last thing the government should do was anything that might undermine business confidence. Consequently, until the transition to responsible bimetallism could be accomplished smoothly and by international agreement, it was "the plain duty of the United States to maintain the gold standard."

V

Bryan delighted to read McKinley's statement. The Democratic challenger—and he did seem the challenger despite the fact that his party currently controlled the executive branch—desired to make as sharp as possible the contrast between the Republican nominee, the representative of the status quo, and himself, the herald of change. Bryan knew that his candidacy was a long shot at best, but it would be longer still if he couldn't show that he offered a definite and decisive alternative to things as they were.

Bryan labored under a number of significant handicaps. One was his age—or rather his lack of it. Though his youthful good looks appealed to many women, this didn't do him much good since women couldn't vote. His youthful energy attracted some people and certainly helped him stand up under the rigors of a hectic campaign, but to many others this very energy betrayed a lack of stability and grounding. A few generations later, youth would be a political asset; in the 1890s, maturity counted for more.

Bryan's character and intellectual gifts also became a matter of contention. The Democratic candidate's admirers couldn't say enough about his virtues. The author Willa Cather described a visit by Bryan to a small Nebraska town just a few months before the Chicago convention. The trip was both political and personal: a friend of Bryan, who happened to be a silver man, had died, and Bryan came to give the funeral oration. "There," Cather wrote, "with an audience of some few hundreds of bronzed farmers who believed in him as their deliverer, the man who could lead them out of the bondage of debt, who could stay the drought and strike water from the rock, I heard him give the greatest speech of his life. Surely that was eloquence of the old stamp that was accounted divine, eloquence that reached through the callus of ignorance and toil, and found and awoke the stunted souls of men. I saw those rugged men of the soil weep like children." Cather followed Bryan to Chicago, as did others who heard him that day. She watched from the visitors' gallery during his Cross of Gold speech. "One of those ragged farmers sat beside me in the gallery, and at the close of that never-to-be-forgotten speech, he leaned over the rail, the tears on his furrowed cheeks, and shouted: 'The sweet singer of Israel.'"

William McAdoo, who later worked with Bryan in the Wilson administration, found him impressive in a different way. McAdoo noted that a large number of Bryan's critics thought him a fool or a clown. "He was nothing of the kind," McAdoo declared. "In many respects, he was one of the shrewdest men I have ever known. In him, unsophistication and sagacity were strangely blended. Along with this, he was truthful and square. His friendships were sincere; one could depend implicitly on his word." McAdoo drew a parallel between Bryan and a famous British statesman. "As I think of him, there comes into my mind what somebody said of Gladstone—that to keep hating him, one had to avoid meeting him. I cannot say if this was true of Gladstone, but it certainly was true of William Jennings Bryan."

As did Gladstone, Bryan evoked negative sentiments among his critics as strong as those positive ones his supporters felt for him. John Hay mocked him as "Baby Demosthenes." David Houston, an associate of Bryan in the Wilson administration, complained that logic and evidence meant almost nothing to Bryan. "One could drive a prairie schooner through any part of his argument," Houston said, "and never scrape against a fact." Other Bryan-watchers were still less charitable. "What a disgusting, dishonest fakir Bryan is!" sneered Elihu Root, later a Republican secretary of war and state. "When I see so many Americans running after him, I feel very much as I do when a really lovely woman falls in love with a cad." Theodore Roosevelt conceded that Bryan possessed some kindly traits but nonetheless felt compelled to exclaim, "What a shallow demagogue he is!" Roosevelt was reminded of one of Bryan's predecessors as party leader. "I do not believe he is a bit worse than Thomas Jefferson, and I do not think that if elected President he will be a worse President. The country would survive, but it would suffer, just as the country suffered for at least two generations because of its folly in following Jefferson's lead." On another occasion, Roosevelt dismissed Bryan as "a mere boy, without intelligence or power."

Roosevelt's comparison of Bryan to Jefferson was certainly apt in at least one regard. Where Jefferson's Federalist opponents in 1800 had bemoaned the nation's prospects in the event he should be elected—predicting everything from bloody revolution to the banning of religion, not to mention drunken orgies in the president's house—so Bryan's opponents told of an equally dire fate should the American people go so far off their heads as to select the Democratic candidate. Hanna detected a "communistic spirit" in the air and warned whoever would listen, especially those who inhabited the boardrooms of corporate America, that business was "all going to pieces." Other Republicans predicted that a Democratic victory would produce chaos across America. The masses would overrun established institutions and demagogues would replace the country's natural leaders. Tyranny likely would follow.

McKinley's boosters asked their listeners to imagine a Bryan cabinet that almost certainly would include such apostles of destruction as Ben Tillman, Eugene Debs, and John Peter Altgeld. Bank depositors were treated to forecasts of their savings being swallowed in a sea of silver, with their years of hard work and self-denial vanishing beneath waves of worthless currency. Credible reports circulated of industrialists and merchants placing orders with their suppliers dependent on Bryan's defeat: the orders would automatically be canceled if Bryan were elected. Employers said they would have to shut down, with at least one manufacturer telling his workers to vote as they pleased but adding ominously that if Bryan were victorious on election Tuesday, "the whistle will not blow Wednesday morning." A journalist covering the campaign—a Bryan sympathizer—remarked afterward, "It was a reign of terror in industrial communities, the like of which never was seen before in this country."

If the Bryan side was trying to calm the fears of voters worried about such prospects, it didn't do a very good job. Pro-Bryan speakers, trying to make the point that their man would conduct a thorough cleaning of the stables of corruption, declared that the plutocrats were right to be running scared. One speaker harangued a large crowd in Louisville that Bryan was "the greatest anarchist who ever lived." A subsequent speaker on the same stage led the audience in a call-and-response session in which the speaker asked who was the possessor of one stellar trait after another, and each time the crowd shouted, "Bryan!" At the climax the speaker demanded, "Who is the recognized leader of anarchists in this country?" The crowd responded exultantly, "Bryan! Bryan! Bryan!" Needless to say, the anti-Bryan press had a field day with such evidence of incipient revolution, straight from the heart of the enemy camp.

Bryan's method of campaigning lent itself to such tactical foul-ups. Although the silver-mining interests contributed financially to Bryan's campaign, the Democratic candidate lacked the millions Hanna raised for McKinley. Consequently the Bryan side was unable to hire the best writers to generate promotional material or sharp-eyed proofreaders to ensure that the material didn't contain potentially damaging statements. Nor could the Bryan organization then run off five hundred thousand copies of a given pamphlet and send them all over the country. While Hanna directed McKinley's campaign as an efficient, streamlined business venture, Bryan resorted to hit-and-miss, low-budget methods. The candidate himself often handled mundane matters like train schedules and mail forwarding.

Moreover, in the days before radio and television, the candidate could be seen by only those people who physically attended his rallies. Getting the message out to the many millions more that the Democrats had to reach in order to win required relying on the services of scores and hundreds of volunteer pitchmen and pitchwomen. Keeping track of what all these people were saying was impossible; it was inconceivable that they be required to clear their comments in advance.

Another circumstance contributed to the confusion. The Bryan movement was a hodgepodge coalition of Democrats, Populists, and silver Republicans. They all agreed on silver but often on little else. A Georgia Democrat backing Bryan might stress certain aspects of the candidate's record and promises, while a Kansas Populist would select others, and a Nevada silver Republican still others. Not surprisingly, different speakers sometimes talked at cross purposes. During the twentieth century, one distinguishing feature of the Democratic Party would be the way it embraced a broad coalition of diverse interest groups; in this respect as in others, the twentieth century got a head start during the 1890s.

Yet through all the confusion Bryan shone brightly as the star of the campaign. At the beginning, the Democratic candidate considered taking a page from Populist history and carrying his quest to every state, as General Weaver had done in 1892. Some members of the Democratic national committee tried to talk Bryan out of such a strategy, asserting that the East was a lost cause. Statements from the Eastern Democratic establishment certainly indicated as much. William Whitney, a prominent member of the Cleveland wing of the party, declared forthrightly that he couldn't back Bryan. *The Nation* of New York, whose readers included many influential Eastern Democrats, called the people who nominated Bryan at Chicago a "collection of inflammatory and reckless men." *The Nation* predicted wholesale defections from the Democratic Party among Easterners in November. Faced with such obvious manifestations of dissatisfaction, several of Bryan's advisers urged him to write off the East and concentrate on the Midwest, West, and South, where his efforts might do some good.

Bryan listened to this advice, then consulted with his wife Mary, whom many people considered the more perceptive of the two. Between them they decided he ought to visit the East to assess the situation personally. In addition, a trip to New York City would offset to some degree the perception that his was a strictly rural candidacy. Bryan boarded a train and headed east. On the way he made a surprise stop in Canton, Ohio, where he joined the disappointed Richard Bland in paying a call on McKinley. The Republican candidate shook their hands, then remarked to Bland that he, rather than Bryan, should have been the Democratic candidate. Bland replied smoothly, "I am satisfied if my party is."

Bryan's swing through New York suggested that those who were telling him to give up on the East might be correct. His speech at Madison Square Garden wasn't up to his usual soul-wringing standards; perhaps because he felt he needed to demonstrate his sophistication to this urban crowd, he clogged his address with statistics that glazed the eyes of many of his listeners. Although Bryan paid the necessary courtesy calls on the Democratic leaders of New York state, they showed conspicuously scant enthusiasm for the Chicago ticket. Bryan did his best to bring Senator Hill, the most prominent of the regular Democrats, into the tent, but Hill balked at the entrance. Following a long meeting with Bryan, Hill refused even to talk to the news correspondents who wanted to know how the session went.

This disappointing reception convinced Bryan to go back west. He boarded a train and commenced a procession that took him to Chicago again and far beyond—18,000 miles in all before the campaign was through. Along the way, Bryan pioneered a new era in American politics. From the time of George Washington, American candidates for office, especially for the highest office in the land, had considered it unseemly to seek out votes. However excitedly their hearts thumped to achieve election, decorum dictated that they pretend not to care whether they were elected or not. Thomas Jefferson, while accomplishing the overthrow of the Federalists in what was often called the (peaceful) Revolution of 1800, hardly stirred from his mountaintop hideaway at Monticello. Andrew Jackson, widely acclaimed as a man of the people and the harbinger of genuine democracy in America, likewise left most of his 1828 campaigning to others. William McKinley in 1896 stood—or sat—in a long tradition of awaiting the call of the electorate instead of traveling about trying to elicit it.

There had been a few exceptions to this rule of affected indifference, the most recent being Weaver in 1892; but Bryan was the first major party candidate to hit the road from the start of the campaign and stay on the road until the election. In doing so, he helped make it acceptable for a candidate to energetically seek the presidency. Naturally, Bryan didn't present himself as seeking the presidency merely for himself; that would have been low and disreputable. Instead, he was seeking it on behalf of the American people, and in particular on behalf of those people effectively disfranchised by the excessive power of the wealthy and well-positioned. During the twentieth century, candidates would have no qualms about drumming up votes for themselves; Bryan led the way in 1896.

Bryan might have benefited from an aspect of twentieth-century politicking that didn't exist in the 1890s: accurate polling of the public opinion. Bryan's decision to write off the East was based on his reading of the leaders of the Democratic Party in states like New York. Subsequently he received reports, from observers whose judgment he had reason to trust, that the situation was more promising than the Democratic chairmen in the East had let on. The people in those states could think for themselves, and they didn't always think the way the state bosses wanted them to. As a result, Bryan changed his mind again and belatedly decided to fight the campaign in all the regions of the country. Had he possessed accurate means of measuring what people were thinking—means beyond the self-interested comments of party officials and other persons relying on vague impressions of the public mood—Bryan might have been better able to direct his energies where they would have the greatest effect. On the other hand, so might McKinley and Hanna, and the effect might have been neutralized. (Hanna actually did hire pollsters, but their results were equivocal and of dubious value.)

Yet even operating in the dark, Bryan threw himself completely into the race. He spoke at every station and whistle-stop along his route. He rose early, bouncing out of his berth to greet farmers on their way to market. He stayed up late, wishing other farmers good night on their way home. He declaimed from the rear of his train to any and all who would listen. He described his down-home roots and convinced his hearers he understood the trials they faced. He explained the need to rein in the monopolists and adjust the tariff for revenue rather than to pad the profits of big business. He condemned the use of injunctions and armed troops to break strikes. He called for an income tax to make those who benefited most from the American system of laws and property relations pay their fair share. And always he hammered home the message of silver: the message of debt relief, of higher prices, of a restoration of the dignity of the farmer and the laborer. This was the message his listeners loved to hear. Questions of antitrust violations, tariff schedules, injunctions, and progressive income taxes often sounded complicated, but when Bryan pledged to place more dollars in the hands of the American people—shiny silver dollars like those they had seen in their daddies' hands—they could immediately understand him and they bellowed their approval. Sensitive to his audiences, Bryan responded by increasingly making silver the centerpiece of his campaign.

Had Bryan not been young and possessed of such tremendous energy, he never would have been able to keep up his killing pace. In addition to traveling more than 18,000 miles—in an era of slow trains—he delivered over 600 speeches, sometimes 30 in a single day. As many as 5 million people heard him speak. Rarely did he manage a full night's sleep; people waited to see him even in the dead of night, and he never failed to oblige them. He survived on his ability to snatch a nap whenever possible: twenty minutes here, an hour there. As would become even more true for candidates in later decades, in his quest for popular approval Bryan lost much of his private life. On one occasion he was shaving in his railcar when a crowd outside demanded to see the candidate. Bryan threw open the window and greeted his supporters, face still lathered and razor in hand. This intimacy, essentially new in American politics, endeared him to the millions who rallied to his cause—and appalled many older, traditional politicians who had no desire to mingle quite so closely with the herd.

Those who knew what a murderous pace Bryan was setting often wondered how he did it. One way was by eating a lot. Bryan consumed food by the tableful, amounts inordinate even by the standards of that era of active people and proud girth. Steaks, sausage, chops, bread, potatoes, pies, cakes—he ate whatever he could get his hands on, usually just as fast as he could get his hands on it. Supporters who brought culinary offerings as a show of support were gratified at his appreciation of their efforts on his behalf, although some took offense at the haste and carelessness of his table manners. Yet even this weakness, if such it was, simply showed that here was a man of the people, an individual who put on no airs and required no special treatment.

Bryan returned to Chicago for Labor Day. The Building Trades Council sponsored a rally in Sharpshooter's Park just outside the city; forty thousand people came to hear the "Great Commoner," as he was frequently billed. Bryan was in top form, castigating the plutocrats and calling on his listeners to join him in a crusade to reclaim America for the people. In the heat of the excitement and the crush of the crowd, some women swooned. Always gallant, Bryan halted the proceedings and sent glasses of water from the platform to revive the ladies.

Chicago's lowlifes enjoyed Bryan's return. Not since the Columbian Exposition had the city's artful dodgers had such an opportunity to ply their trade. They mingled with the crowd, and when hands went up cheering for Bryan, their own hands went into the cheerers' pockets. Perhaps they considered it their contribution to the candidate's efforts to speed the circulation of money throughout the economy.

While those who had their pockets rifled were doubtless miffed, on the whole the Chicago rally was a brilliant success for Bryan, and it fortified him for the final two months of the campaign. Restoring the East to his travel schedule, he backtracked to the Atlantic coast after a long loop through the West and South. Every day brought a score of new stops and thousands of new faces. To all the message was the same: Throw out the fat cats, return government to the people, put money in ordinary folks' hands.

As long as Bryan stayed west of the Mississippi and south of the Mason-Dixon line, it was easy for him to think he could win. Farmers in staple-crop regions, still suffering from low prices, responded to his call, as did miners in the Mountain states. Newspapers in those areas echoed the feelings of their readers. The *Duluth Herald* lauded Bryan's "new battle for freedom," while the *Kansas City Times* praised him as a courageous warrior "fighting for the people."

But the East and the industrial districts of the Midwest remained unfriendly territory. Financiers equated free silver with theft and revolution. Manufacturers demanded the tariff protection McKinley promised. Industrial workers, who might have responded to Bryan's call for restoring power to the common people, often felt they had little choice but to vote their lunchbuckets. Papers in the East shouted their derision of the Democratic candidate. The *New York Mail and Express* called Bryan's campaign message "the hysterical declaration of a reckless and lawless crusade of sectional animosity and class antagonism." This paper went on to assert that "no wild-eyed and rattle-brained horde of the red flag ever proclaimed a fiercer defiance of law, precedent, order, and government." Other journals stressed the theme of the French revolution and its reign of terror. The *Philadelphia Inquirer* declared that Bryan was aiming for "the damnation of the Constitution" and "the exaltation of anarchy," in addition to "private robbery" and "national dishonor."

Bryan tried to counter the criticism by softening his language in skeptical districts. He explained to voters in the East that he was not a revolutionary. "Our campaign has not for its object the reconstruction of society," he said. "We do not propose to transfer the rewards of industry to the lap of indolence. Property is and will remain the stimulus to endeavor and the compensation for toil." Moreover, he recognized the need to make his peace with the men who controlled the Democratic vote in big cities like New York. On a visit to Manhattan he allowed himself to proclaim, "Great is Tammany! And Croker is its prophet!"

Yet though Croker and his henchmen recognized Bryan as the leader of the national Democratic Party, they didn't see enough in Bryan's candidacy to strain themselves getting out the vote. And while Bryan might disavow notions of revolution, it was hard for city-dwelling factory workers to get excited about a movement that had its roots in the soil of the farm belt. Higher prices for wheat and cotton meant little to them except higher prices for bread and clothes. As for the recent immigrants who constituted such a large portion of the population of the cities, they found it hard to see what they had in common with natives of the interior who often didn't disguise their distrust of things and persons foreign.

VI

The campaign moved into its final weeks with no one quite sure who had the lead. Bryan thought he was in front, and many professional politicos supported his view. The West and the South seemed solidly in the Democratic camp while the East and Midwest didn't appear as strong for McKinley as they once had. Bryan took encouragement from the endorsement of labor leaders such as Eugene Debs and Samuel Gompers. These endorsements caused one of Mark Hanna's informants in Chicago to cable a worried message: "The labor organizations are against us to a man. Impossible to teach them. They are more interested in the question of Federal jurisdiction over strikes than the money question." Though Bryan made a point of discouraging excessive rambunctiousness among his supporters—if only to deflect the charges of anarchism—he couldn't help taking some satisfaction from news that his supporters even in such unlikely places as New Haven, Connecticut, were mixing it up with Republican partisans, in this case by throwing rocks at a crowd of Republicans demonstrating in favor of the gold standard.

By the end of September, Bryan had perfected his techniques of preaching democracy to the masses. At rallies he would dismiss his critics' complaints that he lacked the dignity to be president; he would retort that he'd rather be thought lacking in dignity than lacking in the "backbone to meet the enemies of the Government who work against its welfare in Wall Street." He would ask, "What other presidential candidates did they ever charge with lack of dignity?" To which someone in the audience would shout, "Lincoln!" Bryan would respond, "Yes, my friends, they said it of Lincoln." Another voice: "Jackson!" Bryan: "Yes, they said it of Jackson." A third voice: "Jefferson!" Bryan: "Yes, and of Jefferson—he was lacking in dignity too." (Laughter and cheers from all.)

Amid the cyclone that Bryan was generating, it was impossible to know how much of what the whirlwind had picked up was merely dust that would settle before the election and how much was solid material that could do the Republicans real damage. Many Republicans were pessimistic and expected the worst. Mark Hanna, on the other hand, having recovered from his earlier fright, expressed confidence. The Republican Party chairman judged that Bryan was hurting himself by concentrating so heavily on one issue. "He's talking silver all the time," Hanna said, "and that's where we've got him." Though silver appealed to the empty-pocketed farmers of the South and West, it didn't promise enough for the workers of the East and Midwest, despite what some of their union leaders might say. Bryan hadn't succeeded in the essential task of any regional or single-issue candidate: to reach out to other groups and widen the original base of support.

Despite his confidence, Hanna didn't propose to leave anything to chance. The Republican propaganda machine continued to crank out literature explaining that the Republican candidate was, as one of the campaign's favorite slogans put it, "the Advance Agent of Prosperity." To capitalize on the suspicions of urban immigrants toward Bryan, the Republican promotions were published in several foreign languages, including Italian, Polish, Yiddish, and Greek. Friendly academics such as J. Lawrence Laughlin of the University of Chicago (recently established by the Rockefeller family) reiterated the hazards of replacing an honest dollar with one worth only "53 cents."

McKinley remained on his front porch in Canton, greeting the delegations Hanna was sending his way. If Bryan was pioneering one method of modern campaigning by taking his message to the people, McKinley was blazing a trail to another twentieth-century technique: the carefully orchestrated photo opportunity. The people who came to visit the Republican candidate liked the arrangement, for they got a thrill of celebrity and a subsidized (by the railroads or the Republican Party) vacation out of it; Hanna and McKinley liked it, for it generated lots of favorable images and allowed the candidate and his manager to control the conditions under which McKinley spoke, thereby lessening the chance for slip-ups. To lessen the chance still further, McKinley's team frequently supplied the guests with softball questions to pitch slowly and easily to the candidate, who duly swatted them for base hits. A typical McKinley statement summoned disaffected Democrats to vote Republican in an effort to restore the economy: "What we want, no matter to what political organization we may have belonged in the past, is a return to the good times of years ago. We want good prices and good wages, and when we have them we want them to be paid in good money."

Reporters liked the front-porch arrangement as well. In covering McKinley, they didn't have to chase across the country as they did with Bryan. Instead, they could set themselves up at a comfortable hotel in Canton, sleep in the same bed every night, and discover which restaurants they could rely on. They didn't have to go searching for a telegraph station or a telephone to file their copy with their hometown newspapers, and the fact that McKinley, unlike Bryan, kept reasonable hours made it easier for them to meet their deadlines. Bryan might be more colorful at times, but he was also harder to work with.

During the final two weeks of the campaign, Bryan threw everything he had into the fight. Responding to intensified pressure on the part of employers to get their workers to vote Republican, the Democratic candidate suggested that his supporters dissimulate about whom they were voting for, if they thought this necessary to keep their jobs. When some railroad companies circulated anti-Bryan messages in pay envelopes, warning that they would go bankrupt and be unable to meet their payrolls if silver were monetized on the Democrats' terms, Democratic pamphlets responded with the query: "Who are these men who are so solicitous about your wages?" The workers knew: they were the same men who had used injunctions and armed soldiers to enforce reductions in pay. The chairman of the Democratic national committee, J. K. Jones, complained that "the great corporations, with scarcely an exception, and many of the large employers of labor are engaged in a concerted effort to coerce their employees to vote against their convictions." Mark Hanna replied that the charge was ridiculous and offered to personally investigate any such wrongdoing. Jones then urged workers to take a leaf from the employers' book. The employers were threatening wage cuts and job losses in the event of Bryan's election; the workers should demand wage *increases* in case *McKinley* won. Hanna cried foul, blasting Jones's suggestion as "a bold attempt to excite workmen against their employers."

At the end of October, Bryan spoke at a final rally in Chicago, where his quest for the White House had commenced. Hundreds of thousands of Chicagoans and visitors from surrounding regions thronged the avenues of the city to cheer the young man who had become such a phenomenon. Bryan stood in an open carriage acknowledging the applause and support and encouraging his followers to battle to the finish. A number of them took him at his word, attacking Republican counterdemonstrators and creating bonfires of McKinley posters.

Hanna remained confident. On the same day as Bryan's Chicago rally, the Republican manager sent back, uncashed, a generous check from a would-be contributor to the McKinley cause. "It is all over," Hanna predicted. "Reports are satisfactory just where we wanted them most."

Some of those on Bryan's side agreed. Richard Teller, the Silver Republican, believed that the strong-arming by employers in favor of McKinley had proved too much. "Boys, I am afraid it beats us. If I were a working man and had nothing but my job, I am afraid when I came to vote I would think of Mollie and the babies."

For all his confidence, Hanna left nothing to chance. On the Saturday before the election, the Republicans staged a monster parade in New York of merchants, lawyers, corporation officials, and other white-collar types. On election day itself, Hanna's organization directed the most thorough get-out-the-vote effort in American history to that date. Republican district leaders received orders to deliver friendly voters to the polls by any means necessary and were given the money to carry out the orders. They hired carriages, wagons, horses, bicycles, and the occasional automobile. Republican employers, with Hanna's encouragement, granted workers paid leave time to go and vote—presumably for McKinley. Republican local officials supplied voters with lunch and pocket change. The Democratic leaders best positioned to counter these Republican tactics—the big-city bosses like Richard Croker—in most cases did little on Bryan's behalf. Other Democrats who might have done more were handicapped by lack of funds.

McKinley probably would have won even without the last-minute help. Although Bryan received more votes than any Democrat before him, McKinley likewise tallied a larger total than any previous Republican. The margin between the two was some 600,000 votes—7,100,000 for

McKinley against 6,500,000 for Bryan. The vote split clearly along sectional lines. The South voted solidly for Bryan, as did every state west of the Mississippi save Iowa, Minnesota, North Dakota, Oregon, and California. McKinley captured, in addition to those five, every state between the Mississippi and the Ohio rivers and all of the Northeast, plus Kentucky, West Virginia, Maryland, and Delaware. McKinley's states brought him 271 electoral votes, to 176 for Bryan.

"God's in his heaven, all's right with the world," Hanna cabled McKinley, who let it be known to reporters that he greeted the reports of his victory on his knees at the side of his mother's bed. Bryan accepted defeat graciously and philosophically. "We have submitted the issues to the American people," he said, "and their word is law." Privately he felt a certain relief. "If they elect McKinley," he commented shortly before the balloting, "I will feel a great burden lifted off my shoulders." Afterward, reflecting on both his own race and the congressional races, which left the Republicans in firm control of the House and with a strong plurality in the Senate (44 Republicans against 34 Democrats, 5 Populists, 6 Silverites, and 1 independent), Bryan remarked, "I regard it in some respects as fortunate that I was not elected, considering the fact that for four years I would have been confronted by a gold Congress. No free silver bill would have been passed. My hands would have been tied."

Not everyone in Bryan's camp took defeat so phlegmatically. Many charged fraud and intimidation and pointed out that a change of a total of less than 20,000 votes in six states would have put Bryan over the top. The charges were probably exaggerated, and the Republicans could reply that at least three Southern states would have shifted from Bryan's column to McKinley's had blacks not been prevented from exercising their Fifteenth Amendment right to vote.

As a result, both sides went away from the 1896 elections claiming victory of one sort or another. McKinley and the Republicans got the plums of political victory: the presidency, the Congress, and the attendant perquisites of office. Bryan's coalition claimed a moral victory. John Peter Altgeld, who had warmed up to Bryan after his initial skepticism, thought Bryan's side had done remarkably well. The people, Altgeld said, had recaptured control of the Democratic Party, which earlier had been betrayed by Cleveland into the hands of the jobbers and monopolists. Once more the party of Jefferson and Jackson proclaimed democratic principles and espoused the cause of toiling humanity. In the election, the people's movement had been confronted by "all the banks, all the trusts, all the syndicates, all the corporations, all the great papers," Altgeld declared. "It was confronted by everything that money could buy, that boodle could debauch, or that fear of starvation could coerce." Considering these odds, the people should be quite proud of the results they achieved.

As for Bryan, the Democratic candidate's final judgment on the election suggested that nothing was final. "The fight has just commenced," he promised.

Chapter 8

DEMOCRATIC IMPERIALISM

I

For all the rage and tumult the 1890s produced in America's domestic circumstances, the last decade of the nineteenth century witnessed an even greater revolution in American foreign affairs. When the decade began, the United States was a regional power of some note, the preeminent country of the two American continents. This wasn't saying a lot, since the other countries of the region ranged in international significance from the minor to the minuscule. By the end of the decade, however, the United States had announced its desire to assume the status of a global power and had done much to vindicate its claim. It had fought a war in two hemispheres at once and seized an empire with colonies in both. It presumed to tell the great powers of the world how to manage their affairs and wasn't surprised that they often actually listened.

Americans had been preparing for their dramatic entrance onto the stage of world affairs for some time. To the thinking of many Americans, the preparation had been under way since the creation of the world, or whenever it was that God had begun mapping His intentions for the human race. Not uniquely among the world's people, but more intensely than most, Americans inclined to believe that Providence had specially appointed them to spread their values and institutions across the face of the earth. This belief acquired a name—Manifest Destiny—during the mid-nineteenth century, and it was used to justify almost anything expansion-minded Americans wanted to do. Under the aegis of Manifest Destiny, Americans annexed Texas, went to war with Mexico, seized California and New Mexico, and acquired Oregon. After the Civil War—which confirmed, in the eyes of Unionists at any rate, Americans' conviction that they were agents of a heaven with headquarters hovering over the northern half of the Western Hemisphere—they added Alaska to their domain.

Much about the argument of the Manifest Destinarians was self-serving, mere rationalization for American aggression and graspingness; but much about it was entirely sincere. From the days of the Puritans, many Americans had believed they had a duty to regenerate humanity. In spreading American institutions and values—as, for example, by extending America's borders—they thought they were sharing the blessings God had bestowed on them with peoples less fortunate. To refuse to share these blessings would be selfish and unworthy.

John Fiske took this view in a pamphlet entitled, aptly if unoriginally, *Manifest Destiny*, first published in 1885 but still a hot seller during the 1890s. To Fiske, a philosophically inclined popular historian and lecturer, America's special genius lay in a unique combination of racial and cultural inheritance, on one hand, and acquired political aptitude, on the other. Fiske was an ardent Anglo-Saxonist; noting the expansion of Anglo-Saxon influence around the planet during the previous three centuries, he forecast a continuation of the trend. "The work which the English race began when it colonized North America is destined to go on until every land on the earth's surface that is not already the seat of an old civilization shall become English in its language, in its political habits and traditions, and to a predominant extent in the blood of its people. The day is at hand when four-fifths of the human race will trace its pedigree to English forefathers, as four-fifths of the white people in the United States trace their pedigree to-day."

Fiske judged all the English-speaking peoples to be suited to governing broad territories and large numbers of people, but he contended that the American branch of the family had developed these skills more fully than the other branches. The secret to America's success consisted in the concepts of representative democracy, which guaranteed a government answerable to the people, and federalism, which balanced local and national interests. In the United States, these twin ideas had approached closer to perfection than anywhere else. Combined, they produced an effect no less revolutionary in politics than the application of steampower or electricity in the field of industry. "If the Roman Empire could have possessed that political vitality in all its parts which is secured to the United States by the principles of equal representation and of limited State sovereignty, it might well have defied all the shocks which tribally organized barbarism could ever have directed against it."

Bursting with this vitality, Americans would extend their influence and institutions across the globe. In a century or so, Fiske said, the United States would comprise "a political aggregation unmeasurably surpassing in power and in dimensions any empire that has yet existed." American influence would flow most dramatically into the backward regions of the earth, but not even Europe would be exempt. Confronted by America's enormous economic productivity—another indication of American national fitness—the old, tired regimes would give way. "The pacific pressure exerted upon Europe by America is becoming so great that it will doubtless before long overcome all these obstacles." While Americans would benefit, the world would benefit more as the United States spread its empire "from pole to pole" and "from the rising to the setting sun."

John Fiske's enthusiasm for America's glorious destiny was matched by that of Josiah Strong, the general secretary of the American Evangelical

Alliance. Like Fiske, Strong was a regular on the lecture circuit of the expansion-oriented. Strong paid more attention than Fiske to the perils littering the road to glory, as befitted a man of the cloth. Catholicism or Mormonism might divert the righteous, he warned. Unchecked immigration, which was bringing large numbers of papists and Jews to America, might diminish American vigor. Intemperance might cloud Americans' judgment, or socialism sap the nation's productive powers. But God tested even the elect, and by overcoming these trials, Americans would simply harvest the greater victory.

With Fiske, Strong found the Anglo-Saxon race to be singularly suited to dominion over lands and peoples. Strong discerned Anglo-Saxon superiority in two areas above all. First, Anglo-Saxons possessed a "genius for self-government." He elaborated: "The noblest races have always been lovers of liberty. The love ran strong in early German blood, and has profoundly influenced the institutions of all the branches of the great German family; but it was left for the Anglo-Saxon branch fully to recognize the right of the individual to himself, and formally to declare it the foundation stone of government."

The second aspect of Anglo-Saxon superiority was the race's "pure spiritual Christianity." Strong identified a close connection between race and religion. "It was no accident that the great reformation of the sixteenth century originated among a Teutonic, rather than a Latin people. It was the fire of liberty burning in the Saxon heart that flamed up against the absolutism of the Pope. Speaking roughly, the peoples of Europe which are Celtic are Roman Catholic, and those which are Teutonic are Protestant; and where the Teutonic race was purest, there Protestantism spread with the greatest rapidity." In the centuries since the Reformation, much of continental Protestantism had degenerated into formalism, until its adherents became as impoverished in spirit and power as the papists. "That means that most of the spiritual Christianity in the world is found among Anglo-Saxons and their converts; for this is the great missionary race." Getting down to points, Strong declared, "It is chiefly to the English and American peoples that we must look for the evangelization of the world."

Fortunately for the world, the Anglo-Saxons were prolific. "This race is multiplying not only more rapidly than any other European race, but more rapidly than *all* the races of continental Europe taken together." Nowhere did the multiplication proceed so swiftly as in America, where numbers swelled from both natural increase and immigration. Strong had to stretch a bit to accommodate recent shifts in the origins of many immigrants; speaking of the nearly 1 million Germans who left home for America during the 1870s, he predicted that "in one generation their children will be counted Anglo-Saxons." (Strong didn't deal with the even more recent wave of immigration from Southern and Eastern Europe.) Yet whether inherited or acquired, the laudable traits of the Anglo-Saxon character blossomed most fully in the United States. "There is abundant reason to believe that the Anglo-Saxon race is to be, is indeed already becoming, more effective here than in the mother country." Strong insisted that there could be no reasonable doubt that "North America is to be the great home of the Anglo-Saxon, the principal seat of his power, the center of his life and influence."

Interestingly, even contradictorily, in the light of the rest of his argument, Strong attributed the blossoming of Anglo-Saxons in America to the mixing of Anglo-Saxon blood with that of other races—although he drew the line considerably short of what even the most eugenically fastidious would deem miscegenation. Quoting the poet, Strong wrote, "Saxon and Norman and Dane are we," adding that an American Tennyson would have tossed in Celt, Gaul, Welshman, Irishman, Frisian, Flamand, French Huguenot, and German Palatine.

In any event, the Anglo-Saxons, particularly those inhabiting America, would inherit the planet. The Anglo-Saxon displayed "indomitable perseverance" and a "genius for colonizing"; he was "divinely commissioned to be, in a peculiar sense, his brother's keeper." Destiny drew nigh. "God, with infinite wisdom and skill, is training the Anglo-Saxon race for an hour sure to come in the world's future." Lesser races must stand aside or be swept aside. Only a "ready and pliant assimilation" could save them. When the moment arrived, "this race of unequaled energy, with all the majesty of numbers and the might of wealth behind it," would spread itself over the entire earth. Americans had only to accept the challenge and answer the call. Strong was convinced they would. "Notwithstanding the great perils which threaten it, I cannot think our civilization will perish; but I believe it is fully in the hands of the Christians of the United States, during the next ten or fifteen years, to hasten or retard the coming of Christ's kingdom in the world by hundreds, and perhaps thousands, of years. We of this generation and nation occupy the Gibraltar of the ages which commands the world's future."

II

This sense of commanding the world's future wasn't universal in America during the 1890s. There were some who questioned whether the United States (or any other country) *ought* to command the world's future, and others who questioned whether America *could*. Few Americans doubted that their country possessed the material potential to become a leader among the world's nations, but some wondered whether their country possessed the requisite national character.

Theodore Roosevelt was among the most outspoken of this last group. During the 1890s, Roosevelt emerged as a politician to be taken seriously. It wasn't easy, since he didn't fit readily into any existing category of American political leader. In fact, Roosevelt never would fit into any such category; he would create a category all his own. In 1890, Roosevelt turned thirty-two. He was ten years out of Harvard and had spent three terms in the New York state assembly. Though he officially identified himself with the Republican Party, he defined Republicanism pretty much as he pleased, often acting more like an independent than a good party man. When the (relatively) progressive faction within the national party lost out in 1884 to James Blaine and the old guard—and when, moreover, Roosevelt's young wife died in the same year—he retired from political life. He already had one outlet beyond politics for his enormous energies: the writing of history. His 1882 *The Naval War of 1812* had been favorably received, and he had plans for other works of American history. But Roosevelt decided he needed a change of scenery as well as a change of activity, and he took up ranching in Dakota Territory.

Since childhood Roosevelt had been enamored of men who lived strenuous physical lives. He suspected that they were in closer touch with reality than those, like himself, who came from soft, comfortable backgrounds. With many others of his generation (and later generations), he particularly admired cowboys, and he decided to become one. He was an odd sight on the Dakota frontier, with his thick glasses and Harvard mannerisms, but he eventually won the respect of his neighbors through hard work and determination.

He returned to New York and politics after two years, when Republicans there asked him to make a run for mayor of New York City. He lost—Tammany's grip was too tight—and once more devoted his attention to history. In 1889, he published the first two volumes of *The Winning of the West*. But it was Roosevelt's reputation as a reformer rather than a historian that brought him to the attention of President Harrison, who appointed him civil service commissioner. During the first half of the 1890s, Roosevelt filled this post with vigor and some distinction. He also continued to write, publishing the third and fourth volumes of his history of the West in 1894 and 1896. In addition, he contributed frequently to journals and magazines, setting forth his opinions on history and current affairs via reviews and articles.

Roosevelt's opinions on current affairs were as robust as his attitude toward life in general. He subscribed enthusiastically to the Anglo-Saxonism of John Fiske and Josiah Strong, although he put his own interpretation on the idea. Roosevelt believed that the English-speaking peoples had shown themselves to be the most civilized and most competent of all the world's peoples, and he thought it entirely fitting that they should govern the greatest portion of the earth's surface. Observing the progress of European colonization in Africa, Roosevelt declared, "It is to the interest of civilization that the English-speaking race should be dominant in South Africa"—just as, he added, it was to civilization's interest that the United States should be dominant in the Western Hemisphere. At a time of trouble in the Sudan, Roosevelt told a British friend that "England would be doing her duty as a civilized nation if she overthrew the Mahdists and opened up the Sudan." Roosevelt conceded that British rule in places like Africa and

India had benefited Britain; but most of all, he said, it had "advanced the cause of civilization."

Yet while believing that the English speakers were the most advanced race, Roosevelt didn't deny the possibility that other races might catch up. To the extent that he was a racist (racialist might be a better word), he judged peoples on their accomplishments rather than on what might have been their innate strengths or deficiencies. For example, while he disdained the Chinese as demonstrably incompetent in creating a modern society, he had immense respect for the Japanese. "What wonderful people the Japanese are," he said to a friend during the period of the Russo-Japanese War. "They are quite as remarkable industrially as in warfare." He added, "I believe that Japan will take its place as a great civilized power of a formidable type." In other words, Roosevelt was willing to judge peoples on the basis of what they did rather than what they were (or weren't).

It was this attitude that sometimes caused him concern about America's future. Roosevelt had no doubt that Americans held the potential for greatness; he just wondered whether they would live up to their potential. Only sporadically in the past had Americans done so, Roosevelt contended. Thomas Jefferson, according to Roosevelt's researches for his book on the War of 1812, had neglected American military strength at a time of British and French depredations against American shipping and American rights; Jefferson instead chose a course of "cowardly infamy." Roosevelt considered the leaders of the Confederacy during the Civil War to have been traitors pure and simple (although he admired the gallantry of Confederate military men, including some relatives on his mother's side). Opponents of American expansion during the 1890s were hardly better. They shied from war, but their quixotic quest for peace made war only more likely. "Peace comes not to the coward or to the timid," he asserted, "but to him who will do no wrong and is too strong to allow others to wrong him." On another occasion he declared, "A Quaker may be quite as undesirable a citizen as a duelist." No man who was unwilling to bear arms and fight for his rights should be entitled to the privilege of living in a free community. Something similar applied in the international arena. "There is no place in the world for nations who have become enervated by soft and easy life, or who have lost their fibre of vigorous hardiness and manliness." In an address before the Naval War College, Roosevelt stated, "All the great masterful races have been fighting races." Once a race lost the hard, fighting virtues—no matter how clever in commerce or sophisticated in art it might be—it lost its right to stand with the best. "No triumph of peace," he proclaimed, "is quite so great as the supreme triumphs of war."

It dismayed Roosevelt that not all of his contemporaries shared his high opinion of the martial virtues. In fact, many even of Roosevelt's friends thought him a little loony on the subject. A Harvard classmate remarked, "He would like above all to go to war with some one." This college chum added that Roosevelt "wants to be killing something all the time." William James, who had taught Roosevelt at Harvard, asserted, "He is still mentally in the *Sturm und Drang* period of early adolescence." James went on to say that Roosevelt praised war "as the ideal condition of human society, for the manly strenuousness which it involves," and that he treated peace "as a condition of blubberlike and swollen ignobility, fit only for the huckstering weaklings, dwelling in gray twilight and heedless of the higher life." James concluded sardonically, "One foe is as good as another, for aught he tells us." Longtime Theodore-watcher Harry Thurston Peck explained some inconsistencies in Roosevelt's positions by saying that Roosevelt felt that "what is wrong when done by others is right when it is done by him or his friends." George Smalley, a British journalist who followed Roosevelt's career closely, remarked on Roosevelt's inability to accept that others might fairly disagree with him, or other countries legitimately disagree with America. "Roosevelt is as sincere as he is intemperate," Smalley said. "Let us admit, and regret, that he honestly believes it impossible to differ from him honestly."

It was precisely because others differed with him that Roosevelt often felt compelled to put his arguments in the extreme form he did. He thought most of his compatriots sorely required waking up. At a time of tension with Germany he declared, "Frankly, I don't know that I should be sorry to see a bit of a spar with Germany. The burning of New York and a few other sea coast cities would be a good object lesson in the need of an adequate system of coast defenses." When President Harrison reacted less belligerently than Roosevelt thought appropriate to a slight by the government of Chile, Roosevelt privately registered his disgust. John Hay reported to Henry Adams, after talking to Roosevelt: "For two nickels he would declare war himself—shut up the Civil Service Commission and wage it sole." A member of the naval affairs committee of the House of Representatives remarked, following a visit by Roosevelt, then assistant navy secretary: "Roosevelt came down here looking for war. He did not care whom we fought as long as there was a scrap." Roosevelt himself asserted, as relations with Madrid grew strained in the runup to the Spanish-American War: "It is very difficult for me not to wish a war with Spain, for such a war would result at once in getting a proper Navy."

The issue of a navy nearly obsessed Roosevelt, as it did Roosevelt's ideological kin. The most influential of these was Alfred Thayer Mahan, a career navy man and an instructor at the Naval War College. Mahan came by his interest in military matters honestly, being the son of a professor at West Point. He attended the Naval Academy at Annapolis and gradually rose through the ranks to captain. His assignments included stints at sea and ashore, and certain of them allowed Mahan to demonstrate a talent for historical research and writing. In 1886, he received an invitation to teach at the Naval War College. He accepted, and he succeeded so well that he was soon promoted to president of the college. In 1890, he published his lectures on naval history under the title *The Influence of Sea Power Upon History, 1660–1783.*

The book was an immediate sensation in the circles Theodore Roosevelt ran around in. Reviewing it in the *Atlantic Monthly*, Roosevelt called it "distinctively the best and most important, also by far the most interesting book on naval history which has been produced on either side of the water" —the Atlantic Ocean—"for many a long year." What Roosevelt particularly liked about Mahan's work was the case it made for a strong American navy. Roosevelt denounced the notion, popular among many in the United States, "that we could defend ourselves by some kind of patent method, invented on the spur of the moment." He was pleased to note that Mahan's analysis exploded such ideas as "sheer folly." Mahan had demonstrated clearly what was required. "We need a large navy, composed not merely of cruisers, but containing also a full proportion of powerful battleships, able to meet those of any other nation. It is not economy—it is niggardly and foolish short-sightedness—to cramp our naval expenditures."

Roosevelt was equally enthusiastic over the sequels Mahan produced during the 1890s. *The Influence of Sea Power Upon the French Revolution and Empire, 1793–1812*, published in 1892, sold well in the United States and, translated, in several foreign countries. Mahan became a cult figure among big-navy types around the world. In 1893, the British government decorated him, and both Cambridge and Oxford universities conferred honorary degrees upon him. His 1897 *Life of Nelson* returned the favor, while another book of the same year, *The Interest of America in Sea Power, Present and Future*, reiterated his arguments on behalf of a large and powerful American navy. In this book, Mahan contended additionally that overseas naval bases and coaling stations were necessary to continued American security and prosperity. He urged his compatriots to adopt "a Twentieth Century outlook" on the world: a frame of mind willing to project American power across the globe. He conceded that his program wouldn't come cheap; but the alternatives would prove far more expensive in terms of strategic danger, lost commercial opportunity, and national humiliation.

Henry Cabot Lodge of Massachusetts was as enthusiastic an advocate of a "large policy" for America as Roosevelt and Mahan. Lodge was eight years older than Roosevelt and had completed law school at Harvard five years before Roosevelt graduated from the college. Where Roosevelt made politics his profession and history his hobby, Lodge initially reversed the order. During the late 1870s, Lodge lectured on American history at Harvard, and in the 1880s he produced a series of solid biographies of American notables: *Alexander Hamilton* in 1882, *Daniel Webster* in 1883, and *George Washington* in 1889. He also compiled a nine-volume *Works of Alexander Hamilton* and a new edition of *The Federalist*. On the side Lodge commenced a political career. Following an inauspicious start in the Massachusetts legislature, he won election to the United States House of Representatives in 1886. After three terms in the House he graduated to the Senate, where he remained for the rest of his life (until 1924).

Like Roosevelt, Lodge was ambitious—personally and nationally. The two aspects of their ambition dovetailed neatly, for in pushing a large policy for the United States overseas, the young Republicans promoted themselves as spokesmen for that policy. As the expansionist policy took hold, assuming it did, so would their careers. This conjunction of personal and public interests didn't make them any less sincere; it merely gave them additional reason to do what they thought was right.

In the context of the 1890s, American expansionism was tantamount to American imperialism, although Roosevelt, Lodge, and the others generally refused to admit as much. During the debate over annexation of the Philippines in the wake of the Spanish-American War, Roosevelt flatly declared that there was "nothing even remotely resembling 'imperialism' " in America's treatment of the Philippines. Nor had imperialism ever been involved in American expansion. "There is not an imperialist in the country that I have yet met," Roosevelt stated. Lodge concurred. Commenting on American history, Lodge said, "I do not think there is any such thing as 'imperialism.' " He added, however: "But I am clearly of the opinion that there is such a thing as 'expansion' and that the United States must control some distant dependencies."

III

Lodge's labored distinction between imperialism and expansion reflected Americans' uneasiness about the former, despite their incipient embrace of it. He would have made things clearer had he distinguished between territorial expansion and economic expansion. Territorial expansion was what more forthright commentators than Lodge and Roosevelt termed "imperialism": the bringing of foreign territories under the American flag. It was almost always coercive and obviously required government participation. Economic expansion was the spread of American trade and investment abroad. It might be more coercive or less, and involve more or less government participation. Many Americans in the 1890s were not territorial expansionists, but with rare exceptions they were all economic expansionists. Economic expansion seemed simply good business writ large.

Of course, the theoretical distinction between economic and territorial expansion often blurred in practice; and nowhere more than in the events surrounding the annexation of Hawaii. Covetous Americans had eyed Hawaii (or the Sandwich Islands, as they were called by British explorer James Cook, honoring a sponsor of his voyages) since the late eighteenth century. The archipelago became a regular stop in the China trade that both American and British merchants were developing. Ships would leave their home harbors in the North Atlantic loaded with manufactured goods, then sail south around South America, and north again to the northwest coast of North America, where they would barter for seal, otter, and beaver pelts. The ships would proceed west across the Pacific, often wintering in Hawaii. For the crews, the Hawaii stopover was the delight of the journey, as the natives were friendly and comparatively uninhibited. After adding sandalwood to their cargoes, the ships would continue on to China, there acquiring silk, tea, and other luxury items that would fetch high prices back home. With perhaps a stop in the East Indies or India, the ships would complete their circumnavigation of the globe by doubling the Cape of Good Hope and traversing the South Atlantic to the familiar waters of the North Atlantic.

Hawaii acquired such a reputation as a result of the China trade that American Protestant missionaries determined to put an end to the frolics taking place there. The missionaries converted many of the native Hawaiians to Christianity, persuaded them to put on clothes, and generally spoiled the party. The missionaries also brought Hawaii to the attention of adventurous American planters who were willing to gamble that they could grow sugar cane there cheaply. The gamble paid off, and by the latter half of the nineteenth century Hawaii was a major exporter of sugar. Though residents of Hawaii, the planters retained their American connections sufficiently that they succeeded in lobbying Congress to allow Hawaiian sugar to enter the American market duty-free. During an era of high tariffs, this was a significant advantage.

Another reason for the favor that Congress showed Hawaii was that Hawaii boasted one of the finest sheltered bays in the Pacific: Pearl Harbor. Navalists of the Mahan blue-water school looked longingly on Pearl Harbor. During the 1870s and 1880s, the American government tied the special treatment afforded Hawaiian sugar to special American privileges at Pearl Harbor. At first, Washington contented itself with a pledge by the Hawaiian government not to sign over Pearl Harbor (or any other part of the archipelago) to a third country. In 1887, this pledge was strengthened by a positive grant of naval basing rights at Pearl Harbor to the United States.

Events of the 1890s upset this cozy relationship. In the committee-room maneuvering that produced the McKinley tariff of 1890, mainland American sugar producers joined forces with American growers who had plantations in Cuba to persuade Congress to eliminate Hawaii's exemption from the tariff. This action dealt a body blow to the Hawaiian sugar industry and provoked the American community in the islands to plot a counteroffensive. The plan they came up with involved overthrowing the Hawaiian government of Queen Liliuokalani and attaching Hawaii to the United States. Once inside the American political frontier, Hawaii—and the planters' sugar—would be safely inside the American tariff wall.

Although her assistance probably wasn't quite necessary, Liliuokalani aided the plotters by a variety of measures that infringed on what the planters had come to consider their rights. She revoked certain privileges the planters had been granted by her predecessor and attempted to restore the prerogatives of the throne. The Americans had never fully reconciled themselves to living under a monarchy, and they convinced themselves that this reactionary trend justified rebellion.

They also convinced the American minister to Hawaii, John Stevens;

and when, in January 1893, the planters launched their bloodless coup—or nearly bloodless: one shot was fired and one person wounded—Stevens guaranteed its success by landing a squadron of marines from the U.S.S. *Boston*, anchored in Pearl Harbor. The American troops didn't do any fighting, but their presence and the presence of the Gatling guns and artillery they brought ashore and mounted opposite the royal palace helped persuade the queen not to attempt to reverse the rebellion. Speaking on behalf of the American government in Washington—or so he hoped—Stevens immediately recognized the successor regime to Liliuokalani. He declared an American protectorate over the islands, raised the American flag, and urged Washington to ratify his actions lest some other country—Britain, Japan, or even Germany—elbow its way in. "The Hawaiian pear is now fully ripe," he declared, importing a fruit never seen in that part of the Pacific, "and this is the golden hour for the United States to pluck it."

Expansionists in the United States thrilled at the thought. Anglo-Saxonists embraced the opportunity to extend white rule across the Pacific: Roosevelt told a British friend that the United States should take Hawaii "in the interests of the White race." Navalists like Mahan considered Pearl Harbor vital to an effective American presence in the central Pacific. Commercial expansionists pointed to Hawaii's long history as a steppingstone to the Asian market.

But between the deed and its ratification, control of the presidency changed hands. Benjamin Harrison was replaced by Grover Cleveland, who had serious qualms about the manner in which the Hawaiian government had been overthrown. Was this a genuinely democratic revolution, one that the United States should be proud to support? Or was it merely a successful putsch, in which one small group was ousted by another? In annexing Hawaii, would the United States be encouraging the spread of American values, or abetting a criminal conspiracy? Cleveland wanted to know, and so he appointed an investigative commission to examine the circumstances surrounding Liliuokalani's removal.

Cleveland had other reasons for hesitating over annexation. Twenty-five years after the purchase of Alaska, the question of whether a noncontiguous territory could become a state remained open. Previously Americans had shielded themselves from charges of imperialism by replying that territories acquired by the United States soon achieved coequal status with the original thirteen states. This argument was already falling short with Alaska, which appeared unlikely to become a state in any living adult's lifetime. Annexation of Hawaii would strain it still further. Hawaii was very far away, and, more troublesome, it was inhabited mostly by nonwhites. Some ninety thousand persons lived in the islands. Half of these were aboriginal Hawaiians; about half were Asians (mostly Chinese and Japanese). Only a few thousand were of American descent. By annexing Hawaii to the United States, the American government would be taking these tens of thousands of Asians and Polynesians to its bosom. Was this what the majority of the American population wanted? On recent evidence—most tellingly the Chinese Exclusion Act, passed in 1882 and renewed in 1892, which barred Chinese immigration to the United States—the answer was no.

Finally, the same sugar interests that had succeeded in blocking access by Hawaiian sugar to the American market didn't like the idea of annexing the islands and with them the islands' sugar. The issue transcended Hawaii: the continental growers had to consider that if their Hawaiian competitors managed to force their way into the United States, American growers in Cuba might try something similar.

While the Hawaiian question hung fire, the Panic of 1893 seized Wall Street, and the American economy went into its nose-dive. Eugene Debs and the railway workers tied up traffic across the Midwest, and Jacob Coxey led his army from Ohio to Washington. Amid all the confusion, Cleveland decided he didn't need to add to his troubles by getting into a fight over Hawaii. When Cleveland's investigative committee reported that the coup in Hawaii was the work of a very small minority, and that the great majority of the islands' population was hardly clamoring for annexation, the president had additional reason for not seeking to add Hawaii to the United States. He withdrew a proposed treaty of annexation and put the issue aside for the rest of his second term.

IV

Yet Cleveland wasn't so overwhelmed by domestic difficulties as to ignore foreign affairs entirely. In fact, by the time it became evident that the depression wasn't going to lift soon, he began looking to the international arena for relief from his troubles at home. For most of a century—since 1823, when James Monroe had announced what came to be called the Monroe Doctrine—the United States had treated the Western Hemisphere as its particular bailiwick. For an even longer period—at least since the 1760s, when the series of crises that led to the Revolutionary War commenced—Americans had vented their frustrations at the world by complaining about Britain. Sometimes the Britain-bashing had been justified, as during the lead-in to the War of 1812. Much of the time it reflected the same kind of scapegoating that in the twentieth century would make the United States the villain of choice for many countries. As the most powerful nation around, and one with fingers in lots of pies, Britain was a logical candidate for complaint in a wide variety of situations. In any event, when the Cleveland administration started looking for distractions from its difficulties at home, it hit upon one that combined these two aspects of traditional American policy: a proprietary interest in Latin America and antagonism toward Britain.

For many years, the border between Venezuela and the British colony of Guiana on the northern coast of South America had been in dispute. For most of those years, the dispute hadn't really exercised anyone, since there didn't seem to be much in the disputed region to get huffy about. But in the 1880s, gold was discovered—indeed, the largest single gold nugget ever pulled from the ground anywhere, a grapefruit weighing 509 ounces, was found there. This changed the situation entirely. Immediately each side began pressing its claim with great fervor. The British took the attitude that the territory was theirs and that Venezuela could go to hell; Venezuela felt that it was being exploited on account of its weakness.

The United States entered the picture when the Venezuelan government appealed to Washington for help. The Venezuelans were shrewd enough to realize that while an appeal on grounds of justice might not elicit much support from Washington, an appeal on grounds of American interest probably would. The Venezuelan government hired as a lobbyist William Scruggs, a former American diplomat. Scruggs cleverly cast his client's case as involving a challenge to American prestige and security by that notorious international bully, Great Britain. He wrote and circulated a pamphlet entitled *British Aggressions in Venezuela, or the Monroe Doctrine on Trial.* The tract explained that the dispute was a clearcut example of Britain's trying to export to South America the type of strongarm approach it had made a career of in Asia and Africa. The difference this time, though, was that in pushing Venezuela around, the British were violating the Monroe Doctrine, by which the United States government had warned the European governments to stay out of the affairs of the Western Hemisphere.

Scruggs's timing couldn't have been better. The Cleveland administration was reeling from the results of the 1894 congressional elections, as well as from the other vexations of the mid-1890s. Expansionists like Roosevelt, and the Republican Party generally, were lambasting the administration for timidity in foreign affairs, evidenced by Cleveland's failure to annex Hawaii, and now this. Congressional Democrats understood the score: they joined the Republicans in a unanimous resolution demanding that the British accept international arbitration in the Venezuela dispute. They urged Cleveland to get on board. A Democratic representative from Texas, Thomas Paschal, told Richard Olney, now Cleveland's secretary of state, "Turn this Venezuelan question up or down, North, South, East or West, and it is a winner." Paschal, speaking of the economic and political unrest abroad in the country, continued, "Why, Mr. Secretary, just think of how angry the anarchistic, socialistic, and populistic boil appears, on our political surface," and he advised, "One cannon shot across the bow of a British boat in defense of this principle will knock more pus out of it than would suffice to inoculate and corrupt our people for the next two centuries."

Henry Cabot Lodge fired a shot of his own across the administration's bow. Lodge wrote an article in the *North American Review* insisting that the president take a firm stand in Venezuela on the basis of American hegemony in the Western Hemisphere. The administration needed to defend "the supremacy of the Monroe Doctrine," Lodge declared, "peaceably if we can, forcibly if we must." In a letter to Roosevelt, Lodge said that he was "worried and angry beyond words." Should the United States allow Britain to get away with coercing Venezuela, "our supremacy in the Americas is over." In another letter, Lodge explained, "If Great Britain can extend her territory in South America without remonstrance from us, every other European power can do the same, and in a short time you will see South America parcelled out as Africa has been. We should then find ourselves with great powers to the south of us, and we should be forced to become at once a nation with a powerful army and navy, with difficulties and dangers surrounding us."

Roosevelt concurred completely. He praised Lodge for his article and said, "If only our people will heed it!" He linked arms with Lodge in demanding that the Cleveland administration register a protest in the strongest language possible. "The United States cannot tolerate the aggrandizement of a European power on American soil," Roosevelt asserted.

Cleveland got the message. Calling Richard Olney, he had the secretary of state draft a vigorous remonstrance to the British government. Olney had only just moved to the State Department from the Justice Department after his successful work as Cleveland's point man in the fight against Debs and the railway workers; eager to make a favorable first impression in his new post, he wrote a lengthy memo that treated the members of the British government as though they were recalcitrant strikers who needed a stiff lecture on the basic points of law and history. Olney reminded the British of the special interest the United States had long taken in the affairs of its Latin American neighbors. He expressed concern at Britain's demands against Venezuela and at the possibility that the British might be moving toward a protectorate or something similar over Venezuela. Such an outcome would be entirely unacceptable to the United States, not simply on its own demerits but because it might lead to European efforts to partition South America in a manner similar to the partitioning currently under way in Africa.

Olney reviewed the evolution of the Monroe Doctrine from its promulgation in the 1820s, through its successful application against the French in Mexico in the 1860s (when Paris had been persuaded to withdraw the troops that propped up the government of the transplanted Austrian, Maximilian), and on to the present. Olney reminded the British government of the reasoning behind the Monroe Doctrine: "The states of America, South as well as North [to improve his argument, Olney spoke of the two continents as divisions of a single super-America], by geographical proximity, by natural sympathy, by similarity of governmental constitutions, are friends and allies, commercially and politically, of the United States. To allow the subjugation of any one of them by a European power is, of course, to completely reverse that situation and signifies the loss of all the advantages incident to their natural relations with us."

Then came the clincher: "Today the United States is practically sovereign on this continent"—that single American continent again—"and its fiat is law upon the subjects to which it confines its interpretation." Why was this so?, Olney asked rhetorically. "It is not because of the pure friendship or good will felt for it"—although he didn't deny that friendship and goodwill counted for something. "It is because, in addition to all other grounds, its infinite resources combined with its isolated position, render it master of the situation and practically invulnerable as against any or all other powers." Olney concluded by demanding that Britain refer the border dispute to an international tribunal. He left it to British imagination what the United States would do if the British government failed to comply.

Cleveland had wanted a stern note to the British government, but he hadn't expected anything quite this bracing. He later likened Olney's message to a "twenty-inch gun." All the same, the president was pleased. "It's the best thing of the kind I ever read," he told Olney. With minor revisions Cleveland approved the note and directed Olney to send it off. It would surely get Britain's attention, and it would probably quiet some of the criticism of the administration for lack of spine in foreign affairs.

Astonishingly, Olney's note did not get Britain's attention. At least it elicited no reaction, not for months after its delivery. The Olney message was dated July 20, 1895, and was delivered to the British foreign secretary a short while later. Lord Salisbury did double duty as prime minister, and he had much else on his mind at this time. Britain was on the verge of war with recalcitrant colonists in South Africa, and a war there appeared likely to inflame or be inflamed by the developing rivalry between Britain and Germany. The German kaiser was known to be pleased by the growing tension near the Cape of Good Hope and was doing what he could to increase it. Besides, Salisbury guessed—quite rightly—that about 80 percent of the bluster of the American note was intended for an American audience. When the Americans got this way, it was best to ignore them. They had a short attention span and would soon be diverted by something else.

Besides, Salisbury considered the American position to be almost entirely without substance. Britain wasn't bullying anyone. It was merely defending a longstanding and meritorious claim against latter-day efforts by an upstart Venezuelan government—which, like the United States government, was trying to make political hay out of the affair—to take what didn't belong to it. Moreover, Britain possessed a global empire, and it faced dozens of claims like that of the Venezuelan government. Arbitration sounded fine in principle, but to submit the Venezuelan dispute to an international tribunal would make all the other claimants think they should get a similar hearing. There would be no end to the haggling.

So Salisbury let Cleveland and Olney stew in their own juice for four months. And when he did deign to reply, he rejected the American demand for arbitration. He denied that the Monroe Doctrine had anything to do with the matter at hand. "It is not a question of the colonization by a European Power of any portion of America," he said. "It is not a question of the imposition upon the communities of South America of any system of government devised in Europe." Salisbury went on to assert that even if the Monroe Doctrine had been involved, it wouldn't affect Britain's decision a whit, since Britain had never accepted that singular and unilateral declaration of American preferences. The Americans would do well to keep out of a quarrel that was none of their business. The issue was straightforward. "It is simply the determination of the frontier of a British possession which belonged to the Throne of England long before the Republic of Venezuela came into existence."

Salisbury's flippant response made Cleveland "mad clean through," as the president remarked to a friend. The fact that the British prime minister had taken his sweet time delivering his response merely added to Cleveland's annoyance. The president had hoped to be able to include an energetic statement about Venezuela in his annual message to Congress: either a claim of victory or a further demand for British compliance. But the British note didn't arrive in time. As a result, Cleveland ended up not being able to say much at all on the issue and feeling rather foolish.

To try to salvage the situation, Cleveland decided to escalate. Those arrogant English mustn't be allowed to get away with insulting the United States. The president unveiled his rejoinder in a special message to Congress—a mode of communicating with London that underlined the domestic motivation behind his actions. Writing in December 1895, he again emphasized the importance of the Monroe Doctrine as a fundamental principle of American diplomacy. "If the balance of power is justly a cause for jealous anxiety among the governments of the Old World and a subject for our absolute noninterference, none the less is an observance of the Monroe Doctrine of vital concern to our people and their government." Because the British had refused to accept international arbitration, Cleveland said, he was asking Congress to grant him authority to appoint an investigative commission to determine where the true boundary lay. Cleveland strongly hinted at the use of American force to implement the commission's findings. The president granted that it was "a grievous thing to contemplate the two great English-speaking peoples of the world as being otherwise than friendly competitors in the onward march of civilization," but the United States could never countenance "wrong and injustice, and the consequent loss of national self-respect and honor."

The expansionists in the United States, even many who otherwise couldn't stand Cleveland, roundly cheered the president's ultimatum. "I first alone in the wilderness cried out about Venezuela last June and was called a Jingo for my pains," Lodge crowed. "Jingoes are plenty enough now." Roosevelt announced, "Let the fight come if it must. I don't care if our sea coast cities are bombarded or not; we would take Canada." Whitelaw Reid, editor of the *New York Tribune*, detected an opportunity for the United States to run the British nearly out of the Western Hemisphere. "This is the golden opportunity of our merchants to extend our trade to every quarter of Central and South America," Reid declared. Irish-Americans, always eager for a chance to whack Britain, started drilling in preparation for combat duty. In Congress, members of both parties rallied behind the president. The legislature quickly appropriated $100,000 for the commission Cleveland called for.

Yet even as the war whoops resounded across the land, second thoughts began nagging in certain quarters. Many Americans thought it entirely disproportionate for the United States to contemplate war with the most powerful country in the world over a few thousand square miles of jungle in South America. Some business leaders got cold feet when the stock market plunged in response to a pullout by British investors. (This reaction reminded Roosevelt why he could never be just an ordinary Republican. Writing from the vicinity of Wall Street, Roosevelt complained with disgust of the "cowardice, stupidity and selfishness of the great majority of the people I meet here." Lodge described a similar situation in Boston and expressed similar dismay.) The Cleveland administration, having made its point, pondered whether it really wanted a war on top of its other troubles. Besides, after all the grief it had suffered as a result of the depression, it could only view the latest stock slump with grave apprehension.

In Britain, analogous rethinking was taking place. Lord Salisbury belatedly recognized that he had failed to appreciate the depth of American feelings on the subject of the Monroe Doctrine. Even less than the Cleveland administration did Salisbury's Conservative government want war. Indeed, the Tories, realizing the growing threat that Germany was posing to both the security of the British empire and the stability of Europe, decided that with Germany a likely enemy they could use America as a friend. Consequently, Salisbury consented to back down—slightly. He didn't immediately agree to negotiations on the boundary issue, but he did agree to negotiate about negotiations.

This was just the device needed to deescalate the affair gracefully. For several months American and British diplomats held discussions regarding the appropriate forum for a settlement. While they talked, the governments on both sides of the Atlantic found other things to fret over—for Cleveland's part, principally Bryan and silver. In November 1896, after McKinley's election, the negotiators came to terms on a five-person arbitration panel. Two Americans would join two Britons on the panel; the fifth member would be a third-country national agreed upon by the other four. (Venezuela was excluded from the commission—a fact that revealed once more the essentially political nature of the whole business.) The panel conducted an exhaustive investigation that lasted more than two years. By the time it reached a conclusion, almost no one in either the United States or Britain was paying attention. America had fought a war with Spain in the interim, and the British had just started fighting the Boers of South Africa. The commission essentially split the difference between the extreme claims of the two parties—a solution that satisfied Washington and London well enough, although the Venezuelans had hoped for better.

V

The most important lasting consequence of the war flurry over the Venezuela boundary was a rapprochement between the United States and Britain. The years that straddled the end of the nineteenth century and the
beginning of the twentieth produced some remarkable reversals in diplomatic relations, the most spectacular of which was the entente between
those rivals of a millennium, Britain and France. What the fear of God, of
the Saracens, of the plague, and of anyone and anything else had failed to
engender during the long centuries since the Norman conquest of England,
the fear of Germany finally did. Less stunning but no less significant than
the Anglo-French understanding was the Anglo-American entente that the
mutual stand-down over Venezuela made possible.

In terms of domestic American politics, the Venezuela crisis demonstrated the political potency of the expansionists. The fact that the United
States didn't go to war with Britain mattered less than that it considered
doing so. For fifty years, Americans hadn't even come close to a foreign
war. Now, all of a sudden, they were getting hot about a plot of ground
most of them couldn't have located without a good atlas. It didn't take a
genius to discern that the fervor of the American response had less to do
with South American gold than with Populist silver, less to do with Britain
than with Bryan, less to do with an ambiguous Venezuelan frontier than
with the vanishing American frontier. At a time of pervasive national uncertainty, the jingoes knew what they wanted—which got them halfway to
getting it.

The next few years got them the other half. In 1895, as the tussle with
Britain was getting tense, a war broke out in Cuba. Not for the first time:
between 1868 and 1878, Cuban nationalists had fought Spain in what was
called, appropriately, the Ten Years' War. The nationalists had entreated
the United States for protection against their Spanish colonial oppressors,
wrapping themselves in the mantle of self-determination, the American
Declaration of Independence, and the Monroe Doctrine. Their entreaties
drew strong support from certain segments of the American population.
Manifest Destinarians argued for American intervention on grounds of
both the welfare of the Cubans, who would be released from Spanish bondage, and the interests of the United States, which might win control of Cuba
in the bargain. (Needless to say, control of Cuba by the United States would
be an entirely different matter than control of Cuba by Spain was, according to this line of reasoning.) One enthusiast of intervention, J. R. Dabney
of Kentucky, advised President Grant, "For God's sake, let us go in, and
Cuba, voluptuous Cuba, will be the reward." Dabney added, "People
everywhere wish something to stir them up. Times are dull. A war with
Spain would be very popular in this state." Yet times weren't everywhere
as dull as they evidently were in Kentucky, what with Reconstruction in

the South, headlong industrialization in the North, the massacre of the buffalo on the Plains, and the suppression of Indian resistance throughout the West. The Grant administration shook its finger at Madrid, saying that American patience had limits and that Cuba must someday be free, but Grant declined to offer guns or money to the Cuban rebels, and the uprising petered out after Spain promised to be nicer in the future.

Nicer wasn't good enough, and by the 1890s the nationalists were at it again. In 1895, they raised the banner of rebellion once more, vowing this time to fight till liberty or death. The timing of the renewal of the rebellion was due partly to the American Congress, which had repealed the favored tariff treatment of Cuban sugar. As demand for their product plummeted, sugar growers in Cuba laid off thousands of cane-cutters and other workers. Many of these vigorous but now idle and often angry young men joined the ranks of the veteran dissidents. Buoyed by these additions, leaders of the opposition—including José Martí, a refugee from the Ten Years' War who had spent more than a decade in New York—declared war on the regime.

The Spanish government responded with redoubled determination to hang on to this vestige of a once magnificent American empire. Although many well-placed persons in Spain recognized that Cuba was losing its attractiveness as a colony, and would lose even more if the war there lasted very long, the government in Madrid was too precariously situated to be magnanimous. So again it dispatched an army to the island to suppress the rebels.

The rebels' strategy largely dictated the government's. Overmatched in conventional military terms, the rebels fought a guerrilla war, ambushing and harassing Spanish units and attempting to make Cuba ungovernable for Spain. The rebels hid in the mountains and among the people; they came out at night and in small groups to strike against the Spanish and against Cubans loyal to Madrid. As ever with nationalist guerrillas, they didn't need to defeat the Spanish in open battle, although if the opportunity presented itself they wouldn't let it slip; they needed only to demonstrate an ability and willingness to keep fighting longer than the Spanish. Sooner or later, they reasoned, Spain would get fed up with the whole affair and go home.

The Spanish forces, under the leadership of a new commander, General Valeriano Weyler, replied with measures that were as old as guerrilla warfare itself. Called *reconcentrado*, Weyler's strategy was to separate the guerrillas from their supporters among the Cuban people. The Spanish established fortified camps and towns into which Cuban peasants were herded from the countryside; access to these camps was strictly controlled, with the idea that any guerrillas who came into the camps would be unable to get out and cause mischief, and any person who stayed outside must be a guerrilla and therefore would be subject to capture or killing.

The theory of the *reconcentrado* policy was logical enough, but its application was brutal. The uprooting involved in relocating the peasants thoroughly disrupted life in the Cuban countryside, convincing many peasants who hadn't taken a strong stand one way or the other that the Spanish authorities were a greater threat to their welfare than the guerrillas. Conditions in the camps compounded the feeling: food rations were short, sanitation was primitive or nonexistent, and disease was rampant. When the Spanish supplemented the *reconcentrado* approach with scorched-earth tactics outside the camps, the bitterness among the Cuban people mounted still more.

Spain's harsh handling of the Cuban insurrection quickly aroused American sympathies. Humanitarians argued for American intervention for the dual purpose of alleviating the suffering of the Cuban people and teaching the despicable Spaniards a lesson. Expansionists saw an opportunity to eject Spain from the Caribbean and extend American influence southward, either by outright annexation of Cuba or by the establishment of an American protectorate over a nominally independent Cuba. Politicians of both parties saw Cuba as an issue upon which Americans might release the frustrations that were surfacing as labor violence, political unrest, and other manifestations of dissatisfaction with the American status quo. Better that Americans vent their frustrations on a foreign enemy than on each other—or, worse, on their elected representatives.

The Cuban nationalists played on these American sentiments. They established propaganda bureaus and committees of assistance in the United States; a group calling itself the Cuban Junta set up headquarters in New York, while a "Cuban Legation" began conducting diplomatic business on behalf of the rebels in Washington. These pro-nationalist outfits raised money for the cause of Cuban independence and disseminated information calculated to benefit the nationalist movement. The information was often more inspirational than accurate; truth was subordinated to expedience in reporting Spanish atrocities and nationalist triumphs.

The nationalists' press releases found a ready outlet in American big-city newspapers. Recent changes in printing technology had sparked a heated competition among the leading papers in New York, Philadelphia, Chicago, and elsewhere. Hoping to attract the advertising that would allow them to pay off their investment in the new equipment, papers like the *New York World* of Joseph Pulitzer and the *New York Journal* of William Randolph Hearst vied for the high circulation figures the advertisers demanded. Pulitzer and Hearst lapped up the stories the Cuban nationalists disseminated, even the most exaggerated, and added embellishments of their own. They sent reporters to Cuba to discover more misdeeds of the Spanish, and they hired renowned artists, including Frederic Remington, to provide illustrations for the accounts the reporters cabled home. (Remington at first couldn't find much to draw. The guerrilla war in Cuba provided few such obviously dramatic scenes as he was used to depicting from the Indian wars of the American frontier. When Remington pointed this out to Hearst, the publisher cabled back, "You furnish the pictures, and I'll furnish the war"—or words to that effect.)

On the reasoning that stark contrasts of black and white would sell more papers than bland shadings of gray, the reporters painted the Spanish soldiers as unspeakable villains, who committed murder, torture, and rape against innocent Cuban women and children. Hearst's *Journal* reveled in its characterization of the Spanish commander: "Weyler the brute, the devastator of haciendas, the destroyer of families, and the outrager of women." The paper asserted of Weyler that it was impossible "to prevent his carnal, animal brain from running riot with itself in inventing tortures and infamies of bloody debauchery." Pulitzer's *World*, not to be outdone, screamed: "Blood on the roadsides, blood in the fields, blood on the doorsteps, blood, blood, blood! The old, the young, the weak, the crippled—all butchered without mercy." The *World* wondered, "Is there no nation wise enough, brave enough, and strong enough to restore peace in this bloodsmitten land?"

This was an era when news correspondents doubled as adventurers and heroes. Henry Stanley had tracked David Livingstone through the jungles of Africa for the *New York Herald*; cub reporter Winston Churchill was about to start writing dispatches on the Boer War, getting himself captured in the process and then making a dramatic escape, which he wrote up in breathless detail. In the case of Cuba, Hearst's paper received and published a report about a young Cuban woman named Evangelina Cisneros who had been abused and jailed by Spanish soldiers. The story sparked a tremendous outcry in the United States. At Hearst's instigation, thousands of Americans signed petitions demanding that Señorina Cisneros be released. After these failed to secure her freedom, an enterprising Hearst reporter in Cuba slipped into the Havana prison where she was being held, sawed through the bars in her cell, disguised her as a boy, and made off with her to freedom. When the pair arrived in America, the *Journal* fêted both rescuer and rescued. The paper boasted, "An American Newspaper Accomplishes in a Single Stroke What the Best Efforts of Diplomacy Failed Utterly to Bring About in Many Months." The governor of Missouri suggested that Hearst send five hundred correspondents to Cuba and have done with the war right away. In another incident, Spanish soldiers boarded an American passenger ship leaving Havana and searched for rebel communications. Among those allegedly searched were three young Cuban women. To lend human interest to the tale, Remington—who by now was getting the hang of what was expected of him—contributed an imagined illustration of one of the women being stripped naked by the soldiers. "Does Our Flag Protect Women?" the headline demanded.

Meanwhile the contributions of the nationalists to the violence on the island went generally unreported in the American press. Though the rebels' activities provoked many of the Spanish reprisals, they complicated and confused an issue that was more compelling in its simpler form.

The uproar in the yellow press fostered an atmosphere in which the affairs of Cuba became a matter of surpassing interest to millions of Americans. By itself the sensationalism didn't produce American intervention in the Cuban war, but it acted in such a way as to magnify other influences, and the end result was the same.

The magnifying process required some time. The uprising broke out just as the Cleveland administration was getting worked up about the Venezuela affair; unwilling to risk two tangles simultaneously, Cleveland proclaimed American neutrality in the Cuban conflict. This disappointed the nationalists, who hoped for prompt American assistance. The nationalists were disappointed further when the administration sought to dissuade American merchants and shippers from doing business with Cuba, lest such business produce incidents that would suck the United States into the conflict. Arms and other supplies thus became harder to acquire than the rebels had anticipated.

Yet as the fighting continued, with neither side nearing victory, Cleveland and Richard Olney let Madrid know that the United States wouldn't allow the blood-letting to continue forever. Olney summarized the administration's position in April 1896: "That the United States cannot contemplate with complacency another ten years of Cuban insurrection, with all its injurious and distressing incidents, may certainly be taken for granted." The following December, Cleveland warned the Spanish: "The spectacle of the utter ruin of an adjoining country, by nature one of the most fertile and charming on the globe, would engage the serious attention of the Government and people of the United States in any circumstances." The president added meaningfully, "The United States is not a nation to which peace is a necessity."

But by this time Cleveland was a lame duck, and Madrid knew it needn't worry overly much about his remonstrances. The question of real concern was the attitude of the incoming McKinley administration. On the face of things, this attitude didn't appear promising to Spain. Since the beginning of the 1890s, the loudest and most belligerent voices calling for American expansion overseas and American intervention in other people's quarrels had come from McKinley's party—from the likes of Roosevelt and Lodge. McKinley didn't appear to be such a bellicose type, but he couldn't help being influenced by those Republicans who were. Already the influence of the expansionists was making itself felt on the president-elect, who was being pressured to give Roosevelt and his aggressive associates important posts in the new administration. McKinley had reservations about Roosevelt. "I am afraid he is too pugnacious," the president-elect remarked to a visitor who was plumping for Roosevelt. "I want peace, and I am told that your friend Theodore is always getting into rows with everybody." Yet McKinley allowed himself to be persuaded, evidently believing that it was better to have Roosevelt on the inside throwing bricks out than on the outside throwing bricks in.

At first the belligerent influence of the expansionists was offset by caution in another important wing of the Republican Party: big business. Partly as a matter of good fortune, partly because economic cycles always run their course eventually, and partly from the reassuring effect of Bryan's defeat in the 1896 election, the American economy started climbing out of its depression about the time of McKinley's inauguration. The recovery wasn't especially robust, however, and investors remained skittish. The last thing they wanted was a war, which would probably send the American currency into another round of gyrations and cause investors to pull back once again.

McKinley wanted peace, as he said, and initially he was content to be guided by the more cautious elements of his party and administration. The new president assured Carl Schurz, a member of the Republican Party's anti-imperialist wing, that there would be "no jingo nonsense in my administration." McKinley's first secretary of state, John Sherman, was old and ailing and not eager to embark on any foreign adventures either. (McKinley tapped Sherman for the top diplomatic job as a reward for long and faithful service to the Republican Party—and also to open a place in the Senate for Mark Hanna.)

Unfortunately, the troubles in Cuba didn't diminish from being ignored by the American government. On the contrary, the fighting grew worse. And with each flare-up, the danger of the United States being drawn in became greater. Americans owned much property on the island, from sugar plantations to commercial buildings and homes. This property, and in some cases the Americans themselves, got caught in the crossfire between the nationalist rebels, on one hand, and the Spanish and the Cuban loyalists, on the other. The Spanish and the loyalists resented the advice the American government directed toward Madrid; they felt the Americans had no business meddling in an internal affair of the Spanish empire. When this resentment reached a critical level, it flashed into violence against American holdings.

The nationalists had reasons of their own for striking at American property. Some of the nationalists thought the United States was being hypocritical in not supporting Cuba's claims to self-determination. Didn't the natural rights proclaimed in the American Declaration of Independence apply to Cubans as well as to North Americans? In the confusion of battle, it was tempting to take out one's frustration at Washington's inaction by torching an American canefield. More to the point, the nationalists could see that attacks on American lives and property, if blamable on the Spanish and the loyalists (and the American newspapers were obviously willing to blame just about anything on those villains), might well be the straw that broke the back of American reluctance to intervene. If the Americans intervened, the war was as good as won.

Precisely such attacks, of undetermined origin, moved McKinley to dispatch a special envoy to Cuba in the spring of 1897. William Calhoun toured the war zone and returned to Washington in June to render his report. "The island is one of the most unhappy and most distressed places on the earth," Calhoun declared. "I traveled by rail from Havana to Matanzas. The country outside the military posts was practically depopulated. Every house had been burned, banana trees cut down, cane fields swept with fire, and everything in the shape of food destroyed. It was as fair a landscape as mortal eye ever looked upon, but I did not see a house, man, woman or child, a horse, mule, or cow, nor even a dog. I did not see a sign of life, except an occasional buzzard sailing through the air. The country was wrapped in the stillness of death and the silence of desolation."

Calhoun predicted no early end to the fighting. He said that Cuba had been "the football of Spanish politics" for too long for Madrid to accept any reasonable compromise with the nationalists. For their part, the nationalists had made too many sacrifices to stop short of full independence. The Spanish had succeeded in suppressing the rebellion in some provinces, but their success was illusory. Calhoun compared the rebellion to a "smoldering fire" and said that "the moment there is any relaxation of the attempt to suppress it, the flames will break out again with renewed fury."

McKinley responded to Calhoun's report with a public condemnation of Spanish policy in Cuba. The president explained that he was forced to protest "in the name of the American people and in the name of common humanity" against "the cruel employment of fire and famine to accomplish by uncertain indirection what the military arm seems powerless to directly accomplish." McKinley asserted that Americans had the right "to demand that a war, conducted almost within sight of our shores and grievously affecting American citizens and their interests throughout the length and breadth of the land, shall at least be conducted according to the military codes of civilization."

The Spanish government took its time replying to McKinley's statement. Part of the delay was the result of turmoil in Madrid: early in August 1897 the prime minister, Antonio Canovas del Castillo, was assassinated. Reorganizing the cabinet required some weeks. It also afforded a glimmer of hope of a peaceful settlement in Cuba, since Canovas's replacement was bound to be more liberal than that tough old reactionary. In fact, the new government was indeed more liberal than Canovas's, but the realities of Spanish politics were such that no government enjoyed much room for maneuver on Cuba. Madrid told Washington it reserved to itself the right to determine appropriate means for dealing with the insurrection. If the rebels wanted peace, all they had to do was lay down their arms. The United States should mind its own business.

Yet this wasn't Madrid's last word. In October, the Spanish government announced the recall of General Weyler and pledged to move toward a degree of autonomy for Cuba within the Spanish empire. In November, the government promised to terminate the policy of *reconcentrado*.

Unfortunately for the Cuban nationalists and for smooth Spanish-American relations, pledging reforms proved easier for Madrid than implementing them. When the Spanish government got around to supplying the details of its autonomy plan, the arrangement turned out to be largely a smokescreen for continued rule from Madrid. It didn't satisfy the nationalists, and it didn't satisfy the McKinley administration.

In his December 1897 message to Congress, McKinley again declared that the United States had a compelling interest in the affairs of Cuba. He also stated that time was running out on American forbearance. "The near future," the president said, "will demonstrate whether the indispensable condition of a righteous peace, just alike to the Cubans and to Spain as well as equitable to all our interests so intimately involved in the welfare of Cuba, is likely to be attained. If not, the exigency of further and other action by the United States will remain." Precisely what other action the United States would take, McKinley wasn't saying. That would be determined "in the light of the obligation this Government owes to itself, to the people who have confided to it the protection of their interests and honor, and to humanity."

Events soon conspired to force McKinley's hand. In January 1898, Madrid's minister in Washington, Enrique Dupuy de Lome, wrote a letter to a Spanish friend in Cuba. De Lome meant for the letter to be confidential, and in it he unburdened himself of his annoyance at the American government. He characterized McKinley as "weak and a bidder for the admiration of the crowd, besides being a would-be politician who tries to leave a door open behind himself while keeping on good terms with the jingoes of his party." Elsewhere in his letter, de Lome indicated that Spain's seeming concessions to the Cuban nationalists were designed principally to appease the Americans and weren't meant to accomplish genuine reform.

Neither this admission—which was hardly news—nor de Lome's comments about McKinley would have been especially inflammatory had the author not been the representative of the Spanish government to the United States. American critics of McKinley said far worse about the president every day. But diplomats get paid to be more discreet. A rebel sympathizer on the staff of the intended recipient of the letter noticed the return address as de Lome's and decided to open the envelope to see what interesting tidbits it contained. Realizing what a stir the letter would produce if published, the sympathizer turned the letter over to the Cuban nationalist propaganda office in New York. The nationalists clapped their hands in glee at their good luck, with one calling the letter "a great thing for us." From the propaganda office, its contents quickly found their way into the *New York Journal.*

William Randolph Hearst's paper made full use of its scoop. "Worst Insult to the United States in Its History!" the headline blared, above the text of de Lome's letter. Joseph Pulitzer's *World* and other papers picked up the hue and cry. One wit set his outrage to verse:

Dupuy de Lome, Dupuy de Lome, what's this I hear of you?
Have you been throwing mud again, is what they're saying true?
Get out, I say, get out before I start to fight.
Just pack your few possessions and take a boat for home.
I would not like my boot to use, but—oh—get out, de Lome.

De Lome had to resign. Yet the resignation did little to stem the surge of outrage in the United States against Spain. At the same time it made the troubles between Madrid and Washington even harder to resolve, since it left the Spanish government without top-level representation in the United States at a crucial moment in relations between the two countries. Richard Olney, now a former secretary of state, shook his head thinking of de Lome's faux pas. "Poor Dupuy must realize how much worse a blunder can be than a crime," Olney wrote Cleveland. "Here is his country practically unrepresented at Washington at a time when its interests demand a *persona grata* at our capital more imperatively than ever before."

The Spanish government eventually apologized for de Lome's forthrightness, but before it did, another and far more serious provocation developed between the two countries. Since the time when the violence in Cuba had begun to touch American property and threaten American lives, the American consul-general in Havana, Fitzhugh Lee, had periodically requested that Washington send a warship to Cuba in case Americans needed to be evacuated swiftly. As an ardent interventionist, Lee also calculated that a show of American naval power might knock some sense into the Spanish. McKinley had held off at first, but in January 1898 the president gave his approval. The Navy Department—where Roosevelt, who told his sister that "I am a quietly rampant 'Cuba Libre' man," was busy preparing for war— decided to dispatch the *Maine*, one of America's newer mid-sized battleships. The administration requested permission from the Spanish authorities to send the vessel to Havana and invited Spain to reciprocate by sending Spanish ships to visit American harbors. Perhaps the exchanges would help diminish tensions, Washington suggested. Spain agreed to allow the American ship to enter the harbor at Havana, although it did so without enthusiasm. Some Cuban loyalists resented the American intrusion, but their complaints were overruled.

When the *Maine* arrived, Consul Lee called it "a beautiful sight and one long to be remembered." Lee added that the presence of the battleship "greatly relieved" the minds of the Americans in Cuba. The official reception given the ship and its crew by the Spanish officials in Cuba was cordial, and most of the people of the city were pleasant enough. For a time the ship's presence seemed to have a calming effect. The Americans in the Havana area, knowing they had a safe ride out of the country if things got really sticky, had less incentive to demand American intervention.

But on the evening of February 15 a great tragedy—and perhaps a great crime—occurred. A thunderous blast tore through the *Maine*, killing nearly the entire the crew; 266 died in all. The 7,000-ton ship sank within minutes to the bottom of Havana harbor. Only the top of its charred and tangled superstructure protruded from the suddenly oily waters of the bay.

Although no one could tell at the time just what had caused the explosion and all the deaths, the pro-war faction in the United States was quick to pin the blame on the Spanish and the Cuban loyalists. A *New York Journal* headline declared, "The Warship Maine Was Split in Two by an Ene-

my's Infernal Machine!" The Hearst paper added, "The Maine Was Destroyed by Treachery!" The *Journal* printed diagrams showing where the
mine that allegedly sank the ship must have been placed and it offered a
reward of $50,000 for information leading to the identification of those
individuals responsible. (Shortly thereafter, the *Journal*'s one-day circulation topped the one million mark.) Ever competitive, Pulitzer's *World* tried
to send divers to Havana to examine the wreckage. The ploy failed (but
not before boosting the *World*'s circulation to a record of more than 5
million in one week). Smaller papers joined the chorus. The *New Orleans
Times-Democrat* warned McKinley to get moving or get out of the way.
"Mr. McKinley may not have sufficient backbone even to resent an offense
so gross as this, but war in this country is declared by Congress, and no
explanation of the Spanish Government, no offer to make reparation, could
prevent a declaration of war."

McKinley still resisted taking the final step, although he did move closer
to war. The president ordered an inquiry into the causes of the disaster;
simultaneously he underlined his displeasure at this recent turn of events—
and protected himself against a new round of criticism from the war hawks
in the United States—by asking Congress to approve a $50 million package
of war preparations. Congress passed the bill almost at once, to the satisfaction of an increasing portion of the American public.

The passage of the bill flabbergasted the Spanish. "The Ministry and
press are simply stunned," reported the American minister in Madrid. As
had the British government in the case of the Venezuela dispute, the Spanish
had underestimated the seriousness with which the American people and
the American government viewed the current troubles. The Spanish tended
to look on the war fever in America as a matter of domestic politics that
would dissipate as soon as the Americans found another outlet for their
aggressiveness. But when Washington with hardly a second thought voted
$50 million to get ready for war, the Spanish had to believe that the Amer-
icans meant business.

At the end of March 1898, the president's commission of inquiry on the
Maine explosion delivered its report. The commission couldn't identify who
had been responsible for the disaster, but it asserted definitely that
something external to the ship had caused the explosion. In other words,
someone had deliberately destroyed the vessel. (Two subsequent investigations split on the same question. A 1911 inquiry agreed with the 1898
commission that the explosion had been external; a 1976 study thought
the evidence indicated an internal explosion, perhaps caused by coal dust
in a fuel bunker.)

The commission's report increased the momentum toward war. A large
segment of the American public now felt that intervention was necessary;
diplomacy would no longer do. "The people want no disgraceful negotiations with Spain," the *Chicago Tribune* insisted with only modest exag-
geration. "Should the president plunge his administration into that morass,
he and his party would be swept out of power in 1900 by a fine burst of

popular indignation. An administration which stains the national honor will never be forgiven."

Even much of that portion of American opinion that wasn't demanding war was no longer strongly opposing it. American business leaders who previously had feared that war would stifle the economic recovery now began to think that chronic uncertainty regarding the situation in Cuba might be the greater danger. Perhaps it would be better to go in and get the fighting over with.

McKinley himself, who heretofore had hoped to resolve the issue peacefully, likewise was coming to the conclusion that there was no reasonable way to avoid war. The Cuban nationalists appeared determined to keep fighting as long as necessary to drive the Spanish out. The Spanish appeared unwilling or unable to concede defeat. The American minister in Madrid explained that government officials there considered their stand on Cuba vital to the survival of the Spanish regime. "They prefer the chance of war, with the certain loss of Cuba, to the overthrow of the dynasty," he said.

McKinley moved still closer to war when Senator Redfield Proctor of Vermont, a personal friend and formerly an opponent of American intervention in Cuba, returned from a visit to Cuba with grim news. Conditions in the reconcentration camps, he stated, were absolutely horrifying. "Torn from their homes, with foul earth, foul air, foul water, and foul food or none, what wonder that one-half died and that one-quarter of the living are so diseased that they cannot be saved?" Proctor described children with "arms and chest terribly emaciated, eyes swollen, and abdomen bloated to three times the natural size." He added, "I have been told by one of our consuls that they have been found dead about the markets in the morning, where they had crawled, hoping to get some stray bits of food from the early hucksters." Proctor explained how his heart had gone out to "the entire native population of Cuba, struggling for freedom and deliverance from the worst misgovernment of which I ever had knowledge."

Proctor's account pushed many waverers into the war camp. The *Wall Street Journal* declared that the Vermont senator's description of circumstances in Cuba "made the blood boil." The financial paper went on to assert that the report had "converted a great many people in Wall Street." The *Literary Digest* offered its opinion that American intervention was "the plain duty of the United States on the simple ground of humanity."

On March 27, McKinley sent Madrid what amounted to an ultimatum. Spain must agree to an armistice with the Cuban rebels; it must begin negotiations toward a peace treaty; it must accept American arbitration of the conflict if a settlement did not take place within six months; it must definitively end the *reconcentrado* policy; and it must provide relief assistance to the Cuban people. In light of the fact that the rebels were demanding that the Spanish clear out of Cuba and showed no sign of dropping this demand, McKinley's ultimatum implied that Spain must accept independence.

Even if Spain had been disposed to negotiate with the Cuban nationalists, the effrontery of the Americans in delivering such an ultimatum made it nearly impossible for the Spanish government to do so now. Madrid offered to provide relief to Cuba, to terminate *reconcentrado*, and to grant an armistice, providing the rebels asked for one. But it would never accept American arbitration, and it wouldn't grant independence. Several days after delivering this response, the Spanish government modified its position somewhat, consenting to a unilateral suspension of military operations in Cuba.

Madrid's answer didn't satisfy McKinley, and on April 11, McKinley sent a war message to Congress. "The long trial has proved that the object for which Spain has waged the war cannot be attained," the president asserted. "The fire of insurrection may flame or may smolder with varying seasons, but it has not been and it is plain that it cannot be extinguished by present methods. The only hope of relief and repose from a condition which can no longer be endured is the enforced pacification of Cuba. In the name of humanity, in the name of civilization, in behalf of endangered American interests which give us the right and the duty to speak and to act, the war in Cuba must stop." McKinley went on to describe the "very serious injury to the commerce, trade, and business of our people, and the wanton destruction of property" caused by the hostilities in Cuba. The sinking of the *Maine* and the death of its men demonstrated that those hostilities were a "constant menace" to the peace of the hemisphere. The president requested that Congress grant him authority to use American military forces to end the war in Cuba.

Some members of Congress were eager to do more than the president desired. A group of senators pushed a resolution calling on the administration to extend diplomatic recognition to the Cuban rebels. McKinley rejected this idea. The president was pleased at the thought of driving Spain out of Cuba, but he wasn't sure he wanted to commit the United States to backing a government put up by the rebels. There would be time to talk about such things after the Spanish were removed. The administration's allies on Capitol Hill succeeded in sidetracking the recognition resolution.

An amendment to the war measure, renouncing American interest in annexing Cuba, fared better. The amendment was the brainchild of Senator Teller of Colorado, the silver Republican leader from the 1896 election. Teller worried that American imperialistic types might be using the cover of humanitarianism to capture Cuba, and he decided to call their bluff. His amendment declared that "the United States hereby disclaims any disposition or intention to exercise sovereignty, jurisdiction, or control over said island, except for the pacification thereof, and asserts its determination when that is accomplished to leave the government and control of the island to its people." Some of the interventionists grumbled at Teller's maneuver, but they couldn't well oppose the amendment without looking like opportunists out to benefit from Cuba's distress. The amendment passed, effectively guaranteeing at least nominal Cuban independence in the likely event American intervention succeeded in ejecting the Spanish from the island.

Thus amended, the war resolution was approved by Congress on April 19. It proclaimed Cuban independence, demanded the withdrawal of Spanish troops, and authorized the president to accomplish these results by force if necessary. The Spanish government responded two days later by severing diplomatic relations with the United States. When American ships began blockading Cuba, Spain declared war. Three days after this, Congress responded with a war declaration of its own, backdated to the day Spain cut diplomatic ties.

Americans greeted the war declaration with general applause. Rabid pro-war voices shouted in triumph. "We are all jingoes now," ranted the *New York Sun*. "And the head jingo is the Hon. William McKinley, the trusted and honored Chief Executive of the nation's will." Theodore Roosevelt thrilled at the opportunity, as he phrased it, to "put Spain out of the western hemisphere." And though he was an expansionist, Roosevelt wasn't wholly displeased at the Teller amendment. "I should be very doubtful about annexing Cuba in any event, and should most emphatically oppose it unless the Cubans wished it," he explained. "I don't want it to seem that we are engaged merely in a land-grabbing war."

Other voices stressed the humanitarian aspect of American intervention. Indiana Republican and war hawk Albert Beveridge saw American military power as the agent of moral uplift. "At last, God's hour has struck," proclaimed Beveridge, the most insufferably righteous member of the imperialist camp in Congress. "The American people go forth in a warfare holier than liberty—holy as humanity." Lyman Abbott, the noted pastor of Brooklyn's Plymouth Church, sermonized that American intervention in Cuba was the currently appropriate answer to the ever-compelling central question of social ethics: Am I my brother's keeper? George Hoar, an anti-imperialist Republican senator from Massachusetts, said he had expected that the United States would play the role of peacemaker among nations. But circumstances in Cuba were forcing a change of his mind. "We cannot look idly on while hundreds of thousands of innocent human beings, women and children and old men, die of hunger close to our doors. If ever there is to be a war, it should be to prevent such things as that." Hoar said he would do everything in his power to help President McKinley get Spain out of Cuba by peaceful means, even now. Yet if peaceful means didn't suffice, military force was the only answer. "If guns and ships of war are ever to be used, they are to be used on such an occasion."

VI

Americans grew only more enthusiastic as the actual fighting neared. Rallies across the country summoned patriots to the flag; parades gave volunteers a rousing sendoff. Bands blasted their martial tunes, stirring the blood of even those required to remain at home. Contributions to the war effort poured in from all sides. Tens of thousands of young men from every region hurried to enlist, afraid chiefly that the fighting might end before they had a chance to put a bullet or a bayonet through a Spaniard. Famous men stepped forward to accept commissions. William Jennings Bryan headed a regiment of Nebraska volunteers—which, as the Democratic leader explained, was "deservedly called the Silver Battalion because so many of my personal friends are in the ranks." Roosevelt helped organize a cavalry unit called the Rough Riders. The Wall Street community put together an outfit of financier-soldiers. Heiress Helen Gould made up for some of her late husband Jay's shady transactions by donating her yacht and $100,000 to the cause. The Astor family supplied a regiment with equipment and pay.

Orators, politicians, preachers, and other benders of the public ear voiced support for the glorious humanitarian venture upon which the nation was embarked. Most Americans agreed with Senator Hoar that if an appropriate occasion for the use of military power ever existed, this was it. Americans were using their strength to succor the afflicted and chastise malefactors. Even more than in most cases, Americans believed that God rode on their side into battle.

An additional element, often unspoken, motivated the rush to the colors and the overall zest for war. With the exception of frontier skirmishes against the American Indians, America hadn't known war for over thirty years—long enough for the searing reality of war to fade from memory, covered over by a heroic haze, and long enough for a new generation of young men to grow up eager to prove their manhood in this age-old rite of passage. For thirty years these young men had heard their fathers and grandfathers tell tales of service with Grant and Lee, implying or stating outright that kids these days had life too easy. The stories got pretty boring after a while; now the youngsters had a chance to earn bragging rights of their own.

A second result of the long stretch between wars was that the U.S. Army was woefully unprepared to fight. In keeping with the American tradition of defenses manned by ordinary citizens rather than professional soldiers, the Union army had largely disbanded after the Civil War and Reconstruction. Fighting the Indians had required only small numbers of troops, and neither Congress nor the public was inclined to spend the money that maintaining a big army demanded. The few officers who stayed in the army had no experience leading large groups of men, and the troops had no experience of conventional combat. To confound the situation still more, the army's quartermasters hadn't the vaguest notion what supplying an army of almost a quarter-million green recruits would entail. There weren't enough uniforms to go around, and those that did exist were of a motley variety of styles and colors. Rifles were similarly scarce, so that new enlistees had to train with wooden replicas. At a time when even the Spanish—so disdained by their American opponents—used modern smokeless powder in their weapons, American soldiers still relied on black powder, which gave away the firing position of each rifleman.

Despite the handicaps, the War Department at once set to its task of fielding an army, transporting it to Cuba, and defeating the Spanish. The day after he ordered the blockade of Cuba, McKinley issued a request for 125,000 volunteers. The department tried, in the way bureaucrats do, to take advantage of the emergency to enlarge its domain and fatten its budget: it proposed pulling most of these volunteers into the permanent ranks of the regular army. Congress disliked this proposal, as did advocates of the state national guards. But the department got much of what it wanted, including congressional authorization for a regular army of 65,000 men. This would be bolstered by short-term volunteers who eventually numbered 200,000.

Staffing the officer corps of the suddenly enlarged army proved to be a major problem. Partly because there hadn't been a war in so long, partly because the war against Spain promised to be an easy and relatively safe victory, and partly from principled patriotism, would-be Grants and Lees lined up at McKinley's doorstep seeking commissions. His own Civil War experience—he was the last Civil War veteran to hold the presidency—clued McKinley to the troubles political officers could cause. For the most part he deflected the applicants, and he succeeded in keeping the majority of the responsible positions in the hands of professional officers: of his twenty-six promotions to the rank of major general, nineteen were regular army men.

Yet McKinley was too astute a politician to leave war entirely to the real generals. The sectional nature of the vote in the 1896 presidential election had demonstrated that deep suspicions still separated the South from the North—besides demonstrating the weakness of the Republican Party in the South. With the continued spread of the Jim Crow system and the disfranchisement of African-American voters, the party would only grow weaker in the South. McKinley attempted to throw a line across the rift between North and South and to reverse the decline of the Republican Party in the former Confederacy by conspicuously including Southerners in his search for leadership of the Cuba-bound army. "There must be a high-ranking officer from the South," the president explained. "There must be a symbol that the old days are gone." Among his first appointments was Congressman and ex-Confederate Joseph Wheeler—"Fighting Joe" Wheeler of Alabama.

Appointing officers was only the beginning of the McKinley administration's difficulties preparing for war. Contracts had to be awarded for weapons, uniforms, food, medical supplies, and a thousand other items. The Republican Party's record on this sort of thing showed greater concern for private profits than for efficiency, and companies and individuals pushed and shoved to get in on the spoils of war. It didn't help matters that the secretary of war, Russell Alger, had received his appointment as a political payoff for helping deliver the vote of his home state of Michigan to Mc-Kinley in 1896. Alger blew hot and cold about the idea of actually going to war against Spain. Later, after the war ended in victory and all could joke about it, McKinley teased Alger: "I do remember that you had your war days and your anti-war days." Damn-the-torpedoes types like Henry Cabot Lodge agitated for Alger's removal, believing that the army could never be the instrument of a really vigorous foreign policy so long as it remained in the hands of such fuddy-duddy hacks. But McKinley's sense of loyalty caused him to stick by Alger through the war. Besides, it would be an admission of weakness and confusion for McKinley to fire his war secretary just when a war secretary was needed most.

Partly from Alger's failure of oversight, partly from the greed of wartime profiteers, and partly from the hurry with which America went to war in 1898, numerous scandals developed around the provisioning of the troops. The most notorious involved "embalmed beef." American soldiers in the war against Spain were among the first in history to enjoy the luxury of refrigerated meat, which arrived at field camps in almost as good condition as meat arrived at their local butcher shops back home. Previously armies had lived off meat on the hoof, or on canned meat. Driving herds of cattle to where the soldiers were located was a hit-or-miss affair, and canned meat was usually a culinary abomination. Compared to armies in previous wars, American soldiers in the war against Spain lived high on the hog—and cow.

Not all of them, though. The army couldn't ship enough refrigerated meat to feed all the soldiers, and in some locales refrigeration proved impossible. After becoming accustomed to chilled meat in the training camps, soldiers often had to rely on canned meat, usually beef, in the field. Conditions on the battlefield commonly required soldiers to eat the stuff straight from the can, and the canned beef soon became the focus of some of the soldiers' most serious grumbling. Moreover, at a time when the meat-packing industry was on the verge of being a national disgrace—Upton Sinclair's 1906 exposé, *The Jungle*, would make vegetarians out of millions, at least temporarily—packers passed off on the army more than a few lots that would have turned the stomachs of Genghis Khan's troops. Hungry soldiers opened their tins of beef to discover knots of gristle, hunks of rope, and mummified maggots.

Yet, curiously, it was some of the refrigerated beef that caused the greatest uproar. General Nelson Miles, the officer in charge of such matters, heard innumerable complaints about the canned beef and decided to investigate. He directed regimental commanders to submit reports evaluating the rations their men had received, focusing specifically on the canned beef.

As these reports came in, Miles also received a report on the refrigerated meat from a volunteer surgeon on his staff, William Daly, a Pittsburgh doctor. Daly said that in various inspection tours he had encountered refrigerated beef that tasted of boric acid and salicylic acid, chemicals sometimes injected by unprincipled packers into meat to preserve it.

Daly's report became the basis for charges by Miles against army suppliers—and against some of his rivals in the War Department. Miles's charges in turn became the basis for a spate of stomach-churning headlines in the popular press. "Poisons Used in Beef Made the Soldiers Ill," shouted Hearst's *Journal*; "Tons of Bad Meat Sent to Troops in Puerto Rico." The commissary-general of the army, Charles Eagan, vehemently denied the allegations, calling them a "scandalous libel" and branding Miles a "liar." Eagan went on to say, "I wish to force the lie back into his throat, covered with the contents of a camp latrine. I wish to brand it as a falsehood of whole cloth, without a particle of truth to sustain it; and unless he can prove his statement he should be denounced by every honest man, barred from the clubs, barred from the society of decent people, and so ostracized that the street bootblacks would not condescend to speak to him, for he fouled his own nest; he has aspersed the honor of a brother officer without a particle of evidence or fact to sustain in any degree his scandalous, libelous, malicious falsehood." For added emphasis, as if any were necessary, Eagan asserted that Miles had "as black a heart as the man who blew up the *Maine* possessed."

Needless to say, this kind of characterization of his boss—which, though expunged from the official record of the investigation of the affair, was soon retold by reporters present—didn't do anything positive for Eagan's career in the army. The commissary-general was court-martialed on charges of conduct unbecoming an officer and prejudicial to good order and discipline, and convicted. Though McKinley intervened to keep Eagan from being drummed out of the service, his career was finished.

What was ironic about the whole flap was that the investigating commission, after gathering evidence and hearing further testimony, declared that Eagan was right, in substance if not in the particulars of his characterization of Miles. The commission found that Miles "had no sufficient justification for alleging that the refrigerated beef was embalmed or was unfit for issue to troops." This verdict struck many observers as a typical case of the War Department closing ranks against critics, for by the time the judgment was delivered, Miles was at odds with War Secretary Alger over a whole variety of matters. It seemed to some that Miles lost not on the merits of his argument—or the quality of the beef—but because of the greater political weight of his antagonist. To complete the complicated picture, McKinley refused to fire Miles, as Alger demanded, thereby antagonizing the war secretary.

One reason for all the backbiting in the army and the War Department was a recognition by the two bureaucracies of their abysmal failure to maintain safe standards of hygiene in the training camps. This was the real scandal of the war, compared to which the "embalmed beef" brouhaha was trivial. The lack of hygiene gave rise to epidemics of yellow fever, typhoid, and malaria that scourged American soldiers, killing far more than died in battle. To some degree, the epidemics resulted from the inadequate state of medical knowledge at the time. The staff of the army medical department, despite including some of the best physicians in the country and being directed by George Sternberg, one of America's most distinguished research scientists, frequently mistook malaria for yellow fever, and typhoid for malaria. As a result, by the time the doctors recognized what they were up against, their preventive measures were often too late. Moreover, neither they nor anyone else during the 1890s knew with assurance or in detail how these diseases were spread. Malaria was attributed to bad air released when latrine trenches were dug. Typhoid was correctly associated with contaminated water, but the persistence of the typhoid organism and its contagiousness were significantly underestimated. Largely overlooked was the role of mosquitoes in transmitting yellow fever and malaria.

Yet much of the sickness that afflicted American soldiers resulted from bureaucratic bungling. Medical officers in the army were commonly regarded with disdain as quacks who wanted to undermine the spirit of the army by coddling the troops. The army's commanders typically prided themselves on ignoring the advice of their medical officers. At the outset of the war, when both military pride and political considerations required that soldiers be landed in Cuba as quickly as possible, the requisition orders placed by the medical department usually got short shrift. When equipment for sanitation had to compete for War Department dollars with rifles and bullets, the rifles and bullets won out.

Overestimates of the number of soldiers required to defeat the Spanish likewise contributed to the outbreak of disease. Of the more than 200,000 volunteers ultimately requested by the president for service, fewer than one out of six made it into combat. The rest spent the late spring and summer of 1898 in training camps in Florida and elsewhere across the South. The hot weather in that region added to overcrowding to produce horribly unhealthy conditions. Troops lacked shovels to dig latrines, disinfectants to control germs, kettles to boil water. A fundamental principle of troop deployment had always been that soldiers should be spread out in order to minimize the hazard of infection, but the recruits in Florida were crammed together cheek by jowl. As a result, camp kitchens and hospitals were located within yards of latrines and garbage pits. Poor drainage—a Florida trademark—turned the camps into quagmires when it rained.

Conditions were even grimmer among the troops that got to Cuba. Hardest hit was the Fifth Corps, which suffered shocking rates of sickness and death. For weeks after their hurried arrival in Cuba in June, many of the troops of the Fifth Corps went without such basic items as tents and cooking gear. They marched into battle in heavy wool uniforms because the army didn't have enough summer gear to go around. Before a month passed, dysentery, yellow fever, and malaria were rampant in the ranks. By the end of July, the American field hospitals were packed with sick soldiers. So high was the death rate that the commander of the Fifth Corps felt obliged to dispense with the customary rifle volleys at burials lest the incessant reminders of their mortality demoralize the rest of the troops. And only the worst of the diseased were admitted to the hospitals; many more suffered outside, usually from malaria. Unable to digest their food and wracked by diarrhea, the victims grew weaker and more gaunt by the day. The disease didn't spare the buglers any more than it spared anyone else, and as the musicians sickened, the notes that blew over the camps sounded, to the ears of one New York volunteer, like "the ghastly echo of a thinning and dying army corps."

The statistics told the sad story. More than 2,500 American officers and men died of yellow fever, typhoid, malaria, dysentery, and other diseases during the period of the war. This was over ten times the number that died of wounds in battle.

VII

Yet for all the preventable and unpreventable disease and death, Americans could still look on the conflict against Spain as a "splendid little war," in John Hay's assessment. The war produced heroes as well as casualties. The first hero and the greatest one to emerge from the war made his name in a location that surprised most Americans. Ever since the undeclared naval war against France of 1798–1800, the front line of American defense had been the wooden wall of its navy. By the 1890s the wall had become mostly steel, and steam had replaced wind in providing propulsion. Congress hadn't exactly lavished money on the navy, but the admirals—with the help of Captain Mahan—had done far better than the generals in getting what they needed to make the United States a military power to be reckoned with. Compared to their qualms about a standing army, Americans registered few fears about a powerful peacetime navy, both because a navy was more obviously necessary to protect American overseas trade and because no one had ever heard of an admiral sailing his flagship up the steps of a national palace or parliament in an effort to seize the government, the way generals had been known to do with their horses.

It helped the navy get ready for the war that Theodore Roosevelt was assistant navy secretary. As McKinley had dithered over whether to intervene in Cuba, Roosevelt grew increasingly impatient with the president. Roosevelt never suspected that others might be privy to wisdom not imparted to him, and he fumed to friends that McKinley had "no more backbone than a chocolate eclair." He branded McKinley's diffidence "derelict," and in a letter to Mahan he muttered, "I can hardly see how we can avoid intervening in Cuba if we are to retain our self-respect as a nation." While stamping his foot about the president—and shaking his fist at Mark Hanna, as he did at a March 26 dinner where, looking at McKinley's friend and adviser, he vowed, "We will have this war for the freedom of Cuba, in spite of the timidity of the commercial interests"—Roosevelt did what he could to prepare the navy.

It wasn't easy, since he didn't enjoy the entire confidence of his immediate superior, John D. Long, the secretary of the navy. Long had had reservations about Roosevelt similar to McKinley's; he feared that if appointed, the young man would soon be trying to run the whole Navy Department, if not the whole country. But Roosevelt dearly wanted to work in the department, and through an intermediary he passed assurances to Long of complete cooperation. "I shall stay at Washington, hot weather or any other weather, whenever he wants me to stay there, and go wherever he sends me," Roosevelt promised. "My aim should be solely to make his administration a success."

Yet once Roosevelt got the job of assistant secretary, Long found it difficult to restrain him. In public most of his statements reflected the president's and navy secretary's line, but his voluminous personal correspondence showed a decidedly more militant approach. And because Roosevelt's correspondents included many influential people, his letters amounted to a concerted campaign to push the United States into war. In November 1897, Roosevelt explained his thoughts to a well-placed friend in the navy. "I would regard a war with Spain from two viewpoints," Roosevelt said: "first, the advisability on the ground both of humanity and self-interest of interfering on behalf of the Cubans, and of taking one more step toward the complete freeing of America from European domination; second, the benefit done to our people by giving them something to think of which isn't material gain, and especially the benefit done our military forces by trying both the Army and Navy in actual practice." Roosevelt thought a war with Spain would be quite instructive, and he said he would be "very sorry not to see us make the experiment."

Roosevelt's desire for war intensified during the first months of 1898. When the *Maine* went down at Havana, he immediately labeled the disaster "an act of dirty treachery on the part of the Spaniards," and said he "would give anything if President McKinley would order the fleet to Havana to-morrow." Though McKinley wasn't ready to go that far yet, Roosevelt guessed he would soon, and the assistant secretary laid plans to make the most of the opportunity. Ten days after the *Maine* explosion, Secretary Long decided to take an afternoon off from work. Conditions at the Navy Department had been frantic, what with investigating the tragedy and fielding requests for information from senators and representatives, from the press, and from the public. The confusion was calming down somewhat by February 25, and Long thought he could afford a few hours away from his desk.

This was just the chance Roosevelt had been waiting for. It so happened—probably not by accident—that Roosevelt's friend and fellow expansionist Henry Cabot Lodge dropped by the Navy Department that

Friday afternoon when Roosevelt was in charge. The Massachusetts senator cheered Roosevelt on as the latter set about charting American strategy for the looming war, ordering this squadron in one direction, that squadron in another direction, a third squadron somewhere else. Roosevelt's actions stunned Long when the secretary returned to the office the next morning. "I find that Roosevelt, in his precipitate way, has come very near causing more of an explosion than happened to the *Maine*," Long declared. "The very devil seemed to possess him yesterday afternoon." Long added, "He has gone at things like a bull in a china shop."

What Roosevelt had done was to arrange for the optimal placement of American ships in the Atlantic and Pacific, to requisition ammunition (which the navy lacked vessels to transport or warehouses to store), to ask Congress to begin drawing up legislation allowing the navy to enlist an unlimited number of seamen, and generally to clear the navy's decks for action against Spain.

The most portentous of Roosevelt's actions that afternoon was to send a telegram to Commodore George Dewey, the commander of the American Asiatic squadron.

> Dewey, Hong Kong:
>   Secret and confidential. Order the squadron except *Monocacy* to Hong Kong. Keep full of coal. In the event of declaration of war Spain, your duty will be to see that the Spanish squadron does not leave the Asiatic coast, and then offensive operations in Philippine Islands. Keep *Olympia* until further orders.
>
> Roosevelt

Long could have rescinded Roosevelt's directive to Dewey when the secretary returned to work, but he didn't. There wasn't any reason to; the order was entirely logical. Though Cuba would be the cause of the war, the war itself would be against Spain, and American forces shouldn't be obliged to confine their anti-Spanish efforts to Cuba. Even before the explosion of the *Maine*, Roosevelt had suggested an attack on Spain proper. An American "flying squadron," according to this scenario, would enter Spanish waters at night and attack Cádiz. The point would be to keep the Spanish busy and worried at home, thereby preventing the dispatch of reinforcements to Cuba.

The same reasoning applied to the Philippines but with an additional twist. Roosevelt and other expansionists saw the Philippines as a likely target of American expansion. The Philippine archipelago was comparatively lightly populated. Filipino nationalists recently had revolted against Spanish colonial rule, but the revolt had fizzled; they seemed unlikely to put up stiff resistance against an American takeover. Anglo-Saxonists like John Fiske and Josiah Strong contended that the Filipinos could stand some Westernizing, which American rule would bring. More important, the Philippines possessed wonderful harbors, which would provide the American navy with the kinds of foreign facilities Mahan and the navalists were demanding that America acquire. Manila could be made into an entrepot to the entire Far East.

Consequently, an American operation against the Spanish in the Philippines made perfectly good sense from the perspective of long-range American expansionism, as well as for the short-term purpose of preventing the Spanish fleet at Manila from sailing away, either to strengthen the Spanish navy off Cuba or to harass America's West Coast. But just because it made good sense didn't mean it needed to be broadcast publicly, and when Dewey commenced the war for the United States with an attack against the Philippines, many Americans were completely surprised—albeit delightedly so, on account of how the attack turned out.

Spanish officials in the Philippines were less surprised and considerably less delighted. After receiving Roosevelt's February cable, Dewey had asked the American consul in the Philippines, O. F. Williams, to snoop around and gather what information he could regarding Manila's defenses and the Spanish fleet's readiness for war. Williams responded with clumsy diligence, and between his obvious investigations and the overall state of Spanish-American tension, he made himself unwelcome. The Spanish governor suggested he depart, saying his life was in danger from mobs. Williams left, but not before passing along intelligence Dewey characterized as "highly valuable."

At noon on April 25, Dewey received a message from Navy Secretary Long. "War has commenced between the United States and Spain," Long wired. "Proceed at once to Philippine Islands. Commence operations particularly against the Spanish fleet. You must capture vessels or destroy. Use utmost endeavor."

Dewey had just repositioned his squadron from Hong Kong to Mirs Bay, a nearby anchorage where he ran his crews through target practice and various other drills. He waited briefly for Williams and the latest news from the Philippines before raising anchor; on April 27, he led two columns of vessels into the South China Sea, bound for Manila.

Dewey arrived at the entrance to Manila Bay on the afternoon of April 30. His squadron carefully skirted south of Corregidor, the island guarding the approach to the capital. Shore batteries opened fire, which Dewey's *Boston* and *McCulloch* returned. Neither side did much damage. By dawn of May 1 the American vessels had penetrated twenty miles up the bay nearly to Manila, where they came under bombardment from guns in the city and in Cavite to the southeast. At this point, Dewey's six warships commenced shelling the anchored Spanish fleet. Describing the engagement for Washington's benefit, Dewey wrote, "The squadron maintained a continuous and precise fire at ranges varying from 5,000 to 2,000 yards, countermarching in a line approximately parallel to that of the Spanish fleet. The enemy's fire was vigorous, but generally ineffective."

The battle lasted six hours. By noon the Spanish ships were in flames and their guns silent. When the cannons of Fort Santiago, at the mouth of the Pasig River, and of Intramuros, the old walled town at Manila, continued to fire, Dewey sent word to the Spanish governor that unless they ceased he would bombard the city. The Spanish official complied, and by one o'clock all fighting had ended. Three Spanish warships were on the bottom of the harbor and seven more were charred hulks. Spanish casualties numbered in the hundreds. Dewey lost no ships and suffered only seven casualties, all minor. "The squadron is in as good condition now as before the battle," Dewey reported.

The victory at Manila made Dewey a national hero. The navy quickly promoted him to admiral, and his walrus-mustached face graced newspapers and magazines across America. Politicians devised all manner of schemes for being seen with him when he returned to the United States; sculptors carved his features in stone; parents named sons after him. Both political parties inquired into his background and ambitions, wondering whether he might be persuaded to run for office.

VIII

It wasn't Dewey, though, but Roosevelt who really cashed in on the Spanish-American War. The war afforded bumptious Theodore the opportunity he had been desiring for years to test his mettle under fire, and shortly after the outbreak of hostilities he resigned his post at the Navy Department to enlist in the army. His decision to do so puzzled some of his associates. Secretary Long wondered to a colleague why Roosevelt wanted to quit an important job in Washington in order to "brush mosquitoes from his neck in the Florida sands." John Hay remarked, "Theodore Roosevelt, that *wilder verwegener*, has left the Navy Department, where he had the chance of his life, and has joined a cowboy regiment."

The cowboy regiment Hay referred to was the First Volunteer Cavalry, headed by Colonel Leonard Wood, with Lieutenant Colonel Roosevelt as his assistant. The unit, soon christened the "Rough Riders," included one of the oddest assortments of personnel in the history of the American military. Roosevelt was still enamored of cowboys from his Dakota days, and he encouraged the enlistment of horse-wise men from the frontier. Telegrams went out to the territorial governors in the West, seeking individuals who were "young, good shots and good riders." Roosevelt and Wood were soon buried under applications from individuals, as Roosevelt politely put it, "who do not look at life in the spirit of decorum and conventionality that obtains in the East." At the same time Roosevelt turned to the blueblood side of his background for polo-playing recruits from the Harvard, Yale, and Princeton clubs of New York City. The Ivy League responded as enthusiastically as the territories did.

This strangely mixed crew gathered at San Antonio in May 1898. Though the townsfolk weren't particularly impressed, the American news media loved the spectacle. Already Roosevelt had gained a reputation as a colorful character and probably one with a future; he could always be counted on for lively copy. He started generating news immediately upon his arrival at San Antonio. Roosevelt prided himself on his egalitarianism, and after a hot day drilling his troops under the South Texas sun, he announced, "The men can go in and drink all the beer they want, which I will pay for!" The pleased bronco-busters and fox-hunters cheered their leader and headed for the nearest saloon, with Roosevelt in the van.

When Wood heard of the incident afterward, he upbraided Roosevelt for a flagrant breach of military discipline. It was hardly conducive to respect, Wood insisted, for officers to go drinking with the men. Roosevelt saluted abruptly and walked out of Wood's tent. A short while later he returned. "Sir," he announced, "I consider myself the damnedest ass within ten miles of this camp. Good night, sir."

During the few weeks the Rough Riders remained in San Antonio, the locals came to like them (and the business they brought), and when word arrived that the unit would be moving out at the end of May, the town decided to throw a farewell party. The high point of the evening was to be a band concert, conducted by Professor Carl Beck, a first-generation German immigrant to Texas. One of the compositions was entitled "Cavalry Charge"; its climax included the sound of a cannon firing, as a supplement to the percussion section. No one informed the Rough Riders, however, that real gunpowder was on the program, and when the cannon went off several of them concluded that the conductor was under fire. "Help him out, boys!" shouted one of Roosevelt's men. Others leaped to their feet, shooting their pistols into the air. Women and children in the audience screamed and dove under their chairs. In the confusion the electricity failed, leaving everyone still more confused and frightened. Band director Beck declared, the next day: "I was in the Franco-Prussian War and saw some hot times, but I was about as uneasy last night as I ever was in battle." The Rough Riders, after discovering their mistake, judged the affair a great joke and spent the rest of the night celebrating.

Shortly thereafter, Wood, Roosevelt, and their men departed for Tampa, where they aimed to be among the first units shipped out to Cuba. But the wheels of the War Department ground slowly, and it wasn't until the second week in June that they made ready to board the ship that had been assigned to carry them south. To the momentary dismay of the regiment, Wood and Roosevelt learned that the same vessel had inadvertently been assigned to two other regiments as well. Roosevelt described how his fast thinking and decisive action saved the day: "I ran at full speed to our train; and leaving a strong guard with the baggage, I double-quicked the rest of the regiment up to the boat, just in time to board her as she came into the quay, and then to hold her against the Second Regulars and the Seventy-first, who had arrived a little too late, being a shade less ready than we were in the matter of individual initiative. There was a good deal of expostulation, but we had possession; and as the ship could not contain half of the men who had been told to go aboard her, the Seventy-first went away, as did all but four companies of the Second."

It turned out to be a typical military case of hurry up and wait. Once aboard the ship the Rough Riders lingered for almost a week in Tampa Bay, sweltering under the June sun and nearly suffocating from the raw sewage the city regularly dumped into the harbor. Finally, on June 13, their vessel weighed anchor and started for Cuba. "When Colonel Roosevelt heard the news," one of the Rough Riders recalled later, "he could not restrain himself, and entertained us all by giving an impromptu war dance."

The initial American landing in Cuba, opposite a small village called Daiquirí, was enthusiastic but disorderly. Almost no one among the Rough Riders and the thousands who accompanied them had any experience approaching a beach through surf, which was unusually heavy this day. Yet the men were all excited, and they managed to get ashore—except for two unfortunate drylanders who drowned. The highlight of the operation came when General Wheeler, the Confederate hero now a bit past his prime, urged his men forward with a rebel yell and the cry, "The Yankees are running!" Catching himself, he amended his remark: "Dammit! I mean the Spaniards!"

Because space had been so limited on the ship, most of the Rough Riders had been forced to leave their horses in Florida. As the unmounted cavalry marched inland, they renamed themselves "Wood's Weary Walkers." Roosevelt was as ebullient as ever, though, at least partly because he was one of the lucky ones allowed to bring his horse.

After some preliminary skirmishing, the First Volunteers took part in an attack on San Juan Hill near the town of El Caney. By this time an illness of a higher-up had resulted in Wood's promotion to brigade commander, leaving Roosevelt in charge of the regiment. In the assault on San Juan Hill, Roosevelt led his men up a smaller rise, Kettle Hill, adjacent to the main elevation.

It was a glorious moment. "San Juan was the great day of my life," Roosevelt remarked twenty years later. With bravery almost indistinguishable from recklessness, Roosevelt tore about on horseback amid withering enemy fire. He afforded Spanish riflemen a large and conspicuous target, set off from the rest by a blue polka-dot bandanna worn around his sombrero hat. When two of his men hesitated to go forward, he bellowed, "Are you afraid to stand up, when I am on horseback?" An officer of the regular army got in his way; Roosevelt roared, "Let my men through, sir!" Miraculously he escaped the enemy bullets, although a quarter of his men didn't. The costs were high, but the assault was a smashing success. Roosevelt and the Rough Riders captured the hill and put the Spanish to rout.

Roosevelt was thoroughly pleased with himself and his men. "I do not want to be vain," he wrote Henry Cabot Lodge, "but I do not think that anyone else could have handled this regiment quite as I have handled it." He continued, "It has done as well as any of the regular regiments and infinitely better than any of the volunteer regiments; and indeed, frankly, I think it has done better than the regulars with the exception of one or two of the best regular regiments."

After San Juan Hill, the remainder of the war in Cuba was anticlimactic for Roosevelt—and for most of the American expeditionary force. The American Navy shortly defeated the Spanish fleet as it tried to flee Santiago harbor, giving the Americans undisputed control of the waves. The expected crucial battle for the city of Santiago never took place: the Spanish commander surrendered without a fight. This surrender effectively terminated the fighting in Cuba. An American force sent against the Spanish colony of Puerto Rico landed there at the end of July and encountered little difficulty suppressing Spanish resistance.

The Spanish government asked for an armistice, which McKinley granted subject to four conditions: that Spain would grant Cuba unfettered independence; that the United States could keep Puerto Rico (which Teller and the supporters of his amendment had failed to include in their disclaimer); that the armistice should be considered a suspension of hostilities rather than a definitive end to them; and that the United States could hold the city of Manila and its environs until the ultimate fate of the Philippines should be determined by a peace conference. Madrid muttered some objections briefly, especially about the Philippines, but in the second week of August it accepted McKinley's conditions.

IX

When the peace conference began, the Philippines quickly became a sticking point. Most of the stickiness owed to the fact that the Filipinos didn't at all relish being handed from one great (or ex-great) power to another. The Filipinos remonstrated with American leaders to allow them the independence the Americans claimed for themselves and had just guaranteed to the Cubans. Filipino representatives followed American and Spanish negotiators to Paris for the peace conference, and they buttonholed officials of the McKinley administration in Washington. They threatened to fight against the Americans, just as they had fought against the Spanish, to secure their freedom.

McKinley later remarked, somewhat disingenuously, that George Dewey would have saved his country a lot of bother after his victory at Manila if he had just turned around and sailed away. At first McKinley thought about giving the Filipinos what they wanted, but during the late summer and fall of 1898 he grew convinced that the prudent thing for the United States to do was to annex the Philippines. The president defended his decision as the only reasonable one. He rejected returning the Philippines to the Spanish, who had proven themselves unfit to govern other people. He couldn't deliver the Philippines over to a third country, for while Spain might be the worst of the colonial powers, none was much better (nor much more popular among American voters). Besides, the Far East was already on the verge of war among the imperialists, and bestowing a bounty on one party might set teeth gnashing among the rest and trigger the conflict. Moreover, relinquishing the islands to a commercial rival of the United States would be "bad business," McKinley said. As to the Filipinos themselves, the president judged that they were unprepared for independence: lacking the capacity for self-government and self-defense, they would quickly be swallowed by one or more of the imperialist powers. McKinley contemplated annexing just part of the Philippine archipelago but set this notion aside as unworkable. Only annexation of the entire lot by America remained. "There was nothing left for us to do," McKinley concluded, "but take them all, and educate the Filipinos, and uplift and civilize and Christianize them, and by God's grace do the very best we could by them, as our fellow men for whom Christ also died."

Many in America disagreed (not least American Catholics, who wondered just what McKinley meant in saying that the overwhelmingly Catholic Filipinos needed to be "Christianized"). The Philippine question aroused violent feelings throughout the United States. Opponents of annexation—which was the most controversial provision of the treaty the American and Spanish negotiators concluded in Paris in December 1898—decried it as placing America on a par with the predatory imperialists. Charles Eliot Norton of Harvard feared that the acquisition of an empire would bring upon the United States "the misery and the burdens that war and standing armies have brought upon the nations of the Old World." Norton thought that Americans had lost their senses in the flush of military victory. The country was delirious. "All the evil spirits of the Old World which we trusted were exorcised in the New, have taken possession of her, and under their influence she has gone mad." Norton bemoaned the deflowering of America at the hands of the expansionists. "She has lost her unique position as a potential leader in the progress of civilization, and has taken up her place simply as one of the grasping and selfish nations of the present day."

E. L. Godkin, the crotchety editor of *The Nation*, was less surprised than Norton at the recent events but no less dismayed. Godkin forecast endless frustration in the Philippines and beyond. He had long opposed extending the American writ too far too fast; at one point he burst out, "We do not want any more States until we can civilize Kansas." He judged to be overwhelming the present arguments against annexing the Philippines: "the sudden departure from our traditions; the absence from our system of any machinery for governing dependencies; the admission of alien, inferior, and mongrel races to our nationality; the opening of fresh fields to carpetbaggers, speculators, and corruptionists; the un-Americanism of governing a large body of people against their will, and by persons not responsible to them; the entrance on a policy of conquest and annexation while our own continent was still unreclaimed, our population unassimilated, and many of our most serious political problems still unsolved; and finally the danger of the endorsement of a gross fraud for the first time by a Christian nation." After Dewey's victory at Manila, Godkin said, McKinley was "drunk with glory and flattery." Many Americans were following the president into reckless inebriation. America would pay the cost with its future. "I can not help thinking this triumph over Spain seals the fate of the American republic."

Veteran reformer and mugwump Carl Schurz had been through excitements before, including the 1848 revolutions in Europe and the American Civil War. Speaking from that experience, and speaking also as a (German) immigrant who took seriously American democratic principles, Schurz warned that the acquisition of an overseas empire would be the ruin of democracy in the United States. "The character and future of the Republic and the welfare of its people now living and yet to be born are in unprecedented jeopardy," he wrote. The expansionists were trampling on all that the founding fathers had established and all that Lincoln and the Unionists (including Schurz himself) had fought to preserve. The Spanish war was ended, but another war was inevitable: "The Filipinos fought against Spain for their freedom and independence, and unless they abandon their recently proclaimed purpose for their freedom and independence, they will fight against us."

Andrew Carnegie similarly opposed annexation as likely to lead to war. But the war the steelmaker feared most was one between the United States and the imperialist powers. The imperialists were on the edge of war already, and nowhere were they so close to conflict as in the Far East. "It is in that region the thunderbolt is expected. It is there the storm is to burst." By annexing the Philippines, the United States would plunge straight into the tempest. Carnegie derided the notion that annexation would lead to the uplifting of the Filipinos. Far more likely would be the degradation of Americans. "Has the influence of the superior race upon the inferior ever proved beneficial to either? I know of no case in which it has been or is." Soon Americans in the Philippines would be the ones requiring uplifting. "Soldiers in foreign camps, so far from being missionaries for good, require missionaries themselves more than the natives."

Congressional opponents of annexation added to the list of demerits attending such a course. Democratic Congressman Jehu Baker of Illinois predicted that America would come to resemble England. "The English system," Baker said, "rests upon monarchy, inequality, aristocracy and rank. The American system rests upon democracy and equality and severely excludes legalized aristocracy and rank." An imperialistic American policy would erase the difference. Baker continued: "This would be one of the most lamentable self-degradations in the history of mankind. The attempt to suddenly sweep us into a colonial policy similar to that of Great Britain—so suddenly that we have scarce time to note where the leap will carry us—is, in my opinion, the most audacious and reckless performance of jingoism that this or any other country has ever witnessed."

Jerry Simpson, the Kansas Populist, smelled jingoism on the treaty too. Simpson also caught a whiff of something far more sinister. Under Cleveland, the bosses of business had learned to use federal troops to break strikes and intimidate labor; under McKinley, the troops would be used against the people at large. Imperialism was the cover for a design to strengthen the military, which the minions of big business would use to smash dissent. "That is what they want it for, along with a scheme for colonial empire, and to place on the throne in this country William McKinley, President of the United States, Emperor of the West Indian Islands and of the Philippines." Simpson could hardly believe what he was seeing. "Empire!" he cried. "Do gentlemen understand the meaning of the word 'empire' as applied to a republic? It means that we are taking the first step toward the strong centralized power that will finally result in this Republic being turned into an empire."

In the Senate, which had the final power of approval or veto over the treaty, Hernando Money addressed the pocketbook issue of trade in an American empire. The Mississippi Democrat took second place to no man in his patriotic zeal; he said that he had felt "in every ruddy drop that visited my heart a tingling of joyous pride when the great exploits of our sailors and soldiers astonished the world." He experienced a "thrill of exultation" and a "glow of enthusiasm" when the American flag waved above the walls of Manila. But Americans mustn't be deluded by arguments for annexation as necessary to their foreign commerce. "Are conquests and subjugation necessary to the spread of American products?" he asked. "Have we depended heretofore upon those aids so much vaunted in this debate?" Of course not. "The commerce of the United States, fortunately for this great Republic, has been founded more wisely upon the superior skill of its artisans." Driving home this point, Money went on: "That which carries American commerce abroad is not the protection of this Government; it is not that the flag of the fighting Navy of the United States is found on every sea and in every port; it is the skill of the American workingman."

Democrat John Daniel of Virginia raised the issue of race. America had enough racial problems without taking responsibility for millions of dark-skinned Asians. "Today we are the United States of America," Daniel declared. "Tomorrow, if a treaty now pending in the Senate is ratified, we will be the United States of America and Asia." Annexation entailed more than mere political ties, Daniel explained luridly. "It is a marriage of nations. This twain will become one flesh. They become bone of our bone and flesh of our flesh. Henceforth and forever, according to the terminology of this treaty, the Filipinos and Americans are one." This was nonsense, for the treaty said no such thing, but Daniel played the theme of miscegenation to the hilt. The Philippines, he warned, were a "witch's caldron" of races; rhetorically stirring the cauldron for his listeners, he chanted:

> Black spirits and white,
> Red spirits and gray,

> Mingle, mingle, mingle,
> You that mingle may.

With a straight face, Daniel repeated the most preposterous stories about the Filipinos. "The travelers who have been there tell us and have written in the books that they are not only of all hues and colors, but there are spotted people there and, what I have never heard of in any other country, there are striped people there with zebra signs upon them." Perhaps some of these reports were exaggerated, Daniel conceded, but even so they bore scrutiny before America sold its Anglo-Saxon birthright for "this Asiatic mess of pottage."

The opponents of annexation made a powerful case, traversing, as they did, both the high road of republican principle and the low road of racist demagoguery. But they labored under the decided disadvantage of saying no when the great majority of Americans wanted to say yes. After a dismal decade of depression, divisive politics, labor violence, narrowing geographic and psychic horizons, and a host of other inducers of anxiety and related ill feelings, the spectacular victory in the Spanish-American War gave Americans something to celebrate. Celebrating didn't necessarily require seizing the Philippines, but insisting on rejecting the spoils of war made the anti-imperialists look like a bunch of spoilsports. Nobody likes spoilsports.

The advocates of annexation pressed this psychological advantage. They pointed out that refusing the Philippines would mean abandoning what had been won at the cost of American lives and treasure. "We have hoisted our flag," Roosevelt declared, "and it is not fashioned of the stuff which can be quickly hauled down." Henry Cabot Lodge asserted that to withdraw from the Philippines would be an "act of infamy." Lodge, who characterized the war with Spain as "not only righteous but inevitable," described American expansion as similarly inevitable. "We are going to hold possessions over the seas, be they more or less."

Lodge was a central figure in the fight over the Paris treaty. Just as Roosevelt had been the expansionists' agent in the executive branch, Lodge was the expansionists' man in the Senate. The collaboration between the two wasn't lost on the anti-imperialists. Edward Atkinson, a leader of the treaty opponents, said of the Massachusetts senator's relationship to Roosevelt: "Lodge is the Mephistopheles whispering poison in his ear all the time." Not long after the war started, Lodge wrote to Roosevelt registering satisfaction at the general course of the fighting, but warning: "The one point where haste is needed is the Philippines." Lodge fretted that Spain might surrender before the United States had taken all the territory it required. Roosevelt concurred, writing back from the front: "You must prevent any talk of peace until we get Porto Rico and the Philippines." Lodge did his best, and subsequently was able to report, "I think I can say to you in confidence but in absolute certainty that the administration is grasping the whole policy at last." He continued, "Unless I am utterly and profoundly mistaken, the administration is now fully committed to the large policy that we both desire."

As the pendulum swung toward American annexation of the Philippines, Lodge enjoyed the discomfiture of the anti-imperialists. He described the treaty's foes as "very comic," and when an anti-imperialist petition garnered but two thousand signatures, he remarked, "I should hardly have thought it possible that the result should have been so trivial from so much exertion." Lodge didn't mind at all that annexation was proving to be a potent partisan issue. "The drift of public opinion in favor of an imperial policy seems to be absolutely overwhelming," he informed Roosevelt, "and the Democrats here seem to be going to pieces over it."

Roosevelt thought it served them right. The Democrats, he said, demonstrated "a lamentable indifference to the true interests of the nation." For that matter, Roosevelt didn't think much of Republicans who disagreed with him. Anti-imperialist Republican George Hoar particularly provoked the ex–Rough Rider, who deemed Hoar and his ilk "little better than traitors."

During the Senate debate on the treaty, Lodge lambasted the foes of the pact and affirmed the fundamental justice and wisdom of annexation. He ridiculed the notion that the United States was stealing sovereignty from the Filipinos. "There was no sovereignty there whatever except the sovereignty of Spain, and we succeeded to the sovereignty." He likewise dismissed Democratic charges of American oppression of the Filipinos. "There has never been an act of oppression against the Filipinos by any American soldiers or by the American forces of any kind in the Philippine Islands. . . . Their oppression exists solely in speeches in the United States Senate." If anything, the United States had been too lenient toward the Filipinos. "They have been treated with the utmost consideration and the utmost kindness, and, after the fashion of Orientals, they have mistaken kindness for timidity."

Lodge's defense of annexation displayed logic and some emotion, but for purple passion it paled beside the oratorical excesses of Albert Beveridge. The Indiana Republican informed his Senate colleagues that theirs was an age of imperialism. Prizes like the Philippines were rare and becoming rarer. "This island empire is the last land left in all the oceans," Beveridge asserted. The Philippines held the key to the "illimitable markets" of China. "Our largest trade henceforth must be with Asia. The Pacific is our ocean. More and more Europe will manufacture the most it needs, secure from its colonies the most it consumes. Where shall we turn for consumers of our surplus? Geography answers the question. China is our natural customer. She is nearer to us than to England, Germany, or Russia, the commercial powers of the present and the future." China's trade would soon reflect the immensity of her population. "That statesman commits a crime against American trade—against the American grower of cotton and wheat and tobacco, the American manufacturer of machinery and clothing—who fails to put America where she may command that trade." This was where the

Philippines came in. As the "Gibraltar of the Pacific," the islands were placed to "command the commercial situation of the entire East."

God had smiled on few regions of the earth as warmly as He had smiled on the Philippines. "I have cruised more than 2,000 miles through the archipelago, every moment a surprise at its loveliness and wealth," Beveridge continued. "I have ridden hundreds of miles on the islands, every foot of the way a revelation of vegetable and mineral riches. No land in America surpasses in fertility the plains and valleys of Luzon. Rice and coffee, sugar and coconuts, hemp and tobacco, and many products of the temperate as well as the tropic zone grow in various sections of the archipelago." Minerals were no less abundant. "I have a nugget of pure gold picked up in its present form on the banks of a Philippine creek. I have gold dust washed out by crude processes of careless natives from the sands of a Philippine stream."

Yet the Philippine issue transcended trade or physical endowments. "It is elemental. It is racial. God has not been preparing the English-speaking and Teutonic peoples for a thousand years for nothing but vain and idle self-contemplation and self-admiration." On the contrary. "He has made us the master organizers of the world to establish system where chaos reigns. He has given us the spirit of progress to overwhelm the forces of reaction throughout the earth." Americans would deny their destiny if they declined the opportunity now facing them. That would be the easy and cowardly course. Americans must accept the challenge of empire. The world would gain if Americans grasped their fate, and so would America. "It holds for us all the profit, all the glory, all the happiness possible to man."

Beveridge's flights of oratory may have moved a few foes of annexation to change their minds, yet as matters turned out, the anti-imperialist cause was done in not by one of its enemies but by one of its friends. William Jennings Bryan opposed an American empire for the same reasons adduced by Jerry Simpson and others who warned that imperialism would further strengthen the forces that already oppressed the common people of America. But at the same time, Bryan feared that the imperialist debate would distract the people from the more essential domestic issues on which he hoped to fight the campaign of 1900, now little more than a year away. Consequently, he desired to push the annexation question off the table, the better to concentrate attention on the trusts and silver.

Bryan, rationalizing mightily, contended that the Senate must ratify the Paris treaty, if only to terminate the state of war that still technically existed with Spain; the United States could then deal with the Philippines at leisure. Bryan's argument made just enough sense, and he possessed just enough pull, to convince several otherwise skeptical senators to suspend their doubts and vote in favor of the treaty. As a result, the treaty passed the Senate—and the United States embarked on a career of undisguised imperialism—by a margin of 57 to 27, one vote more than the necessary two thirds.

EPILOGUE

♦

I

The debate over annexation of the Philippines revealed a rift between two visions of America's role in the world that paralleled the two visions of America's domestic life. The imperialists embraced a future in which the political values and industrial energy that had tamed the North American continent would spread beyond its shores to the world at large. America's frontier hadn't vanished but rather migrated across the Pacific. The westering sun was not setting on the United States but rising on a new ocean of opportunities for Americans.

By contrast, the anti-imperialists took their guidance from the past. Fearing involvement in world affairs, they looked to a time when the United States had held itself aloof from the world. Such a time had never actually existed, any more than Jefferson's yeoman farmer had ever existed as a meaningful model of actual American life. But if the anti-imperialists' memories were mainly myths, their concerns were real. They witnessed what chronic intercourse with other nations had brought the great powers of Europe, and they wanted nothing of the sort for the United States. They saw the face of imperialism in Africa and Asia, and its predatory visage put them off. Believing that America had to choose between democracy and empire, they clung to the former and shunned the latter.

Events of the few years after the annexation of the Philippines indicated that the anti-imperialists were correct in perceiving a contradiction between American democratic values and American imperialism. Almost simultaneously with the Senate approval of the Paris treaty, Filipino nationalists launched attacks against American troops in the vicinity of Manila. Filipino leaders, including the charismatic Emilio Aguinaldo, felt used and betrayed by the United States. Aguinaldo had hitched a ride home with Dewey from exile and organized a resistance movement against the Spanish that contributed materially to the American victory over Spain in the Philippines. When the McKinley administration thanked Aguinaldo and his comrades by seizing the islands for the United States, they vowed to oppose the Americans with even greater determination than they had opposed the Spanish.

No one then or later thought of calling the fight for the Philippines a "splendid little war." The struggle was brutal and demoralizing. As the opponents of annexation had predicted, the United States found itself in the same position Spain had been in with regard to Cuba. The Filipinos initially tried to defeat the Americans by conventional means; when this failed, they adopted a guerrilla strategy. The Americans responded with anti-guerrilla tactics that proved chillingly similar to General Weyler's *reconcentrado* policy. American soldiers and some of their Filipino allies—the war divided Filipino society as deeply as Cuba had been rent by the anti-Spanish war there—resorted to torture of suspected guerrillas and sympathizers. The most notorious method of extracting information was the "water cure," by which interrogators forced a gallon or more of water down the throat of a suspect until his stomach was all but bursting, and then pummeled and kicked the bloated belly. More than a few people died under the treatment. Although such atrocities nagged the consciences of some of those responsible—and provoked congressional inquiries—many Americans were willing to accept that in a war between the white race and a colored race harsh measures were necessary. (Sixty years later, when American troops again were fighting in Southeast Asia, some of this same sentiment would return to haunt America—and do more than haunt Vietnam. Meanwhile, the concentration camps U.S. troops had created in the Philippines would be resurrected as "strategic hamlets.")

The Filipinos fought gamely until the first part of 1902, when an American officer named Frederick Funston devised a plan for capturing Aguinaldo. Funston dressed some friendly Filipinos as rebels and disguised himself and a few other Americans as their prisoners of war. The bogus rebels would pass themselves off as reinforcements Aguinaldo had requested—the Americans had intercepted his message—and would escort Funston and the other Americans into Aguinaldo's camp, where they would spring their trap. A snag developed when Aguinaldo told the fake reinforcements to leave the Americans behind, since he didn't want them to learn the location of his camp. Yet Funston wouldn't be frustrated so easily. He and the Americans dropped to the rear of their Filipino collaborators but followed at a distance. The collaborators entered Aguinaldo's camp and were greeted with enthusiasm. With Aguinaldo's guard momentarily down, they began shooting the soldiers protecting the insurgent leader. Funston and the Americans rushed up and took Aguinaldo prisoner. They whisked him away to the coast where they were met by an American warship, which carried them and Aguinaldo to Manila.

The Filipino insurgency was already showing signs of strain before Funston accomplished his coup, and Aguinaldo's capture intensified it. When shortly thereafter Aguinaldo called on his followers to lay down their arms and declared allegiance to the American government, most of the fight drained out of the resistance movement. By the summer of 1902 the conflict was over.

The suppression of the Filipino insurgency was, for American imperialists, a case of winning the battle and losing the war. The United States governed the Philippines directly until the mid-1930s and indirectly for another ten years. As exercises in colonialism went, American rule of the Philippines was comparatively benign, and when Washington granted independence to the Republic of the Philippines in 1946, most Filipinos had warm feelings for Americans. But the Philippine war had soured the American public on imperialism. Many Americans had been willing to go along with annexing territory overseas as long as annexation was cheap and easy; the war of resistance in the Philippines demonstrated that it could be expensive and hard. In doing so, the war poisoned the well of American public opinion for similar ventures elsewhere. After the turn of the new century the United States contented itself with acquiring informal influence over foreign territories rather than formal control and responsibility.

Still, informal influence sufficed to make the United States the most powerful player in the game of nations during the next ninety years. For the first half of that period, much of the same ambivalence that characterized the debate over the Philippines persisted; only after two world wars would a solid majority of Americans convert to a conviction of the need for sustained engagement in international affairs. But even that victory for the philosophy of Mahan and Lodge and Roosevelt wouldn't be permanent, or at least it wouldn't be unassailable. When American intervention in Vietnam turned out to be more than its backers bargained for, many Americans criticized the policy of global engagement, often in terms strikingly similar to those employed by the anti-imperialists of 1898.

The debate that developed around American foreign policy during the 1990s also echoed certain of the themes of the final decade of the previous century. At the end of the Cold War the United States was the world's only superpower, and one might have thought that Americans would take advantage of that superiority to enforce their will globally. When wars broke out in Somalia and Bosnia and Rwanda, some Americans did call for intervention, on the same humanitarian grounds that had elicited American intervention in Cuba in 1898. These calls sufficed to send American troops briefly to Somalia. But other voices warned that the United States needed to get its own house in order before it tried to rearrange the furniture elsewhere, much as the anti-imperialists had contended a hundred years before. Some of the more historically minded pointed to the Philippine war as evidence of what happens to hubristic nations that undertake foreign adventures lightly. As of mid-1995, the historically minded, or at any rate the cautious, were guiding American policy.

II

Amid the cautious mood of post–Cold War America, it was sometimes hard to remember that Roosevelt and the advocates of a "large policy" had won the debate during the 1890s. But Roosevelt's side *had* won the debate, and that wasn't all Roosevelt won. The Rough Rider emerged from the Spanish-American War a great hero, not least because of his virtuosity at self-promotion. Roosevelt quickly turned his wartime experiences into the bestselling *Rough Riders*. Readers could have been forgiven for thinking that there had been only one Rough Rider, namely the author, assisted by a following of subalterns and aides. Rumor had it that the printer of the book ran out of type pieces for the capital letter "I." Humorist Finley Peter Dunne's character Mr. Dooley described Roosevelt's book to his sidekick Hennessy, calling it (in his Irish brogue), "Th' Biography iv a Hero be Wan who Knows." Mr. Dooley paraphrased Roosevelt's account of the regiment's actions at the front:

We had no sooner landed in Cubia than it become nicessry f'r me to take command iv th' ar-rmy, which I did at wanst. A number of days was spint by me in reconnoitring, attinded on'y be me brave an' fluent body guard, Richard Harding Davis [a noted war correspondent and author]. I discovered that th' inimy was heavily inthrenched on th' top iv San Joon hill immejiately in front iv me. At this time it become apparent that I was handicapped be th' prisence iv th' ar-rmy. . . .

Wan day whin I was about to charge a block house sturdily definded be an ar-rmy corps undher Gin'ral Tamale, th' brave Castile that I afterwards killed with a small ink-eraser that I always carry, I r-ran into th' entire military force iv th' United States lying on its stomach. "If ye won't fight," says I, "let me go through," I says. "Who ar-re ye?" says they. "Colonel Rosenfelt," says I. "Oh, excuse me," says the gin'ral in command (if me mimry serves me thrue it was Miles) r-risin' to his knees and salutin'. This showed me 'twud be impossible f'r to carry th' war to a successful con-clusion unless I was free, so I sint th' ar-rmy home an' attackted San Joon hill.

Ar-rmed on'y with a small thirty-two which I used in th' West to shoot th' fleet prairie dog, I climbed that precipitous ascent in th' face iv the most gallin' fire I ever knew or heerd iv. But I had a few r-rounds iv gall mesilf an' what cared I? I dashed madly on, cheerin' as I wint. Th' Spanish throops was dhrawn up in a long line in th' formation known among military men as a long line. I fired at th' man nearest to me an' I knew be th' expression iv his face that th' trusty bullet wint home. It passed through his frame, he fell, an' wan little home in far-off Catalonia was made happy be th' thought that their riprisintative had been kilt be th' future governor iv New York. Th' bullet sped on its mad flight an' passed through th' intire line, fin'lly imbeddin' itself in th' abdomen iv th' Ar-rchbishop iv Santiago eight miles away. This ended th' war.

Mr. Dooley went on to remark that he didn't object to Roosevelt's efforts on behalf of his own reputation. "No man that bears a gredge again' himsilf 'll iver be governor iv a state. An' if Tiddy done it all, he ought to say so an' relieve th' suspinse. But if I was him I'd call th' book 'Alone in Cubia.' "

Mr. Dooley's review of *The Rough Riders* was printed in newspapers throughout the country. Roosevelt read it and sent Finley Peter Dunne a note: "I regret to state that my family and intimate friends are delighted with your review of my book." Somewhat later, when Roosevelt encountered Dunne on a train, he related a story about a reception he had recently attended, at which a young lady had gushed over him, explaining that she had read everything he had ever written. Roosevelt had asked her which of his books she liked best. She replied, "Why, that one, you know—*Alone in Cuba.*"

Roosevelt could afford to tell jokes on himself, considering his career trajectory at the time. Upon his return to New York after the war he announced his candidacy for governor. Several of his Rough Rider mates lent moral support on the campaign trail, and a bugler blew the charge before each of his stump speeches. He was swept into office, much to the chagrin of New York's regular Republicans, who didn't at all like Roosevelt's irregular—which was to say, reformist—approach to government. They hadn't suffered him long before they decided that the only way to get rid of him was to kick him upstairs to Washington. They lobbied successfully to have him nominated to replace McKinley's vice president, Garret Hobart, who had died in office. Mark Hanna harbored grave reservations about this strategy and about Roosevelt, whom he called "that damned cowboy." Hanna complained, "Don't any of you realize that there's only one life between this madman and the White House?" But after a rousing show for Roosevelt at the 1900 Republican convention, Hanna acquiesced in the nomination. McKinley was healthy, and Hanna could hope that Roosevelt would silently fade into the scenery as other vice presidents had done before him.

The 1900 election was, in many respects, a replay of the 1896 election. William Jennings Bryan won the Democratic nomination again and ran the same kind of barnstorming campaign he had run four years earlier. He still advocated free silver and now added a denunciation of imperialism. Bryan's anti-imperialism rang a little hollow after his backing of the Paris treaty of 1898, and free silver had lost much of its luster since the earlier campaign. New discoveries of gold in the Yukon and South Africa and improved refining techniques were enlarging the historical cube of gold William Harvey's Coin had sketched for his audience, thereby expanding the American currency even without the reintroduction of silver. The return of prosperity since the 1896 election further undercut Bryan's message. McKinley won, by a wider margin than before.

But the Republican president didn't have long to savor his reelection. In September 1901, while attending the Pan-American Exposition in Buffalo, McKinley was shot by an anarchist named Leon Czolgosz. He died eight days later, and Roosevelt became president.

The damned cowboy soon began fulfilling Mark Hanna's worst fears. With Roosevelt's accession to the presidency, the Progressive movement, which had started with such local efforts as campaigns to oust city bosses like Richard Croker, gained a national leader. To some extent the Progressive movement was a house-broken version of Populism. There were important differences, to be sure. The Progressives tended to come from cities and towns, whereas the Populists had hailed from the countryside, and the Progressives were mostly of the middle and professional classes, where the Populists had been farmers and their economic kin. The Progressives didn't share the Populists' obsession with silver, which by the turn of the century had become largely a moot issue. Nor did they embrace the Populists' conspiratorial outlook on the American political economy, largely because they were better educated and more aware of how the world of bright lights and tall buildings really worked.

Yet Progressivism, like Populism, was essentially an attempt to employ the tools of government to restore a balance to society that rapid industrialization had knocked awry. The Progressives distrusted big business, just as the Populists had, and they worked to collar the captains of industry. Roosevelt flummoxed J. P. Morgan in 1902 by bringing an antitrust suit against Morgan's Northern Securities railroad trust. Morgan must have thought he was still dealing with Grover Cleveland, for he told Roosevelt: "If we have done anything wrong, send your man to my man and they can fix it up." Roosevelt replied, "That can't be done," and proceeded with the prosecution. Roosevelt wanted to make the point that the president of the United States wasn't simply a rival operator and that Morgan had to play by the same rules as everyone else. In 1904, the Supreme Court decided in Roosevelt's favor and against Morgan, delighting the Rough Rider and outraging the great financier. When Roosevelt left the White House in 1909 and set off for an African safari, Morgan was reported to have wished the lions happy hunting. Roosevelt's successor, William Howard Taft, continued the antitrust offensive. In 1911, Taft's Justice Department won a suit against the Standard Oil Company, mandating the breakup of John D. Rockefeller's brainchild. Although Rockefeller didn't like the verdict, it didn't exactly bankrupt him: two years later he established the Rockefeller Foundation with a gift of $100 million.

The Progressives adopted a number of other measures favored by the Populists. They supported an income tax and succeeded in amending the Constitution to allow it. They advocated direct election of senators and likewise rewrote the Constitution to effect it. They demanded a reduction of the tariff and accomplished it. They wanted currency reform—though not as drastic as the free coinage of silver—and established the Federal Reserve System to produce it. They sought regulation of the railroads and passed the Elkins and Hepburn acts to provide for it.

Another issue that percolated through Populism to Progressivism was immigration reform. Populist distrust of the cities often translated into nativist suspicion of immigrants, those teeming masses who were portrayed by Jacob Riis and who made the cities even more foreign than they otherwise would have been. The Progressives blamed the immigrants for providing the votes that kept the Crokers and Plunkitts in power. The shift of immigrant origins in the 1880s and 1890s from the familiar lands of Northern and Western Europe to the more exotic locales of Southern and Eastern Europe added a racist element to anti-immigrant sentiment—beyond the anti-Asian feeling that had produced the 1882 Chinese Exclusion Act. Yet for all this, it was only during the anti-foreign and anti-radical frenzy of World War I and its aftermath that Congress passed the first comprehensive immigration restriction measure.

For a time the 1924 National Origins Act seemed to settle the immigration issue. But American freedoms and the American standard of living continued to attract foreigners, some who arrived legally, others who didn't. By the 1990s, their absolute numbers (though not their proportion of the American population) surpassed the immigration statistics of the late nineteenth and early twentieth centuries. As a result, immigration remained as live an issue as it had ever been.

The immigration question and the Progressive reforms weren't the only legacies of Populism that lasted into the 1990s. The strength of Populism had been its appeal to ordinary people; its weakness had been its appeal to some of the worst instincts in those people. Circumstances of the 1990s that mirrored those of the 1890s—especially changing economic conditions and the apparent breakdown of traditional institutions—evoked a new populism that displayed the best and worst features of the old. Calls by conservatives for the people to recapture control of government from out-of-touch elites promised to produce a rebirth of democracy, but the conservatives' demonization of opponents and their conspiratorial attitude toward an ill-defined liberalism threatened to generate something darker. Where the first Populists had split the country sectionally, with the West and South shearing off from the North and East, the new populists seemed to be aiming for a new sectionalism, one that alienated the suburbs and rural regions from the inner cities. Where the first Populists had fought to keep the race question out of the arena of politics, but ultimately failed, the new populists didn't even try. Obliquely, but in a manner no one could miss, they played on racial fears and hostility in hopes of consolidating their coalition. The old Populism had broken apart on the race question; the new populists saw it as their cement.

IV

Although the Progressives were more proficient than the Populists in effecting reform, they were also more boring—which doubtless had something to do with their effectiveness. The Progressive movement lacked the passion of Populism, and it never brought forth individuals with the color and flair to match Ignatius Donnelly, Mary Lease, and Jerry Simpson. Theodore Roosevelt came close. Roosevelt certainly knew how to play a crowd. In 1912, running on the Progressive ticket, he was attacked by a would-be assassin. Only benevolent fortune and Roosevelt's verbosity saved him: the bullet intended for his heart plowed into the thick manuscript of a speech he was about to give. Bleeding, but from a merely superficial wound, Roosevelt went on with his speech, to tremendous applause from his audience.

Among those cheering that day may have been some partisans of organized labor, who recalled Roosevelt's support for labor in the big anthracite strike of 1902. Roosevelt's action marked a major switch in government labor policy since Cleveland and Olney had taken the part of management in the Pullman strike. In the aftermath of that contest the railroads had determined to break the American Railway Union, just as the steel manufacturers had broken the Amalgamated union after the Homestead strike. The railroads refused to hire union members; employees seen speaking with A.R.U. representatives were summarily dismissed. For a while the union went underground in its organizing activities: recruiters approached workers only away from their jobs, and new members weren't required to attend meetings or do anything that would give away their membership. But it was no use. The companies were too strong and the workers too intimidated. In June 1897, the A.R.U. held its last convention.

Ironically, the railway union collapsed just when its prospects might otherwise have started improving. By 1897 the depression was ending, and as the economy strengthened, so did labor's opportunities. In that year organized labor achieved one of its few triumphs of the 1890s, after coal miners in Pennsylvania, Ohio, Indiana, and Illinois went out on strike. During the previous few years falling prices had driven wages down by a quarter, and the continuing influx of immigrants had made organizing difficult. In 1897, the United Mine Workers, which had about ten thousand members at the time, decided to take advantage of the business upturn to press for improvements in wages and working conditions. Some of the mine operators accepted the U.M.W. demands, unwilling to risk a shutdown that would send new orders elsewhere. Others held fast against the miners. The U.M.W. called a strike against the holdouts and asked nonmembers to honor their picket lines. The response was astonishing: nearly one hundred thousand workers left the mines in just a few days, with the stoppage spilling beyond the states originally involved into Kentucky and Tennessee.

The recalcitrant owners quickly caved in. They granted some of the union's demands at once, and during the next year worked out agreements on others, including an eight-hour day and a uniform wage scale. Not surprisingly, U.M.W. membership soared, gaining some 1,000 percent.

On the whole, however, the 1890s were a dismal decade for organized labor, and the improvements of the decade's last years couldn't erase the memory of the defeats at Homestead and Pullman. The election of Republican McKinley in 1896 promised no good for unions, although, considering the conservatism of Cleveland and Olney, it couldn't do much worse. A slow-moving federal investigative commission appointed to examine the causes of the Pullman strike and recommend ways to prevent similar disputes in the future delivered a report urging compulsory arbitration to resolve labor-management deadlocks, but the Republican-controlled Congress wouldn't touch any such infringement on the rights of property. Government remained on the side of management, which itself remained as determined as ever to resist the demands of labor.

About the sole comfort labor could derive from the struggles of the 1890s was the hope that the excesses of the owners would contribute to solidarity among workers. "They are as blind as the fools of power have always been," Henry Demarest Lloyd wrote to Clarence Darrow in the aftermath of the Pullman strike. "It is only by the aggressions of the enemy that the people can be united. Events must be our leaders, and we will have them. I am not discouraged. The radicalism of the fanatics of wealth fills me with hope. They are likely to do for us what the South did for the North in 1861."

Theodore Roosevelt didn't agree with Lloyd on many things, but he concurred in scorn for the fools of power. In the spring of 1902, miners in the anthracite fields of Pennsylvania walked off the job, demanding a pay hike, an eight-hour day, and recognition of the United Mine Workers as their bargaining agent. The owners refused to meet the union's demands; indeed, the owners at first refused to meet the union's representatives. George Baer, the most prominent of the owners, chiefly on account of his capacity for looking reasonably intelligent while spouting idiocy, declared that "God in his infinite wisdom" had given control of the property interests of America to the directors of the country's large corporations; for workers or anyone else to meddle in management's affairs was tantamount to questioning divine authority. Roosevelt grew livid at what he called the "arrogant stupidity" of Baer and the other owners. The president suppressed his anger long enough to summon the owners to meet with representatives of the union in his presence, but he nearly exploded when, in response to a union offer to submit the dispute to arbitration, the owners not merely said no but called for federal troops to break the strike, as in the Pullman affair. Roosevelt very quickly let the owners know that he wasn't Cleveland. He told them that if federal troops were used at all, they would be used against the owners rather than against the miners. After Mark Hanna and J. P. Morgan assured them that Roosevelt meant what he said, the owners agreed to arbitrate. A presidential commission split the difference between the miners and the owners.

Roosevelt's assistance in the anthracite strike hardly solved all the problems of organized labor. While the trade unions associated with the American Federation of Labor continued to gain membership and influence, industrial unions of the type Eugene Debs had tried to organize with the American Railway Union encountered difficulties. Some of these difficulties the industrial unionists brought on themselves by actions and policies that were too radical for the middle-of-the-road tastes of the majority of Americans. The most radical of the important industrial unions was the Industrial Workers of the World, founded in 1905 and comprising miners, loggers, farm workers, textile hands, and anyone else who liked the idea of "one big union" devoted to taking power away from the owners and giving it to the workers. Many of the Wobblies, as I.W.W. members were labeled, didn't stop short of advocating violence against the capitalist oppressors. The Wobblies waged a few successful strikes, as in 1912 in Lawrence, Massachusetts, against textile companies there, but the antiradicalism of World War I and after sent the I.W.W. into terminal eclipse. (It also sent Gene Debs to jail for opposing the war. Yet Debs's sincerity shone even through the bars of his cell: while still imprisoned, he polled more than 1 million votes as the Socialist candidate for president in 1920.) It wasn't until the era of the New Deal that industrial unions gained a prominent place in the American economy.

But few issues are ever settled forever in politics or life. Though unions flourished for a time, by the last decade of the twentieth century they once more were in decline. Some of the reasons for the decline were similar to the reasons for the unions' troubles in the 1890s. The Republican administrations of the 1980s and early 1990s were conspicuously unfriendly to unions; certain historically conscious observers likened Ronald Reagan's brusque handling of a 1981 air traffic controllers' strike to Cleveland's treatment of the railworkers' walkout. More important, the American economy was undergoing a transformation as sweeping in its effects as that of one hundred years before. Analogously to the manner in which the skilled jobs of the mid-nineteenth century had given way to the unskilled labor that predominated at places like Carnegie's Homestead during the 1890s, the manufacturing jobs of the mid-twentieth century gave way to the service jobs—also usually unskilled—of the 1990s. Organized labor had required time to adjust to the new circumstances of the end of the nineteenth century; it was hardly surprising that labor was requiring time to adjust to the new circumstances of the end of twentieth century.

V

Unlike Eugene Debs, who died in 1926, Jacob Coxey lived long enough to see his short-term failure yield longer-term success. The march of Coxey's army did not prod Congress to forceful action to alleviate the plight of the unemployed during the depression of the 1890s, but it did raise that plight to the level of national public concern. Prior to the 1890s, the thought of marching on Washington to protest unemployment made about as much sense to most Americans as the thought of marching on Washington to protest drought or flood or fires. Depressions were commonly classed as acts of God. But during the last decade of the nineteenth century, large numbers of people began to draw connections between government policy decisions and the state of the nation's economy. The precise nature of the connections was unclear, despite the claims to clarity of the silverites and their comrades. It would require a few decades more for these perceived connections to have a decisive influence on public policy, but after Coxey's army invaded Washington no American administration could count on the out-of-work to suffer in silence.

As with organized labor, the breakthrough occurred during the 1930s—not coincidentally, during the only depression in American history worse than that of the 1890s. The New Deal included several programs inspired by Coxey's good-roads vision. Coxey himself spent the early years of the 1930s as mayor of Massillon, where he attempted to put his program into effect on a local level. But his issue of $200,000 in small-denomination bonds failed to find subscribers, and in 1934 he was ousted from the one public office he ever held. Meanwhile, though, millions of unemployed Americans—precisely the kind of people who had followed Coxey from Ohio to Washington in 1894—took government jobs building roads, bridges, dams, irrigation works, and any number of other projects that warmed the old Commonwealer's heart.

Again as with organized labor, the pendulum subsequently swung back, and by the 1990s the notion that government should guarantee employment often elicited ridicule. But the basic problem that Coxey had highlighted—of making sure that the American economy generated sufficient jobs for the American people—remained. It underscored arguments on all manner of topics, from free trade and the Federal Reserve to welfare and farm subsidies and tax breaks. Coxey had wanted to start a debate; he succeeded beyond his dreams.

VI

A more noticeable, if not so noteworthy, legacy of Coxey's army lay in the realm of political tactics, as distinct from economic substance. So sensational was the march on Washington in producing publicity that numerous other groups adopted the approach as a way of gaining recognition for their own causes. None utilized the technique of marches on Washington—and elsewhere—more effectively than the civil rights movement of the twentieth century.

At the beginning of the century the jury was still out on which of the two opposing strategies for African-American betterment—the accommodationist approach of Booker Washington or the confrontational style of

W. E. B. Du Bois—would be the more effective. At the time there was strong reason to question whether either strategy, or any other, would work. The tide of American prejudice was flowing more strongly than ever against anything smacking of racial equality. The Jim Crow system proliferated across the South, and African-Americans found themselves shut out of almost all public social contact with whites. Decreasing numbers of blacks dared to vote even where poll taxes, literacy tests, and white primaries didn't legally exclude them. Violence extended the reach of prejudice beyond the law, with lynchings and lesser forms of intimidation a commonplace. Segregation also occurred in the North, although there it tended to be informal rather than written into statute. Nor did the South have a monopoly on anti-black violence, a fact evidenced by race riots that broke out in 1908 in, of all places, Abraham Lincoln's Springfield, Illinois. But until World War I, when hundreds of thousands of African-Americans left the South for the factories and cities of the North, tension and trouble between blacks and whites remained a predominantly Southern problem.

The declining political and social condition of African-Americans reinforced Du Bois's belief that Washington's accommodationism was sterile and self-defeating. In 1905, Du Bois and others of similar persuasion organized the Niagara Movement, which called for immediate efforts to gain full equality for blacks. The movement won support from white liberals and in 1909 merged with the newly chartered National Association for the Advancement of Colored People. Ultimately the N.A.A.C.P. would become the most influential civil rights organization in America; and, ironically, what was born as a radical alternative to Booker Washington's cautious conservatism would find itself branded as timid and chained to the status quo. By then, however, Du Bois would have given up on America and emigrated to Ghana, where he died in 1963.

Du Bois gave up too soon, for during his last years the wheel was starting to turn against the segregationists. In 1954, the Supreme Court overturned the 1896 Plessy decision, ruling that, in an American context, "separate but equal" was a contradiction in terms—just as Justice John Marshall Harlan had predicted it would become. The court's unanimous decision in *Brown* v. *Board of Education of Topeka* knocked the first props out from under the Jim Crow system; the 1964 Civil Rights Act flattened most of what remained. And the 1965 Voting Rights Act guaranteed that Jim Crow wouldn't get back up again by enforcing the Fifteenth Amendment, finally securing to African-Americans their right to vote.

In the end it was hard to say whether Du Bois or Washington had been correct. Du Bois had accurately forecast that acquiescence in the Jim Crow system would lead to additional erosion of black rights, and he accurately anticipated that if blacks waited for whites to extend equal rights voluntarily, they would probably wait forever. On the other hand, Washington understood that the obvious obstacle to advancement for the majority of African-Americans was poverty. Frustrating as it was for Du Bois's talented tenth to be denied the opportunity to climb to the top of the hill of American society, for most blacks the primary problem was to keep from being ground into the mud at the bottom. For them, basic education in the means of earning a living was more immediately important than social and political equality. Moreover, Washington recognized that African-Americans' minority status in the United States rendered them ultimately dependent on the goodwill of the white majority; whatever the Constitution ostensibly guaranteed to blacks, those guarantees would have to be enforced by whites—white courts, white legislators, white sheriffs. Absent the goodwill of whites, constitutional guarantees meant nothing. If history vindicated Du Bois regarding the continued erosion of black rights, it also confirmed Washington's judgment about the need for white cooperation. While the civil rights reforms of the mid-twentieth century wouldn't have happened without the agitation Du Bois demanded, neither would they have happened without the support of the whites Washington courted.

The jury in the Washington–Du Bois dispute was still out as the end of the twentieth century neared. By most measures Du Bois's talented tenth had succeeded beyond his ambitions, grand as those sometimes were; Du Bois's heirs in academia, to cite his chosen field, often found themselves in greater demand than whites. At the same time, however, economic equality for the majority of African-Americans remained but a hope for the future, and often a distant hope. Although no black leaders any longer advocated acquiescence in inequality, nearly all appreciated the importance of the self-help Booker Washington had urged.

The debate between Washington and Du Bois also lived on in the controversy over affirmative action, which split the African-American community (not to mention Americans more broadly) just as the fight between Washington and Du Bois had, and for similar reasons. On one side were those who contended that the legacy of slavery and legal segregation remained so powerful that active efforts by government to overcome them were required. Affirmative action, while hardly ideal, was necessary. On the other side were those who rejected preferential treatment as paternalistic and degrading. Affirmative action, rather than elevate blacks in the eyes of either the white majority or African-Americans themselves, did just the opposite, for it tarnished the achievements of even the best and most qualified with the suspicion that such achievements were unearned. In addition, it afforded an opening to white racists to charge reverse discrimination.

It was hard to tell where Washington or Du Bois would have come down on the question of affirmative action, had they lived so long. Washington's concern for the masses of black people might have inclined him toward accepting affirmative action, which acknowledged the obstacles that often kept ordinary African-Americans out of schools and jobs. On the other hand, his emphasis on self-help and his comparative apathy toward politics would have disinclined him to look to government for black advancement. Du Bois's confrontational streak might have demanded affirmative action as a recompense for centuries of discrimination; then again, his elitist soul would have rebelled at the thought that he or others of the talented tenth needed help from the government or anyone else, and it would have shunned the shadow that such help would cast over their achievements.

VII

The difficulty of determining who had the better of the Washington–Du Bois debate reflects a larger difficulty in deciding which of the two competing visions of America in the 1890s was the more accurate. Was the genuine America really in the past, as Frederick Jackson Turner and the Adams brothers and the trade unionists and the Populists and the anti-imperialists and innumerable others declared or implied? And did current trends indicate a destiny of decline for the United States? Or was the true America the land of the future, as Josiah Strong and John Fiske and J. P. Morgan and John Rockefeller and Thomas Edison and Henry Cabot Lodge and A. T. Mahan and Theodore Roosevelt indicated, in their various ways? And consequently was the future to be a time of triumph for American ideals and American institutions?

Compelling contemporary evidence certainly supported the declinists. The labor violence, the squalor of the slums, the hypersensitivity of the nation's financial markets, the rise of suffocatingly powerful trusts, the blatant corruption of the big-city bosses, the radicalization of agrarian politics—these were damning indictments of the direction the country was headed. To Americans raised on the notion of individual initiative and America's blessed freedom from the ills of the Old World, it appeared patent that America's best days were gone. On current trends, conditions could only get worse.

In certain respects they did. Individual opportunities taken for granted during most of the nineteenth century continued to diminish. Free land vanished, and along with it nearly everything having to do with Turner's beloved frontier—except memories that strayed farther and farther from reality. While the courts broke up the biggest trusts, the consolidation of American industrial life continued, leaving the individual increasingly at the mercy of the corporation. What had happened in the steel and oil industries repeated itself elsewhere: the automobile industry, the type specimen of American business in the twentieth century, was born in a hundred toolsheds but matured on the assembly lines of only a handful of giant firms. And the fratricidal troubles of the Old World increasingly intruded upon Americans, to the extent that the United States twice felt obliged to rescue Europe from self-destruction.

Yet events of the twentieth century also bore out the predictions of the American triumphalists. The economic recovery that began during the last part of the 1890s presaged long-term economic growth that made the United States far and away the wealthiest nation in world history. This prosperity eased much of the strain on labor-management relations, answered many of the complaints of the farmers, and prevented the polarization along class lines that during the 1890s had appeared ominously imminent. The American political and legal system learned how to deal, albeit not perfectly, with both the city bosses and the corporate bosses: the former through Progressive political reforms and public services that stole the bosses' clients, the latter through antitrust legislation and enforcement. And while America's imperial adventure in the Philippines didn't quite lead to the glorious millennium predicted by Josiah Strong and Albert Beveridge, neither did it utterly subvert the Republic. The anti-imperialists had wrung their hands over the prospect that the imperialist impulse would overwhelm American democracy; as things turned out, something closer to the opposite occurred.

The fact of the matter regarding America's future after the 1890s was that there were lots of facts of the matter. One set of facts showed the declinists to have been correct; another confirmed the triumphalists' clairvoyance. America went to hell in a handbasket after the 1890s; it also went to heaven in an airplane. Whether a person concentrated on the former journey or the latter turned as much on individual taste and temperament as on anything else. By all aggregate accountings, Americans were wealthier and more powerful in the twentieth century than before; this future had been evident in the 1890s to anyone with eyes to see, even Brooks Adams. For some Americans, wealth and power were enough; others demanded additional blessings, including unfettered individual opportunity and widespread social, economic, and racial equality. On these counts, for greater or less time and in greater or less degree, America proved wanting.

A hundred years later, as Americans approach the end of another century, a single verdict on the 1890s debate between the declinists and the triumphalists remains as problematic as ever. That it does so—that a century of evidence leaves the issue still in doubt—ought to recommend modesty to latter-day debaters on the same subject. Odds are that their own debate will be unresolved another century hence. A reader of Edward Gibbon's *Decline and Fall of the Roman Empire* once asked the author for a judgment on Rome's lasting significance. Gibbon replied that it was too soon to tell. Observers of American history—whether that of the 1890s or the 1990s—could do worse than recall Gibbon.

Still, history speaks, even if not as unambiguously as Gibbon's reader desired. And America's experience of the 1890s *can* offer some guidance to Americans of a century later. It can serve as a reminder, for example, of the power of populist politics: the thunder unleashed by the Populists echoed down the decades well into the next century. But with this reminder comes another: that not even Jove can control the rains that follow the thunder. The Populists wanted to fortify government to curb the power of big money; their great-grandsons wound up as suspicious of big government as the great-granddaddies ever were of big money. And in one of the real ironies of American politics, millions of the modern populists cast their votes in the 1992 presidential election for one of the biggest-money men in the country, an information-age Rockefeller.

A second lesson has to do with the intractability of certain problems. It doubtless would discourage Booker Washington and W. E. B. Du Bois to know that the race question is as troublesome today as during the 1890s. Jacob Riis would have no difficulty writing a sequel about urban unfortunates in the 1990s. On the other hand, the very persistence of such problems suggests that the world won't end, nor the Republic dissolve, if they aren't solved tomorrow.

As to economic change: the costs of change are usually more apparent than their benefits. The Homestead strikers could feel what the shifts in the steel industry were costing them in the 1890s, but they couldn't know that their sons would be making more steel in fewer hours and at higher wages a generation hence. This might afford at least a modicum of solace to middle managers rendered redundant during the corporate restructurings of the 1990s.

Perhaps more than anything, the experience of the 1890s reveals the resilience of America. The apocalypse seemed nigh during that reckless decade to the many who couldn't conceive that the country could long survive the political, economic, racial, and cultural forces that were tearing it apart. Survive it did, however, and indeed emerged more buoyant than ever. This is no guarantee that a similar outcome will succeed the 1990s—history offers no guarantees. But it does offer perspective, which can be the next best thing.

BIBLIOGRAPHY

◆

A book of this kind obviously depends on the work of other historians. The titles below indicate some of that work. They have been chosen, as well, to guide the interested reader to additional information on the 1890s and the surrounding years. The list also includes memoirs and other volumes in which the principals speak for themselves.

Adams, Brooks. *The Law of Civilization and Decay: An Essay on History.* 1896; New York, 1943 ed.

Adams, Henry. *The Education of Henry Adams.* 1906; New York, 1931 ed.

Addams, Jane. *The Social Thought of Jane Addams.* Christopher Lasch, ed. Indianapolis, 1965.

———. *Twenty Years at Hull House.* 1910; New York, 1960 ed.

Alexander, De Alva Standwood. *A Political History of the State of New York.* 4 vols. New York, 1906–23.

Allen, Frederick Lewis. *The Great Pierpont Morgan.* New York, 1949.

———. *The Lords of Creation.* New York, 1935 ed.

Allen, Robert L. *Reluctant Reformers: Racism and Social Reform Movements in the United States.* Washington, D.C., 1974.

Arnold, Thurman W. *The Folklore of Capitalism.* New Haven, Conn., 1937.

Bailey, Thomas A. "Was the Election of 1900 a Mandate on Imperialism?", *Mississippi Valley Historical Review,* 1937.

Bardolph, Richard, ed. *The Civil Rights Record: Black Americans and the Law, 1849–1970.* New York, 1970.

Barnard, Harry. *Eagle Forgotten: The Life of John Peter Altgeld.* Indianapolis, 1938.

Barnes, Donna A. *Farmers in Rebellion.* Austin, Tex., 1984.

Barnes, James A. *John G. Carlisle.* New York, 1931.

———. "Myths of the Bryan Campaign," *Mississippi Valley Historical Review,* 1947–48.

Barry, David S. *Forty Years in Washington.* Boston, 1924.

Beale, Howard K. *Theodore Roosevelt and the Rise of America to World Power.* Baltimore, 1956.

Beer, Thomas. *Hanna.* New York, 1929.

———. *The Mauve Decade: American Life at the End of the Nineteenth Century.* New York, 1926.

Beisner, Robert L. *Twelve Against Empire: The Anti-Imperialists, 1898–1900*. New York, 1968.

Beringause, Arthur F. *Brooks Adams*. New York, 1955.

Bicha, Karel Denis. "Jerry Simpson: Populist Without Principles," *Journal of American History*, 1967.

Billington, Ray Allen. *Frederick Jackson Turner*. New York, 1973.

Blackmur, R. P. *Henry Adams*. New York, 1980.

Blair, Lewis H. *The Prosperity of the South Dependent Upon the Elevation of the Negro*. 1889; reprinted as *A Southern Prophecy*, edited by C. Vann Woodward. Boston, 1964.

Bodnar, John E. *The Transplanted: A History of Immigrants in Urban America*. Bloomington, Ind., 1985.

Brands, H. W. *Bound to Empire: The United States and the Philippines*. New York, 1992.

Bridge, James H. *The Inside History of the Carnegie Steel Company*. New York, 1903.

Broderick, Francis L. *W. E. B. Du Bois: Negro Leader in a Time of Crisis*. Stanford, Cal., 1959.

Brody, David. *Steelworkers in America: The Nonunion Era*. Cambridge, Mass., 1960.

Brown, Dee. *Bury My Heart at Wounded Knee*. New York, 1970.

Brownell, Blaine A., and Warren E. Stickle, eds. *Bosses and Reformers: Urban Politics in America, 1880–1920*. Boston, 1973.

Bryan, William Jennings. *The First Battle: A Story of the Campaign of 1896*. Chicago, 1896.

———. *Memoirs*. Philadelphia, 1925.

Buder, Stanley. *Pullman: An Experiment in Industrial Order and Community Planning, 1880–1930*. New York, 1967.

Burgoyne, Arthur G. *Homestead*. Pittsburgh, 1893.

Burns, James MacGregor. *The Workshop of Democracy*. New York, 1985.

Byrnes, Joseph F. *The Virgin of Chartres: An Intellectual and Psychological History of the Work of Henry Adams*. Rutherford, N.J., 1981.

Cable, George W. *The Silent South*. 1885; Montclair, N.J., 1969.

Callow, Alexander B., Jr. *The Tweed Ring*. New York, 1965.

Carnegie, Andrew. *Autobiography*. Boston, 1920.

———. *The Empire of Business*. New York, 1902.

Carosso, Vincent P. *The Morgans: Private International Bankers*. Cambridge, Mass., 1987.

Cash, Wilbur Joseph. *The Mind of the South*. New York, 1941.

Champernowne, Henry. *The Boss: An Essay Upon the Art of Governing American Cities*. New York, 1894.

Chudacoff, Howard P. *The Evolution of American Urban Society*. 2nd ed. Englewood Cliffs, N.J., 1981.

Clanton, O. Gene. *Kansas Populism*. Lawrence, Kan., 1969.

Clark, Champ. *My Quarter Century of American Politics*. New York, 1920.

Cochran, Thomas C., and William Miller. *The Age of Enterprise*. New York, 1942.

Coletta, Paolo E. "Bryan, Cleveland, and the Disrupted Democracy, 1890–1896," *Nebraska History*, 1960.

———. *William Jennings Bryan*. 3 vols. Lincoln, Nebr., 1964–69.

Conot, Robert. *Thomas A. Edison*. New York, 1979.

Contosta, David R. *Henry Adams and the American Experiment*. Boston, 1980.

Cook, Fred J. *American Political Bosses and Machines*. New York, 1973.

Corey, Lewis. *The House of Morgan*. New York, 1930.

Cornell, Robert J. *The Anthracite Coal Strike of 1902*. New York, 1971 ed.

Cosmas, Graham A. *An Army for Empire: The United States Army in the Spanish-American War*. Columbia, Mo., 1971.

Croly, Herbert. *Marcus Alonzo Hanna*. New York, 1912.

Dale, Edward Everett, and Jesse Lee Rader, eds. *Readings in Oklahoma History*. Evanston, Ill., 1930.

Daniels, Roger. *Coming to America: A History of Immigration and Ethnicity in American Life*. New York, 1990.

Davis, Allen F. *American Heroine: The Life and Legend of Jane Addams*. New York, 1973.

———. *Spearheads for Reform: The Social Settlements and the Progressive Movement, 1890–1914*. New York, 1967.

Dawes, Charles Gates. *A Journal of the McKinley Years*. Chicago, 1950.

Degler, Carl N. "American Political Parties and the Rise of the Cities," *Journal of American History*, 1964.

Destler, Chester McA. *American Radicalism, 1865–1901*. Chicago, 1966.

———. *Henry Demarest Lloyd and the Empire of Reform*. Philadelphia, 1963.

Diamond, Sigmund. *The Nation Transformed: The Creation of an Industrial Society*. New York, 1963.

Diamond, Wilbur. "Urban and Rural Voting in 1896," *American Historial Review*, 1941.

Doenecke, Justus D. "Myths, Machines, and Markets: The Columbian Exposition of 1893," *Journal of Popular Culture*, 1972.

Dozer, Donald M. "Benjamin Harrison and the Presidential Campaign of 1892," *American Historical Review*, 1948.

Du Bois, W. E. B. *Correspondence*. Amherst, Mass., 1973–78.

———. *The Souls of Black Folk*. Chicago, 1903.

———. *Writings*. New York, 1986.

Dulles, Foster Rhea. *Labor in America*. New York, 1955.

Dunn, Arthur Wallace. *From Harrison to Harding*. 2 vols. New York, 1922.

Dunne, Finley Peter. *Mr. Dooley in Peace and War*. Boston, 1898.

———. *Mr. Dooley: Now and Forever*. Louis Filler, ed. Stanford, Calif., 1954.

Durden, Robert F. *The Climax of Populism: The Election of 1896*. Lexington, Ky., 1965.

———. "The 'Cow-Bird' Grounded: The Populist Nomination of Bryan and Watson," *Mississippi Valley Historical Review*, 1963.

Dusinberre, William. *Henry Adams: The Myth of Failure*. Charlottesville, Va., 1980.

Dyer, Frank Lewis, Thomas Commerford Martin, and William Henry Meadowcroft. *Edison: His Life and Inventions*. 2 vols. New York, 1929.

Eckler, A. Ross. "A Measure of the Severity of Depression, 1873–1932," *Review of Economic Statistics*, 1933.

Eisenstein, Sarah. *Give Us Bread But Give Us Roses: Working Women's Consciousness in the United States, 1890 to the First World War*. London, 1983.

Ellis, Elmer. *Mr. Dooley's America: A Life of Finley Peter Dunne*. New York, 1941.

Faulkner, Harold U. *Politics, Reform and Expansion, 1890–1900*. New York, 1959.

Filler, Louis. *The Muckrakers.* University Park, Pa., 1976 ed.

Fite, Gilbert C. "Republican Strategy and the Farm Vote in the Presidential Campaign of 1896," *American Historical Review,* 1960.

———. "William Jennings Bryan and the Campaign of 1896," *Nebraska History,* 1966.

Foner, Philip S. *History of the Labor Movement in the United States.* 8 vols. New York, 1947–.

Freidel, Frank. *The Splendid Little War.* Boston, 1958.

Friedman, Milton, and Anna Jacobson Schwartz. *A Monetary History of the United States, 1867–1960.* Princeton, N.J., 1963.

Garraty, John A. "Bryan," *American Heritage,* 1961.

———. *Henry Cabot Lodge.* New York, 1953.

———. *The New Commonwealth, 1877–1890.* New York, 1968.

Ginger, Ray. *Age of Excess: The United States from 1877 to 1914.* New York, 1975 ed.

———. *Altgeld's America: The Lincoln Ideal versus Changing Realities.* New York, 1986 ed.

———. *The Bending Cross: A Biography of Eugene Victor Debs.* New Brunswick, N.J., 1949.

———, ed. *The Nationalizing of American Life, 1877–1900.* New York, 1965.

Glad, Paul W. *McKinley, Bryan and the People.* Philadelphia, 1964.

———. *The Trumpet Soundeth: William Jennings Bryan and His Democracy.* Lincoln, Nebr., 1960.

Gompers, Samuel. *Seventy Years of Life and Labor.* 1925; Ithaca, N.Y., 1984 ed.

Goodwyn, Lawrence. *Democratic Promise: The Populist Moment in America.* New York, 1976.

Gordon, John Steele. "The Magnitude of J. P. Morgan," *American Heritage,* 1989.

Gould, Lewis L. *The Presidency of William McKinley.* Lawrence, Kan., 1980.

Hackney, Sheldon, ed. *Populism.* Boston, 1971.

Hagedorn, Hermann. *Leonard Wood.* 2 vols. New York, 1931.

Handlin, Oscar. *The Uprooted: The Epic Story of the Great Migrations That Made the American People.* Boston, 1952.

Harbert, Earl N. *The Force So Much Closer Home: Henry Adams and the Adams Family.* New York, 1977.

Harlan, Louis R. *Booker T. Washington.* 2 vols. New York, 1972–83.

Harvey, George. *Henry Clay Frick.* New York, 1928.

Harvey, William H. *Coin's Financial School.* Chicago, 1894.

Hays, Samuel P. *The Response to Industrialism, 1885–1914.* Chicago, 1957.

———. "The Social Analysis of American Political History, 1880–1920," *Political Science Quarterly,* 1965.

Healy, David F. *The United States in Cuba, 1898–1902.* Madison, Wis., 1963.

Hendrick, Burton J. *The Life of Andrew Carnegie.* 2 vols. Garden City, N.Y., 1932.

Hendrickson, Kenneth E., Jr. "Reluctant Expansionist: Jacob Gould Schurman and the Philippine Question," *Pacific Historical Review,* 1967.

Hibben, Paxton. *The Peerless Leader: William Jennings Bryan.* New York, 1929.

Hicks, John D. *The Populist Revolt.* Minneapolis, 1931.

Hidy, Ralph W., and George S. Gibb. *History of Standard Oil Company (New Jersey).* 3 vols. New York, 1955–71.

Higham, John. *Send These to Me: Jews and Other Immigrants in Urban America.* New York, 1975.

———. *Strangers in the Land: Patterns of American Nativism, 1860–1925*. New Brunswick, N.J., 1955.

Hoffmann, Charles. *The Depression of the Nineties: An Economic History*. Westport, Conn., 1970.

Hofstadter, Richard. *The Age of Reform: From Bryan to FDR*. New York, 1955.

———. *The Progressive Historians: Turner, Beard, Parrington*. Chicago, 1968.

———. *Social Darwinism in American Thought, 1860–1915*. Philadelphia, 1945.

———, and Michael Wallace, eds. *American Violence: A Documentary History*. New York, 1970.

Hoselitz, Bert F. "The City, the Factory, and Economic Growth," *American Economic Review*, 1955.

Hughes, Thomas, P. "The Electrification of America: The System Builders," *Technology and Culture*, 1979.

———. *Networks of Power: Electrification in Western Society, 1880–1930*. Baltimore, 1983.

———. "Thomas Alva Edison and the Rise of Electricity," in Carroll W. Pursell, Jr., ed., *Technology in America*. Cambridge, Mass., 1981.

Jackson, Stanley. *J.P. Morgan*. New York, 1983.

Jacobs, Wilbur R. *The Historical World of Frederick Jackson Turner, with Selections from His Correspondence*. New Haven, Conn., 1968.

Jaher, Frederick Cople, ed. *The Age of Industrialism in America: Essays in Social Structure and Cultural Values*. New York, 1968.

Jones, Stanley L. *The Presidential Election of 1896*. Madison, Wis., 1964.

Jones, Virgil Carrington. *Roosevelt's Rough Riders*. Garden City, N.Y., 1971.

Josephson, Matthew. *Edison*. New York, 1959.

———. *The Politicos, 1865–1896*. New York, 1938.

———. *The President Makers*. New York, 1940.

———. *The Robber Barons*. New York, 1934.

Katzman, David M., and William M. Tuttle, Jr., eds. *Plain Folk: The Life Stories of Undistinguished Americans*. Urbana, Ill., 1982.

Keller, Morton. *Affairs of State: Public Life in Late Nineteenth Century America*. Cambridge, Mass., 1977.

Ketchum, Richard M. "Faces from the Past," *American Heritage*, 1963.

Keyssar, Alexander. *Out of Work: The First Century of Unemployment in Massachusetts*. New York, 1986.

Kirkland, Edward C. *Dream and Thought in the Business Community, 1860–1900*. Chicago, 1964.

———. *Industry Comes of Age*. New York, 1961.

Klein, Maury. *The Life and Legend of Jay Gould*. Baltimore, 1986.

Koenig, Louis W. *Bryan*. New York, 1971.

Kolko, Gabriel. *Railroads and Regulation, 1877–1916*. New York, 1970 ed.

Kraut, Alan M. *The Huddled Masses: The Immigrant in American Society, 1880–1921*. Arlington Heights, Ill., 1982.

LaFeber, Walter. "The American Business Community and Cleveland's Venezuelan Message," *Business History Review*, 1960.

———. "The Background of Cleveland's Venezuelan Policy," *American Historical Review*, 1961.

———. *The New Empire: An Interpretation of American Expansionism, 1860–1898*. Ithaca, N.Y., 1963.

Lasch, Christopher. "The Anti-Imperialists, the Philippines, and the Inequality of Man," *Journal of Southern History*, 1958.

Lears, T. J. Jackson. *No Place of Grace: Antimodernism and the Transformation of American Culture, 1880–1920*. New York, 1981.

Lee, James M. *History of American Journalism*. Garden City, N.Y., 1923.

Leech, Margaret. *In the Days of McKinley*. New York, 1959.

Lester, Julius, ed. *The Seventh Son: The Thought and Writings of W. E. B. Du Bois*. New York, 1971.

Lewis, David Levering. *W. E. B. Du Bois*. New York, 1993.

Licht, Walter. *Working for the Railroad: The Organization of Work in the Nineteenth Century*. Princeton, N.J., 1983.

Linderman, Gerald F. *The Mirror of War: American Society and the Spanish-American War*. Ann Arbor, Mich., 1974.

Lindsey, Almont. *The Pullman Strike*. 1942; Chicago, 1964 ed.

Litwack, Leon F. *North of Slavery: The Negro in the Free States, 1790–1860*. Chicago, 1961.

Livesay, Harold. *American Made: Men Who Shaped the American Economy*. Boston, 1979.

———. *Andrew Carnegie and the Rise of Big Business*. Boston, 1975.

Lloyd, Henry Demarest. *Lords of Industry*. New York, 1916.

———. *Wealth Against Commonwealth*. New York, 1894.

Lodge, Henry Cabot. "Thomas Brackett Reed," in Lodge, *The Democracy of the Constitution and Other Addresses and Essays*. 1915; Freeport, N.Y., 1966 ed.

Lofgren, Charles A., *The Plessy Case: A Legal-Historical Interpretation*. New York, 1987.

Logan, Rayford W., ed. *W. E. B. Du Bois: A Profile*. New York, 1971.

Lynch, Denis Tilden. *Grover Cleveland*. New York, 1932.

Marcus, Robert D. *Grand Old Party: Political Structure in the Gilded Age, 1880–1896*. New York, 1971.

Martin, John Stuart. "When the President Disappeared," *American Heritage*, 1957.

Marx, Leo. *The Machine in the Garden: Technology and the Pastoral Ideal in America*. New York, 1964.

May, Ernest. *American Imperialism*. New York, 1968.

———. *Imperial Democracy: The Emergence of America as a Great Power*. New York, 1961.

McCall, Samuel. *The Life of Thomas Brackett Reed*. Boston, 1914.

McClure, J. B., ed. *Edison and His Inventions*. Chicago, 1879.

McElroy, Robert. *Grover Cleveland*. New York, 1923.

McGurn, James. *On Your Bicycle: An Illustrated History of Cycling*. New York, 1987.

McKelvey, Blake. *American Urbanization: A Comparative History*. Glenview, Ill., 1973.

———. *The Urbanization of America*. New Brunswick, N.J., 1963.

McMath, Robert C., Jr. *Populist Vanguard: A History of the Southern Farmers' Alliance*. Chapel Hill, N.C., 1975.

McMurry, Donald L. *Coxey's Army*. 1929; Seattle, 1968 ed.

McPherson, James M. *The Abolitionist Legacy: From Reconstruction to the NAACP*. Princeton, N.J., 1975.

McSeveney, Samuel T. *The Politics of Depression: Political Behavior in the Northeast, 1893–1896.* New York, 1972.

Merrill, Horace Samuel. *Bourbon Leader: Grover Cleveland and the Democratic Party.* Boston, 1957.

Miller, Nathan. *Theodore Roosevelt.* New York, 1992.

Millis, Walter. *The Martial Spirit.* Boston, 1931.

Miner, Curtis. *Homestead.* Pittsburgh, 1989.

Monkkonen, Eric H. *America Becomes Urban: The Development of U.S. Cities and Towns, 1780–1980.* Berkeley, 1988.

Morgan, H. Wayne. *From Hayes to McKinley: National Party Politics, 1877–1896.* Syracuse, N.Y., 1969.

———. *William McKinley and His America.* Syracuse, N.Y., 1963.

———, ed. *The Gilded Age.* Syracuse, N.Y., 1970 ed.

Morris, Edmund. *The Rise of Theodore Roosevelt.* New York, 1979.

Morris, Lerona Rosamond, ed. *Oklahoma Yesterday, Today, Tomorrow.* Guthrie, Okla., 1930.

Mott, Frank L. *American Journalism.* New York, 1950 ed.

———. *A History of American Magazines.* 5 vols. Cambridge, Mass., 1930–68.

Muller, Dorothea. "Josiah Strong and American Nationalism," *Journal of American History,* 1966.

Nagel, Paul C. *Descent from Glory: Four Generations of the John Adams Family.* New York, 1983.

Nevins, Allan. *Grover Cleveland.* New York, 1932.

———. *John D. Rockefeller.* 2 vols. New York, 1940.

Nugent, W. T. K. *Money and American Society, 1865–1880.* New York, 1968.

Olcott, Charles S. *The Life of William McKinley.* 2 vols. Boston, 1916.

O'Leary, Paul. "The Scene of the Crime of 1873 Revisited," *Journal of Political Economy,* 1960.

Oliver, John W. *History of American Technology.* New York, 1956.

Olsen, Otto H., ed. *The Thin Disguise: Plessy v. Ferguson.* New York, 1967.

Otis, D. S. *The Dawes Act and the Allotment of Indian Lands.* Norman, Okla., 1973 ed.

Painter, Nell Irvin. *Standing at Armageddon: The United States, 1877–1919.* New York, 1987.

Parker, George F. *Recollections of Grover Cleveland.* New York, 1909.

Passer, Harold C. *The Electrical Manufacturers, 1875–1900.* Cambridge, Mass., 1953.

Peck, Harry Thurston. *Twenty Years of the Republic, 1885–1905.* New York, 1917.

Peffer, E. Louise. *The Closing of the Public Domain.* Stanford, Cal., 1951.

Peters, Ronald M. Jr. *The American Speakership: The Office in Historical Perspective.* Baltimore, 1990.

Pollack, Norman. "Hofstadter on Populism: A Critique of *The Age of Reform,*" *Journal of Southern History,* 1960.

———. "The Myth of Populist Anti-Semitism," *American Historical Review,* 1962.

———. *The Populist Response to Industrial America.* Cambridge, Mass., 1962.

———, ed. *The Populist Mind.* New York, 1967.

Pratt, Julius. *Expansionists of 1898.* Baltimore, 1936.

Pringle, Henry F. *Theodore Roosevelt.* New York, 1931.

Rayback, Joseph G. *A History of American Labor.* New York, 1959.

Regier, C. C. *The Era of the Muckrakers*. Chapel Hill, N.C., 1932.

Ridge, Martin. *Ignatius Donnelly*. Chicago, 1962.

Riis, Jacob A. *How the Other Half Lives*. New York, 1890.

Riordon, William. *Plunkitt of Tammany Hall*. 1905; New York, 1948 ed.

Robinson, William A. *Thomas B. Reed*. New York, 1930.

Rockefeller, John D. *Random Reminiscences of Men and Events*. New York, 1909.

Roosevelt, Theodore. *Autobiography*. New York, 1920.

———. *The Letters of Theodore Roosevelt*. Edited by Elting E. Morison. 8 vols, Cambridge, Mass., 1951–54.

———. *The Rough Riders*. New York, 1899.

Rosenzweig, Roy. *Eight Hours for What We Will: Workers and Leisure in an Industrial City, 1870–1920*. New York, 1983.

Rothman, David J. *Politics and Power: The United States Senate 1869–1901*. Cambridge, Mass., 1966.

Rudwick, Elliot M. *W. E. B. Du Bois: Propagandist of the Negro Protest*. New York, 1969.

Russell, Francis. *The President Makers: From Mark Hanna to Joseph P. Kennedy*. Boston, 1976.

Rydell, Robert W. *All the World's a Fair: Visions of Empire at American International Expositions, 1876–1916*. Chicago, 1984.

Saloutos, Theodore. *Farmer Movements in the South: 1865–1933*. Berkeley, 1960.

Salvatore, Nick. *Eugene V. Debs*. Urbana, Ill., 1982.

Satterlee, Herbert L. *J. Pierpont Morgan*. New York, 1939.

Schlereth, Thomas J. *Victorian America*. New York, 1991.

Schlesinger, Arthur M. *The Rise of the City, 1878–1898*. New York, 1933.

Schwantes, Carlos A. *Coxey's Army*. Lincoln, Nebr., 1985.

Shannon, Fred A. *The Farmers' Last Frontier: Agriculture, 1860–1897*. New York, 1945.

Sherman, John. *Recollections of Forty Years in the House, Senate and Cabinet*. Chicago, 1895.

Silverberg, Robert. *Light for the World: Edison and the Power Industry*. Princeton, N.J., 1967.

Simkins, Francis Butler. *Pitchfork Ben Tillman*. Baton Rouge, La., 1944.

Smith, Henry Nash. *Virgin Land: The American West as Symbol and Myth*. Cambridge, Mass., 1950.

Smith, Page. *The Rise of Industrial America*. New York, 1984.

Spencer, Samuel R., Jr. *Booker T. Washington and the Negro's Place in American Life*. Boston, 1955.

Stead, William Thomas. *If Christ Came to Chicago*. Chicago, 1893.

Stealey, O. O. *Twenty Years in the Press Gallery*. New York, 1906.

Steffens, Lincoln. *Autobiography*. New York, 1931.

———. *The Shame of the Cities*. 1904; New York, 1957 ed.

Stein, Leon, ed. *The Pullman Strike*. New York, 1969.

Strong, Josiah. *Our Country*. New York, 1885.

Tarbell, Ida M. *The History of the Standard Oil Company*. 2 vols. New York, 1904.

Tax, Meredith. *The Rising of the Women: Feminist Solidarity and Class Conflict, 1880–1917*. New York, 1980.

Thelen, David P. "Social Tensions and the Origins of Progressivism," *Journal of American History*, 1969.

Thoburn, Joseph B., and Muriel H. Wright. *Oklahoma: A History of the State and Its People.* 2 vols. New York, 1929.

Thomas, John L. *Alternative America: Henry George, Edward Bellamy, Henry Demarest Lloyd, and the Adversary Tradition.* Cambridge, 1983.

Tindall, George Brown, ed. *A Populist Reader.* New York, 1966.

———. *South Carolina Negroes, 1877–1900.* Columbia, S.C., 1952.

Trachtenberg, Alan. *The Incorporation of America: Culture and Society in the Gilded Age.* New York, 1982.

Tuchman, Barbara. *The Proud Tower: A Portrait of the World Before the War, 1890–1914.* New York, 1966.

Turner, Frederick Jackson. *Early Writings.* Madison, Wis., 1938.

———. *The Frontier in American History.* New York, 1920.

———. *The Significance of the Frontier in American History.* 1893; Ann Arbor, Mich., 1966 ed.

Utley, Robert M. *The Indian Frontier of the American West, 1846–1890.* Albuquerque, N.M., 1984.

———. *The Lance and the Shield: The Life and Times of Sitting Bull.* New York, 1993.

Vincent, Henry. *The Story of the Commonweal.* 1894; New York, 1969 ed.

Wall, Joseph Frazier. *Andrew Carnegie.* New York, 1970.

Ward, David. *Cities and Immigrants: A Geography of Change in Nineteenth-Century America.* New York, 1971.

Washington, Booker T. *The Booker T. Washington Papers.* Edited by Louis R. Harlan et al. Urbana, Ill., 1972–.

———. *Up from Slavery.* New York, 1901.

Welch, Richard E. *The Presidencies of Grover Cleveland.* Lawrence, Kan., 1988.

Wendt, Lloyd, and Herman Kogan. *Lords of the Levee: The Story of Bathhouse John and Hinky Dink.* Indianapolis, 1943.

White, Leonard D. *The Republican Era, 1869–1901.* New York, 1958.

White, William Allen. *Autobiography.* New York, 1946.

Wiebe, Robert. *The Search for Order, 1877–1920.* New York, 1967.

Williams, R. Hal. *Years of Decision: American Politics in the 1890s.* New York, 1978.

Williamson, Joel. *After Slavery: The Negro in South Carolina During Reconstruction, 1861–1877.* Chapel Hill, N.C., 1965.

———. *The Crucible of Race: Black-White Relations in the American South Since Emancipation.* New York, 1984.

——— ed. *The Origins of Segregation.* Boston, 1968.

Wolff, Leon. *Lockout: The Story of the Homestead Strike of 1892.* New York, 1965.

Woodward, C. Vann. "The Birth of Jim Crow," *American Heritage,* 1964.

———. *Origins of the New South, 1877–1913.* Baton Rouge, La., 1971 ed.

———. "The Populist Heritage and the Intellectual," *American Scholar,* 1959–60.

———. *The Strange Career of Jim Crow.* New York, 1974 ed.

Wykoff, Walter A. *The Workers: An Experiment in Reality.* New York, 1899.

Wynes, Charles E., ed. *Forgotten Voices: Dissenting Southerners in an Age of Conformity.* Baton Rouge, La., 1967.

———. *Race Relations in Virginia, 1870–1902.* Charlottesville, Va., 1961.

Yellen, Samuel. *American Labor Struggles.* New York, 1936.

Zink, Harold. *City Bosses in the United States.* Durham, N.C., 1930.

INDEX

◆

Manufactured by Amazon.ca
Bolton, ON

25417254R00222